AUTUMN and THE ANGEL

AUTUMN and THE ANGEL

Juanita Diane Friend

Kravitz and Sons LLC
1301 Farmville Blvd, Suite 104
Greenville, NC 27834

Published by Kravitz and Sons LLC.

ISBN: 979-8-89639-078-7 (sc)
ISBN: 979-8-89639-077-0 (e)

Library of Congress Control Number: 2025902009

Table of Contents

Dedication

My book, Autumn and the Angel, is dedicated to my precious husband, John.

John, thank you for your encouragement and belief in my project. I truly appreciate your patience, understanding, and guidance, which have helped me achieve my dream. You are the most wonderful gift God has ever given me, second only to my Savior, Jesus Christ. I love you today, I will love you tomorrow, and I will love you forever.

Thank you to my Grandfather, William Abraham Lehman, who loved me more than life.

Thank you to my Uncle Walter Lewis 'Charlie' Lehman for the gift of John Milton's child edition of *Paradise Lost*. It ignited my young imagination and inspired me to write a story about a realm I dream of living in when my days on Earth end.

CHAPTER 1

The Wraith

Autumn Dawn Carter sat in her screened gazebo, her legs crossed, her notebook propped against her bent knee. Alone with her thoughts her written words flowed free and colorful from her pen's moist tip. Autumn was not a professional writer; she was the wife of David Carter, owner of Carter Heating and Air Conditioning. She didn't live in the big city, or a prominent neighborhood. She inherited David's family home in Florida and though they were not wealthy, she lived a comfortable life and was well-known in her community. Right now, David was working and she was alone on her ten acres of sunburned property. Today, she planned to write her outline and pen the book that lived inside her heart.

Autumn was writing down the description of her characters when lightning struck in the distance. A storm was predicted, but until it moved closer, she would remain in the gazebo she named Almost Heaven. The muted sound of thunder rumbled in the distance. She glanced through the screen that separated her from the sun's hot rays. That was when a streak of blue-white streak of lightening, more brilliant than the sun's light, brightened the sky. Curious, Autumn lowered her notebook to the glider's seat and walked to the gazebo's screened door.

Across the acres of burnt grass and wilted plant life, she saw what appeared to be a huge white crane.

"Poor bird," Autumn whispered.

With her right hand, she lifted her thick, long hair away from her perspiring neck, caught it in her left hand, and expertly tied hair with hair so that her mane cascaded down her back. Brushing strands of stray hair from her damp cheeks, she said, "Fan your wings all you want, precious bird. You'll find no relief from this dreadful heat."

Autumn rose to her feet, walking to the gazebo's screened door. Shading her eyes, she searched for the bird. "There it is," she sighed. She tried the gazebo's latch. As always, it was set in place and refused to turn. Narrowing her eyes, she gasped, "What's that?" She hurried to the small stand, pulled open the drawer, and retrieved small binoculars from it. Setting the glasses to her face, her eyes widened in fear.

A ghost, glowing brilliantly in the glare of the sun's cruel light, moved slowly and deliberately toward the gazebo. Golden flames lifted like a wavering crown from the ghost's head. Its garments whipped silently against the breeze that drenched the air, adding to the horribleness of its presence. Slack-jawed and trembling, Autumn dropped the small red binoculars she held in her hand. Stumbling backward, she caught her foot in the iron coils of David's handcrafted coffee table. Falling to the floor, she reached for the miniature field glasses.

"No! No!" Autumn sobbed. She reached into her skirt's deep pocket, but it was empty. "I left my cell phone on my dresser. Oh no, there's no one here but me."

Sprawled across the floor, paralyzed by fear, a terrible thought crossed her mind: what if this apparition had come for her? She had never been in such a dreadful state. Forcing herself into a sitting position, she scooted across the floor until she could peer out from behind the structure's lattice wall. A startled gasp closed her throat. The ghoul was less than three-quarters of an acre away. Her breath quickened. Her frenzied mind struggled to clarify the urgency of her situation. Why didn't this harbinger turn away or dissolve into the air? Why was it here? Worse, why did it keep walking in her direction?

The terror that quickened Autumn's heart sent her blood racing through her veins. Bitter bile rose in her throat, a result of her anxiety. She turned to the small stand beside her glider rocker and reached for the pitcher she had brought from the house. Pouring iced tea into one of the plastic disposable cups stored in the stand's drawer, she gulped down the drink in one long swig. In desperation, she scanned the gazebo for a hiding place. Autumn closed her eyes and covered her face with her hands; her perspiration, more from fright than heat, soaked her clothes. Whining like an abandoned puppy, she scooted backward across the floor until her back rested against the two-seater glider. Turning her throbbing head, Autumn focused her glistening eyes on the oversized cushions of the glider. She found her hiding place, but first, she needed to see where the ghoul was now.

Trembling, Autumn crawled across the floor of the gazebo. Staying low, she knelt behind the lattice wall that rose three feet high on all six sides. The gazebo's screen was thick, so when the sun shone at certain times during the morning and afternoon, it acted like a curtain, concealing anyone inside the structure. Autumn glanced over her shoulder at the clock. Unfortunately, the sun had moved, and she could now be seen by anyone who wasn't blind.

Sucking in a deep breath, Autumn peeked through one of the many latticework slots. "Oh no," she whispered. Clasping her hands over her mouth, she forced herself to calculate the distance between the intruder and herself. "I'd say," she whispered, "I'd say, he's less than an eighth of an acre away." Shaking from head to toe, she crawled across the floor. Crouching low, she pulled an old afghan from its hook and threw it over the glider's seat. The cover's loosely crocheted fabric fell to the floor like a netted barrier between two enemies. "I should have worked inside today."

Curiosity teased Autumn. She had to have just one more look. Creeping from behind her stockade, she crouched behind the latticework and peeked out to see where the ghoul was now. It was almost upon her.

"Oh! Oh, heaven help me!" she gasped. Tears streamed down her cheeks as she inched her way across the wooden floor to cower behind the glider. Autumn rubbed her knotted stomach. Never before had she felt fear like this. With her forehead pressed against the glider's frame, she closed her eyes and hoped the intruder would not sense her presence.

A noise at the gazebo's door caused every muscle in Autumn's body to tighten. Brushing her long hair off her wet face, she peeked out from behind the glider's cushions. She was certain that she would see the skeletal face of the Grim Reaper. Instead, she saw the silhouette of a tall man. Though she couldn't make out his features, she could see that he wore a long white robe girded at the waist with a blue sash.

Autumn shrank, trembling against the bars that supported the glider's cushions. Bent at the waist, her cheek pressed against the floor, she watched the oddly dressed man through the afghan's delicate weave. A sickening wave of panic surged through her when the intruder cupped his hands around his eyes and peered through the screen as though he were looking for something or someone. Autumn felt that he saw her, but instead of calling to her as she expected him to do, the man turned away and took the path that led from the gazebo.

Autumn sat still. Hardly breathing, she peered out from under the glider's chassis. Yes. He was leaving. Relieved that she had out-smarted the intruder, Autumn pressed her forehead against the double-seated chair's warm iron frame and exhaled for the first time since the ordeal began.

Sitting upright behind the glider, Autumn kept her eyes trained on the man who had frightened her. He was walking toward the house. He disappeared from view when he stepped onto the back porch. Good. He would see no one was home, and he would leave.

Again, curiosity made Autumn leave her hiding place. Standing now, half hidden behind a support beam, she watched the stranger weave his way through the trees that shaded the path to the gazebo. As he made his way to the house, a low breeze moved the branches of the trees, allowing the sun to cast its full glow against the intruder's back. Autumn shaded her eyes against the glare of the man's brilliant white garments.

"What is he wearing on his back?" Narrowing her eyes, she studied her uninvited guest. "Oh my," she gasped aloud, "he has wings!"

A fickle breeze tickled the trespasser's ear with the feather-soft whisper of a human voice. Shaking his head in amusement more than disgust or anger, the winged man turned away from the house and peered toward the gazebo.

"Autumn," he called. "Autumn Dawn Carter, I am here to speak with you."

Though mortal and spirit were separated by distance, with shrubs and trees between them, their eyes locked. Ensnared by the man's powerful gaze, Autumn grew anxious.

From where the spirit stood, he saw the woman run her trembling hands through her damp hair while she turned in circles. "Autumn Dawn Carter, I mean you no harm. I come on a mission of peace." For a brief moment, the other-worldly creature felt the woman would succumb to his will, but his certainty passed when Autumn screamed for him to go away. "Only the One who sent me can relieve me of my mission."

Autumn's flesh crawled. Oblivious to the man's friendly overtures, she whimpered, "I have to get out of here!"

In a desperate attempt to escape her garden retreat, she struggled with the door's stubborn latch. As always, it refused to work for her. Licking her dry lips, sweat oozing down her face, her breath coming in rapid gasps, she sobbed mournfully, "I'm trapped inside this stupid gazebo!" Then a thought crossed her mind: if she couldn't get out, the man couldn't get in. Turning her gaze toward the house, she saw the man had not moved from where he had been when he discovered her.

"He's afraid of me," she mused aloud. Feeling smug, she called out, "You better go away! I called the police. They are on their way to my house as I speak."

Her body convulsed when the intruder lifted from the ground and flew through the air in her direction. Suddenly, she knew how Dorothy from *The Wizard of Oz* felt when she saw the wicked witch's flying monkeys. A sob escaped her throat. She stumbled across the floor to her hiding place.

Scrambling behind the glider's plush cushions, she knelt with her forehead pressed against the floorboards. She held her breath and waited for the intruder to enter the structure. The sound of her blood surging through her veins drowned out the click of the screen door's latch and the nimble footsteps of the one who searched for her.

Autumn stiffened. The wraith was with her in the gazebo. Unseen but felt, the intruder's presence was overwhelming. Autumn wiped her eyes with her dirty hands to clear her vision. She cocked her head to one side so she could see the stretch of floor that led from the door to the area in front of the glider. From where she crouched, she could see the sandals the stranger wore. A scream rose in Autumn's throat—the visitor's sandaled toes were pointed right at her.

Chapter 2

Secrets Revealed

Autumn lay behind the glider, partially hidden by the afghan, her tear-stained face pressed tightly against the gazebo's wooden floor. Though her eyes were closed, she knew the intruder was looking at her - his gaze was that intense.

The angel, who had seen war and who had been a victim himself, sought to ease this precious creature's fear of him. "Child, take my hand," he said softly. "I mean you no harm." He extended his huge hand over the back of the glider. Again, he spoke encouraging words. "I come in peace. Your Father in Heaven sent me to this place to speak with you in private."

Mustering her strength, Autumn rose to a sitting position. Her heart was warmed by the comforting tone of the angel's voice. She let go of the afghan's tattered hem. Forcing her eyes open, she glanced upward. Her lips parted slightly when she saw the angel's handsome face. When their eyes met, Autumn just knew that the entire world had turned a brilliant shade of blue.

Calmer now, she reached for the angel's outstretched hand, cringing a bit when his long, tapered fingers closed around hers. On legs made weak by fear, she made her way from behind the glider to stand before her powerful guest. Awkward and inferior, she lowered her eyes to the floorboards. Should she kneel? Should she speak first or wait until she was spoken to? Cool, comforting hands cupped her face. A soft voice laced with understanding urged Autumn to look at him while he spoke.

"I am Archangel Kaela," the heavenly being said softly. "I mean you no harm. I am here on a mission for God."

Sobs weakened Autumn. She collapsed on the floor, hugging the great angel's ankles. Try as she would, she could not stand. "Should I kneel before you?" she heard herself ask.

"No living creature in the universe kneels before anyone, but God and Son," was the angel's reply.

Autumn sank closer to the floor, trembling as a new wave of fear washed over her. Strong arms lifted her from where she lay. Cradled against the angel's chest, she inhaled deeply. The scent of citrus and flowers forced her eyes open. Expecting to find Florida had been drenched in a miraculous rain that revived the fruit trees and flowers, she turned her head to gaze through one of the gazebo's screened walls. Instead, her narrowed vision revealed a sea of burned grass, dying bushes, leafless trees, and palms with dried fronds. Autumn turned her frightened eyes to the angel's face. He was smiling. Seconds later, she felt herself being lowered onto the seat of the glider. She sat stock still while Archangel Kaela wiped away her tears with napkins he found on the serving tray. Both Autumn and the angel were quiet for a long moment.

At last, the angel said, "I am sorry I frightened you." He lifted her sweaty glass from the end table and urged her to drink. Autumn sipped tea warmed by the sun-heated air and weakened by melted ice. She breathed in deeply. Seeing she was all right, Archangel Kaela rose from where he had been kneeling and stood before her. "My assignment is to instruct you in the ways of God so you will allow no one to doubt His existence. Today, you will write what you learn and put it in a book."

Autumn whispered, "Surely, somewhere on Earth, there is someone more deserving to tell your story than I am?" The sweet scent of bananas, berries, citrus, flowers, and the freshness of new fallen rain replaced the stale, musty scent of the gazebo's interior. Autumn inhaled deeply. Could this be the ambrosial scent angels were rumored to carry on their wings? "Would you like a glass of iced tea?" She asked her uninvited guest. "I don't know how cold it will be, but I have plenty of it."

"Iced tea?" Archangel Kaela mused. He took a seat on the glider, resting his back against its plush cushions. "I have never tasted iced tea but could use something wet. Thank you."

He watched as Autumn filled their glasses with half-melted ice cubes and tea. His hostess set a bowl on the coffee table before him. When the lid was removed, he saw the bowl filled with fine, gritty, white sand. The Archangel's brows rose high on his forehead when Autumn filled her spoon with the white substance and stirred it into her tea. He accepted the unused spoon she offered and prepared to use it to sweeten his tea to his taste.

From her rocking chair, Autumn watched as Kaela mirrored her actions by wiping the hollow of his spoon with a napkin before dipping it into the sugar bowl. But when he lifted the teaspoon from the bowl, he did not empty it into the glass as she had expected. Instead, the angel spilled a fraction of its contents into the palm of his hand, and like a tourist in a foreign restaurant who dared to sample a new exotic food, the archangel lifted the sugar in his hand to his mouth and tasted it. A dreamy expression crossed his face. With a contented sigh, he emptied the teaspoon into his glass, stirred, and tasted. Several teaspoons later, Autumn's guest returned the sugar bowl to its tray.

Kaela's pink tongue licked his upper lip. Sugar was not as tasty as Heaven's nectar, but it would do until he returned home.

"You are undoubtedly curious about my presence here." Autumn nodded. Like a backyard gossip, the angel motioned his hostess closer. "You have been chosen to pen the secrets of God's universe. Take up your writing material; listen closely to what I say. If you have questions, ask, and I will answer them. When our work is finished today, you must put what I tell you in a book and present it to mankind."

Autumn lifted her notebook from the stand and opened it to a new page. With her pen's tip pressed hard against the page's top line, she nodded to let the angel know he could speak.

"Have you ever felt that a day was too short? Or that a night would never end?" Kaela asked. He smiled at Autumn's enthusiastic nod. "Mankind attributes boredom or imagination to these fluctuating time periods when, in fact, they have experienced an anomaly in Earth's time continuum. Correct time depends on the consistency of the globe's gravitational pull. When the flow of gravity is interrupted, it causes an abnormality in time. Mankind is too busy in his daily life to notice when Earth speeds up or slows down. And time-pieces, even the most sophisticated time-pieces, are incapable of making the proper changes unless someone programs them to do so. Therefore, the fluctuations in time remain unaccounted for, and they are lost to mankind forever."

"Are you saying the fluctuations in this planet's gravitational pull put us hours ahead or hours behind the time we think it is without us even being aware of the change going on around us? Do the anomalies make our calendars wrong too?" Autumn asked.

Kaela nodded. "By Father's estimation, the anomalies have slowed Earth's time by nearly a century. It is good for you to know that Earth's timetable was altered when natural disasters occurred after its creation, like say, when meteorites, comets, and chunks of dead worlds struck its surface. Father's Word made the appropriate corrections, allowing Earth to rotate so its days equaled twenty-four hours and its years equaled approximately three hundred and sixty-five days, but because of its change in location, Earth's time continuum leaves much to be desired."

"Earth changed its location?" Autumn asked.

"Yes, when God saw that Earth could support life, He created mankind. Adam's first sin caused the planet to withdraw from its position in space and seat itself far away from where it sat on the day of its creation," the angel explained.

"Please help me to understand how Adam's sin changed Earth's time." Autumn cringed, realizing that she had interrupted the powerful angel's account. "I'm sorry. Please excuse me. I was under the impression that sin is a crime committed against one or more of God's laws. I had no idea sin had the power to change Earth's position in space, even affecting its orbit around the sun."

Autumn glanced to where the angel sat. He was gone. As quickly as she discovered Kaela's disappearance, the roof of the gazebo evaporated, and her eyes beheld a sky filled with angels. Some were dressed in long white robes girded at the waist with pastel-colored sashes; others were attired in outfits resembling the military garb worn by ancient Roman soldiers.

In a nearby thicket, she saw a man who was probably in his mid-thirties. He was naked, covering his private parts with both his hands while he shouted accusations at his mate. The woman, a beautiful young thing whom Autumn estimated was in her late teens, was crouched over at the waist, trying to hide herself from her husband's angry eyes. Both were sobbing. Both were shouting.

"How could you do it, Eve?" The man's voice, more hopeless than angry, shouted, "We have lost everything because you are vain ... and I am weak. We were wealthy, now we are poor and desolate." Horrible sobs escaped his throat. "I wish I never met you. You are deceitful, and I hate you for what you did. And I hate myself more for allowing you to do it."

"Adam, you were my teacher." Eve wept bitterly. "You should have taught me what I needed to know about life, but you kept some things to yourself. So now you want to condemn me for what the snake made me do. Where is the love you promised me when I became your wife? Where is the support you gave me when times were good?

"If you really loved me, you would have watched over me morning to night, but you let me wander through this garden alone. I was taken advantage of by God's enemy, and you were not there to defend me. You love God more than you love me. You spent hours with Him, leaving me with nothing but my chores."

Mankind's first father turned his back to his wife's accusations. "You could have come to me. We could have gone to God, our Creator. The angels would have rid this garden of the snake before it deceived you, but you" - he turned to face his accuser - "you enjoyed keeping company with a creature that was not of our world. There must be a name for a woman like you. If there is none, as king of this world, I shall surely find a name that fits your deception."

"Please forgive me, Adam." Eve sobbed. "I would not have eaten the forbidden fruit if you had been more attentive to my needs. Every day while I worked with my plants, you wandered off to hear the angels teach God's lessons. When I met the snake, he was so sweet. I fell for his words of encouragement. You called me wife, he called me Goddess. You told me I would learn more as time passed, the snake called me wise. He emphasized my brilliance. He adored my beauty. You were too busy trying to please your Creator to worry about my needs. Your only concern was that my chores were done right. You scolded me for staying out late. You worried that I might cross your God by doing something to embarrass you. So when the snake said, 'Eat the fruit from the tree of knowledge.' I obeyed his order."

Adam was on his knees. "Eve, do you see what you have done?" He rose and took her hands in his. He studied her face. Her jaw was set. Her eyes were cold. "No. You blame me for what happened between you and the snake. Have you forgotten the nights I searched for you, fearing the worse had happened? You willfully chose to ignore me when I said, 'If you see a stranger in our garden, run home.'

"While I listened with all my heart to my Creator's words, you made wreaths of flowers for the angels to wear in their hair. You had no interest in what they told us, so you did not fear the unknown." Adam covered his face with his hands and sobbed bitterly. "All we had is lost to us now."

"According to the snake," Eve whispered, "the whole world awaits us. We will no longer be prisoners in the garden, the angels will no longer be our guards, and God will no longer be our jailer. We will be free."

Adam stared at his wife in disbelief. "We are free, Eve."

"We are free only because I ate the fruit from the tree of knowledge," Eve scoffed. "I have surpassed your wisdom. Now I refuse to live with a man who knows less than I. Therefore, either you will eat the fruit I am offering you, or I will leave you forever." Eve pushed a ruby red apple into her husband's trembling hand.

Adam dropped the fruit to the ground. "I have to speak to my Lord before I eat this horrible thing." He ran down the tree-shaded path to a clearing. "Father, I need You!" he called anxiously. "Father, I need to speak with You."

"My precious child, what is it?" God's voice sounded like the rustling of leaves in the trees.

"Father," Adam said as he wiped burning tears from his eyes. "If my wife ate the forbidden fruit, what would become of her?"

"She would surely perish," the Lord replied.

"Would her fate remain the same if she was deceived by someone who invaded our peaceful garden and encouraged her to eat?" Adam asked.

"Yes, Eve would perish since she is well aware of my one law for mankind," Father said, knowing that Adam was fearful of losing his beloved wife. "Her voice would fade from Earth, never to be heard again. She would be unknown to this world's future generations. And the one who tricked her into eating the forbidden fruit would be hated by humans forever," God explained. As the Holy Father prepared to leave the garden to return to Heaven, He warned, "Adam, do not eat the fruit that grows on the tree of knowledge. My law firmly states that it is forbidden to you and your wife."

God's words tormented Adam. If Eve were to perish, he would never hear her voice again. If she ceased to exist, he would never hold her in his arms again. What good was life without Eve? Would another Eve come to live in the garden, or would he be alone as he had been before God created this woman for him? Could he love another Eve as he did this one? Tears welled in Adam's eyes. He could not let God take from him the only gift that brought him joy. Though Eve still lived, Adam grieved her passing. With his head lowered, his shoulders bent, Adam crept timidly down the path toward the tree of knowledge where his wife awaited his return

"What did our Keeper say, sweet husband?" Eve asked.

"He said nothing that concerns us, dear wife," Adam said, sadly aware that he had told his first lie. He took Eve in his arms, wondering if he would lie to her for the rest of his life to spare her feelings. Or would he, one day in anger, blurt out the truth? He embraced his wife for a long moment, then he knelt, and with one trembling hand, he reached for the fruit he had rejected earlier. Lifting the brilliant red apple from the ground, he bit through its firm skin.

"Oh, this is horrible," Autumn wept. She wiped her tears on the back of her hand.

From behind her, a voice replied, "When Lucifer was purged from Heaven his name was changed to Satan meaning, darkness. God's fallen angel charmed the woman with his lies." Autumn turned swiftly to see an angel whose skin, hair, and eyes were as golden as the robes he wore.

"Satan convinced Eve that she was a Goddess. He told her that she was wise beyond her years. He convinced her that Adam was envious of her though Adam loves Eve more than life itself. Love and admiration can be mistaken for envy since, like the envier, the one in love hopes never to lose sight of the object of his interest. Confused, Eve mistook Adam's pure love and rightful concern for her safety as envy. Her youthful lack of common sense caused her to befriend her Creator's enemy. Under Satan's guidance, Eve became conceited, suspicious, greedy, and discontent. Worse, Satan convinced Eve to commit adultery. The woman is with child. Adam is unaware of her condition, since he has yet to know Eve sexually. Woe to the inhabitants of Earth, for Satan is the father of the globe's first infant!"

"Oh," Autumn sighed. Her gray eyes brimmed with tears. "Eve cheated on Adam with Satan. And now, she has convinced her husband to break God's one law for mankind." She narrowed her eyes. "So, Adam is not the guilty one."

"Eve was deceived into eating the forbidden fruit through Satan's power of persuasion," the golden angel told her. "Adam, who is older and wiser in God's ways, chose to believe his wife's lies over God's truthfulness. He willfully put his love for Eve before his trust in God. Due to Adam's act of willful disobedience, the earth has suffered a wound that will never heal. Adam plagued his generations with a sinful nature that will follow it from the womb to the grave." He raised his eyes to the sky. "Our Lord has ordered His sons back to Heaven before He delivers His punishment on Adam and every living thing on this globe." Having said his piece, the angel ascended, joining the others on their trek to glory.

Autumn stood in the clearing, gazing up toward the sky, her eyes fixed on the band of fleeing angels. Wisps of clouds, almost transparent, added to the beauty of their ascent to Heaven. More clouds moved in, slowly at first, but as the breeze that carried the sweet fragrances of woodland flowers in its hems grew stronger, the clouds quickened their pace. Warm air, almost tropical in its invisible touch, grew cooler. Within moments, the sky grew darker. The clouds lost their snowy appearance, turning silver before they turned a dismal shade of gray. Earth's landscape grew gloomy and foreboding. The wind blew violently.

Autumn turned her head away from torrents of air that robbed her of her breath. Around her, trees of all shapes and sizes were torn and tossed in the savagery of the chaotic storm. Gasping, Autumn fell to her knees, turning her head against the raging current. Her hair lifted high above her head, falling, whipping, slapping against her face until a deluge of rain plastered it to her head, shoulders, and back. Lightning streaked across the sky. Thunder shook the earth. Uprooted trees fell onto the path before her.

In Heaven, Father cut the golden cord that bound Heaven to earth. Sensing its release, the trembling planet spilled its seas onto dry land while its ice-capped mountains imploded. Blustering gusts of wind bent and snapped the thickest trunks of the strongest, tallest trees, distributing their branches from one end of the world to the other. Frigid rain filled with cutting ice pelted the ground as rolling clouds tumbled frantically through a sky that flash white then black. Thunder, trapped within the atmosphere, roared with deafening loudness across the globe.

Every creature living on earth's surface feared for its life. Fish of the sea, large and small, sought the safety of the oceans' floors. Four-legged beasts ran blindly through the forests and across the meadows as though trying to out-run the chaos that threatened to swallow them, and smaller, slower animals and birds of all species hugged the ground. The globe did not stop falling until it reached an undiscovered region where it joined a collection of uninhabited planets in their foreign dance around an alien sun.

Terrified of the violent tempest wrought by God's anger toward Satan, Autumn stretched out on the ground. Tears streamed down her face. "Father, why?" she shouted over the storm's din. "Father, why is it so cold? Father, stop the wind, stop the rain! Please! It's so cold."

"Are you all right?" someone asked.

Shivering, Autumn loosened her grip on sunburned grass and glanced up to see Archangel Kaela gazing down at her. He wore an expression of pure amusement.

"Holy smokes," Autumn gasped. What was she doing lying on the ground outside the gazebo, sobbing like an idiot? "I'm sorry. I must have had some kind of spell." She stood, wiped the sand from her knees and elbows, and went inside. Gulping down the tepid tea she had poured earlier, she shook her head. "Earth was beautiful at first, and then this storm moved in. I was pinned to the ground … I was out in the elements … and I was afraid."

"God's wrath is a horrible thing to experience," the archangel said, lifting his glass to his lips. He sipped the warm liquid and set the glass on the stand. "Father was upset to know that Adam would not sacrifice Eve to keep his word. Adam didn't trust his Creator enough to confide in Him." Kaela reached for his tea. "Our Lord loves you, Autumn, because you talk to Him every day. You always confided in Him, but recently—"

"I talked with a golden angel," Autumn interrupted. She didn't want to hear what Kaela had to say. She was well aware that Father knew her mind; He knew that someone had suggested she remove Him from the miracle of restored health, and she knew she was wrong to even consider such a foolish notion.

"You met Uriel," Kaela told her.

Autumn smiled. "I met Uriel. But who is he? Who is this Uriel, this golden angel?" She lowered herself into the rocking chair, mopping her face with a napkin.

Kaela returned to the glider. Leaning toward Autumn, he said, "Uriel is God's fire. His duty is to keep all the gaseous globes in deep space glowing. In my opinion, Father entrusted mankind's well-being to Uriel since he is responsible for keeping Earth's sun lit so that it warms and nourishes this world. You will learn more about Uriel and his years in Heaven later. Feel honored, dear child, for your vision put you in the presence of a great and powerful spirit." With a nod in her direction, Kaela sat back against the glider's plump cushions and crossed his legs.

"So I had a vision," Autumn said with a smile. She lifted her notebook and pen from the floor. "Come to think of it, it wasn't so bad. I thought I was a goner there for a minute. I couldn't breathe. The wind was so strong it took my breath away, and all the while, it pushed me closer to the ground. The air was so cold I thought I'd freeze."

"Think of how the Adams and Eves of Earth felt," Kaela said, his eyes glowing with excitement. "They were naked, acclimated to tropical weather, happy in their gardens, and they were visited daily by loving angels and a doting Creator. Their faithful obedience to God and Son determined humankind's destiny." He noticed Autumn's brows were raised, her eyes fixed on his face. "Yes, I am speaking in plurals when I speak of Adam and Eve.

"Father created His first couples in all sizes, shapes, and colors. Each couple fell from grace in its own sweet time. Not all the women were attracted to the image of a snake. Most Eves liked Earth's furry four-legged creatures. Try as he would, my fallen brother could not mingle his essence with the cells of a wolf, lion, or bear. Satan could only possess reptiles. So he took the form of a talking snake."

"A talking snake," Autumn giggled. "I guess the devil couldn't become a chimp or an ape either."

"Satan was cursed," Archangel Kaela replied. "As he tumbled through deep space from Heaven to Hell, Father called him a snake. God's first angel arrived in Hell devastated by his loss of titles and position, crippled by physical injuries from his fall, and yet he somehow managed to maintain his power of persuasion. When he arrived on Earth, he convinced the globe's Eves that he was divine. Satan often changed from the caricature of a sleek, beautiful snake to a crimson-and-ebony dragon. Astonished by his ability to change form, the women secretly proclaimed him a God. Being wise and old, Satan persuaded them to doubt their husbands. He told each woman he pursued that she was a Goddess and her powers would grow if she proved her obedience to him by acting on everything he said.

"Satan began his hateful lesson by pointing out the physical differences between the women and their husbands. He encourage each Eve to seduce her Adam. But Father was not ready to populate the earth with human infants. There was so much more He wanted His created children to learn before becoming parents. And so the Adams, though receptive to their wives' bold advances, chose tender kisses, sweet hugs, and soft endearing words to raw sex. Satan convinced the women that their men had rejected them when, in fact, the Adams of Earth were visited every day in their gardens by God's trusted sons, who educated them on the basics of life. Earth's Eves took comfort in the snake's words and heeded his advice because they had begun to doubt their husbands' ability to keep them happy.

"It took time and patience, but Satan successfully persuaded Earth's Eves that the men who loved them were beneath them, intellectually and physically. One by one, the women became infected with deceit and vanity. They believed that envy, not love or concern for their safety, was the reason their husbands encouraged them to stay close to home. Each one, in her own time, rebelled with lies and behaved shamefully in Satan's presence. Aware of their baser feelings, the women willfully committed adultery with God's fallen son.

"Seeing how easy it was to turn Earth's Eves against their husbands, Satan complained about the daily visits God and his angels made to each garden. He convinced the women that God was their keeper and His angels were visiting the garden to spy on them for Him."

"Well, then, it was Eve's sin, not Adam's, that changed the world," Autumn stated.

"No," Kaela replied. "As Archangel Uriel told you earlier, the Eves of the world were gullible. Being much younger than their husbands were, they, in good faith, took Satan at his word. Through his power of persuasion, the devil convinced the females that they were wiser than they actually were. Satan accused their husbands of being foolish men, who envied them. He introduced the women to their most carnal emotions, and then he encouraged them to seduce him."

"They seduced him?" Autumn gasped. "I thought they were poor, innocent children."

Kaela shook his head. "They were innocent when they were faithful to their husbands and when they worshipped their Creator. But Satan praised them when they did his bidding. He told them stories of the life he had once lived and of the beautiful Goddess he made his wife. The devil spoke lovingly of his son and the power he had over mankind. Satan convinced the women if they honored him with the forbidden fruit of their wombs, he would make them Goddesses." The angel sipped his tea. "Amazingly, by appealing to her vanity and teaching her distrust, Satan convinced each of Earth's Eves to deceive her husband and her Creator, so she would lie with him as his wife." Kaela grew quiet for a moment, and then he said, "When Adam bit into the apple, the hills and valleys of this globe resounded with the cries of human babies. Satan's sons and daughters were born. As a final blow to God, who created him, Satan held up his arms and shouted, 'Earth is mine!'"

"Earth will never belong to Satan," Autumn snorted. She read what was written in her notebook. "Adam's first lie was not to Eve. He lied to God when he was asked if the woman had eaten the forbidden fruit. That was Adam's first deception. His first disobedience happened the moment he bit into the apple Eve offered. We are born into sin because Adam betrayed God while he lived in Eden."

She glanced across the gazebo at Kaela. "Adam wasn't envious of anyone. Satan was envious of him. He disrupted Adam's home-life. He seduced Eve with flattery to encourage her to commit adultery so that she would break God's heart by having his child, not Adam's." Her hand flew to her mouth. "Earth's first-born children were fathered by Satan. That's why our Bible tells us that God favored Abel. Cain envied Abel's relationship with God, and that is why he killed his brother."

CHAPTER 3

Hell

To Autumn, this day felt special. When she fell asleep beside David last night, she pictured herself sitting in the gazebo alone, writing her outline for the book that would remove God from the miracle of restored health. Today, the arrival of this wonderful angel proved her wrong. She was learning more about God's plan for mankind than she had ever imagined possible. Autumn smiled. She studied the angel's face for a brief moment. "Tell me about the son Satan claimed he had with a beautiful Goddess and the power that he had over mankind."

Archangel Kaela nodded. "I can tell you what happened after Lucifer was purged from Heaven." He raised his brows, nodding once in Autumn's direction. "Would you like that?"

"Yes, please," Autumn urged. She placed her pen's point on the notebook's page and raised her eyes to let him know she was ready to record his account.

"Lucifer fell to Hell from Father's love and mercy for nine brutal days," Kaela said, his eyes brimming with unshed tears. "And for nine days, we heard his screams in Heaven. The screaming stopped when my eldest brother fell into Hell's Lake of Fire, where he lay bruised, broken, and burning. During that time Father changed Lucifer's name to Satan. When Satan emerged from the lake's fiery waves, he was unrecognizable. Most of his scalp had been burned off. His hair was gone. His eyes were red, their lids crusted with dried bloody tears. Satan's face was so badly burned that the muscular structure that lay hidden beneath the missing skin was clearly visible. He was so transformed that Beelzebub, who loved him most when they lived in Heaven, did not recognize him when they met in Hell."

The angel closed his eyes. "For forty days and forty nights, Satan tried to prove his identity to hordes of his former followers. At last, he asked the one question that proved he was not God's spy or some Hell-born thing: Satan demanded that someone tell him where he could find the daughter that he birthed at the base of God's throne. When no one could tell him where Sin was, he stormed off, determined to find her. But before he left, he promised his supporters that he would find the path that led from Hell to Earth, where they would rule as kings."

"Well, that's awful," Autumn said to no one there. The gazebo's walls fell away, and the light of day was replaced by darkness. She found that she was in a place where the flames that shot up around her gave off heat, not light. Crinkling her forehead, she studied the dreadful landscape that stretched out for miles around her.

"This must be Hell," she whispered. From nearby, a figure approached. A man, for lack of a better description, trudged over Hell's molten ground in her direction. He was a hideous thing, but though he was burned and badly injured, he moved past her with great determination. "That must be Satan," she gasped, pressing her fingertips to her mouth.

Hours past like tiny eternities, and Hell's climate was taking a toll on Autumn. Her flesh burned from the prison's extreme heat. Perspiration peeled from her body in sheets of salt. Her hair was dry and had begun to fall out. Her eyes burned under their lids, and her vision was so blurred that she feared she would be blinded by Hell's intense climate. Inhaling, she filled her sore, scorched lungs with the heated air that engulfed the region. "I would like to go home now," she whispered, hoping her angelic guest would hear her plea.

Beside her, the fiend who fell from God's grace went up to the ceiling, returning to the ground before the scent of smoldering brimstone overwhelmed his senses. He walked a while before rising again to inspect Hell's ceiling for what seemed like the millionth time. Now Autumn saw what Satan was seeing - a broad, smooth, flat surface that was hardened by Hell's intense heat and covered with soot. The ceiling, probably miles thick, reached further than her eyes could see. A close inspection of the ceiling's surface revealed that it was free of fissures and left little hope for escape. The devil returned to the ground to continue his journey through Hell.

Time passed slowly, Autumn was about to make a new appeal for Archangel Kaela to take her home when she heard Satan mumble, "Hell's gates."

The bars on Hell's gates were made of a combination of brass, iron, and hard rock. They were at least a foot in diameter, and they were burdened with dozens of heavy chains. Each chain was secured by a large, thick, strong lock. Autumn watched as the fiend inspected the gates. Anxious to escape Hell's furious heat, Satan reached for one of the gate's many locks but quickly withdrew his hand. Hell's heat had saturated the locks and chains that secured the gates so intensely that they glowed red-hot and were engulfed in flames. The fiend stepped away from the gates, and so did Autumn.

Hellish demon and blessed mortal stood in the miserable prison, both wanting to escape and neither knowing how to accomplish their desired feat. It was now that Autumn saw a female form seated on a throne by the gate close to where she stood. The woman was normal to the waist, but the lower half of her body was distended in width and length. Mournful howls rose up from the woman's lower abdomen, the anxious cries of hounds waiting to be born. Autumn watched in stunned horror as a litter of three-headed full-grown hounds ripped free from the woman's womb. They whined pitifully as they licked the blood from their bodies with their large hungry mouths. Within minutes after they were born, the hounds fed on the afterbirth that nourished them while they were in the womb and then, they forced their way back inside their screaming mother's body.

Hourly, the hounds were born, and mid-way through each hour they returned to the safety of their human mother's womb. Even inside the warm, moist walls of their hideous kennel, the hounds howled in continued discontent. The woman shifted her body, hoping in vain to find a more comfortable position. It was then that Autumn and Satan notice something else - the key that opened Hell's gates dangled from the woman's side.

Something moved at the opposite end of the gates. Autumn focused her eyes on what could only be described as black velvety shadow. On its head, the monster wore a kingly crown, and its scepter contained a dreadful dart. The shadow's eyes, burning pits of fire, were fixed on Satan. The scowl on its face was so fierce that Hell grew darker. Autumn searched the area for a hiding place. Finding none, she took several steps backward. Satan did not move. Instead, he unsheathed his sword, glaring defiantly at the phantom.

Through gritted teeth, the creature growled, "So you are Lucifer, God's former son of light. You are the traitorous angel who broke the Lord God Jehovah's tender heart. You are the liar who deceived one-third of Heaven's sons into waging a vain war against their powerful King. You are the rebellious brother who, with his army of insurgents, was cast out of Heaven by God. How does it feel, deceptive one, to be sentenced to eternal pain and despair?"

Satan was left speechless by this creature's description of his crimes against God.

"You are the one God renamed Darkness," the shadow said. "You are the one who can no longer call yourself an angel from Heaven. You are a demon, doomed to Hell, and you dare to be defiant in my presence. I am Hell's king. This entire region belongs to me. Show me respect, or my scepter's dreadful sting will show you misery, the likes of which you will regret. Speak your piece, traitorous spirit, and then return to the Lake of Fire, the place of your rightful punishment." The shadow grew larger in stature and more frightening with each word he spoke.

The two mighty enemies frowned so hatefully at each other that Hell trembled. Satan glared fearlessly at the great shadow, his eyes blazing like fire. He could recall only one other time when he met such a formidable foe. That, however, was in the past. Now, it was time to rise to a new challenge. Satan lifted his sword, and moving hypnotically, he circled the shadow, daring him to strike.

"Father!" the mother of the hounds cried out. "Stop what you are doing!"

Satan turned slightly to see the awful witch, the keeper of the sought-after key, draw nearer to where he stood. The shadow lifted its scepter, exposing its powerful barb. Satan reaffirmed his grip on his sword, hoping to strike the fatal blow but before the sword met its mark, the sorceress placed herself between the one she called father and the ghoul. Satan lowered his sword. The ghoul returned to his seat by the gates.

Autumn listened intently to a family reunion that proved to be more interesting than she had thought at first. A lot of men doubted they fathered a child, and many cited reasons for their doubt, but no one Autumn knew ever told a child that she was too ugly to be his. She smiled to herself when Sin accused Satan of fathering the shadow she called Death.

"Prove to me that I am your father," Satan challenged. "Tell me what you know about the day that you were born."

Autumn listened as the guardian of Hell's gates described a day when God hosted a festival for His sons of light. It was a day of great joy. The northern emperor Lucifer, Heaven's first crowned prince, and his loyal subjects were guests at the Holy Castle. Throughout that glorious day, the northern citizens were entertained by wandering minstrels and games at the stadium, and they enjoyed an endless feast. They dined in the castle's main dining hall after which they went to the auditorium where they delighted in Israfel's choir and Zephon's orchestra. Lucifer was seated in the family booth on the third-floor mezzanine with God, his seven virtuous sisters, and the holy scribe, Excelsa. At one point in the concert, Heaven's King rose from His seat, pausing the festivities long enough to set a princely crown on Archangel Michael's bowed head.

"You thought the festivities were done to honor you," Sin said quietly. "You rose up in anger, ordering your followers to return to the North. Before you left the Sacred Region and God's Holy Castle, you went to the King's outdoor throne room with the intention of destroying His great white throne. During your tantrum, I was born. I had lived in your heart for many months, and at last, I was free to adore you as your daughter, your lover, and your queen. We lived a life of crime and perversion. But you were not contented with what we had. You declared open war on God. We were captured and cast into this horrible prison."

"Enough," Satan said. "You are my daughter, and I caused your suffering. My envy of all things good and righteous burdened us with this misery."

Sin continued her story. "Before I was sentenced to eternal doom by Heaven's hateful King, He gave me this key with the ominous revelation that only I have power over it. His orders were that Hell's gates must remain locked forever. No one can pass through these gates without my permission."

Sin grew quiet for a moment. She smiled at her former lover, her twin, her father … the angel who broke God's law that read, "Angels shall not procreate." "Sitting here, alone, I thought about the child you put in my womb. My belly grew enormous, and our unborn child was never still. My labor was long, and the pain I suffered was horrendous. When I gave birth, the child I carried tore from my womb so forcefully that the bottom half of my body was deformed. Your new-born son tried to kill me with his scepter's poisonous sting. I ran away, but Death was faster. He caught me, tossed me to Hell's smoldering floor, and he had his way with me. His curse will follow me from now to the end time."

"His crime against you is the reason for the hounds?" Satan asked.

"Yes." Sin wept. "The hounds tear at my insides when they are kenneled in my womb. When they are born, they feed on my blood. Death calls them off before they taste my flesh. He knows, if the hounds devour me, he will perish." Sin saw hope spring into her former lover's blood-stained eyes. "Do not think that what you learned makes Death inferior to you. Only God is immune to Death's sting. Even Immanuel will fall victim to Death for a little while."

Satan remained silent, his eyes fixed on the shadow who sat at Hell's gates. Thoughts turned over in his mind. How could he have fathered such a horror? How could this shapeless thing be his flesh and blood? How could God be immune to Death's sting, but not Immanuel? Did Hell's climate warp Death into what he became at the moment of his birth? What if one condemned to Hell became what lived within his heart? That might explain Death's outward appearance since his first act at the moment of his birth was to brutally attack his own mother.

Satan's mind questioned why God would allow His only Son to perish under the sting of Death's powerful sting. *Perhaps God knows He was mistaken to put Immanuel on my throne.* "I wonder, should I return to Heaven to claim what is mine?" Satan whispered softly to himself.

"Father, God put clay beings on a new world that is tied to Heaven with a golden cord," Sin said, breaking the silence that fell over her conversaion with her father. "I long to find that world. I dream of infecting those beings with my venom, but I never had the courage to leave Hell until now. Death hopes to enter God's new world to feed on the life-force that courses through the veins of all the creatures that live there." Sin deliberately touched the key that dangled at her side. She saw her father's eyes move from her face to the key she held between her fingers. "I can help you leave this place. I have the power to determine who should use this key. And only I have the power to allow a resident of this prison to walk through those gates. But if I help you, you must help me and my son by taking us with you to God's new world."

Autumn was back in the gazebo. Kaela opened his eyes. "Satan convinced Sin that he had to accomplish his mission alone. He persuaded her to wait in Hell for him by promising to return for her and Death when he secured Earth as his own. Sin gave him the key and her permission to leave Hell. When he was outside Hell's gates, Satan returned the key to Sin for safekeeping. He warned her that she should not release anyone else from God's prison." The angel smiled, his blue eyes searching Autumn's face. "What?" he asked.

"Did God know that Satan escaped from Hell?"

"Of course Father knew," Kaela said with a nod. "He saw Satan's reunion with Sin, heard their conversation, and watched His hateful son leave Hell. Father called a council meeting moments after Satan arrived on Earth. Against my sisters' advice, Father allowed the fallen angel to explore the planet. He told us that Satan would act as the gauge by which He would measure mankind's faith and devotion to Him."

The angel sighed heavily. "Father was devastated when He saw how the Adams of Earth betrayed Him to protect their mates. Aware that mankind was infected by Sin and fearful that one day, the race would enter our realm uninvited, our Lord cut the cord that tied Earth to

Heaven. Cut free, Earth careened through the universe, stopping only when it reached this gentle galaxy."

"God created mankind … Why didn't He uncreate our race?" Autumn asked.

"Father will never destroy what He creates," Kaela revealed. "He is the epitome of love and forgiveness. But in time, mankind will stand before his Judge, and he will be so afraid. When humans are questioned by the angry Son, truth will pour from their mouths like water. They will not stop admitting their sins and describing how they felt when they committed crimes against others until the entire truth is known. Judgement Day will be a frightening, deadly day for sinners. But it will be a day of rewards and victories for righteous souls."

CHAPTER 4

More Secrets

Archangel Kaela, second lieutenant in Prince Michael's sainted army, stirred his iced tea to sweeten it with the sugary syrup that lay at the bottom of his glass. "I would like to blame mankind's grief on Satan," the angel replied somberly. "But Satan is not that powerful. When Father created Earth's Adams and Eves, He was so pleased with them that He sent His angels to Earth to aid in their development. The healers among us acted as guides to ancient mankind, teaching members of its race how to reset limbs that were accidently broken, settle upset stomachs, cure allergies, and soothe aching heads with herbs. Your ancient ancestors did not know debilitating diseases the likes of which modern mankind suffers. No poisons polluted the water ways, the air they breathed, or the ground they used to grow the food they ate. Earth was a paradise when it was new."

"Satan admitted to Sin that his envy of all things good and righteous put him in Hell," Autumn said.

"Yes, envy is worse than hatred," Kaela said, nodding. "When we hate someone, we simply forget about them. They live their lives, and we have no idea what they are doing. Better still, we could care less about their well-being, where they live, or who they keep as friends and acquaintances. But when we are envied, we become a target. Our envier wants what is rightfully ours. He harbors bad feelings when he knows we are happy. He disregards our accomplishments, he hates that we love, or are loved. He enjoys our times of sorrow and he hopes whatever makes us sad is just the start of our problems. And worse, the envier always keeps his target subject in sight." Kaela lifted one eyebrow. "Envy is a powerful emotion that leads to nothing but distress for both the envied and the envier. Now, are there any questions?"

"Can angels marry mortals?" Autumn asked.

The angel leaned forward. "During Enoch's time, Semyaza, a soldier in Prince Michael's army, came to Earth at God's request. When he returned home, he revealed that mankind had multiplied as its Creator hoped it would. He told Father, humans were showing signs of progress but suggested that they could use angelic instruction on perfecting their skills. That evening, Semyaza met in secret with two hundred angels in his charge. 'Let's go to Earth and mate with mankind's daughters,' he suggested, fully knowing that doing so would violate Father's rigid law that states 'Angels shall not procreate.' Spurred by lust, Semyaza led his troops to Earth. Lust transformed two hundred angels into demons. They mated with Earth's women and fathered children that were giants among men."

"They were giants among men!" Autumn interrupted. Her thoughts turned to Goliath.

"The women who lived with the angels thought they were better than their righteous sisters. Trained by their celestial husbands, they learned to use make-up to enhance their beauty. They became vain, hateful beings. The demon-angels taught them how to cast spells so that they could level plagues against their enemies and make the strong feeble. They taught the men to make weapons to conquer nations. Meanwhile, their giant-sized children slowed progress by tainting crops and introducing famine to the regions surrounding their homeland."

"What became of these giants?" Autumn asked.

"Noah's flood."

"They drowned?" Autumn gasped. "That's awful!"

Kaela nodded. "It was awful. I was Gabriel's second in command when Father ordered us to gather our troops. We came to Earth and captured Semyaza and his angels. We separated them from each other, and one by one, we confined them to the many valleys on this planet to await judgement. Then Noah's flood happened. All the corrupt angels perished. A few of their giant-sized descendants survived. The huge people formed a tribe, calling themselves Nephilim. They did very little to help mankind's progress. In fact, they hindered the race's growth by creating havoc wherever they went. If Semyaza and his troops had been faithful to God's law concerning angelic procreation, the Nephilim would not have existed. So it is not wise for angels to mate with mortals."

"Why did God create people in different colors?" Autumn asked.

"People are one species, they just come in a variety of colors," Kaela said with a slight smile on his lips. "Father loves all His created sons. He hopes that, someday, the members of mankind will stand like a shining rainbow before His throne. He did not expect the colors of mankind to engage in sexual relations. Interracial children have redefined the way people look, but their parents are not sinners. They, and those humans who procreate outside their race, should not be condemned, nor should the races condemn each other with hateful names or slurs. They should love each other as Father loves them."

Autumn lowered her head. Glancing at Kaela, she said, "Our government tells us that we must accept a multitude of perversions, lest we injure someone's sensibilities."

Kaela sighed, shifting his weight on the glider. "Some people are born with perverse tendencies, and they exhibit perverse behavior that is unacceptable to people of faith. Keep in mind that some people are born with the desire to take that which does not belong to them, and others are born with a yearning to commit murder. If a mortal being or an angel chooses his sinful desire over God's common-sense laws, he will answer for his sins when he is judged by Heaven's angry Son. But if he turns away from his sin and sincerely seeks Father's forgiveness, he will be saved from eternal damnation." Kaela thought for a moment, before adding, "Those who condone evil-doing are as guilty as the sinners."

Autumn sipped her warm tea. Sitting her glass on the end table closest to her glider rocker, she asked, "Is it possible to purge our world of evil?"

"To do that, righteous souls must use fortitude, which is the purest essence of moral courage, and they must openly exhibit their spiritual strength, which is faith." The angel leaned toward Autumn. "Father cannot stop Satan in his tracks, mankind must do that. Just as Satan was the gauge by which Father tested Adam's fortitude, he is the gauge by which Father's justice will judge the human race. Here are a few examples of how Satan sends his advocates to Earth to turn mortals against each other.

"The demon Belial, the one destined to become the false prophet, influenced Aleksandr Friedmann and George Lemaître to remove God's name from universal creation. The demonic possession of Charles Robert Darwin led him to believe people evolved from monkeys. Hell's fallen angels are still angry that they failed to rob Father of all His possessions while they lived in Heaven. In their effort to break God's heart, these demons disguise themselves as humans so they can persuade certain members of your society to become atheists and agnostics, who strike out at those who love God and Son. These unGodly souls emphasize mortal misconception over divine facts."

"Are there other Gods besides the Lord God Jehovah and His Son, our Savior, Jesus Christ?" Autumn asked.

"Father's first law to mankind says, 'Thou shalt have no other Gods before me,'" the archangel told Autumn. "Doubting souls might read this verse and think that there is more than one God in the universe. But that is not so. The Bible, God's written Word, clearly states that there is no other God but Jehovah. If many Gods existed, the sacrifice Jesus made for mankind would be in vain since there would be many paths to Heaven." Kaela saw that Autumn was still confused, so he asked, "How do you believe?"

"I'm a Christian," Autumn said proudly. "I believe in the Father, the Son, and the Holy Ghost. I believe that anyone who does not worship as a Judeo-Christian is an idolater. And I believe any religion that is steeped in violence and promotes lying is a fabrication by demons from Hell." She smiled. "My faith in God and Son is strong. My visions have confirmed what I learned when I was young about the existence of Satan on Earth and his influence over my ancient parents. But I have a request: will you share all you know about Earth's creation so I can write an accurate account of what happened?" Autumn urged.

Chapter 5

Sacred Secrets Revealed

A dizzying feeling captured Autumn in its grip. It was the feeling we get when we ride a merry-go-round or sit on one of those space swings in a kiddie park. Nausea threatened to ruin this new experience. Instinctively, Autumn closed her eyes. When she opened them, she saw that she stood in the center of a beautiful ebony-robed universe. Before her, millions of stars glistened like diamonds throughout the dark abyss. Planets of all sizes, in shades of the deepest grays and browns to the lightest hues of blues and pinks, moved about the region in a graceful dance that signified a different rotation for each world. Clouds of crimson towered upward through the darkness, lighted from within by newly forming stars. Meteors and asteroids, spinning wildly, passed existing globes, narrowly missing them. While Autumn marveled over the beauty and depth of deep space, the darkness split in half and parted like a curtain. A brilliant Being, whose personage rippled like the clearest waters from the purest lake or river, appeared.

"Deep space, be still," the Being commanded, "for I, Immanuel, come by order of my beloved Father to bring life to this region of the universe."

At the sound of the mighty deity's voice, planets stopped turning, stars steadied their glow, and meteors and asteroids paused their journeys through the vast expanse, holding their position as if frozen in mid-air. Even the crimson clouds stopped their billowing. Within seconds of Immanuel's command, a broad untamed waterspout, an enormous whirlwind of dust, a rotating pillar of fire, and a raging hurricane of pure air arrived to present themselves to their Master. With His right hand, Immanuel reached deep into the raging inferno, taking from it a portion of its blistering flame. After rolling the spark into a ball, He set it gently in the black velvet night that spread out around Him. "Dust, cover the fiery sphere with your rich particles."

Obedient to her Creator, the dust storm lent her particles to Immanuel who, in turn, wrapped them around the small, raging ball of fire. Heated by fire's warmth, dust particles formed ores that burned red-hot in some places and glistened white-hot in others. The Master added more dust until the blaze was hidden from sight. Now, the wind arrived to blow his breath across the surface of the globe, and for a moment, the newly forming planet became a fiery comet. Without encouragement, the waterspout poured its wealth of fluids onto the surface. Steam rolled up in thick billowing clouds that cloaked the globe in dense fog. Rain fell until the fire was smothered. Earth changed from a fiery comet to a global ocean.

"Land that sleeps beneath this global sea, awaken," Immanuel commanded. "Arch your back to the sky to form this world's hills, valleys, and mountains."

Far beneath the quiet waters, the ocean's floor heaved upward as a great mountain sought release from its dark, wet prison. Land struggled to free itself, causing towering waves to roll across the ocean's surface. With powerful thrusts, the sandy floor pushed upward against the churning waters until a chain of islands broke through the global brine. While the immature knobs of land reached half-way around the globe, the ground that lay submerged beneath the ocean's depth remained a mystery.

Encouraging the land to rise up in defiance of the sea, Immanuel commanded, "Islands, your continued growth will form this world's hills and mountains, fields and valleys." In Earth's desire to obey its Creator, the newborn ground threw off its fluid sheet. Growing broader, the chain of islands lunged up toward the sky to form one great spiny bank that encircled the entire world.

Desperate to rid themselves of the barrier that divided it into two angry seas, the waves launched an extensive battle to erode the tender land. Towering above the mountain range, great waves of water crashed down on the hill's highest peaks. Soil, mixed with the ocean's brine, slid down the muddy slops. Though the strongest of the mountains endured the sea's brutal punishment, the gentlest of hills and some newborn islands succumbed to its cruel abuse. Broad portions of hillsides and strips of land fell away, forming narrow chasms. Eager to reunite, the seas swept through each trembling gorge at once.

While on the surface of the ocean, waves threatened to drown the land, the shifting sand at the sea's depth drilled holes in the foundations of the mightiest mountains, threatening to topple them into the raging waters. Penetrating the ranges' soggy bases, the abrasive silt formed the globe's first aquatic caverns. The tunneling sand pushed further through the soft earth, causing the water that rested against the ocean's floor to become restless and discontent.

After a futile struggle, a fraction of the sea plunged down the cavern's descending slope. When it entered a narrow passage, the water pounded against walls made of shale, rock, and ore. The sand, as much a victim of the flood as the land above the sea, was forced by the pressure of the water to burrow even deeper.

Led by the sand's drilling motion, the surging water continued its descent until it reached the restricted channel's end. There, like one fluid body, the water spilled into one of the cavern's many rooms. Frantic for release, the brine formed a crack in one of the walls. Spraying through a narrow opening, the body of water slowly emptied from one cell into another, thus beginning its eternal quest for freedom.

From His throne in Heaven, God saw that the flood continued to feed on the globe's immature hills and valleys. To end the ocean's assault on the world, He ordered Immanuel to calm the seas. "Let the submerged ground form basins, deep and shallow, and let the water that covers this globe drain into those basins to form the planet's seas and waterways."

At Immanuel's command, a fraction of the newly formed ground sank to the depth from which it sprang. While the mighty flood spilled its wealth of fluid into the deepest basins, waves raised high from the raging water's surface to beat against newborn shores. Inland, the ground formed smaller basins that became the globe's rivers, lakes, and streams. With the flood tamed, dry land appeared. The unclaimed water that pooled in low shallow areas evaporated and returned as sweet nourishing dew, veiling fog, and rain.

Pleased with what He saw, the Universal King called to His beloved Son, "I command you to cover the surface of my new world with grass, herbs, and every kind of tree and plant that bears fruit. Let each species of vegetation carry within itself the seed that will promise its continued existence."

Immanuel blessed the soil that made up the land so it would be fertile. Then He called out, "Nature, carpet Earth's hills and valleys with sweet, tender grasses." An entity unlike anything one could imagine arrived on a breeze. Nature, adorned in robes of verdant greens, decorated with fragrant herbs and flowers, and trimmed with colorful autumn leaves, knelt before her Creator. As she bowed her head, her golden hair fell forward, hiding her pleasant face. After receiving Immanuel's blessing, Nature rose to her full height. It was then that a portion of her white gown appeared between the hems of her cloak's flowered lapels, revealing that this spirit was robed in all the colors that represent Earth's four seasons.

The entity reached deep within one of her cloak's many pockets and withdrew a handful of seeds that would grow into leafy trees and bushes. From another pocket, Nature withdrew the seeds of flowering plants. With God's permission, she scattered the seeds freely on the earth below. From another of her cloak's pockets, she took the seeds of every species of fruiting tree and bush and scattered them freely on the earth below. Atop the fertile soil, the tiny seeds uncurled and sprouted roots which anchored them firmly in place. The seedlings stretched their minute limbs upward, pushing through the ground's soft crust. Within moments after they were sown, full-grown trees stood straight and tall, their branches adorned with emerald green leaves, fruit, and fragrant blossoms.

At God's command, Immanuel seeded Earth with hardwood trees that formed the globe's mighty forests. He awakened the seedlings of the hearty pines, scattering them throughout the land. Wherever a seed fell, it swiftly sprouted. While Immanuel created trees and plants designed to grow in swamps and wetlands, Nature painted the globe's new foliage every shade of green. God saw Nature's artistry and urged her to paint the petals of every flower that grew on His new world. To the King's delight, Nature took from her core a wide variety of sweet perfumes. Sprinkling the flowers, trees, and bushes with different scents, she gifted Earth's foliage with the gentle fragrances that distinguished one plant from the other.

Outside Heaven's gates, angels, awed by Immanuel's might, used their powerful vision to watch Him create God's new world. While they watched, so did Lucifer and his followers.

"Fill the lakes and streams with fish of all sizes and shapes," the Lord Jehovah commanded Immanuel. "Cause the oceans and seas to become abundant with creatures, great and small. Fill the sky and trees with birds fashioned after every bird in Heaven. Fill the mountains, hills, valleys, and meadows with beasts, large and tiny. All these life-forms will reproduce without my intervention. To assure their reproduction, let the females of every species of creature that walks on the earth, flies through the air, and swims under the sea, give birth soon after her creation."

In humble obedience, Immanuel obeyed His Father's command. Throughout the Earth its streams, lakes, rivers, seas, and oceans swelled with newly hatched fish and other newly born aquatic creatures.

In land, birds and fowl built nests in the branches of green leafy trees or on the ground behind thick shrubs as their mates prepared for motherhood. Soon the limbs and branches of trees, bushes, and shrubs were filled with birds, newly created and newly hatched. Warbling, chirping, screeching, and tweeting rang out, melodious, across the land as birds of all species tossed back their heads and praised their Creator in song.

Beasts, large and small, filled the earth. Within moments after their arrival, the mountains, hills, valleys, and meadows were filled with the howling, grunting, braying, and bellowing of every species of animal as they celebrated their creation and the birth of their young. God's promise of reproduction without divine intervention had been fulfilled throughout the world.

Autumn's heart thundered with the excitement of witnessing Earth's creation.

Then Immanuel commanded, "Let the soil part to release every kind of bug, worm, and reptile. Let them reproduce to fill the earth with their kind."

Before Autumn's eyes, wasps, bees, earthworms, beetles, spiders, and snakes broke through the soil to slither, fly, or creep across the ground, disappearing into the underbrush and trees.

"So it is done. Earth is fertile and resembles Heaven where the angels live, just as my Lord wished."

Autumn sighed. She was back in the gazebo.

"According to Heaven's journals, Immanuel caused a golden chain to reach out of Earth's very core, and He used it to attach Earth to Heaven," Archangel Kaela was saying. "And that is where your planet stayed until Adam chose Eve over God."

"Your account was wonderful," Autumn breathed. "More perfect than you will ever know. But I'm afraid that I didn't write one word of what you said." She shuddered when the angel extended his hand in her direction and sternly snapped his fingers. He wanted her notebook. She closed it and took it to him. Like a schoolgirl, Autumn watched Kaela open the notebook and examine its pages. Would he be angry when he realized his account of Earth's creation went to nothing since not one word he said was written down?

"Everything I told you is here," Archangel Kaela said with a smile. "You have everything written down, and in great detail, I might add." He returned her notebook to her and motioned for her to take her seat. "I understand now what Scribe Excelsa means when he says he 'gets zoned out' while he works on Father's journals." He noticed Autumn's questioning look. "Excelsa is God's holy scribe. He sits in the throne room with our Lord during the day, and in the evening, he occupies a desk in God's inner sanctum. You will learn more about Scribe Excelsa with the passage of time. For now, however, do you have questions for me?"

Autumn examined the callous forming on her finger. "I know that Adam was created from dust and to dust mankind will return," she said, "but I know nothing of angelic creation." She smiled shyly. "Some people think that angels just pop out of the clouds."

"No! Angels don't pop out of the clouds," Kaela gasped, though his eyes twinkled at the thought. "First, let me say this: angels are angels, mankind is mankind. Good mortals do not become angels when they die. After they are judged by God's Holy Son, righteous members of mankind will live in a heaven prepared for them on Earth, the New Jerusalem. Father may choose a few fortunate souls to live with Him in Heaven where they will be equal to the angels. The people who remain on Earth will know God's angels well since we will come to minister to our Lord Immanuel and teach mankind how to be productive in the best of ways. But that has not happened yet," Archangel Kaela said with a wave of his hand.

"If you are interested in learning what *will* happen, read Revelation. We are talking about what *has* happened." He sighed and relaxed his back against the glider's thick comfortable pillow. "Long before angels were created, Father and His Word, His inner Companion, created Heaven. The globe is sacred since our Lord's image dwells there. The only difference between Heaven and Earth is, this world is left to the mercy of the elements and is warmed by an alien sun. To sustain the life that lives here, Father wrapped your world in a protective layer of ozone. My world has no need for ozone or a sun since its light comes from within."

"Heaven's light comes from within?" As though in answer to her question, the page on which Autumn wrote divided in half. In the void that lay between the halves' jagged edges, a misty vision appeared. Her eyes widened. Through the pale twilight, she saw a golden throne. It sat in the center of what looked to be … Yes, it was an outdoor throne room. Across the room from where the throne sat, she saw a high-arched doorway. Through it, a beam of light appeared. Dim at first, the light grew ever brighter until at last, it became so brilliant that Autumn slammed her notebook shut.

"Wow!" she exclaimed, pinching the corners of her eyes with her fingertips. "I'm sorry. What were you saying?"

"I said," the archangel sighed, "Heaven's day begins when Father takes His throne atop the castle's highest peak. At the eleventh hour, Father commands the clouds to lower themselves to the ground around the Holy Castle. As His light dims, the globe's birds and beasts prepare for sleep. On the twelfth hour, Heaven's King retires to His castle's inner sanctum. Father's absence from His outdoor throne room creates the realm's pale night."

"Do angels sleep?" Autumn asked.

"Yes, we sleep. Slumber is necessary to our well-being. Eight to twelve hours of sleep puts our minds at ease, heightens our awareness, and makes us more attentive to others. During our restful state, our blood flow slows so that our vital organs receive the nourishment they crave. Our heart resets its rhythm, and our damaged cells regenerate themselves. While we sleep, our dreams help us solve our daily problems."

Autumn studied her angelic mentor's face.

"What?" he asked.

"Nothing, I'm just anxious to hear about angelic creation," Autumn replied.

Kaela turned slightly in his seat, stretching his leg across the glider's unused cushion. Earth's gravity was almost as brutal as Hell's. With his left foot planted firmly on the floor, he rocked the glider at a slow and steady pace. "According to Scribe Excelsa's book, which is entitled *Angelic Creation*, night was half over when Father left the castle for His laboratory. This night, our Lord, His Word, and my sisters would combine their skills to produce Heaven's first created citizen."

Archangel Kaela's voice faded. Did he doubt that she was listening? Autumn glanced up from her notebook to assure her angel that he had her full attention. Her jaw dropped. She was no longer seated in the glider rocker in her gazebo. She was standing on a path that wove its way across a landscape that looked nothing like Florida. Here, the lawn, bushes, and trees were so vigorous that their green leaves glowed with good health. While she admired her surroundings, a fog fell gently from above to settle around her. The fog moistened Autumn's skin. She ran her fingers across her arm. Her skin felt creamy to the touch. Her mosquito bites were gone, so where the red scratch marks that made the bites turn from bumps to welts.

Autumn ran her hands through her hair. Her tresses felt strong and full, and when she tossed her head, her hair bounced with renewed health.

"This fog is Heaven's nourishing dew," she marveled. "It heals everything it touches." Autumn extended her arms, threw back her head, closed her eyes, and turned in circles several times. "I love this place," she whispered softly to herself. When she opened her eyes, she gasped. The fog she admired had grown so very thick that it blocked out everything around her. For a moment, Autumn was confused about which way to go. But then, the fog cleared enough for Heaven's pale night to reintroduce her to her surroundings.

Autumn turned on the path to face the lawn that she had found so beautiful when something in distance caught her eye: a beam of light, shrouded by the heavy mist but still bright enough to see from where she stood.

Without hesitation, Autumn walked toward the beam, its rays leading her to a rustic structure whose opened door allowed the brilliant light from within to illuminate the fog outside.

Brimming with curiosity, Autumn entered the structure's lighted room. From where she stood, she saw the tables, tools, and utensils stored here were far more advanced than those in any of Earth's modern-day clinics. All was quiet except for the sound of muffled voices, followed by echoing laughter that filtered through the building. Autumn determined that she was in someone's laboratory. Hoping to find the owners of the voices, she began a search that took her past tables burdened with scientific equipment unlike any existing on Earth. Her trek led her to a room where seven feminine spirits stood.

The spirits were identical to each other. Each wore a silver robe, girded at the waist with a sash made of a material so brilliant that the sight of it hurt Autumn's eyes. The spirits' long, thick hair shone like the terrestrial moon at its fullest. One by one, they turned to face her. The blush on their pearlescent skin told her that she had been discovered.

"Good evening," Autumn said as she walked toward one of the girls. "I'm Autumn Dawn Carter, I come in peace."

She was about to offer her hand in friendship when a light from behind blinded her. Cupping her hands over her eyes, she turned toward the overwhelming glow. With eyes narrowed, she peered through the fine spaces between her fingers to see the luminous image of a divine being. Autumn knelt in humble reverence before her Lord. With her head lowered, her eyes closed, the palms of her hands pressed together, she whispered his name, "Father."

As suddenly as the light appeared, it faded. Autumn opened her eyes fully expecting to see Archangel Kaela studying her in amusement. Instead, she saw the deity surrounded by His loving daughters. No longer was the Holy Father the effulgent being who stood before her. He had reduced His brilliance to a glowing outline of Himself.

Autumn rose to her feet and walked to where God and the seven spirits labored over a glimmering substance. Stationed at the foot of the slab, she watched her Maker pour a mass of cells onto its chrome top. A hand unlike any hand she had ever seen before shadowed the shimmering substance that lay beneath its palm. "I command my Word to fashion a being whose physical body is similar to mine." In humble obedience, the Word sent His creative powers through His Host's fingertips.

Powered by the current that flowed from God's almighty hand, the cells bonded to form a spinal column. From that bony ladder, a pair of collarbones and two pelvises emerged. The long bones that fashioned the creature's limbs developed. At the top of the spine, neck bones appeared and a skull formed. Inside the skeleton's rib cage, a bubbling brew churned. Autumn sucked in her breath. The unsightly concoction boiled until the being's heart, lungs, and vital organs were developed. Within the hollow of the skull, a magnificent brain formed. From the skull's bony sockets, two crystal-blue eyes stared unseeing into Autumn's face. She blinked and wiped her sweaty palms on the thin material of her dress.

Like a witness at a gruesome scene, Autumn watched fibers of muscles weave their way through the creature's organs and penetrate its skull. Cords of muscles wound themselves around its bony limbs and wove their way over and through the joints. A thick swell of muscle mantled the being's chest and swept up toward his collarbones. The sinewy vest was less noticeable at the creature's shoulders. Autumn rubbed her eyes and stared in disbelief, for though the being remained face-up on the slab, she saw the muscles make their way down his back. Deep rooted in the back's sturdy wall were the wings that made Heaven's sons unique.

A bloodless heart sent its network of arteries and veins throughout the being's body. Vessels as thick as reeds and as fine as hairs wove themselves through the creature's brain, his vital organs, and worked their way through, over, and around the muscular structure. When the vessels ended their journey at the being's fingertips and toes, they retraced their route back to the heart.

"Robe this hideous sight in flesh!"

Hearing the Lord's command, a single cell appeared at the crown of the being's head and spread like a glow to the soles of his feet. Autumn reached out her trembling hand to touch the creature's arm. His skin was soft and cool; smooth as silk, but firm to the touch. Autumn smiled and lowered her hand to her side.

"Father, give our brother all the senses you gave us," Wisdom said. "How else can he be whole?"

Heaven's King commanded the fibers that lived beneath His son's skin to awaken and become the conduits that carried the tactile senses to the brain. Nerves awakened and penetrated the angel's organs and muscles and wove themselves around his bones. From deep within his flesh to just beneath his skin, the fibers wove their way through every cell of his being. When the nerves finished their journey, the Word gave the creature facial features and covered his bare scalp with thick golden curls.

Leaning over the slab, Autumn looked into a face that was far more beautiful than Kaela's. "His wings are bare," she whispered. As the words fell from her lips, long and short, broad and narrow white feathery plumes fringed in God's sacred gold covered the creature's naked wings.

"Created full-grown and wise, my eldest brother lay in a coma-like sleep," the archangel was saying. "His dreams introduced him to his holy family, to his environment, and to Heaven's laws. So it is for all angels. Tenderly, God whispered, 'Rest, gentle angel,' thus naming my race. Father honored my brother's radiance by naming him Lucifer, which means 'light.'"

Kaela grew quiet. Perhaps he was waiting for Autumn to ask another question. Maybe he was just collecting his thoughts. Whatever his reason, there was a noticeable lull in his account. Autumn glanced toward the gazebo's big plastic clock. Well, now, that had to be wrong. Mickey Mouse's fingers were pointing to the same numbers they pointed to when Kaela arrived. Autumn assumed the clock was broken or that its battery had died. Shrugging, she turned her attention back to her guest.

Kaela sipped his tea and licked its sweetness from his lips. As he straightened his back, he said, "None of Father's blood flows through my veins or the veins of any angel. We are the product of every trace element and mineral existing in Heaven. The essence that gives our skin its glow is genesis. Genesis is a mixture of living organisms taken from the vortex of Infinity. During our creation, the Word seeded us with God's conscience so that we would know the difference between right and wrong. God's Word also determines our characteristics and our physical traits.

"Like mortals, we enjoy freedom of self-expression, the drive that keeps us productive. In ancient times, the angels had the freedom of choice. That gift was revoked when some of Heaven's citizens sought to use their freedom of choice against Father."

"Were the angels created one at a time or in droves?" Autumn asked.

"Angels are created in flocks," Kaela answered. "I am one of the several thousands of sons created of God's first flock. Lucifer was the only angel to be created alone. During the early years of his life, my eldest brother was as documented as he was loved. Before the rebellion against Father, volumes of texts defining Lucifer's creation lined the shelves of the castle's main library. The scientific descriptions revealed the realm's first angel was an experiment. But written in our Lord's own hand are the words, 'Lucifer's thirst for knowledge, his angelic grace, and his outstanding beauty made me want more sons.'"

At this point, Autumn interrupted. "I'm not trying to be rude, but being a female, I have to ask, did God ever create more daughters? If He didn't, was it because He loved your brothers more? And one last question, do your sisters have wings?" Before Kaela could speak, Autumn held up her hand to indicate she had still another question. "Why were your sisters created?"

"Father so loved the entity Nature that He requested her presence during Heaven's creation," Archangel Kaela said. "It was Nature who carpeted our landscape in her favorite shades of green, painted each flower's petal with her love, and cloaked our beasts and our fowl in their colorful furs and feathers. While Father is the giver of life, Nature is the deliverer of the wildlife's young. To honor His beloved entity, Father created daughters who resembled her."

"Yes," Autumn agreed. "Now that you mention it, your sisters do resemble Nature, though their hair color and flesh is much different from hers."

Kaela's clear angelic voice took Autumn from her earthy garden retreat to a room that lay deep within the confines of God's laboratory. The room's walls were lined with shelves that were filled with supplies. Its counters' stainless steel tops lay burdened under books and scientific tools. In the corner, at the far side of room, there sat a piece of furniture that was seemingly out of place in comparison to all the modern equipment that surrounded it.

"What is that?" Autumn whispered, creeping nearer to her find. It looked to be … Yes, it was … an empty old cradle.

Curious, she knelt to study the cradle's exterior. "This isn't wood," she whispered to no one there, "and it sure isn't metal." Her fingertips pressed against the cradle's smooth, dull outer surface. "It feels like … skin."

Autumn rose to her feet, leaning over the ancient crib. Through narrowed eyes, she studied the cradle's shimmering interior. Without hesitation, she ran her hand over one of its glistening walls. "*Ugh!* What is this stuff?" Her upper lip curled in disgust.

The cradle's interior was covered with a layer of thick mucus. Gagging, Autumn looked for something to wipe her hand on. Finding nothing, she reluctantly wiped the gunk on the skirt of her dress. "Well, that should dry stiff." She leaned over the crib again. Its interior no longer appeared shimmering or glistening. It just looked slimy. A thick piece of mucus peeled off the side, slid to the center of the crib's curved floor, and disappeared through a circular opening. More of the mucus that covered the cradle's interior peeled away.

Autumn gasped. The realization of what she saw made her eyes grow wide. She staggered backward. The part of the cradle she had touched was shedding its lining, cleansing itself like a womb. Within seconds after being touched the cradle's interior healed itself, taking on its original appearance.

Autumn was about to leave when her Creator entered the room.

Shielding her eyes with her hands, Autumn peered through the cracks between her fingers. She watched Heaven's King spill a vial of His pure essence on the cradle's glistening floor. The organisms that lay dormant inside the crib's once-shimmering interior awakened. Mini storms raged within each divine cell's nucleus until its tough exterior ruptured. Colorful displays of currents were visible beneath the bassinet's pale lining as the organisms divided and quickly multiplied. United by an unseen force, the cells interlocked to form the links of seven sacred chains. Once more, the mini storms raged to separate the cells' pure essence from that which was unGodly. As the holy cells bonded, a sweet ambrosial fragrance filled the room. Autumn turned swiftly on her heel, expecting to see Kaela. Her abrupt movement sent her spinning back to the gazebo.

"Before Father's eyes, a spirited wind lifted from the cradle. Caught within the wind's spirals were pure and impure cells alike," Kaela explained. "The small cyclone pressed its funnel end against the floor and rotated around the room. Though the twister carried seven holy spirits within its swollen body, it vented its rage on everything that lay within its path. The wind ripped shelves from the laboratory's walls, flung equipment madly through the air, and up-ended several heavy work-tables. Hoping to relieve itself of the souls that lived within it, the cyclone slammed its body against the room's ceiling and floor."

With debris falling all around her, Autumn leaped to her feet, screaming. The howling of the temperamental wind stifled her voice.

What a time to return to the laboratory! Terrified that a flying shelf or a tumbling table might strike her, she cowered behind her Lord. The cyclone might have destroyed the entire interior of the structure if God had not commanded, "Spiraling wind, stand before me." As though entranced, the twister stationed itself before its Master. "Release the seven spirits you have locked within your whorl."

In humble obedience, the wind slowed its rotation. From the clutches of chaos, seven silver Goddesses emerged. Like row flowers bent by a gentle breeze, the feminine spirits knelt before their beloved Father. Autumn saw the Goddesses' beautiful faces, and to her astonishment, she knew their names—Wisdom, Truth, Inspiration, Mercy, Faith, Charity, and Love.

Autumn returned to the gazebo. She sat quietly for a moment. "The pure cells became your sisters. What happened to the impure cells? Did they vanish or what?" In answer to her question, Kaela explained that God collected the bad cells and locked them away to safeguard Heaven's peace. "If the cells were a threat to Heaven's well-being, why didn't God destroy them?"

"As my account progresses, you will have your answer," Archangel Kaela told Autumn. He smiled at her disappointment. "Do you have any other questions?"

"Why were the Goddesses created?"

"My sisters were created to teach their virtuous lessons to Heaven's future citizens."

"Did the Godly cradle have a name?"

"It is called the Cradle of Conception, the nurturing place of future Gods. The cradle set idle in Father's laboratory until my sisters were created. It was used only once after their creation. Much later, you will learn who sprang from the holy bassinet and why."

Kaela rose from the glider. "I need to stretch my legs. This planet's gravity is tremendous." He walked around the gazebo, admiring the workmanship that had been put into its construction. "Did your husband build this gazebo?"

"Yes, he did," Autumn said with a smile. "I helped a little. I handed him his tools, measured some of the planks, and I even hammered a few nails."

Kaela smiled at her words as he took his seat on the glider. Lifting his glass to his lips, he said, "It is really hot and dry here." He studied Autumn's flushed face. "You know, I patrol Hell from time to time, and the climate there is far more burdensome than it is here. In Heaven, there is very little gravity. We are bound to the globe by God's love. Today, I felt Earth's gravity, and I asked Father to lessen the burden so I could better concentrate on telling you my story."

"We are telling your story?" Autumn asked. Did her angel blush?

"Yes." Kaela smiled at her from the glider. "Father believes if I tell my story, you will see how my flocked progressed and how Lucifer's envy changed Heaven from a peaceful realm to a violent one."

Autumn cleared her throat. Setting her pen's point on her page, she said, "Well, let's get started. You told me that you were created of God's first flock of angels." Kaela nodded. "While you slept, what did you experience? What did your dream tell you?"

"First, I experienced a soothing, velvety darkness," Kaela revealed, "until a blinding flash of light that originated, seemingly from nowhere, pierced my eyes. The sharpness of the light dimmed slightly, and it began to swirl. As it swirled, it filled my dream with many colors that were, simultaneously, soft and brilliant. Then my dream began. I saw myself as a carpenter and knew if I applied myself, I would become a master of my trade. My dream showed me the tools I would invent, how those tools would improve my skills, and how I would use them to teach others my craft.

"A voice called my name. I opened my eyes to see Father looking down at me. Clouds shrouded His brilliance, and though I could barely see the gentle outline of His features, I can honestly state that Father is the most beautiful entity in all the cosmos. Embracing the gift of life that God offered me, I sat up on the slab. My sister Inspiration encouraged me to stand while Charity clothed me in the garments my Lord provided. Clothed in my new robe and sandals, I wandered outside, fully aware of everything around me. Nothing felt new. It was as though I had always been in Heaven.

"I knew each of my brothers on sight. I threw my hand into the air and greeted them by name. When the greetings and the courteous conversations ended, scores of us made our way to the village that lay at the foot of the Holy Mount. Each of us knew where we would live. My cottage is at the back of the village, close by the forest that opens to the dirt road that leads to the Holy City."

"That sounds beautiful," Autumn said with a sigh. She thought for a moment and then asked, "How many angels were created before you? Are you among the youngest or the oldest of your flock?"

"Not many sons were created before me." Kaela laughed. "I was numbered close to the oldest in my flock. Excelsa is my second eldest brother in Heaven. He was created to record Father's miracles. My sisters, the Goddesses, were created before Lucifer. They framed the laws we live by. Lucifer was supposed to be our guide, our mentor. He was created wise. Some say that Lucifer's wisdom equaled God's in Heaven."

"Did Lucifer witness your creation?" Autumn asked.

"Very few have witnessed angelic creation," Kaela said with a nod. "Let me think of who I know that witnessed angelic creation: Father, His Word, my seven lovely sisters, God's holy scribe, and you." Kaela smiled at how his words moved Autumn's heart. Her face glowed with love while her gray eyes filled with shimmering tears. "You are honored to be the only mortal on Earth chosen by God to witness so many of His miracles. You have more in common with Heaven's royal family and their holy recorder than any being living in all the galaxies found in deep space."

Autumn swallowed back her humble tears of gratitude. "I'm overwhelmed," she said, her voice stifled by a quiet sob. "But back to our book, you told me that you are a saint in Prince Michael's army. I have to believe that you have many military accomplishments to your name, but being a civilian myself, I have to wonder what you consider to be your greatest civilian accomplishment in Heaven."

"My greatest accomplishment as a civilian was renovating Father's house," Archangel Kaela answered.

"Was it a real chore? Was the work hard? Were the days tiring? Did you begin your work soon after you were created, or did you wait until you got more familiar with your carpentry tool? Did you work without notes, or did you have to work your plans out on paper?" Autumn asked. "Or, did our Lord create a miracle that lightened the burden of your task?"

"Most mortals believe that since God is the master of all miracles, and that angels let Providence provide for them." Kaela shook his head. "Nothing could be further from the truth. In Heaven, the largest boulder is as light as a dandelion's fluff. A seemingly impossible chore takes an angel as much time to complete as it takes a mortal to pluck a flower from its stem. So is it any wonder that Heaven's productive sons longed to provide for their loving Father?"

Kaela smiled at Autumn.

"Sit back and relax while I describe my first audience with God."

CHAPTER 6

Renovations and Visions

A new revelation enveloped Autumn, making her feel dizzy, almost faint. Struggling to stand, she pressed the palms of her hands against the lithe wooden arms of her glider rocker but toppled backward into the chair's cushioned lap instead. Her fall snapped her neck back, tilting her face up until the crown of her head brushed against the center of the chair's high-arched back. It was then that she noticed the gazebo's ceiling was dissolving. Heavy wooden panels, one-by-six-by-eight foot planks melted away and ten-penny nails rained down from on high, falling to her feet like stars. Above her, the sun shone brightly in a cloudless blue sky. Unseen hands cupped her shoulders, sitting her upright. A male voice spoke comforting words that her ears could barely hear and that her mind could not comprehend. Autumn's head wobbled on her neck. Her eyes, rolling in drunken circles, caught fragments of the gazebo's walls fading against the sun burnt lawn. Never before had she been so assaulted at the onset of a vision as with this one. She blinked rapidly in a desperate effort to force the vision to present itself or leave. Unable to fight the mysterious feeling that enveloped her body and dimmed her mind, Autumn closed her eyes and breathed deeply. How much longer must she endure this dizzying madness?

A brief moment passed before the maddening sensation left her. She opened her eyes to survey her surroundings. The scenery beyond the platform on which she sat was more beautiful than anything on Earth. The foliage, no longer burnt orange, was lush and green, and a refreshing breeze carried on its hems an assortment of perfumes that it lifted from the fragrant petals of colorful flowers. Longing to be there instead of here, she reached out, grasping a handful of air. Once more, unseen hands steadied her. Autumn knew that Archangel Kaela was nearby; she could smell the sweet ambrosial scent he carried on his wings. Slowly, the dizziness subsided, her vision sharpened, and her mind became alert. She felt as if she were awakening from a drugged sleep. Autumn looked down to see what her hands rested on. It was a table top. She was in someone's cottage, and judging by Kaela's behavior, the cottage belonged to him.

"Would you like more grapes?" her angel asked. Autumn reached out her hand, helping herself to a vine that was abundant with amber-green balls of fruit. Glancing around the table, she saw that she was in the presence of two unknown male angels. They were tall and muscular, like Kaela. Both angels were handsome, and she guessed that they were probably about twenty-five Earth years old.

"I knocked, and when Lucifer didn't answer"—Kaela popped a grape into his mouth, chewing and swallowing the fruit before speaking—"I put the blueprints for the saw-mill, the lumber-yard, and our request to renovate the castle under his door."

He rose from the table and walked to a small counter where several rolled and bound scrolls lay. Retrieving them, Kaela passed them out to his friends with the exception of Autumn. "These scrolls hold Heaven's hopes and dreams." Unrolling one scroll, he studied it for a moment, then said, "On this one, I sketched instructions to myself on how to build looms and spinning wheels for the fabric shop that Origen hopes to set up in the city. He is anxious to train others his craft." Unrolling another of the scrolls, Kaela pointed to musical instruments he designed. "Someday talented angels will use these instruments to entertain Father and His royal family."

Abdiel closed the scroll he studied. Tossing it down on the table's polished top, he grumbled, "Lucifer isn't going to allow all this progress to happen unless it has his name on it."

Joniel studied the sketches. "Lucifer probably threw the prints aside, never mentioning them to Father."

Never had Autumn seen three sadder faces. "I know I'm not included in the conversation, but—" She was cut short by apologies and invitations to speak. “Thank you.” She took a deep breath. “Why must we take our plans to Lucifer? Why can’t we by-pass him and take our plans directly to Father?”

“So you’ve been talking with Kaela!” Abdiel’s impatience with Kaela was obvious. “Child, we must take our plans to Lucifer because Father lives in unapproachable light to avoid the likes of us.” He saw her shocked expression. “Not just the four of us, but all of Heaven’s citizens.”

“Who told you that? Lucifer! And you believed him?” Autumn gasped. She had half a notion to tell these unsuspecting angels that Lucifer would, one day, be the devil. “As I see it, if Father can put up with Lucifer all day long, He can put up with us for a few minutes.” She waited for them to stop laughing. “I’m glad you find all my thoughts so amusing.” She studied their smiling faces through narrowed eyes. “Maybe this talk of building a saw-mill, fulfilling Origen’s dream of a fabric shop, and making musical instruments is just table conversation between friends. Fluff! Nothing serious! I just think that we would be wise to mention our plans to the One we call King.” Autumn’s audible sniff was the period that ended her sentence.

“If we approach Father,” Abdiel said, leaning toward Autumn, “who among us is willing to accept the brunt of His anger should He find us more annoying than Lucifer?”

“Is that it? You’re afraid of Father? You’re afraid of what He might do if He finds us annoying?” Autumn spoke those words with a feigned grin. “I find that assumption to be absolutely incredible. If Lucifer is correct, our Lord already finds us annoying, and He has done nothing about it to date. If we continue to be cowards as Lucifer hopes we will—Heaven will never progress.” Autumn bit down gently on her lower lip, chewing it tenderly as she mulled over unspoken thoughts. She felt safe in God’s presence. It was He who shielded her from the anger of the spiraling wind when He permitted her to witness the Goddesses’ creation. Of course, she couldn’t tell her brothers about that experience either.

“I will accept the brunt of our Lord’s anger,” Kaela said. All eyes focused on him. “I agree with Autumn when she says Heaven will never become productive if Lucifer has his way. How will we know what Father wants for Heaven and for His sons if we never converse with Him?" Kaela stood, and Autumn followed suit. "We, two, will go to the castle. We will speak with Father and show Him our sketches. When we return, we will tell you Father's decision about the renovation and the saw-mill. If we don't come back, you may assume that we've been uncreated."

"Well, that made my flesh creep." Joniel groaned. He rose to his feet. "I'm going with you, Kaela. You befriended me on the day of our creation, you taught me our trade, and I am only too happy to accompany you on your quest to aid in Heaven's development."

Abdiel stood at the table. "What happens to one happens to all. Count me in."

The foursome left on foot for Father's house early that afternoon. When they reached the Holy Mount, they ascended the broad woodland staircase that Nature built for God's sons to use when they chose walking over flying. Their conversation was filled with laughter and hope. Kaela rehearsed what he would say to Father when he stood before His throne. When he forgot to mention the looms for the fabric shop in the city or the musical instruments he hoped his brothers would learn to play, he began his speech anew. With each practice, Kaela's words grew more eloquent and wise. By the time they reached the castle's gates, Kaela had his speech memorized. But now, as they crossed the fore-hall and drew nearer to the castle's main doors, Joniel grew weary.

"Maybe we should think about this visit a little longer," he said to himself.

Autumn heard her brother's words as she entered Father's house, and she might have answered if what she saw had not left her speechless. Birds, large and small, flew to nests that cluttered the staircase leading upward. Nests were built on the main floor's crumbling window ledges too. Straw, dried grass and bird droppings littered the stairs, their banisters, and the foyer's tiled floor. Beyond the open circular lobby with its row of empty shops was a corridor that led to more vacant rooms in the castle. The corridor's air was filled with dust, and spider-webs clogged the hallway. Small critters scampered everywhere as if they owned the place. The entire main floor was foreboding in appearance; nothing here resembled how Autumn thought God's Holy Castle would look.

"Stay close to me," Kaela told her. "And watch where you walk." Autumn nodded, lifting her gown to her knees. Glancing up, she noticed her angel was peering at something behind her. She turned to see Abdiel standing in the main lobby, pointing out flaws in the structure to Joniel. When they finished their inspection, they walked to the foot of the stairs where she and Kaela waited. "It will take a lot of work to make this house more comfortable for everyone who lives here."

"Who lives here besides Lucifer, our sisters, and Father?" Autumn asked.

"Scribe Excelsa, Gabriel, Michael, Uriel, Uzziel, Evangeline, Israfel, Zephon, Sonnet—many of our brothers live in Father's house," Abdiel said, resting his hand on her shoulder. "Look! Kaela has tired of waiting for us. If we hurry, we can catch him." Autumn walked with Joniel and Abdiel, and when they reached Kaela, she grasped the back of her angel's robe so that she would not become separated from him again.

Halfway up the stairs, she heard a low, guttural noise that sounded very much like a growl. "What is that?" Autumn asked.

Kaela reached with one hand, grasped her arm, and moved her from behind him so she could see. Horrified, she watched a pride of lions descend the same stairs she and her three brothers climbed. With a tiny, almost inaudible whine, Autumn crept behind Kaela, burying her face in his back. The thought of being eaten by a wild beast the size of a mini-van unnerved her. Shamelessly, she stumbled up the stairs as close to Kaela as she could manage without tripping them both.

In the hallway of the first floor, a wolf pack tended its young. Autumn gasped when Kaela took one of the six sucking pups away from its mother. He snuggled the whining wolf cub, returned it to its former spot among its siblings, patted the father's head, and went on his way. The foursome continued down the hallway toward the stairs. Frogs, toads, crickets, and birds were quite at home here. Pale grass grew in thick dust that was probably centuries old. As Kaela, Autumn, Joniel, and Abdiel approached the staircase leading to the second floor, a sweet chipmunk scampered ahead of them, disappearing behind a cracked door. Curious to see the room the chipmunk chose as its hiding place, Autumn pressed her palm against the door's oak surface and pushed gently.

"Get out of here," a muffled voice warned. Without a word, Autumn ran up the hall to the staircase where she bumped into Kaela, who stood in the shadows waiting for her.

"Did you see him?" Kaela asked, "Did you see Lucifer?"

"No," Autumn replied. "I didn't"

"None of us have."

Her mind reeled to learn that no one, not one created brother, had seen Lucifer in all these many years. "How will we know him when we see him?"

"Love tells everyone that Lucifer is the most beautiful angel in Heaven." Kaela replied.

Since the stairway to the second floor was wide and inviting, Autumn expected to see an abundance of every kind of wildlife roaming its hallway. But even before they left the staircase, she noticed a marked difference in the air; it was fresh and comfortably cool. There was a discernible difference in the hallway's appearance too. The floors were remarkably clean and dust free. Grass, bugs, birds, wolves, lions, and all other four-legged creatures were absent from this floor. The walls were clean and free of spider-webs. Autumn wondered if the brothers who lived here were responsible for the difference between this floor and the castle's main and first floors.

The third floor, the floor that housed the seven Goddesses, proved to be even cleaner. Could it be that Lucifer's indifference toward progress was powerful enough to adversely affect the lower stories of God's house, making the castle seem foreboding and unapproachable to anyone who might wish to enter?

The staircase leading from the castle's third floor to its outdoor throne room was steep and bright. Kaela and his friends climbed the many stairs in silence. When they reached a wide landing, Kaela held up one hand as a signal for everyone behind him to stop. He turned and faced his brothers. "We have only seven more steps to take before we leave this staircase and walk into full view of Father's high seat. Anyone who is uncertain about moving forward should say so now."

Joniel asked Kaela to recite what he had memorized. Abdiel asked him what he hoped to accomplish now that they had come this far. "I hope to accomplish much in this visit with Father," Kaela said. "I will not leave here until Father permits me to move forward with my plans." Joniel's expression turned from relaxed to fearful. "If any of you are afraid to move forward with me, stay here until my visitation with Father ends." He lowered his eyes to where Autumn stood. She was trembling; tears spilled down her cheeks. "If you are frightened, little one, you can stay here and await my return."

"I want to go," she said in a quick whisper. "I'm not afraid. It's just been so long since I last saw Father." Her voice broke. She buried her face in Kaela's robe to muffle her sobs of joy.

"Well, then, follow me," Kaela said.

When he turned to ascend the last seven stairs, he saw Wisdom, Inspiration, and Faith standing there, smiling down at him. Without fear or hesitation, he left his friends on the landing to climb the stairs to greet his beloved sisters. They took his hands in theirs, smiling into his face, and returned his greeting before escorting him onto the polished floor of Father's outdoor throne room. "We are here with plans to improve our Lord's castle and to modernize our Holy City," Kaela told his sisters.

"Come with me, I will escort you to Father's throne," the silver Goddess named Inspiration said. "Because Father's light is so brilliant, I would advise each of you to shield your eyes with your wings now and throughout the rest of your visit." She turned her attention back to Kaela. "Tell me your plans. Tell me how you hope to make life more comfortable for Heaven's citizens."

The two locked arms, and while they walked, they shared ideas and moments of laughter, the way loving family members do when they are together. Joniel, Abdiel, and Autumn followed behind Kaela, flanked by Faith and Wisdom.

"I can see," Abdiel whispered. "Can you?" He nudged Autumn.

"Yes," she said softly. She could see outlines of things, almost as though someone had drawn the entire throne room on bright white paper with a No. 2 lead pencil. To ensure her eyes were properly shielded from God's effulgent light, Autumn moved the tips of her wings closer to the bridge of her nose.

"Remember what you see," Abdiel urged.

Autumn's hungry eyes feasted on the outer bounds of the throne room that stretched out before her. It looked very much like a schematic, but without the grid. Seven pedestals, each topped with a throne, sat in a semi-circle around a light that was too bright to look on even with one's eyes shielded. Truth, Hope, Love, and Charity occupied four of the seven thrones; the other three thrones were vacant, probably belonging to Wisdom, Inspiration, and Faith. Autumn's searching eyes discovered a handsome angel, whose long thick hair tumbled freely over his shoulders.

"Is that Lucifer?" she asked, studying her brother through narrowed eyes. Wisdom identified him as the holy scribe. "Excelsa," Autumn spoke his name with admiration and respect. Heaven's citizens believed that Excelsa was the eldest of God's first flock of angels. Father created him first so that he might witness the miracle of life and write what he saw in a book. "God's holy scribe!" A sob closed her throat. Never had she felt so honored. Never had she felt so at home. Kaela and Inspiration kissed each other's cheeks and parted. Autumn watched her angel approach God's throne and kneel like a knight or a nobleman before his King.

With his head bowed in a reverent manner, Kaela said, "My precious Father, Father to us all, my mighty King, King of all living creatures throughout the universe, my wise and patient Creator, Creator of all things great and small, my Lord, Lord of this world and worlds unknown to me." While speaking these words, Kaela went from kneeling to lying prostrate before God's effulgent image. "I am humbled by Your magnificence and feel unworthy to be in Your presence, but I come with plans to move Heaven forward so that You might be more accepting of Your sons of light."

Father leaned forward on His throne. "Please know that my children are worthy to stand before me and that I am accepting of them as long as they acknowledge my worth in Heaven and throughout the universe as freely as you did, Kaela." God said affectionately, "Arise and speak again so that I may enjoy the sound of my son's voice."

Kaela rose to his feet to stand trembling before his Lord, his eyes shielded with his wings. Joniel, Autumn, and Abdiel remained face-down on the floor behind him. "Father, when You created me, You gave me a wonderful gift. You made me a carpenter. Over these past years, I have learned much, and today, I come before Your throne to ask permission to use my skills to make Your house a home for all who reside in it with You. Please, Father, know that if my request angers You that I, alone, am responsible for this visit. I am ready to suffer whatever punishment You feel is necessary."

"You are very brave, Kaela," God said in a comforting voice. "But you have nothing to fear from me. Your heart is as gallant as your mind is wise, and it pleases me that you would seek my approval before taking on your task. I am aware of your plan to modernize Heaven, Kaela, and I approve of it, for I am the maker of your hopes and dreams. Fashion the tools of your trade. Build your logging mill on the river Courage. Teach your brothers your skills. Improve their living conditions. Fill the shops in the Holy City with your inventions, so others may become productive. Then you and your apprentices may renovate my home."

Kaela knelt again on one knee in humble reverence before his mighty King.

"I glory that you are proficient in your trade, Kaela," Father told His beloved child. "If I had a son, a product of my cells, I would want him to be a carpenter like you. For centuries, I longed to see my sons advance, but I gave my children the gifts of choice and self-expression. I cannot force my sons to use their talents. They must perfect their skills and use them willingly and responsibly."

The Holy Father smiled at Autumn, who peeked at Him every chance she got. "Wisdom, Inspiration, and Faith are the keys to success, Kaela. You have all that, plus a sense of angelic adventure. Go with my blessings, encourage others to learn your trade. When you return, I will expect a report on your accomplishments."

Back at the gazebo, Kaela was saying, "In compliance with our Lord's wish, we taught over five thousand apprentices our carpentry trade. Under our careful guidance, they helped us build a saw-mill along the river Courage. Soon, the river's swift current carried the trees we harvested to the millponds where they were stored. Following our example, Azazel, a master metallurgist, encouraged our brothers to learn his craft. He and his apprentices fashioned the equipment that lifted the logs we cut from the millponds, shaved them clean of their bark, and sliced them into sheets and planks. The wood dust that fell from the logs was combined with tree sap to produce paper, particleboard, hardboard, and chipboard." Kaela smiled. "Now all we needed was a—"

"Lumber-yard," Autumn said brightly.

Kaela nodded. "Yes, a lumber-yard, a place to store our wood products. We needed a dry place where the wood would be safe from rot and termites. The river's banks were too damp for our chipboard and particleboard, and the village was out of question. A lumber-yard there would be unsightly. So we put our lumber-yard on the farthest outskirts of the Holy City." Kaela paused for a breath. "Joniel, Abdiel, and I had forgotten about Lucifer. We were so wrapped up in our work. And now, there was this magnificent town we passed through each day on our way to the lumber-yard.

"One evening, I brought out my blue-prints and instructions for building spinning wheels and looms," Kaela told Autumn. "I introduced my plans to my apprentices. They were so excited by what they saw that they insisted on building the machines for the city's fabric shops. Throughout the city, we laid hardwood floors and built shelves, cabinets and counters designed to hold the goods our brothers would produce. When the city was opened to the public, we renovated Father's house, naming each of its rooms and designing the proper furnishings for them.

"We used wood from the cypress trees throughout the castle. When each piece was finished, Joniel, Abdiel, and I etched elaborate designs into the backs of chairs and on the front panels of stands and buffets. We stained the furniture to highlight its wood grains and when we finished that task, we polished each piece until we could see our reflections in it."

With a contented sigh, the angel rested his back against the glider's plump, firm cushion. "One day, while we were working in the lumber-yard, Michael approached. He commissioned us to build stables to hold the unicorn and flying horses that he and his apprentice, Gabriel, had tamed. They worried the animals might wander away. Because Michael and Gabriel live in the castle, Father had given them permission to put a corral on the castle's grounds. The corral was fine for the unicorn, but it could not hold the flying horses.

"Since our work had slowed, I ordered my apprentices to build a stable in the field that lay beyond the Holy Castle's great court-yard. As payment for our services, Michael taught us to ride the horses, winged steeds, and unicorns that he and Gabriel trained." Kaela smiled to himself at the thought of gliding through the air on the broad back of a winged horse. "That's how it's done in Heaven—we use our talents and skills to repay each other for services rendered. "Everyone learns a skill," Kaela told Autumn. "When an unskilled brother realizes his worth, he usually seeks out all those who did for him and repays them. No one is ever in a hurry to collect the payment that he is owed. He is simply glad that he could put his skill to use to help someone else."

Autumn thought a moment about what Kaela told her. "That's nice," she said softly. "That is really nice." She smiled shyly at her beloved brother. "Was it hard for you to learn to ride a horse?" She really wished she had been in Heaven when Michael was teaching his brothers to ride. Autumn always wanted a horse but was afraid that if she got one, it might bite her.

"Learning to ride is hard only when you think you know more than your instructor." Kaela laughed. He glanced at Autumn, her eyes were glowing. "Let's go to Heaven," the angel suggested. He reached for Autumn's hand, and as their fingers touched, they were transported from the gazebo in Florida to the lumber-yard in Heaven where they were surrounded by Kaela's horde of new apprentices.

"We are finished here today," Autumn's angel was saying. He was focused on the many faces that stood before him. "Tomorrow, Joniel and Abdiel will teach you the art of etching elegant designs into the smooth surfaces of cedar, oak, and cherry-wood." He wiped his hands on the apron he wore over his clothing. "We spoke with Father last night. Abdiel gained our Lord's permission to take my students on a private tour through His house. While you are there, you will be given access to the median rooms. Believe me—you will be delighted by what you see there." He glanced at Autumn, then back at the apprentices. "If no one has questions for me, class is dismissed."

"Will I see the median rooms?" Autumn asked. Kaela implied that she would be busy elsewhere. "Yeah, but I really want to see those rooms." She snorted. "You know I didn't work there. For some oddball reason, I was working by myself, remodeling Chynella's kitchen." She watched the last of the apprentices leave the lumber-yard. "Michael is still offering riding instructions to anyone interested in building a second corral in Father's field. Gabriel sent invitations to those brothers he thought might be interested in learning to use their angelic vision to see far-off distances. He sent us both an invitation. Azazel is teaching metallurgy in his shop. Origen is teaching interested brothers to weave and blend fabrics. Zephon mastered the musical instruments you designed and built. He is giving lessons too. In fact, he is working with Israfel, who is teaching our brothers how to sing, write songs, and sway in time with Zephon's music."

"Well, there is never a dull a moment," Kaela said with a wink. "Let's take Gabriel up on his invitation to teach us how to use our vision to see more clearly. Maybe it will help us improve our carpentry skills."

Autumn signed up for many classes. To her surprise, she found Azazel's metallurgy classes to be very interesting and informative. Merging her skill as a carpenter with her newly learned metallurgy craft, she helped Kaela build a shop that rivaled the stables in size. The shop's back room served as a private office where she, Joniel, and Abdiel met with Kaela to discuss new projects for the apprentices to work on. When she wasn't at the lumber-yard instructing students, she worked at the saw-mill with her brother lumber-jacks. In her spare time, she drew up blueprints for fun projects she hoped to build in her back-yard.

Brothers who lived in the city and the village at the base of the Holy Mount grew curious when they saw Autumn carrying long planks and sheets of wood home with her every evening. Her hammering drew their attention to the cottage she shared with Kaela. Neighbors from near and far gathered in the street outside her home to watch this tiny little angel build a spacious gazebo on her lawn. Now everyone wanted a gazebo of his own.

Autumn moved her material and her tools from one location to the other with ease. She was well paid for her work. Origen gave her the tapestry that hung in his shop window, the one she had always stopped to admire on her way to the lumber-yard and on her way home in the evening. She amassed a small fortune when she built a large gazebo on the castle's grounds. Zephon gave her a flute. Israfel invited her to join his choir. Michael offered her riding lessons. Gabriel taught her to use her angelic vision to see objects up to one mile away. The Goddesses commissioned Nature to teach her gardening and so much more. Her dear brothers—Sonnet, a singer in Israfel's choir, and Bernella, a musician in Zephon's orchestra—taught her to write poetry and how to turn her poems into songs praising God.

CHAPTER 7

Signs of Unrest

Though Autumn never lived in Heaven, she knew the angels' names without ever having been introduced to any of them. She was aware of their talents and skills. And they knew her well, too, though they insisted on calling her brother. Autumn knew that while she was here, her physical body sat in a gazebo in Florida, listening to Kaela's account and writing his every spoken word. So if she had never been here before, where were these memories of friendships and associations coming from? She would talk to Kaela this evening. Maybe her angel could shed some light on this strange set of circumstances.

It was while they prepared for bed that night that Autumn posed her question to Kaela. "How long have I been here?" she asked, smiling at his surprised expression. "I have memories I can't explain, and here I am, getting ready for bed. Days are passing. Nights are coming and going. Has it been this long on Earth? Am I just sitting in the gazebo, frozen in time and no one there can communicate with me, or is this a vision?" She was thoroughly confused and a bit worried about what was going on back home.

"A minute has hardly passed on Earth since you arrived in Heaven," Kaela said with a slight smile. He fluffed his pillow. "I have a feeling that Father is the One familiarizing you with your surroundings and introducing you to our brothers so that you know them when you see them."

"At first, I was amazed that I knew our brothers." Autumn sighed, slipping between the sheets on her bed. Gazing across the room at Kaela, who lay staring at the ceiling, she added, "I am even more amazed at how much I know about you. I remember you … This is so mysterious."

Kaela turned on his side. "Be glad that you are well-liked and popular." He yawned. "I almost look for Father to call on you for help sometime. I just can't figure what He will ask of you or when that day will come." He turned on his side. "Let's get some sleep. Dim your lantern or extinguish its wick." The sound of rustling leaves filtered through the bedroom windows. "Isn't that the most beautiful sound you ever heard?" Within seconds of making his comment, Kaela was asleep.

Autumn lay in her bed, surrounded by pale darkness. Outside, while the nightingales called to one another from the treetops, a gentle breeze carried God's nourishing dew from the Holy Mount to the valley below. "What a contradiction Heaven is," Autumn whispered to herself. Her eyes moved from one corner of the room to the other as thoughts turned over in her mind.

Heaven was a mixture of ancient and modern times. Each cottage was equipped with modern plumbing, but lanterns were the angels' only source of light at night. The shops were as modern as the shops on Earth, but all the items were handmade or fabricated on old-fashioned looms and spinning wheels. The machines at the saw-mill were treadle machines, powered with a foot pedal. But those machines produced as much in a day as the equipment on Earth did that was driven by powerful generators. The castle's auditorium was equipped with acoustics that eliminated the need for microphones and speaker systems. Zophiel was Heaven's only source of news since there was no media or newspapers that delivered Father's thoughts to His sons. But while Zophiel was a mere angel, his message was heard by every ear on the globe. Yes, everything in Heaven, from the great to the small, was a contradiction of itself somehow.

The sweet comforting scent of lavender filled the bedroom. Autumn yawned and breathed in the perfume, her mind drifting back to memories of her life in Heaven. Snuggling her pillow, she pulled her downy blanket over her shoulders. She never thought of Lucifer. He was a thing of the past. All her thoughts were filled with hope and happiness.

"Kaela, are you awake?" She knew he wasn't. "Kaela," she called a little louder. She saw him turn in his bed to face her. "Did I always live with you, or is this something new?" Autumn asked.

"Dear child, you never lived with me." Kaela said, fluffing his pillow and straightening his sheet. "You never lived in Heaven. You never worked in Father's house. You were never a carpenter, though I think you enjoy the work. I don't know whose life you are living. Maybe Father is allowing you to live your life here as you might have lived it if He created you in Heaven and not on Earth." Kaela sighed. "Now go back to sleep."

Days passed. Autumn felt as though she belonged in Heaven. No task was too great for her. No question was too hard for her to answer. To coin a phrase, Autumn was in her element.

It was one those peaceful days when the voices of Israfel's choir filled the region with songs praising Father. Autumn was working with Abdiel, building a piece of furniture she designed for their brother Sahaqiel. Michael approached. He walked passed the two carpenters without speaking. He was clearly on a mission. He entered the shop and was there for some time before he returned to the lumber-yard. Kaela followed close behind Michael. The pair didn't stop until they reached the area where Autumn and Abdiel worked.

"Michael gained Father's permission to put another stable in His field behind the Holy Castle. It will be located close to the one we built." Kaela nodded in Autumn's direction. "Since you are a proficient designer in furniture and gazebos, I am putting you in charge of designing and building our new stable."

Autumn rose to her full height, wiped her hands on the rag she took from her apron's pocket, and humbly acknowledged Kaela's decision to make her the project's foreman. "I am honored by your decision. You won't be unhappy with your choice." Smiling broadly, she returned to her work. Autumn already knew how large the stable would be and what it would look like. That evening, before leaving the lumber-yard, she met with her many apprentices. From among the students gathered before her, she chose Kamyel, a tall, muscular brother who was new to carpentry. With his assistance, Autumn's team of builders hauled the material they needed from the lumber to the work site before going home for the day.

Building the new stable took longer than Autumn anticipated, and maybe because so many brothers relied on her judgement while they worked, it was the most tedious job she ever had. She found that the stable and its design consumed her every waking hour, even causing her to lose sleep at night. It wasn't the same kind of stress that she might have felt on Earth. She knew whatever she did was done correctly—it was as though no one made mistakes in Heaven—but here she sat, in the middle of the night, with Kaela's blue-prints opened on the table before her. Soon she would leave the house, go to the stable, and in her lantern's light, she would compare her angel's blue-prints to the work her apprentices did the day before. When she was satisfied that her students did their work correctly she would return to the cottage to sleep until morning.

When the stable was finished, Michael and Gabriel brought their horses inside. Autumn stood with her arms folded across her chest, smiling broadly as her brothers led unicorns and flying steeds to their stalls.

"The work you did is professional and unique," Kaela told her. "I am very proud of you, Autumn. The confidence you had in yourself and your apprentices is revealed in every plank and nail that went into this project."

Autumn's thoughts turned to her apprentices. "I might have my students over to the house for a party or—"

She was interrupted when Zophiel appeared in the sky like a flash of lightning. "He isn't bringing a message from Father," Autumn said. "If he was, he would be shouting it from the sky for all to hear. Something is going on, Kaela. Maybe you should go over there and see what he wants."

Kaela spoke briefly with Zophiel. When he returned to the stable, he told Autumn, "I have some work to do in Father's house. When you are finished here, go to our cottage, lay out our clothes, and be ready to leave when I get home. We will be dining at the castle."

Kaela could see by Autumn's expression that she was pleased. The castle's dining hall was the place to be when one wanted to sit in the presence of good company. The angels met there daily, taking their meals while enjoying table conversation with brothers who shared their interests. Many good ideas were exchanged over honeyed fruit, spiced vegetables, and room-temperature nectar.

Kaela and Autumn arrived at Father's house at what might have been supper-time Earth time. They were both freshly bathed so that their ambrosial scent wafted pure and clean from them when they past others in attendance. Autumn wore a pale-green robe topped with a sleeveless pale-yellow cloak. Kaela wore his favorite colors—white and blue. They entered the hall, exchanging greetings with their brothers as they made their way to their table. When they were seated, Chynella joyfully set plates, forks, and knives on the table before them. Kitchen cherubs arrived with trays of honeyed fruit, spiced vegetables, several small bowls of edible flowers, and goblets filled with warm nectar. Autumn and Kaela filled their plates. With napkins spread across their laps, they each filled their forks with fruit, savoring the taste of the delicious feast their Father prepared for them.

Autumn lifted her knife, setting the prongs of her fork against the soft flesh of a spiced carrot that lay on her plate. She was about to slice the vegetable into bite-sized pieces when a trumpet's blare called her attention from her meal to Zophiel. "Attention! Attention, one and all!" The glowing white-haired angel called out. It was obvious that he was about to read from the unfurled scroll he held in his hands. "A Festival of Light will be held in the Holy Castle tomorrow evening. All created sons of God will gather in the main dining hall where a bountiful dinner will be served by Chynella and his kitchen cherubs. After the dinner, attendees will retire to the theater where Zephon's orchestra and Israfel's choir will entertain the royal family. Our gracious King will present awards to those brothers who have contributed their time and skills to assure Heaven's progression into the future."

"Wow!" Autumn whispered. The place was so quiet she could hear her heart beating. "We're invited to Father's Festival of Light. You will probably receive an award. Without your inspiration and wisdom, Heaven never would have progressed to where it is now." She lifted up her fork from her plate. "Azazel fashioned eating utensils—I'll bet he receives an award too."

Kaela turned back to his meal, smiling. "Eat and listen while I talk," he ordered. "This afternoon, when Zophiel visited the stables where you worked, I was informed Joniel, Abdiel, and I would be honored at the Holy Castle. Origen, Bernella, Zephon, Israfel, Azazel, and some of their apprentices will receive honors too." Kaela filled his fork with honeyed fruit. "Gabriel will receive an award for his discovery of our powerful angelic vision. The other day, while he and Michael were training their students, one of the flying horses lifted off the ground, disappearing from view. Gabriel followed after him, determined to ride him back to the field outside the Holy Castle. Our bold brother reached heights that no other angel dared to scale, and he made a wonderful discovery.

"Heaven is round and glows pure white, but from that terrific height, no angelic eye can penetrate its light. When he returned to our atmosphere, he noted that the portion of the globe on which we live is small compared to its uncharted regions." Before Autumn could speak, Kaela said, "Father forbids space exploration. He said it is too early, too soon for us to be flying around in the soupy atmosphere of deep space, but He gave Michael and Gabriel His permission to explore Heaven. Scribe Excelsa will document their discoveries." He stopped talking when he saw Michael walking in his direction. "Michael," he called when his brother reached his table. "I heard the exciting news about the exploration."

"Yes, and when a date is set, I would be honored to have you join us on our journey," Michael said, pausing briefly to speak with his talented brother. "That is, if you are interested."

Kaela smiled at his young brother. "Yes," he said, "we are interested—more than interested—in joining your expedition. Count us in. When will we be leaving?"

"There is much to do," Michael told him. He admired Kaela's enthusiasm. "Father wants everyone trained in survival methods. That means our sojourners must obey my rules once they are made. I will teach them skills so that if they become separated from our party, they will know what to do. My survival classes will teach our future explorers how to cross rivers where overhanging tree branches will not permit flight, and we will explore some of the caverns in this area to get the feel of being underground for long periods of time. Based on how well we do, our quest could begin within the next few years."

"What will you be doing until then?" Autumn asked.

"I spoke with Father this evening," Michael said with a smile. "I have obtained His permission to have a stadium built behind the castle, on His north lawn. He suggested that I commission the best carpenter in the area to build the stadium for me." Michael leaned toward Kaela. "Say you will do it."

"I'll do it." Kaela laughed. "I can begin as soon as I draw up the plans and go over them with Joniel and Abdiel. This will be a good lesson for my apprentices too."

"We will train for the exploration at the stadium," Michael said. "Gabriel and I plan to hold equestrian contests, and Azazel is drawing up plans for athletic equipment that will be used in the contests. We will exhibit our wrestling skills, running skills, and riding skills in the stadium."

"I'm looking forward to helping you accomplish your goal." Kaela laughed. "It sounds very exciting."

Michael rested his hand on Autumn's shoulder. "When our dinner ends this evening, I will be going back to the stables. I have students coming for late-night lessons. You should enroll, Kaela. The world looks different at night. It is easy to get lost. Sometimes, my students become so confused about where they are that I must light a torch so they can find their way back to the stables."

Listening to Michael talk, Autumn thought of how dark Earth's nights can be. She wanted to say something about it. She wanted to compare her planet's dark, moonless nights to Heaven's pale nights, but remained quiet. There were things that the angels could know, and things they had to find out for themselves. Michael turned to leave. "I hope to see you after the awards ceremony tomorrow evening."

"Until tomorrow," Kaela and Autumn said in unison.

"We have worn every formal piece of clothing hanging in our closet," Autumn mumbled. "We need something special to wear to

Father's upcoming festival and awards ceremony. We need new robes, cloaks, and sashes, and we need new sandals too. Maybe it's time to pay Origen a visit."

The following evening, Kaela stood in the living room of his small cottage admiring Autumn, who could never reveal her gender to anyone since it was Father's plan for everyone in Heaven to see her as a male angel. "You look beautiful tonight," Kaela told her. She had chosen a pink robe and a mauve cloak as her attire, and of course, she wore matching sandals on her feet. Kaela was clothed in shades of blue, white, and gold.

"Thank you," Autumn said with a delighted smile. "Why can't our brothers know I'm a girl?" she asked while her angel straightened the sash that girded her waist.

Kaela smiled at her question. "If our brothers learn that you are a female, they will think you are a Goddess. My sisters are the only females in Heaven, and they are Goddesses. To reveal that you are a female who is not a Goddess would put you in peril. And since you are Father's guest, He wants to keep you safe."

"I notice that no one has called you archangel," Autumn said, studying her angel's face. "Why is that?"

"I haven't accepted the title yet," Kaela told her. "My promotion to archangel comes much later in Heaven's history. But Father will promote one son to that high rank soon, very soon."

At the castle, Autumn left Kaela surrounded by his beloved apprentices. Her brothers needed time to share their thoughts with their mentor without any interruptions from her. She walked through the castle's fore-hall to the courtyard where she saw Nesroc and Mammon standing in the shadow of a tall oak tree. A crowd of youngsters had gathered round them and were listening to them speak.

"Lucifer sits unblinking in God's effulgent light, which proves that he is royalty," Nesroc was saying. "Think about that—can you look upon Father's face without shielding your eyes? And if Lucifer is not royalty, why must Heaven's master craftsmen gain permission from him to put their skills on display?" The children from God's newly created flock listened intently to what they were being told. "God commanded your eldest brothers of the first flock to build this kingdom to please His best-loved son, Lucifer, who—"

"Your words are false, Nesroc," Autumn said in a challenging tone of voice. "Our Lord did not command my brothers to build a kingdom to please Lucifer. This kingdom was here when we were created." She looked into each child's face. "I am created of God's first flock. I know for a fact that Kaela was the first of our kind to approach our Lord with a request to renovate this house, the village, and the city." She glared at her false brothers. "Lucifer is not a member of the royal family. He may sit in Father's presence, but he has no divine powers. Lucifer is an angel. He is a brother, not a God. The only difference between us and Lucifer is, Father created him first, and he is not a member of a flock." She studied one youngster's face. "You didn't know that, did you, child? You actually believe that Lucifer is some kind of God. Believe me, he's not. There is only one God and seven Goddesses in Heaven, never forget that."

"And just how would you know that, Autumn?" Thummuz, a brazen youngster and a son of God's fifth flock, asked.

"I was present among those who knelt before our mighty Father's throne, and I heard Kaela's request with my own ears," Autumn answered. The children gasped and spoke softly among themselves.

"Who will you believe?" Mammon asked. "Will you believe Autumn, who seeks glory through the accomplishments of others? Or will you believe Nesroc, who you all admire for his height and masculine good looks?"

"Don't challenge me, Mammon!" Autumn warned. To her young brothers, she said, "I speak the truth. I was with Kaela on the day he knelt before God and made his request. And I have worked with him, Abdiel, and Joniel all these many years to make Heaven more comfortable for Father, my beloved sisters, and my precious brothers." Through narrowed eyes, she studied her Lord's adversaries. "Let this be a warning to you, Nesroc. Never speak falsehoods about God in my presence again. We are sons of a great, kind, generous Father who deserves our obedience and our respect." She cast all of them a leveling glance. "Now let's pretend this was a friendly conversation among brothers. Be on your way, all of you."

"I don't know who you think you are—" Mammon snarled.

"That is why we are pretending this conversation was a friendly one, Mammon," Autumn boldly stated, "because you don't know who I am." A hand rested gently on her shoulder. She turned, expecting to see Kaela, but saw Love instead. "My sister, what can I do for you?"

"I am so excited," Love said sweetly. She took Autumn's hand and they walked together toward the main entrance of the Holy Castle. "You and Kaela will be seated with us tonight. We will share a large round table in the center of the dining hall. Scribe Excelsa and Wisdom will be joining us." Love studied Autumn's face. "You are sad?"

"No, I'm fine. Really," Autumn said, aware that only God knew of Heaven's impending unrest. "Love, my sweet sister, what would Father do if something threatened Heaven's peace?"

Love locked arms with Autumn. "I know of nothing that can disturb Heaven's peace. But put your question to Wisdom, she may reply differently. It is my opinion that nothing can happen that will not serve Father's purpose. Therefore, if He decides that something is impractical, it will not happen." Love's answer, simply put, was God's will be done. "Be glad. Rejoice. Be obedient to your Father, who loves you."

"I will accept whatever our Lord wants for me," Autumn said softly, "and thank you for your thoughtful words. My heart is truly comforted." Arm in arm, Love and Autumn walked to the dining hall together.

When Kaela turned away from his apprentices and saw that Autumn was gone, he searched the courtyard, asking everyone he met if they had seen her. The hour was growing closer to when they would be expected in the dining hall, and he had no idea where they would sit. Standing in the courtyard, he used his angelic vision to scan the area beyond where the stadium would sit. She was nowhere to be found. But he did see his beloved sister Inspiration wandering among her brothers, teaching them her lesson so that one day they would receive an award from Father. He called to the silver Goddess, asking, "Have you seen Autumn?"

Inspiration arrived at his side. Taking his hand in hers, she said, "Autumn is in the castle with Love and Mercy. Our small brother is awaiting your arrival. I will escort you to the dining hall."

Brother and sister walked in silence until they entered the castle. In the main foyer, Inspiration turned to him, saying, "This ceremony serves many purposes, Kaela. First, we will feast on Nature's bountiful harvest. Second, we will share an evening of fellowship during which Father will be strengthen by our faith. Third, the awards given tonight will encourage others to work for Heaven's good. And while we sit in Father's presence, He will cleanse and nourish us with His pure light."

Inspiration guided Kaela through the dining hall's high-arched doorway to the large table that sat in the center of the room. "You and Autumn will share this table with Father's scribe and his assistant. My sisters and I will join you when we have finished seating our brothers."

Kaela took the chair closest to Autumn. "Michael and Gabriel will sit at a table with Uriel this evening," he said, leaning close to her ear. "See the tall angel seated at the fourth table from the door? He's the one wearing a dark-blue cloak and a light-blue robe." Autumn nodded, her eyes fixed on the angel's face. "That is Semyaza, the one who, in the future, will fly to Earth to check on its progress for Father, and after making his report, he will return to Earth to mate with the daughters of man." Semyaza sat with Azazel. Both angels had chiseled good looks, both were tall, and both were muscular; but Semyaza had a piercing gaze that was disarmingly seductive.

Kaela caught Autumn's attention by leaning closer to her. "Here comes Dubbiel. Faith is dropping him at a table he will share with Rahab and Sammael. Someday, Father will make them the guardians of Earth's troubled nations. Dubbiel will become the guardian of Persia, and for a little while, Father will allow him to guard Israel. But those events will take place far off in the future." He grew quiet for a moment. Kaela's eyes narrowed and he rose to his feet when Nesroc shoved Faith from his path and set his course for their table. "Well, this should be interesting."

"Yes, very interesting," Autumn mused aloud.

Nesroc ignored Kaela, who remained standing. With a menacing sneer, he leaned across the table, peering into Autumn's face. "Never contradict me while I am speaking with others. Do you understand?"

"Then stop telling falsehoods in my presence," Autumn retorted, her voice flat, but strong. "Otherwise, I will, without hesitation, continue to correct your false stories concerning Father and my brothers."

Nesroc rose to his full height and faced Kaela. "You had best speak with your apprentice about the change that is coming to Heaven. Autumn should know that, soon, one of us will rise up to challenge the King's authority and—"

"He will regret the day of his creation throughout all eternity," Autumn interjected.

Nesroc pointed his finger in Autumn's face. "I am watching you!"

"And I am watching you, Nesroc," Autumn told him. She smiled when he turned on his heel and stormed away.

"What was that?" Kaela asked, his brows knitted and his eyes riveted to Nesroc's back. When he learned of Autumn's encounter with Nesroc and Mammon in the courtyard, he said, "Let me handle the rebellious types. They won't act out until Lucifer walks among us."

"You make Lucifer sound like one of the living dead." Autumn laughed. She nodded to Nesroc, who turned in her direction at the sound of her voice. "I'm still watching you!" she called.

"Don't antagonize him, Autumn," Kaela whispered. "For now, he is harmless."

"Maybe physically he's harmless, but vocally, he's a menace." She glanced around the room. "Our table is the only one not filled—oops! Looks like the party is about to begin," Autumn said, nodding toward the entrance.

Zophiel's trumpet blared. The room quieted. God's messenger called out, "Attention, one and all! I have the privilege of announcing the arrival of God's holy scribe, Excelsa, who is being escorted to his table by our beloved sister Wisdom. The scribe is accompanied this evening by his apprentice, Effiel, who is being escorted to his table by Faith. They will be joined by Evangeline, the historian, who is being escorted to his table by Truth." The trumpet blared again. "I have the honor of presenting our beloved sisters Charity, Love, Inspiration, and Mercy!"

Wisdom wound her way through the tables with Scribe Excelsa on her arm. They were engaged in a private discussion, and judging by Excelsa's expression, their conversation was a heated one. Faith escorted Effiel, who believed in his heart that everyone was here to honor God. Evangeline, who walked with Truth, was a surprise to his brothers. No one had really heard much about him, and now, he was tagged with the title historian. Wisdom and Excelsa neared the table where Autumn and Kaela sat. Being in the presence of the Goddesses, Kaela stood respectfully at his chair. Autumn followed suit. Anyone within hearing distance could tell by the tone of Excelsa's voice that he was not happy.

"You and your sisters never see anything the scamp does!" he grumbled under breath. "If you were more attentive to your duties today and less concerned about perfecting your appearance for this evening's event, you would have heard Lucifer's awful demands." Excelsa's voice was more of a growling hiss in Wisdom's ear than a whisper. "When our Lord presents these awards, Lucifer will go insane with jealousy. This award ceremony is going to send him over the brink."

His eyes narrowed as he studied Wisdom's expressionless face. "Why am talking to you? You are as blind to Lucifer's arrogance as Father is." Scribe Excelsa waited as Wisdom chose a seat at the table for him. He plopped into his chair, shocked that the Goddess stationed him as far from herself as she could. "Well, I see our conversation has ended." Excelsa snorted. He waited until his sisters were seated. "Either you move closer to where I am, Wisdom, or I will shout my discontent with Lucifer all over this dining hall!"

Wisdom exchanged seats with Mercy. "I am telling you, Lucifer is bored," she said in the scribe's ear. "He has no interest in learning Father's business. He has no desire to rule—" She stopped speaking and glanced around the table. "We will discuss this in your suite after tonight's ceremony." Wisdom leaned back in her chair and forced a smile for the sake of the others seated with her.

"I have one more thing to say," Excelsa said, reaching for his water glass.

Wisdom leaned toward him.

"Compare today's notes with Father's ancient scrolls. I tell you, if Lucifer gets what he wants, we may as well kiss blissful peace good-bye." Excelsa lifted the glass to his lips and sipped from it. With his brows knitted, he looked up at Kaela. "Are you coming or going?" he asked. "If you intend to dine with me tonight, please be seated."

Kaela dropped into his seat.

Autumn, who was in a terrible mood herself thanks to Nesroc, studied the handsome scribe for a moment. "I know you sit in the presence of God, and you are his holy scribe, but I am not familiar with your obligations to your office. Could you enlighten me, please?"

"I am obliged to properly record Father's every word," Excelsa answered with a smile, "to correctly chronicle Heaven's daily progress and to, without error, translate our Creator's ancient scrolls into modern angelic dialect. To assist me in my duties, I chose Effiel, who is wise beyond his years."

"Your duties are very impressive," Autumn said, her eyes twinkling with admiration. "But tell me, please, which of the duties you just described gives you the right to insult a brother who finds you so admirable that he stands in your presence and forgets to sit down when you are seated?"

Kaela's mouth dropped open. "Autumn, show some respect!"

"I thought this was Heaven." Autumn snorted. "I have been accosted by Nesroc and had to be content to put that behind me in honor of our precious Father, who is the epitome of all good things, only to be additionally offended by hearing the holy scribe insult my mentor. I make no apologies for my statement."

"No apologies accepted." Scribe Excelsa laughed. "You've got spirit, Autumn. I like you." He turned to Kaela. "I am sorry for being so short with you, Kaela. Your apprentice is wise and truthful. My duties do not give me the right to injure the feelings of others. I should have put the day behind me as Wisdom has been urging me to do. I should have arrived this evening filled with peace and harmony for all." His smile faded. He leaned across Kaela to speak with Autumn. "But you were not present in the throne room when Lucifer made his demands, emotionally blackmailing Father with his temper tantrums and—"

"Excelsa, sit back in your seat!" Wisdom scolded. "The cherubs will serve us soon."

"So that is it!" Scribe Excelsa straightened in his chair. "Sit here and shut-up. Well, thank you very much." He grabbed the napkin from the tabletop and spread it across his lap.

"Ignore Excelsa's sour mood," Effiel said. "I can attest that it has been a very long day, with much to do and too little time to get it all done. Excelsa is especially perturbed at Lucifer's bad behavior toward Father, and I fear my mentor's anger has over-stepped its bounds."

Scribe Excelsa leaned slightly behind Kaela. "I am troubled that God and Goddesses overlook the scamp. I am disturbed that whatever Lucifer wants, Lucifer gets. I could just" the scribe's puffed cheeks glowed red—"Lucifer comes snooping around my desk, getting into my private books, looking up events that happened long before his creation, and uses what he learns to—oh, never mind."

"So how do you feel about receiving an award this evening?" Effiel asked Kaela.

"I am honored that Father found my work worthy of recognition," Kaela replied. "I am honored, too, that Autumn and I can share a table with you, my sisters, and God's personal recorder." The scribe rested his arm across the back of Kaela's chair.

"Your appreciation for Scribe Excelsa delights me," Effiel laughed. "My greatest fulfillment is to arrive at his third-floor suite and find that he has not yet left to spend his day with Father." The assistant trained his adoring eyes on his mentor. "I am honored to be Excelsa's humble student."

"Oh, the child is too modest," Excelsa said, patting Kaela's shoulder. "My student, as he calls himself, knows Father's ancient language as well I do. Effiel is intelligent, patient, and hardworking. If I were not so vain, I would relinquish my title and the duties of my office to my assistant without delay. Effiel records the names and the accomplishments of the realm's many angels. Presently, he is recording Heaven's daily progress." The scribe winked at Wisdom. "Ask the Goddesses, they know that I would be lost without my assistant." Excelsa looked around the room. "Effiel, you can make your announcement now."

The scribe's student rose to his feet and loudly proclaimed, "Welcome, brothers. I know you are as delighted to be here as I am. Now that everyone has taken their seats I respectfully call upon Chynella and his kitchen cherubs to serve us. While they fill our glasses with sweet nectar and our plates with candied fruit and spiced vegetables, let us thank Father for this feast. After our meal, we will retire to the grand auditorium where we will enjoy the evening's entertainment and where we will sit in the presence of Heaven's mighty King." Effiel took his seat and smiled at his mentor's expression of admiration.

Chapter 8

Sin Is Released in Heaven

Autumn tapped Kaela's arm. "I need to return to the gazebo. I have a question that is going take considerable explanation." Instantly, the dining hall grew quiet. Autumn looked around. The cherubs, with their trays of food, stood frozen in mid-step. The scribe faced Eiffel, his one hand lifted and his mouth paused on the word *now*. Mercy and Charity had been sharing a joke. The sisters' lips were parted in silent laughter, their amused expression frozen on their faces. Wisdom's unblinking eyes were riveted to Excelsa's face. Truth's hand rested, unmoving, on Evangeline's shoulder, who sat stock still while they listened to Faith's unspoken words. Everyone was frozen in place. Autumn turned back to Kaela. "I need to know where and how all this anger entered Heaven. It doesn't make sense to me. I feel like I'm back on Earth, having dinner with my parents and my in-laws."

"Remember when you witnessed the Goddesses' creation?" Kaela asked Autumn. Seeing her nod, he said, "Do you remember the impure cells that fell from the circling wind's spirals? And how Father gathered those cells, put them in a vial, and set them on a shelf in His laboratory? Father knew that though the rejected cells were benign, they would become malignant only when they mingled with a disrespectful mind." He studied Autumn for a moment. Her wide gray eyes were fixed on his face. She was ready to learn more about the decline of Heaven's peace. "What I will reveal to you has been secreted from mankind since God created Adam."

Autumn lowered her head for a moment, thinking. Did she really want to know this ancient secret? She had been content believing Lucifer's fall from grace was wrought by his desire to steal his Father's coveted throne. Was there more to that story? And did she really need to know the truth right now? Her head spun. Her palms grew damp.

"I … I really don't think I'm ready for this," she said. "Maybe you should keep God's secret a little longer." But her appeal came too late. She was no longer in the dining hall preparing to enjoy a fine meal with the globe's most prestigious angels; she was alone in a room filled with wooden file cabinets and desks whose tops were littered with rolled scrolls and oversized journals.

"What place is this?" Surely, it was not the library. According to Kaela's description, that room was located on the castle's first floor. Autumn leaned out the window. "Wow! Look at that fog!" Never before had she seen fog like this. This had to be the darkest night in Heaven's history. Autumn's gaze traveled down the outer wall of the castle. Autumn counted the windows below the room she occupied. She was on the third floor. A noise in the room caused her to turn swiftly on her heel. Her eyes widened; she was no longer alone.

Across the room from where Autumn stood, Scribe Excelsa took his seat at his desk. He had the awesome duty of correctly recording information into God's many journals. Tonight, he seemed quite confident as he opened the book and lifted his quill from its inkwell. The light from his lantern illuminated his work area so that its golden glow embraced his face. When he finished his work, he pulled a stained cloth from his desk's drawer and pressed it gently to his newly written words. Autumn saw by his expression that he was clearly concerned about the paragraph he just entered. He read it once. Then he read it again as though he could not comprehend its meaning. With a heavy sigh, he closed the journal, lifted it in his arms, and left the room.

Fearful that she might be seen by angelic eyes or her footsteps heard by angelic ears, Autumn followed the scribe through the castle at a safe distance until they reached God's inner sanctum. Without knocking, the scribe entered Father's sacred den. Autumn stepped inside the room before the door closed. There, in semi-darkness, she took the time to study her surroundings. The sanctum's ceiling was extremely high. From its center there hung an oversized golden chandelier. The lamp's hundreds of flickering candles barely lit the room below, but the candles' dancing flame drew Autumn's attention to the elegant woodwork that framed the ceiling; it was white with gold trim. Midway down the sanctum's wall, the chandelier's light grew so dim that it was hard to determine if the walls were bright white or pale blue in color. The furniture that was constructed from the wood of sturdy cypress trees was dwarfed by the room's immense size.

Seven delicate white thrones set in a semi-circle in the center of the room behind a golden altar. Beyond the altar sat a great white throne that was trimmed in Heaven's purest gold. The throne was remarkably similar to the one in the outdoor throne room. Close to the throne, Scribe Excelsa sat at his desk, waiting for Father to return to His inner sanctum.

"Where is Father?" the scribe asked his sisters, his question echoing through the room to where Autumn stood.

"Father is on the west lawn, close by His laboratory," Wisdom answered. "He says He has pressing business there."

Without a word, Excelsa rose from his seat with God's journal tucked under his arm. He walked in Autumn's direction. She was certain he had seen her, but he didn't stop, even when he was close enough to touch her. Instead, he walked past her through the door to the lobby where he paused a moment. It was almost as if he were encouraging her to follow him.

Autumn took the scribe up on his invitation. She followed Excelsa from the inner sanctum, over the tiled floor of the wide-open circular lobby, past the dining hall with its adjoining shops, to the patio that stretched from the entrance of the castle's fore-hall to the amphitheater—or as Kaela called it, the theater's porch.

Autumn stepped off the patio's glistening floor into the grass that carpeted the court-yard. The fog that rose up around her made it impossible for her to see more than a few feet beyond where she walked. Benches, trees, flowering shrubs, and the sound of a bubbling fountain—she was in God's garden, but where was Excelsa? There, a flash of white, most probably a glimpse of the scribe's cloak. Training her eyes on the white object, she moved cautiously through the garden's labyrinth of outdoor furniture and foliage until she stood a few feet from God and Scribe Excelsa.

"Father," Excelsa called as he drew nearer to his Lord, "my sisters told me that I would find You here. I have a question that concerns the foul cells You spoke of during our session today. I thought You said that the cells were poisonous." The holy scribe paused for a moment. "And then, I thought I heard You say that You planned to release them into Heaven's thin air." He paused again. When Father did not answer, Scribe Excelsa grew anxious. "I think I may have misunderstood Your entire statement."

Our Lord smiled at His scribe's questioning glance. After a long moment of silence, the King said, "Tonight, though I am loath to do it, I will release the essence of my eighth daughter into the air. She will test my sons' faith in me, for unlike her sisters whose virtuous lessons are designed to enhance angelic grace this creature's carnal knowledge will reveal my doubting sons to me."

The universal King sighed. "This child's name shall be Sin, which in my ancient language means 'iniquity.' Sin is benign. She becomes malignant only when her essence mingles with a disobedient mind. Her venom will not affect righteous angels. And Sin will never raise her hand against her Father. Sin will act as the gauge by which I will measure my beloved sons' inborn sense of honor. Inherent obedience is much more powerful than faith. When one is faithful, he is virtuous. When one is obedient, he is dutiful. When faith fails, obedience prevails."

Father took a vial from His cloak's pocket. "Here is the test that will forever change Heaven. Nocturnal Sin will visit each of my sleeping sons in the hope of seducing them with her lies. Corrupt sons will turn away from their loving Father, and in time, they will break my laws. Infected by Sin's venom, they will become evil. Sin will encourage them to rebel against me. And one son, whom I love with all my heart, will lead them in a vain effort to rob me of my throne."

In the darkened calm of the castle's courtyard, the Holy Father uncapped the vial and tossed its contents into the air. Cells capable of destroying Heaven and its angels sprayed upward, spreading themselves thick and heavy above the Holy Mount. Angered by the sight of them, God's Word commanded, "Bad cells, stand before me!" Had the angels rose from their downy beds to gaze lovingly toward Father's house, they would have marveled at a brilliant display unlike any witnessed in Heaven until now.

Autumn stood unnoticed in the garden, shading her eyes from gleaming electrical currents that surged against the fog's obscure hems. Lightning flashed through the air, crashing to the ground, barely missing Scribe Excelsa. In reply to the cells rebellion, God's pure light grew brighter, stronger, blinding Autumn so that she fell to her knees on the dew-drenched grass, hiding her face in her trembling hands. Nausea spread over her like a warm blanket, and for a moment, she thought she would be sick. Then darkness prevailed; the war between good and evil ended as quickly as it had begun.

Once more, God's Word gave His command. "Bad cells, stand before me!" The cells spun until their outer shells bonded. Lacking substance, they formed a thick black mist. In the shape of a crown that was dark with shame, the mist positioned itself above the head of Heaven's righteous King. "Show yourself, foul spirit. Present yourself to me." The mist took the shape of God's spiteful daughter.

"Father," the spirit hissed, her long black tongue flicking from between her thin gray lips. "Bless me so I might seduce your sons with my beauty." Autumn moved closer to where Sin hovered. The ghoul's appearance was frightening. Sin's head was bald and misshapen, as though someone had beaten it with a club. Her flesh hung from her bones, and her black eyes rolled in their sockets with each word she spoke. Terrified, Autumn scrambled to where Excelsa stood, cowering behind him. "How can I fulfill my mission if my brothers see me as I am?"

"Father, I beg You, return the witch to the vial. Do not turn her evil loose on Heaven's sons," Excelsa pleaded. He left Autumn standing alone while he approached God. "As Your faithful servant, I ask You; please do not test Your children in this dreadful manner."

Father turned away from Sin to speak to His scribe. "The witch will not destroy Heaven, though she will destroy many lives by encouraging my doubting and disbelieving sons to use their freedom of choice and self-expression against me," God said softly. "If righteous angels cannot contain her or quell the riots that will rise up against me by their rebellious brothers, I will intervene.

"You see, Excelsa, this test is not singular in nature. My sons of light, my precious angels, were created full-grown and wise. They know that by adhering to my common-sense laws, they can end a problem before it begins." He smiled at the trembling scribe. "I am curious to see how far they will allow evil to progress before they rise up in my name against it. And have no fear, if my righteous sons fail, I will save them from Sin's wrath. But first, Heaven's angels will learn that they are responsible for maintaining the safety of their globe and everything in it, or they will lose their peace of mind and their own well-being.

"If my obedient sons try but fail to do what is right by their Father in Heaven, I will raise up an army against the witch and her followers. Should I find there is not one son of light who puts his Creator before himself, I will allow this world and everything in it to end." The Holy Father turned His attention to the witch. "Nocturnal spirit, go forward and test my sleeping sons. Visit them by night, rest by day, and report to me when you have completed your awful task."

Kaela's voice penetrated the fog that veiled the courtyard. "No one but Father knows what Sin did or where she went. The fact remains that the witch's deeds changed Heaven forever."

Autumn turned on her heel. She hoped to find Kaela had joined her, but she was alone. God and Scribe Excelsa were gone. The pure white fog that had been dense when she first arrived had grown dark and was thicker than smoke. Autumn's heart pounded so that she could hear its hammering in her ears.

"I have to avoid being seen by that witch," she whispered to no one there. Peering through the billowing mist, fearful that she might be seen by God's monster, she crept through the garden. Hiding behind trees and bushes, her eyes fiercely searching her surroundings, she found her way to the theater's porch. Huddled in the darkness against one of the theater's arched doors, Autumn closed her eyes and prayed that she would return to Earth. A noise like the cracking of a branch forced Autumn to open her eyes. Nothing had changed. She was still in Heaven, and it was still a spooky, foggy night. Autumn took a deep breath and rose to her feet.

"Well, that's it," she whispered. "I have to find that witch." Her statement made no sense to her since only a moment ago she harbored the fervent hope that Sin would pass her by unnoticed.

"I'm in Heaven, nothing can hurt me here," Autumn whispered, her words coming in anxious gasps. "God loves me. God is the main source of my happiness. He is the giver of my blessings and the maker of my dreams. I live within His sacred heart, and He will protect me." With each word she spoke, she grew bolder until, at last, she had wandered from where Sin was released, past the theater's porch, through the castle's serene garden, and to the path that wound down from the Holy Mount's high plateau to the village below.

The stairs Nature carved in the four sides of the Holy Mount were straight and descended from the mountain's broad crest to its broader base. Between those stairs were miles of ground that could easily serve as a hiding place for a witch. The farther down the path she went, the more Autumn thought about what God had said.

Father called Sin a nocturnal spirit. He said she was released into Heaven to test his sleeping sons, and He ordered her to rest by day. Autumn realized, then, that Sin is only powerful when God's light can't reach her. Therefore, she must do her work at night.

A sickening odor filled the air. It was mild at first, but it grew stronger by the second. Autumn turned in the direction of the ghastly smell. Sin was walking behind her. Heart pounding rapidly, her mouth dry with fear, Autumn fell face-down trembling in the dirt and she did not breathe until the witch stepped over her, continuing on her way.

Autumn rose slowly to her feet, prepared to follow after Sin, but the stench that hung heavy and foul in the air left her gagging and perspiring. Cupping her nose with her hand, Autumn followed the misshapen form, keeping a reasonable distance between them. At the base of the mountain, Sin's mission was clear. She hoped to infect as many angels in the village as possible with her poisonous venom before Father took His throne on the castle's highest peak. Autumn, curious to learn how the witch would entice her brothers away from God, followed Sin to a cottage located at the very base of the Holy Mount.

The witch lifted from the ground, entering Zuriel's cottage through its wide-open window. Autumn hoisted herself up on the window's sill, dropping to her feet on the floor below. From where she stood, she could hear Zuriel gasping, choking, and coughing. A black mist made its way into the room Autumn occupied. She fell to her knees, cowering behind a piece of furniture that she noticed bore Kaela's signature. From her hiding place, she watched the mist in the form of a thin black sheet of fog float out the window overhead. Suddenly, Autumn realized that the witch had transformed herself into black mist during her visitation, but why?

Autumn followed Sin, always arriving too late to catch her at work. Then, several cottages into Sin's visitation, Autumn devised a plan. She watched the pattern the witch took on her journey through the village. After figuring where Sin would go next, Autumn hurried to the cottage she knew the witch would visit. Standing at Rathanael's bedside, she awaited Sin's arrival. Without a sound, the foul spirit entered the room. Autumn stepped back into the shadows, her eyes fixed on the witch's form. Autumn jaw dropped open when Sin transformed herself into a black mist that entered the sleeping angel through his slightly parted lips. Within an instant, Rathanael sat up in bed, gagging, choking and coughing. Still asleep, God's righteous son gasped, "Be gone dark spirit. Never look my way again."

"That explains it," Autumn whispered to no one there. "Sin turns into a mist so that she can easily infect my brothers with her toxic venom. The brothers who expelled the witch's poison from their bodies remain pure, but what happens when one accepts her venom?"

At Buer's cottage, Autumn's question was answered. Autumn was first to arrive at Buer's bedside. Again, she watched the witch transform into a thick black mist before entering into the sleeping angel's body through his mouth. Autumn waited. It had never taken this long with the brothers she visited before, but then, she had only seen a few instances of the witch's strange ritual. Moments later, Sin reappeared as dark mist through Buer's nostrils. Autumn expected her sleeping brother to sit up in bed, gagging, choking, and coughing; but he remained asleep. Buer was among those brothers who became infected by Sin.

"So that is how Sin does it." Autumn whispered. "Righteous brothers expel the venom and reject Sin from their systems, while evil brothers accept the venom and Sin leaves their bodies without disturbing their sleep."

Throughout the night, Autumn visited her brothers' homes, noting what happened before, during, and after Sin entered their bodies. In some cases, Sin would transform into the mist Autumn saw earlier. In other cases, Sin would simply breathe her venom into a sleeping angel's mouth. No matter, the righteous ones rejected the mist while they slept, coughing up the venom and mumbling a warning for Sin to leave and never come back. Brothers who did not reject the mist most likely would remain infected until they turned to Father, asking Him to cleanse them of their iniquities.

Together, Autumn and Sin had walked miles of jasper sidewalks that lined streets of purest gold, visiting many cottages. But nothing that happened so far this evening sickened Autumn more than the sight of the cottage the witch would enter next. Filled with dread, Autumn followed the foul spirit to a bungalow sitting at the farthest edge of the village, closest to the forest whose one broad path led to the Holy City. Sugar maples, oaks, and birch trees with their glowing white trunks lined the property they were about to enter. Kaela had grown these trees from seeds he gathered on his way to the lumber-yard. The trees' rustling leaves lulled him to sleep at night.

Standing at the bedside where her precious angel lie sleeping, Autumn prayed to Father to save him from the hateful venom Sin offered. Kaela slept soundly in his bed, his sheet drawn between his muscular legs. Bare to the waist, his arms lying at his sides, fingers curled slightly against the sheet that covered him to his knees, his toes pointed outward, Kaela was unaware that evil had entered his room. Sin leaned, pressing her slimy lips against his, breathing her poison into his mouth. Autumn waited for Kaela to stir, to cough, to reject the venom, but he did nothing. At last, as a dark mist lifted from between his parted lips, she heard him utter, "Go away, evil spirit. Bother me no more."

"Thank you, Father," Autumn whispered. At last, she could breathe freely. Leaning, she kissed her beloved angel's cheek. Turning to where Sin had been standing, she saw that she was alone. Autumn ran from the cottage. Standing on the porch, she scoured the area before her, but could see only a blanket of soft pink haze. The fog was lifting. Father was about to enter His outdoor throne room to create Heaven's perfect day. A break in the fog allowed Autumn a glimpse of the witch. Sin was hobbling down the jasper sidewalk as swiftly as her misshapen legs could take her. She was heading toward the Holy Mount. Autumn followed Sin to a cavern under the mountain, where the witch was safe from God's pure light.

Throughout the long day, Autumn sat in the cave, guarding the unsleeping witch. She dozed off a few times, but when she woke, she saw the witch still sat with her back against a jagged rock, her eyes fixed on the cavern's entrance. Sin avoided the light that threatened to enter the mouth of the cave until God retired to His inner sanctum on the main floor of the Holy Castle. Only then did the witch crawl slowly to the cave's entrance to look outside. The clouds that billowed downward from the mountain's crest shrouded the valley below in their moist, thick folds. Heaven's pale light faded, and the night grew as dark, if not darker, than it had been the night before.

Now, the witch rose to her feet. Leaving the cavern's dark interior, she fixed her sights on the street that led to the village. Autumn followed close behind her, knowing that soon Sin would visit God's sleeping sons who lived in the Holy City. That night, the pair visited the apartments above the city's shops and the city's town houses. Autumn watched Sin transform into a black mist, enter into her brothers through their mouths, and leave without a backward glance at her victims. Throughout Heaven's long twelve-hour night, Sin searched for angels whose minds were one with hers. When Father took His outdoor throne to create Heaven's bright new day, Sin was already safe inside her cave.

The cave's interior darkened, growing more ominous with each passing second. Autumn turned, her eyes searching the darkness behind her, fearful that the fallen angel who seduced Eve was close by. Blessed night fell softly, almost going unnoticed by the occupants in the cave until a lively bat took its leave. Sin rose to her feet. Autumn did the same. Together, the pair stepped onto the staircase that led to the Holy Mount's high plateau. Ascending upward, shrouded by thick fog, Sin made her way across the field that opened to a path that led to Father's house. The pair entered the Holy Castle, walked boldly through the main lobby, passed by the sanctuary where God conversed with His daughters and His scribe, and ascended the stairs that led to the first floor; but Sin did not start her quest there. No. The witch began her search for sour minds on the castle's third floor where brothers who taught and mentored God's sons slept.

Autumn held her breath when the witch sought to make Michael, Gabriel, Effiel, and Evangeline her own. The four righteous sons of light, like Uriel, Uzziel, and a youngster named Raphael, expelled the witch's venom, sending her on her way. With Autumn following close behind, the witch left the castle's third floor to visit the angels who lived on the second floor of Father's house.

Among doubtful and disbelieving others, Belial traded his love for God to become Sin's faithful servant. On the first floor, several angels fell for Sin's promise by accepting her venom. Among the traitors were Moloch, Mammon, Nesroc, and Thummuz, who encouraged the children created of the sixth and seventh flocks to question Father's miracles. Night was almost over. God was about to take His throne, but there was one more room to enter, one more angel to visit.

"Lucifer," Autumn whispered.

Sin had saved the Lord's best-loved son to be her last victim. Autumn watched as the witch transformed to mist, but before Sin slipped through the keyhole, Autumn turned the knob and opened the door.

"Here, let me get that for you," she said. The witch seemed to see her for the first time.

Together, they entered a room so dark it that rivaled the darkness that loomed outside the fog-shrouded castle. Autumn used her outstretched hand as a gauge to measure the depth of the gloom surrounding her. It was thick. She could barely see her arm to its elbow. Groping her way across the room with hands out-stretched before her, she found the wall. She fumbled about until she came to what she believed was a window. It was covered with a wide, heavy piece of musty-smelling cloth. "No wonder it's so dark in here," Autumn whispered to herself. She pulled the cloth from the window, dropping it to the floor at her feet.

Dim light filtered in. She moved to another window and removed its covering. There. That was better. The pale light from outside revealed Lucifer's sleeping form. Autumn peered around the room in search of the witch and found her where she left her, standing by the door. Within a second of Autumn's discovery, Sin moved across the room like a snake, her tongue flicking from between her thin gray lips, which were covered with the life-changing venom she reserved for her victims. At Lucifer's bedside, she leaned and kissed his lips.

Visions of hate, lust, and glorious victories filled the sleeping angel's head. The witch pulled away, staring at Lucifer's beautiful face. Sin would have left him to his hateful dreams, but Heaven's first-created son breathed in so fiercely that he forced the witch's misty body into his mouth. Sin struggled to free herself, but the angel inhaled, drawing her deep into his lungs. The witch had more than met her match; she met her new father, her new creator, her new king. Lucifer swallowed hard, completely devouring the monster. Without awakening, the angel turned over on his side to dream of ruling Heaven from God's coveted throne.

As quickly as the vision began, it ended. Autumn was back in the dining room now. She leaned toward Kaela.

"It was horrendous," she whispered. "I could not believe my eyes. Lucifer devoured Sin. I have to think that his desire to rule this world is so great that he is the most evil creature in the entire universe." She studied Kaela's face for a long moment. "Lucifer is inherently evil. I believe our eldest brother was created evil, or maybe Father made a mistake during his creation that rendered him evil."

"God doesn't make mistakes," Kaela said firmly.

"Believe what you want," Autumn said. "But I know for a fact that Father made a mistake long before He created our flock, and judging by the many brothers who accepted Sin's venom willfully, He made a lot of mistakes after He created our flock." She studied Kaela's face for a moment. "Perhaps that explains why some of our brothers are so hostile toward others who have done nothing to offend them. It is almost as though hypocrisy has moved from Earth to live in Heaven." Autumn's cheeks grew red with the realization that she was the only one here who fell into the category of being a hypocrite. It was she who pretended to be something she was not. "Am I to blame for all this unrest and hatred?"

Kaela patted Autumn's hand. "You are simply here to witness the course of events that led to Lucifer's fall. Your presence here cannot change history for the better or for the worse." He nodded across the table at the empty chair Lucifer would have occupied. "Envy is the presence of unfounded hatred and resentment—the desire to own something that is not yours. Deceit leads to betrayal. The ability to exercise your right to freedom of choice and self-expression without taking responsibility for your words and actions opens the door to hypocrisy. None of these faults sit with us tonight since our eldest brother is absent from our table."

Autumn smiled, nodding toward Scribe Excelsa, who dominated the table conversation, commanding the attention of those who sat with him. "Does vanity exist at this table?" she asked. Ignoring Kaela's firm expression, she added, "Father released Sin into the air to act as a tool that will define which of our infected brothers will encourage others to betray Him. Lucifer will be the gauge by which Father will measure our loyalty to Him." She tasted her food. "The sweet potatoes are very good."

Throughout dinner, Autumn sat quietly listening to Scribe Excelsa talk with her sisters about the events of the day. When the meal ended, she and Kaela left the dining hall for the auditorium where the awards ceremony would be held. "I feel honored that Father chose me to write His book. And I am awed that I actually experienced a vision within a vision."

Kaela leaned close to his beloved Earth angel's ear. "In Heaven, we call an experience such as yours double vision." Autumn threw her head back and laughed aloud. "You liked that, huh?" Smiling down at her, Kaela proudly escorted Autumn through the open doors of God's amphitheater to their assigned seats.

Chapter 9

The First Archangel

The auditorium was packed with skilled angels from all God's flocks. Autumn sat in the second row from the front with Kaela at her side. She looked over her shoulder at the masses attending Father's ceremony. Some faces were new, others not so new, and many were the familiar faces of her flock.

"Kaela," Autumn called over the confusion, "about how many flocks would you say our Lord has created so far?" Kaela turned and studied the crowd. His answer was drowned out by the excited voices all around them. She narrowed her eyes, as if doing that would help her hear what her angel said. "Well, how many angels do you think are present tonight?"

Kaela shook his head, pointing to his ears. He couldn't hear her either.

"Someone should invent angelic hearing aids." She burst out laughing. Kaela smiled at her before turning his attention to the stage. There was nothing there to see since the long, blue velvet curtain was drawn with its center hems pulled tightly together. "Makes you wonder what's going on back there, doesn't it?" Autumn asked. When Kaela continued facing front, she simply shrugged and faced front too. The sound of Zophiel's trumpet quieted the room. Autumn took this opportunity to pose her first question to Kaela again. "How many flocks are in Heaven, now?"

"Let me think, our flock was created fifteen hundred years after Lucifer's creation," Kaela said. "The members of Father's first flock were created to be Heaven's inventors, architects, metallurgists, and craftsmen. The Goddesses Inspiration, Charity, and Faith encourage us to build and improve our surroundings. Father waited another fifteen hundred years before creating His second flock of angels," he told Autumn. "Wisdom and Truth encourage the brothers created of God's second flock to become writers, poets, composers, messengers, teachers, and historians. Israfel, Zephon, Effiel, Evangeline, and Zophiel are members of the second flock."

Kaela thought for a moment. "Father waited two thousand years after the second flock arrived in Heaven to create His third flock of angels. The brothers created of the third flock are inspired by Truth, Wisdom, and Inspiration. They are the globe's equestrians, athletes, outdoorsmen, and seekers of adventurer. Michael, Gabriel, Dubbiel, Eae, Moloch, Belial, and Nesroc are members of God's third flock of angels.

"Two thousand years after the third flock was created, Father created His fourth flock of sons," Kaela told Autumn. "Charity, Love, and Mercy encourage them to work for Heaven's good. They are cooks, weavers of cloth, and runners of errands. Chynella, Atella, and Origen are members of the fourth flock. Since Lucifer fell short of Father's expectations, Heaven's first four flocks were created to mentor our younger brothers so that they would become productive by learning our skills."

"Are there healers in Heaven?" Autumn asked.

"Why would we need healers?" Kaela asked. "Father heals us with His light. So there are fifteen hundred to two thousand years between each of our Lord's created flocks. And I would estimate that we have seven flocks of brothers residing in Heaven."

"And they learned their skills because we taught them what they know," Autumn whispered softly. When Kaela did not acknowledge her statement, she focused her attention on the stage. This was all too confusing for her to think about right now. Still, she couldn't help wondering what career the youngsters of the fifth, sixth, and seventh flocks such as Raphael, Citadel, Phillip, and Stephon, would choose to follow. Only time would tell. She pulled Kaela's sleeve. "About how many of us are there?"

"We are innumerable," Kaela responded.

"Innumerable," Autumn repeated in awe. "So where does everyone live?"

Kaela smiled. "Well, dear, we live in the village that has grown to surround the base of this high hill. All the castle's rooms are taken, save for the median rooms whose doors are locked, and in the city, the apartments above the shops are filled." He smiled. "Heaven is teeming with life."

"But the rest of the globe, for the most part, remains unoccupied," Autumn mused aloud. She nudged Kaela. "Look, something is happening on stage."

Effiel crossed the stage to where the podium stood. Without a glance at the audience, he leafed through the pages of his opening speech, pausing only to study the program that listed the evening's events. Behind Effiel, the blue velvet curtain was still tightly drawn. Behind the curtain, preparations were under-way, which promised to make the evening a grand one. Israfel was positioning his choir members so that when they sang, their voices would blend in perfection. Brothers carried large vases holding beautiful flowers gathered from the garden outside, the flowers' colorful petals filled the air with sweet perfumes. God's daughters hurriedly tied transparent lacy bows trimmed in the globe's purest gold around the vases' bulging bellies. Candelabras were lit, and a golden rug was laid where the recipients of tonight's awards would stand.

The trumpet's blare drew the angels' attention from Effiel, who was too busy to notice that all eyes were on him, to the back of the room where Zephon's musicians had gathered. Their march down the auditorium's main aisle to the orchestra pit at the base of the stage was a grand one. The closer the musicians came to the stage, the more deafening was the applause they received. Zephon seated the members of his orchestra and, after taking a well-deserved bow, took his position at his podium.

As grand as the musicians' entrance had been, Zophiel's arrival on stage brought the audience to its feet. Pure white from head to toe, clothed in a white robe that seemed to glow, the herald read the message Father had prepared for His sons. This was when Autumn noticed Zophiel's physical attributes. On Earth, the angel would be described as being an albino since his skin, hair, and eyes were snow-white. The robe he wore reached only to his mid-thigh as did his cloak. Zophiel's two sets of wings were transparent. They were seen only when he was in flight. One set of wings reached from his shoulders to his waist, and the second set of wings reached from the middle of his back to about inch off the floor. It was during this discovery that Autumn noticed the small pair of wings that shadowed each of Zophiel's ankles.

"So that's why he walks so fast," Autumn said, nudging Kaela's ribs. "I never noticed Zophiel's many wings until now."

A trumpet sounded, and all eyes focused on Effiel. The angel walked to the lip of the stage and, in a loud voice, announced, "My brothers, welcome to our Lord's Festival of Light. Gatherings like these will be held every fortnight on the castle's grounds. Presently, Father and our sisters are conversing with the scribe and Lucifer about this evening's festivities. Their arrival to the family booth on the third-floor mezzanine will be heralded by the sound of Zophiel's trumpet. Please remain seated until that time. Thank you."

Autumn sat staring at the stage while Effiel spoke, but the moment he turned away from the crowd and took his position behind the podium, she nudged Kaela. "I'll bet Lucifer's acting up." She pulled on Kaela's cloak to make him lean in her direction. "Excelsa was so upset with our eldest brother that he could barely eat." Autumn turned and gazed toward the family booth on the third floor. "I think we are going to have a—"

The deafening blast of a trumpet echoed through the auditorium, announcing the arrival of the King, His daughters, and the scribe. Effiel called excitedly, "Please rise! And join me in extending a hearty welcome to the royal family and our Lord's holy scribe, Excelsa." Autumn stepped into the aisle, applauding. She was looking for Lucifer, who was obviously absent. When the applause died, Effiel made a second announcement. "Please welcome our eldest brother to the stage."

Heaven's eldest son received a thunderous applause as he strolled across the stage to the podium. Effiel backed away, smiling at Lucifer, who ignored him. Had this happened on Earth, flash-bulbs would have put the stars in space to shame; fans would have been screaming, smiling, and nodding in approval; TV cameras would have rolled in for a close-up of Lucifer; and then the stations would have taken time to identify themselves.

But this was Heaven. Soft music interrupted angelic applause; one lone, beautiful, haunting voice sang a sweet song of praise to God; and everyone in the auditorium turned their attention to the third-floor mezzanine where their Lord sat veiled in clouds. Kaela, Autumn, and many of the ancient angels fell to their knees, bowing their heads, while young angels lifted their arms upward and outward as though they longed to bring God closer to them.

When Israfel's song ended, Effiel asked everyone to be seated. Lucifer stood at the podium, silently waiting for the scribe's assistant to relinquish his duty to him. When Effiel was well out of the way, Lucifer spoke. "Welcome, my brothers." He paused, encouraging his brothers' applause. Smiling, Lucifer said, "Welcome, my sisters." He waited through a second applause. When the room grew quiet, he shouted, "Welcome, Father!" A deafening thunderous applause shook the auditorium. Again, Lucifer waited. He appeared to be reading his notes, studying what he would say next. "Tonight, we gather to thank our brothers who, through their skills and talents, made Heaven productive. I will relinquish the floor to Effiel, who will host our award's ceremony. Thank you for your patience. Please enjoy the rest of the evening." Those words finalized Lucifer's first public appearance. The applause was great, but this time, it was for two angels, not one. As Lucifer took his leave, Effiel approached the podium.

Autumn had been studying Lucifer. Compared to Kaela, Michael, Gabriel, Joniel, and Abdiel, Heaven's eldest son was girl pretty. His face was not masculine; it was beautiful. Lucifer's large eyes were bright blue and fringed with thick, dark lashes. His brows were shaped into two symmetrical arches, as though they had been plucked to perfection. Lucifer mouth was wide. His lips were cherry red. His nose, straight and stately, was turned up at its tip. All these features were framed by a heart-shaped face. Layers of blond curls haloed Lucifer's head and bounced with each word he spoke. Though he was tall, he was not muscular, but lithe like Excelsa, Belial, or Evangeline.

Autumn used her angelic vision to focus on his hands. From what she saw of them, his palms were short with long, tapering fingers. Kaela's masculine hands had generous palms and long thick fingers. Kaela's were the hands of a worker, not the hands of a pampered pet. Everything about Lucifer offended Autumn. Probably because she knew that one-day soon, her eldest brother would begin an evil campaign against God.

"My wonderful heavenly family," Effiel said with a smile, "please join me in listening to songs praising Father as presented by Israfel's choir accompanied by Zephon's orchestra." The room grew quiet, and strains of a sweet violin and Israfel's lovely soprano voice filled the auditorium. When the choir sang their final song, Scribe Excelsa escorted his sisters to the stage, where they stayed while he returned to the family booth to sit with Father and Lucifer.

Effiel walked to the lip of the stage. "Our sisters will present this evening's awards. I have the honor of introducing each brother and the pleasure of revealing how he graciously contributed to our globe's progress through his talents and skills."

The ceremony was gracious, beautiful, and elegant. Each talented brother was escorted to the stage by the Goddess whose virtues he emulated throughout his life.

Wisdom described the golden medallion she would present as an award. "This medal is crafted from the purest gold known to this universe. Father is responsible for the medallion's design. In the center of the medallion is the all-seeing eye, a reminder that our Lord sees all we do. Flecks of Urim and Thummum, precious gems taken from Father's cloak, have been ground into the smallest particles and have integrated into the outer circle of the medallion. On the back side of the medallion are the words *Good and Faithful Son.* The name of the one receiving the award is engraved below those words. And below his name is the name of the Goddess who instructs him."

Wisdom presented the medallion to the first of God's sons. She set the clasp of the golden chain, securing it so that the medallion lay gently against the chest of its wearer. "The gold in this medallion comes from Father's sacred heart."

Watching the Goddess escort her brother to his seat, Effiel added, "The receivers of the awards presented tonight should proudly wear and display their medallion for all to see, for around their necks they wear a solid piece of Father's deepest love and appreciation of them."

Throughout the presentations, Autumn expected Kaela's name to be called next. She imagined how great the applause would be when Inspiration left the stage to escort her angel to the podium. But the hour was growing late, and the ceremony was winding down, and so far, Kaela skills remained unrecognized. Autumn took his hand in hers. She glanced up at Kaela to find him smiling down at her. He nodded toward the stage, where Origen had just received a medallion for his skills as a weaver and teacher of his trade.

"Have we overlooked anyone who should have been honored this evening?" Effiel asked. He seemed to scan the audience for anyone who might lodge such a grievance.

"I know of one such brother," a voice called out. The voice belonged to God's holy scribe. The audience turned their faces toward the third-floor mezzanine to see Excelsa standing on the balustrade that surrounded the family booth. The scribe spread his wings, leaving Father's side to join Effiel on the stage. "The brother of whom I speak is created of God's first flock. Accompanied by three of his most beloved apprentices, he left his cottage in the village to kneel before our Lord's throne. In his hand, he held a rolled scroll of blueprints he drew up that revealed his desire to improve our region through his talent, skills, and craftsmanship.

"If you haven't guessed the name of the brother I have described, let me tell you who he is," Scribe Excelsa said, his words lifted the excitement of everyone in the room. "I am speaking of our beloved brother, Kaela, one of Father's most productive sons!" Applause and cheers thundered throughout the auditorium. "Wisdom and Inspiration, the sisters who advise Kaela will escort him to the podium."

The room grew quiet as the Goddesses left the stage for where their brother sat. Kaela rose from his seat, stepping past Autumn into the aisle. While the Goddesses accompanied their trembling brother to the stage, Scribe Excelsa gave a brief history of the changes that were made after Kaela met with God that wonderful new day in Heaven.

"Created of God's first flock of angels, our brother, Kaela, is famous for his proficiency in carpentry and invention," Excelsa told the audience. "His faith in Father led him to the outdoor throne room, where he knelt before Heaven's throne as only royalty kneels before royalty. Kaela opened his request by recognizing our Lord's great achievements. With each word Kaela spoke, the might of God's power weighed on him until he laid face-down on the floor."

The auditorium exploded in applause when the Goddesses crossed the stage with Kaela. Wisdom and Inspiration walked slowly to give Excelsa the time he needed to finish his account of their brother's accomplishments. "Here was a humble carpenter who brought with him three friends and sketches drawn by his skilled hand, fearfully addressing the Object of his respect and admiration. What a historic moment in time that was!

"Even more historic was Father's confession to Kaela: 'If I had a son, a product of my cells, I would want him to be a carpenter like you.'" The auditorium was dead silent. "Join me in welcoming our brother, Kaela, who I greatly admire." Scribe Excelsa turned away from the audience to face Kaela. "Please, Kaela, address our brothers."

With Effiel standing at his left and Excelsa at his right, Kaela stood silently at the podium, gazing around the auditorium. "*WOW*! This place is big!" Angelic laughter filled the theater. When silence reigned, Kaela said, "I am of the belief that if one wishes to accomplish something, he must start at the beginning by taking the first step. The first step is the most important one because it involves laying the plans that will eventually lead to the finished product. Where one goes from there depends upon how much he enjoyed his chore.

"I enjoy being a carpenter, and I thank Father for etching that skill into my mind. Without my craft, and without my apprentices, I would be idle. But without my Lord, my King, and my Creator, I would be nothing." He added in a soft, loving tone, "Please do not credit me with the advancements made here these many centuries. Credit Father. Without our Lord's loving guidance, His universal understanding, and

His great patience, everything would cease to exist." Kaela focused on the family booth and, in all sincerity, said, "Thank you, Father."

Amid the rich ovation Kaela received for his humble speech, Autumn leaped to her feet, slipped the tips of her fingers into her mouth, and let a shrill whistle that reverberated throughout the auditorium nearly deafening the angels who sat nearby. When God's sons returned to their seats and the theater grew quiet, Autumn wept with immense joy. Her tears streamed down her cheeks so swiftly that they dripped off her chin, falling like liquid diamonds onto her lap. With abandon, she wiped her nose on her cloak's sleeve and breathed in deeply in an attempt to regain her composure. Through glistening eyes, she saw Kaela, Effiel, Excelsa, and the Goddesses walk to the center of the stage where they knelt in humble admiration of their Creator. Autumn turned and focused on the family booth.

God was seated between Lucifer and Excelsa's empty seat, His glorious form shrouded by clouds, thicker than those that hid the witch when she made her rounds that fateful night. All of Father's faithful children rose to their feet, faced the family booth, and knelt before their Lord. All, that is, except Lucifer, who remained seated. The haze that cloaked the King's glory shone like Earth's sun as He lifted His arms and blessed everyone in His presence. The auditorium felt energized, the air seemed purer, and angelic minds were more at ease—such is the feeling of God's perfect love. Scribe Excelsa, Kaela, and Effiel rose to their feet with the others in attendance.

"My children," God's said. "What could please a father more than having his faithful sons praise him with their songs? Your devotion to me is surpassed only by the love I have for each of you."

Israfel's choir, accompanied by Zephon's orchestra, burst into a joyful song that commemorated God's love for His children.

When the choir finished singing, Father said, "Tonight, my scribe, Excelsa, will place my Medallion of Achievement on Kaela's chest so that he knows my great appreciation for his faith in me and for his accomplishments." Father watched as Excelsa unclasped the chain on which the medallion hung, put the chain around Kaela's neck, and set the clasp. Tenderly, the scribe placed God's medallion against his brother's heart before turning him to face the family booth. "Kaela, this award is yours to wear forever. Let it be a daily reminder of my love for you."

Father asked Lucifer to stand at His chair. "Lucifer, my first-created angel, first angel of an entire race of angels, first son of God, I award you the title of archangel, making you the first to hold that title in Heaven. Lucifer, your title empowers you to supervise and oversee work that is being done in my name. And the title of archangel gives you constant access to my throne, my journals, and implies that you will mentor your brothers in ways that encourage them to remain faithful to me."

A few angels applauded at first, but then the applause grew so loud that it rivaled the applause of the brothers who were awarded God's Medallion of Achievement. Autumn's jaw hung open; she did not applaud Lucifer. He had done nothing she was aware of that deserved her admiration. Father was saying something; the choir had begun to sing. Mechanically, Autumn knelt with her brothers while God, His scribe, and the Goddesses took their seats. Lucifer was nowhere to be seen. When she rose to her feet, she turned toward the stage to see Lucifer standing there. Dropping into her seat next to Kaela, she focused her attention on Heaven's first archangel.

Kaela reached for Autumn's hand. He was smiling down at her. "How could Father do this to us?" she asked. "Lucifer is like a stranger. If my memory serves me right, Lucifer never once visited our work area when we renovated the castle. He never dined with us. He never gave us advice to improve our skills. Kaela, Lucifer never accomplished anything in his entire existence in Heaven. So now we have this arrogant entitled thing standing over us with his twisted ideas and—"

"Watch your mouth, Autumn," Mammon said, leaning over the back of her seat. "Lucifer—Archangel Lucifer—is on stage, and he is looking at you."

Autumn turned away from Kaela and glanced toward the stage. Sure enough, Lucifer was focused on her. How loud had she been talking? Did he hear her every word she said about him, or was he simply waiting for her to finish her conversation with Kaela? Did everyone hear what she had to say, or was Mammon eaves-dropping like he always did? Autumn put a smile on her lips and kept her eyes glued to Lucifer's face. He blinked and turned to the notes that lay on the podium before him.

"Now that our brother, Autumn, has expressed his disdain at my promotion," he said, making it clear she was overheard by one and all. "I would like to express my great appreciation to Father, who saw fit to promote me to the position of Heavens first archangel. I earned this title, Autumn by sitting in God's presence and by learning my Father's business—which is none of your business, Autumn—but it is Heaven's business which I have been learning since I was created." He paused, lowering his head as though perplexed. "If any of you feel I do not deserve this promotion and, therefore, do not care to hear the rest of my speech, you may leave the auditorium with my blessing."

To everyone's astonishment, Autumn left her seat, walking up the aisle toward the auditorium's closed doors. She turned before leaving the theater and said, "Pray that God is with us now, for He has bestowed a powerful title on one who knows nothing of angelic grace, and that one will burden all of Heaven's sons with the power of his title and his disobedience to Father's laws." Kaela abandoned his seat, racing up the aisle to where she stood. He opened the door for her, and together, they left the building.

Autumn burst into tears the moment the doors closed. "I'm sorry. I was wrong to speak out like that." She buried her head in her angel's chest and sobbed helplessly. "But I know Lucifer is evil throughout. Why? Why would Father do this?"

"It is not like you don't know the story," Kaela said softly.

"I wish I never would have opened my mouth." Autumn wept. "I wish I could turn time back to when you reached for my hand—" They were back in the auditorium. Kaela reached for Autumn's hand and sat smiling down her. She began to speak, but said nothing when she saw her angel press his finger to his lips. Without a word, Autumn turned away from Kaela and looked toward the stage. Lucifer stood there, his eyes riveted on Autumn's face, an arrogant smirk on his lips. Had she spoken out of turn? Was he waiting for her to finish her insults so he could chastise her before Father and her sisters? She sighed and sat back in her seat, giving Heaven's first titled angel all her attention.

"Good evening," the archangel said with a sweet smile. "Father has honored me by promoting me to a high position that requires an understanding of all angelic hopes and dreams. I intend to be more interactive with each of you. I want to know your needs, your wants, and your cares. I will be dining in your presence. I will be visiting the Holy City. I will be attending festivals such as this one so that I can be closer to God's flocks."

Archangel Lucifer continued speaking until he had the angels squirming in their seats from boredom. Not once did he refer to himself as their brother. Not once during the speech did he comment on their talents or how proud he was of them. Not once did he mention the castle's renovation or give the angels an idea of how he would handle his position or what his duties were. Half-way through the speech, Autumn leaned her head against Kaela's arm and fell asleep. Several angels fought to keep their eyes open. Lucifer saw that the body of the auditorium was either sleeping or staring slack-jawed at him, but he kept talking. It was important now that he stood before Heaven's citizens to make it known to them how fortunate they were to have him as their archangel.

Father rose from His seat. Zophiel's trumpet sounded. Lucifer stopped talking, and the dozing angels woke up.

"My children," the mighty Lord of the universe began, "the hour has grown late, and I must be about my business. But before I go, I have a few announcements. An arena will be built on the castle's northern lawn. An arena is a walled-in playing field where games of friendly competition are held. Kaela and his co-workers will be responsible for building the arena, and if anyone here wishes to improve his carpentry skills, he may speak with Kaela about joining his team of carpenters.

"Michael approached me on another matter. It seems that this region has become more crowded than it should be. Michael has received my permission to lead an expedition from this region to Heaven's unexplored territories. Uzziel will chart the newly discovered regions so future journeys to them from the Sacred Region can be more easily made. Survival classes will be held in the arena that will be built. Anyone wishing to join the expedition must take Michael and Gabriel's survival courses. I understand there will be lessons in horseback riding, among other things. Some classes will be held outside the arena in the wooded areas near my house and elsewhere on the Holy Mount.

"As for me, I will see my sons here in a fortnight. My blessing I bestow upon each of you until we meet again."

When Father's speech ended, He left the theater for His inner sanctum. The angels rose to their feet, making their way from the theater too, leaving Archangel Lucifer on the stage, staring after them.

Back at the cottage that night, Autumn stuffed their soiled clothes into the hamper while Kaela prepared for bed. He was asleep when she finally drew her blanket to her chin. She glanced across the room to where her angel lay perfectly still, apparently exhausted from the evening's festivities. He slept so soundly that it looked as though his mattress had eaten him alive. Autumn sat up. Maybe he had gotten up and his bed was empty. No. He was there, but he was really zonked.

"I need someone to talk to," Autumn whispered to herself. She closed her eyes, and prayed silently. "Father, I have no idea what Your plan is, but if You feel You did right by making Lucifer an archangel, then I will respect Your decision, but I will not respect anyone who becomes disrespectful toward You. Help me to be courageous in the days ahead. Help me to be thoughtful and wise, patient and truthful. Bolster my faith. But more importantly, my precious King, make me inherently obedient to Your laws. I ask for obedience because when wisdom dims, faith falters, patience wears thin, and truth wanes, obedience never fails. I pray this in Your name, my Lord. Amen."

Chapter 10

Meeting Lucifer

The morning following the awards ceremony, Autumn and Kaela were about to sit down to breakfast when a knock sounded at their door.

"I'll get it," Kaela said, rising from the table. "It's probably Joniel and Abdiel."

Every morning, the four brothers walked together from the village to the lumberyard. But today would mark a new moment in Heaven's history. Kaela opened the door, expecting to greet his beloved brothers; instead, he found Archangel Lucifer standing on his porch. For a brief moment, he said nothing. After an awkward and bewildered silence, he said, "Please come in." He called Autumn to the living room. "We have an honored visitor."

"Good morning," Archangel Lucifer said, "I try not to associate with anyone but God and His daughters, but I felt inclined to come here to make my request in person."

"We just sat down to eat breakfast," Autumn told Earth's future devil. Gesturing toward the kitchen, she added, "If you wish, you can pull up a chair at the table and eat with us."

In the kitchen, Autumn and Kaela ignored their food to better concentrate on the reason for the archangel's visit. "I came here because I learned that Autumn is an accomplished carpenter. I have had the pleasure of seeing the gazebos our small brother fashions"—he smiled in her direction—"and of course, I visited the stable. You have excellent workmanship, Autumn. I have decided that you will renovate my suite of rooms. You will start your work immediately."

"Of course Autumn will renovate your apartment," Kaela said, patting her hand. "He is one of my best carpenters." He turned to Autumn, who glared at him from across the table. "Well, what do you think?"

"*How about not speaking for me?*" Autumn could have growled, but instead she asked, "How do you know I don't have other plans?" She turned to Archangel Lucifer. Averting her eyes from his gaze, she explained, "The renovation of your suite will have to wait. I must assist Kaela in the construction of the arena behind Father's house."

"It is impossible for you to turn down my request," the archangel said, rising from his seat. "You see, I did not ask you to renovate my suite. I said that you will renovate my suite of rooms at the castle."

"Yeah, well, you came here with a request." Autumn sighed. "I suggest that you take your request—"

"I am Heaven's first and only archangel. I am trying to be fair with you," Lucifer told the desperate cherub. "My request became a decision—one that you will honor. You will do the work that is required, or you will face the consequences of your disobedience to me."

Autumn rose from her chair, positioning herself behind Kaela.

Archangel Lucifer walked to where she stood. He reached as though he would touch her shoulder, but he dropped his hand to his side. Leaning into Autumn's face, he stated, "You will report to me when you finish your meal."

The archangel walked toward the living room. Kaela hurried to open the door for him; he held it until Lucifer left the porch. Closing the door, he studied Autumn's face. What was she doing? Was she sniffing the air?

"It stinks in here." Autumn sniffed. The room smelled like a damp basement or a musty closet. The breeze that carried the sweet scent of lilacs through the room's open windows was absent today, and with its absence, the kitchen smelled strangely stale. Autumn sniffed the air. "Archangel Lucifer made our house stink." Every time she saw him, she remembered how her eldest brother deceived Eve, caused Adam to betray God, and burdened mankind with a sin that followed the human race from the womb to the grave. Snorting out through her nostrils to relieve her nasal passages of Lucifer's dreadful stench, she told Kaela, "I am going to the lumber-yard. I will see you when you get there."

Kaela returned to the table. "Let's eat first. We have a lot to discuss." He watched as she took her seat and he waited while she helped herself to the bowl of stewed peaches before he opened his mouth to speak on Lucifer's behalf.

Breakfast at the cottage was horrendous. Autumn whined, cried, and pleaded with Kaela to find someone else to renovate Archangel Lucifer's apartment, but he remained adamant, telling her, "The archangel chose you to do the work; therefore you must comply with his wishes. Are you done eating? If so, leave for the castle now, and don't come back until your work there is well under-way."

Autumn refused to leave the kitchen. Clinging to the tabletop, she warned Kaela, "Don't touch me!"

He pried her fingers loose, forcing her to her feet, struggling to keep her standing while she resolutely pushed herself down into the chair's wooden seat.

"Autumn, you will go to the castle, and you will comply with the archangel's wishes," Kaela snarled.

Autumn glared into her angel's face, sobbing. "Tell me why you're siding with Lucifer."

Kaela stepped back, freeing Autumn of his grip; he studied her for a moment. He knew how she felt. She loathed doing anything for Earth's future devil, but it was imperative that she complete this chore since it would earn her, her brothers' admiration.

"You must do this, Autumn," Kaela said softly, "so that I can give my account without interruption. If we quit here, we will return to the gazebo—"

"Good! Send me back to the gazebo," Autumn snarled. "What do I care?"

Kaela refused to tolerate her stubbornness another moment. He wrestled her from the kitchen to the living room where, with great effort, he tried to open the door. Autumn kicked it shut. He opened the door again. Again, it was kicked shut. Throwing Autumn over his shoulder, he opened the door and tossed her onto the porch. Seeing her rise to her feet, he slammed the door and held it closed. When Autumn stopped pounding and kicking, he leaned into the door and, in a stern voice, told her, "If you refuse to renovate Lucifer's suite, find somewhere else to live. And don't expect me to return you to the gazebo either."

Autumn stood on the porch, staring at the closed door through narrowed eyes. She wanted to yell "I hate you," but that emotion didn't exist in Heaven yet. She wanted to stomp off the porch, find a rock, and toss it at the house. But instead, she turned away in defeat, walking slowly through the yard to the sidewalk. She paused there, hoping the door would open and Kaela would call her inside. The door remained closed. All right, she would go to the castle, report to Archangel Lucifer, and do whatever it took to renovate his suite of rooms, but she had no intention of arriving early. Autumn chose to walk to the castle very slowly, rather than fly.

She made her way through the village, returning her brothers' greetings with a frown and a lame wave of her hand. Anyone seeing her knew without a doubt that she was unhappy. But not one heavenly soul approached to ask the reason for her discontent. Maybe they already knew that she had been duped into renovating the archangel's apartment. Dread grasped her in its terrible clutches as Autumn drew on memories of a past life she had never lived.

"When we remodeled Father's house, Lucifer never visited our work sites. He never dined with us when our work day ended, and he never gave us one good word of encouragement." She lifted her eyes from the ground long enough to see she where she was. Lifting one small foot, she stepped onto the staircase Nature had carved into the four sides of the Holy Mount.

Autumn took the stairs, knowing they led her closer to the object of her fear. Yes, she feared Lucifer. He was evil. The archangel's dark spirit made it hard for her to look at him, let alone work in close proximity to him. "Our request to renovate Lucifer's rooms was denied. If we could have gained his permission to remodel his suite, our work at the castle would have been completed, and we could move on to projects that require our immediate attention." She wept softly for a few minutes. Wiping her eyes and nose on her robe's sleeve, she took a deep breath. "Now, because Lucifer feels its time, I have been elected to work in,"—she lowered her grumbling to a whisper—"the devil's lair."

Filled with a dread that she had not known until now, Autumn continued on her way until she stood in the first-floor hallway outside Lucifer's apartment.

With great apprehension, Autumn raised her fist and knocked gently at the archangel's door. She waited. When there was no answer, she knocked again, this time with a tad more forcefulness. Once more, her knock went unheeded. Taking a step backward, Autumn wondered if it was Lucifer's intention to shun her as he had shunned the carpenters, weavers, and cleaning cherubs during the castle's renovation. Or was he conducting business with Father in the outdoor throne room?

Autumn stepped up to the door and knocked a third time. For a third time, her knock went unheeded. Confident that the globe's eldest angel was absent from his quarters, Autumn pounded the door with both fists, amazed that she felt no pain in her hands.

"Lucifer, are you in there?" she shouted. Her voice echoed through the hallway, down the stairs, into the foyer below, and returned as a whisper to where she stood.

"Oh well! I tried," Autumn said, hoping Father heard her words. She was pleased with herself for having come this far. How many of her brothers would put themselves in a situation where they might actually come face to face with their world's future devil? That action, in itself, took guts. Autumn turned away from the door, lifted her tool kit, and started down the hall toward the stairs. She was on the first step down, ready to descend onward to the foyer, when she heard a latch turn, a door open.

"Autumn," a clear, almost musical voice called out. Autumn turned swiftly, gazing up the hallway, expecting to see the owner of the lilting voice looking back at her, but no one was there. She wondered if she should go back and try the door again. Or should she leave the castle and return to the safety of Kaela's lumber-yard? As badly as she wanted to leave, her curious nature urged her to try Lucifer's door once more.

Cautiously, as though approaching the den of a dangerous animal, Autumn crept up the hallway. The door stood open. Her flesh crawled. A chill raced from the back of her neck down her spine. With eyes wide, Autumn peered into the once-forbidden room. Fresh air swept in from the hallway, mingling with the perfumed breeze that entered the room through its northern window. Together, the air and the breeze disturbed layers of dirt that had accumulated over the centuries. As a result of the disturbance, the top layer of dirt formed a dust cloud that rose from the chamber's floor, blurring Autumn's vision. Within the floating particles, there stood a shadowy figure. The scene was reminiscent of a soul emerging from the fog on a moonlit night on Earth. Autumn remained in the hallway until the dust settled.

"Come in," Archangel Lucifer called. "I want to get this started and over with as quickly as possible."

Autumn entered the room. "Yes, Archangel, so do I."

"Good, then we are of a like mind," Lucifer said, a charming smile on his lips.

Autumn looked the room over from its ceiling to its floor. It was a huge room, big enough to be three rooms in one. An arched doorway beckoned to her. She walked through it to find what she considered a nicely sized room. Another arched doorway led her to a third and last room. It was bigger than the middle room, but way smaller than the front room. When Autumn returned to where Lucifer stood, she noticed his appearance. The archangel was unkempt and sleepy-looking. Her jaw dropped. Lucifer hadn't answered his door when she knocked at it because he had been sleeping. "I can start in this room," she told him. "We will have to move that box of straw out of here—"

"That box of straw is my bed," Lucifer said sharply.

Autumn's brows darted high on her forehead. Lucifer slept in a box filled with straw while the angels he frowned on slept in the comfort of real beds? Whatever! "I see." She sighed. "So you plan on keeping the … your bed where? Not in this room?"

The archangel tossed his golden curls. "I commissioned you to do a chore for me, and you accepted the task. Therefore, I am putting all decision-making in your capable hands."

Autumn studied the front room for a long moment. "All right, this room will be the kitchen, dining room, and living room. When one enters your apartment, the kitchen will be located to his left. I will build wall cabinets for storing your dishes and counters for storing your supplies and eating utensils, such as knives, forks, and spoons. You can eat in, or out, at your discretion." She reached into her tool kit and pulled out a tape measure. Walking to the area, she measured the back wall where she would put the counters and cabinets she would build.

"Will I have water in my room? Like my sisters and Scribe Excelsa?"

"I don't plumb kitchens and baths," Autumn replied. "But I know a brother who does, and I will bring him here before I set in the sinks, tubs, showers, and the commode. Right now, I'll draw up some sketches to show you the changes I can make, and then I will rough in my plans. When you are satisfied, we will begin."

"I want to begin now," Archangel Lucifer said. "Inspiration told me that you are a fine carpenter, and I agreed that you would be the one doing the work. As I said before, the details for this project are in your capable hands."

Autumn sighed. "All right then, let's get started. I will have to send Zophiel to Azazel's shop. He is our metallurgist, but he has apprentices working under him who are proficient in plumbing houses." Autumn began her work by stepping off the kitchen to where the dining room would be. Making a mark in the dust, she snaked her tape measure to the back wall. Wiping the dust away with a rag she found, she set her mark on the floor.

"The kitchen's width will reach from here to there. Then the dining room will start here. You may want a hutch for your plates, which I am sure you will receive when we have open house."

"An open house," Lucifer mused. "What is an open house?"

"I will invite our brothers to come and admire your quarters, and they, in turn, will bring gifts you can use in your new apartment,"

Autumn said. She smiled at Lucifer's pleased expression. So the devil likes gifts? Who would have thought that? "The dining area is open to the kitchen, with no wall between, but I need to get a lay of where it may be, since it would be nice to set the table here, under the window."

The archangel sat down on the corner of the box he slept in and watched Autumn work.

"Okay, the dining room will be a bit bigger than the kitchen, if that pleases you. A larger dining room will give you a nice piece of wall for a tapestry and a place for your hutch. Now, the living room will be way bigger." Autumn made her mark on the floor where the dining room ended and the living room began. She snaked her tape measure over three-fourths of the room before she ran out of tape. "Lucifer, go over there and put your finger on that tape until I can get there. I don't want it to move."

"You were commissioned for the task," the archangel snorted.

"Here's how it is," Autumn said, turning her face in his direction. "I can do this right because I'm a good carpenter. Or I can measure this wrong because you are a bad archangel." Lucifer's face grew dark with anger. "Now if you want me to say I did this room with absolutely no help from you, I will. This is the biggest job I've ever done alone. So I will get pats on the back, all kind of praise, and maybe even win a medallion from Father. Who knows where the glory I receive will end? I may have to get used to hearing my brothers call me Archangel Autumn. Or I could say that without your help, I would have made mistakes, and the accolades will go to you." She moved her gaze from the archangel's astonished face to the end of the tape measure that lay humped on the floor. "It's your call."

Lucifer rose to his feet and walked the length of the tape until he reached the end of it. Kneeling, he set his finger on the tape and waited for Autumn to relieve him from his chore. Standing, he watched while she used her rag to wipe away the dust and set her mark on the floor. She snaked the tape again until it touched the wall just to the right of the arched doorway.

"Wow! You are going to have a large living room," she said, rising to her feet. "Our tape measure only handles twelve feet at a time. That's why I needed your help. Thanks." Autumn went on with her work.

From the other room, she shouted, "This middle room will make a nice office. You could set a desk here, a couple chairs, a nice sofa, a few stands." She grew quiet for a moment. "This back room will be your bedroom. You will have the privacy you need, a nice bathroom, and walk-in closet. I have a nice large room to play with in there."

Autumn walked to the front room. Archangel Lucifer was standing where she left him. "You have a nice place here. It's very spacious, with five big windows and the perfect view of the new stadium when it's finished. I know you will be pleased with the improvements on your apartment when my work is done." Autumn picked up her tool kit and headed for the door.

"Wait a minute! Where are you going?" Lucifer asked. "You are not done here."

"I'm going to the lumber-yard to get the material I need to begin the job," Autumn explained. "Unless you would like to take my list to Kaela and have what I need delivered to the castle." She walked to a rustic settee. "I'll just sit here and wait." She plopped down on the bench's rough seat.

"No, go on," Lucifer said, waving his hands toward the door. "I simply thought you were shirking your duties."

"I don't shirk my duties, Archangel," Autumn said as she past him. "I know of only one brother who ever shirked his duties. His disinterest in Heaven's future leaves me cold."

For weeks, Autumn reported to Lucifer's apartment. She left the cottage to report for work as Father took His seat on the castle's highest peak, and she did not return home until the last angel, bird, and beast was sleeping soundly. Her major complaint when she and Kaela met at the breakfast table was the archangel's constant presence.

"He never leaves the apartment," Autumn said as she sipped room-temperature nectar. "Before I started remodeling the archangel's quarters, I thought he sat at the foot of Father's throne all day, doing who knows what. But Lucifer is always home. It's like having a spook skulking around, gaping at you while you work. He gets so close when I'm measuring and cutting boards that I can feel him breathing down my neck. And I can tell you this, spending a day with Lucifer is like spending a day without God's healing light." She smiled when Kaela laughed aloud.

The light outside grew brighter; fog swirled past the kitchen window, lifting upward and dissipating—the perfect sign that God had taken His outdoor throne. "Well, I'm off to see the wizard." Autumn said with giggle. She rose from her chair and walked to the living room where she set her tool kit. "Don't wait up for me. I'll see you tomorrow morning."

This day, as Autumn walked to work, she prayed. "Father, I don't know if I'm doing right by this task or not. I'm an author, not a carpenter. But I thank You for the knowledge You have given me and the chance to extend my talents to improve another room in Your home. I ask Your guidance so that when I finish my work, You, not Lucifer, will be pleased. I am Your child, Your servant, Your subject, and I will love You until the end of time. Amen."

For three long months, Autumn labored to modernize the archangel's spacious apartment. At one point, to end the many trips she made daily to the lumber-yard, she brought her building material into the castle and set it in the hallway. So that she had quick access to the supplies she need, she let the door to Lucifer's room stand open. Several brothers who lived in the castle stopped in the hallway to look in on her while she worked. Some braved Lucifer's hostile glare and entered the apartment to visit with Autumn. While they were there, they made pleasant conversation with her, commenting favorably on her carpentry skills.

God's seven virtuous daughters and His scribe were her most devoted fans. They *oohed*! and *aahed*! over every piece of kitchen furniture she built, complimenting her on her detail work when each piece was finished. As Autumn applied the stain to the wood surfaces, her royal spectators marveled at how the oils she used emphasized the wood grains.

Scribe Excelsa asked, "Did you polish all the cabinets and counters by hand?" When Autumn said she had, the scribe turned to the Goddesses with a smile and a nod of approval. Brothers who gathered to stand in the presence of their virtuous sisters and God's holy scribe commented on how each piece of furniture Autumn made caught and reflected Father's pure light!

Kaela's visits were the best part of Autumn's days. She looked forward to going to lunch or dinner with him. Lucifer was usually bored with her by mid-afternoon and was glad to see her go. Seated in the dining room at a table with her angel, Autumn ignored her plate of food, hungry for shoptalk.

"So how is the work on the arena going?" She listened intently while Kaela told her about the stadium's excavation and how the blueprints had changed since he first drafted them. "How long do you think it will be before it's done?" Kaela estimated another couple weeks to a month before the games could begin.

"Good grief," Autumn gasped, dropping her fork into her plate. "It's taking me longer to do Lucifer's apartment than it's taking you to build an entire stadium from scratch."

Kaela reminded her that she worked alone while he had more than one thousand laborers helping him.

"Well, knowing that makes me feel better, but I should be one those laborers helping you."

Within days after the stadium was finished, Lucifer's apartment was done. Autumn kept her word about inviting her brothers to view it. Zophiel announced an open house in the morning, and by afternoon, thousands of curious angels longing to see the living quarters of the globe's first titled angel formed a line from the village to the castle's first-floor hallway. Autumn and Lucifer stood at the door, greeting their brothers while Octaviel led them on a tour through the newly renovated suite. Just as Autumn predicted, many of Lucifer's visitors came with gifts. Octaviel and Cybel brought dinnerware and serving trays. Azazel arrived with a box of chalices and eating utensils made of Heaven's most glittering ores. Kaela, Joniel, and Abdiel arrived early, before the staircase and hallway filled with fascinated visitors, to deliver and set in place the furnishings they made for the dining room, living room, small office, and bedroom. Origen's silk tapestries, woven rugs, and plump pillows added a cozy air to each of the rooms.

By evening's end, Autumn stood at the door with Archangel Lucifer seeing the last of his visitors off. Kaela waited down the hall by the stairs.

"I have to say that my first solo project worked out pretty good for both of us," Autumn told Archangel Lucifer. "I enjoyed the time I spent here. I've learned so much about carpentry and myself since I began. But now, it is finished, and it's time for both of us to move on. If there is any way I can serve you in the future, please don't hesitate to ask." Autumn stepped into the hallway.

Lucifer reached out, almost touching her shoulder, but he withdrew his hand as quickly as he had extended it. Leaning his cheek against the doorframe, he said, "Those are the sweetest words ever spoken to me by a commoner. Thank you for the work you did here. And I want you to know that I absolutely refuse any credit you may heap upon me for the part I played in making your project successful. Let us keep it to ourselves that without my keen intelligence and wherewithal, this renovation would have failed miserably."

Autumn narrowed her eyes. She remembered the first time she entered this suite. Dust, dirt, and straw from his bed were everywhere. The place smelled musty, and she was pretty sure Lucifer was the source of the odor. Had it not been for Origen's weavers, the archangel would still be wearing the same filthy clothes he wore when she arrived outside his door that first day. And, without her expertise, Lucifer would still be hanging his robes on pegs that once protruded through the walls of the front room. The Goddesses encouraged him to bathe in sweet-scented water and to wash his tangled mass of curls so that they glimmered like gold in God's light. But, that was then.

"Thank you for allowing me this experience," Autumn said curtly. She turned away from her haughty brother and walked to where Kaela stood.

"So?" Kaela asked, draping one arm over her shoulder before they began their descent to the main floor. "What did he say?"

"He practically told me I never would have been able to complete this project without him." Autumn lifted her face when she heard Kaela's snicker. Suddenly, they were both laughing aloud. "And I thanked him for the experience." She gasped, leaning her head against her angel's rib. Again, they burst out laughing.

When they reached the castle's fore-hall, Autumn turned and tugged at Kaela's cloak. He leaned closer to hear what she was about to say. "Thank you, dear angel," she whispered as she kissed his cheek and hugged his neck. "Thank you for giving this opportunity to test my carpentry skills and for allowing me to know Lucifer, Father's horrible adversary."

Kaela repaid her gratitude with a gentle pat on her back and a kiss on her forehead. "Let's go home."

Chapter 11

The Games and the Exploration of Heaven

Autumn sat at the table listening to Kaela, Joniel, and Abdiel address the plans Michael had for the stadium. "He says that he and Gabriel are training brothers who exhibit their inborn athletic skills. I guess that means those of us who are carpenters, weavers, and musicians are out." Kaela shook his head, sipped from his goblet, and in a voice so soft that he could barely be heard, said, "I really wanted to take part in Heaven's exploration."

"I'm going to go to the stadium, and if Michael is there, I'm going to ask him if I can sign up for the exploration," Autumn told her brothers. "Only a chosen few from each flock has inborn athletic skills. And I'll bet that on the first day of training, thousands of us will be turned away."

She studied the faces seated at the table. "What?" she asked. "If we don't let Michael know we are interested in his survival training classes, we won't have a chance of being considered for the exploration." She nudged Kaela with her rolled fist. "Remember when we talked to Michael in the dining hall the night before you received your award? He asked you if you were interested in exploring Heaven with him and Gab. You told him you were; now you're worried that you won't make the team. Well, I'm worried that if I don't try out, I won't make the team either." Autumn rose to her feet. "I'm leaving for the stadium. If you want to stay here, do it. But I'm going to explore Heaven. I'll tell you all about it when I get back."

Kaela, Joniel, and Abdiel rose to their feet. "What one does, we all do." Abdiel sighed.

The stadium was packed with curious brothers who longed to know what this place was, why it was built, and what it would be used for. When Michael saw Kaela and his crew walk through the wide-open gates of the arena, he called to the brothers who were gathered there. "The one who oversaw the construction of the stadium has arrived. He will tell you my plans for it." Michael walked to where Kaela stood. "Tell *them* what I told you."

"Michael and Gabriel intend to hold contests on this field!" Kaela shouted, turning as he talked, he walked to the center of the stadium's dirt floor. "The stadium will be used for equestrian contests, to compare marksmanship, to evaluate wrestling skills, and to compare brothers' ability to toss the javelin." Kaela turned toward the row of seats where the royal family would sit during the exercises. "See those seats that are within the bounds of the balustrades? Father, our sisters, the scribe, and his assistant will sit there. We will be honor by our Lord's presence throughout the games." He held his arms out to his sides and turned to face all those who listened to what he told them. "Right now, I am here to sign up for survival training classes so that I can join Michael on his exploration of our globe." To Michael, he shouted, "Sign me and my crew up for your classes so that we can leave with you when you go off to explore our world!"

Autumn smiled. She was ready for a new adventure. But she was unaware of how grueling training could be. What started in the stadium that she found comparable to classes being taught by a teacher in a classroom expanded to the river Courage, where Michael instructed his brothers on ways to cross large bodies of water without flying over them. They learned to use their angelic vision at night while they rode their ponies over uneven ground. The biggest challenge the students faced was exploring the caverns in the Holy Mount. Michael's instructions began the moment Father took His seat atop the castle's highest peak and ended when Father entered His inner sanctum. But it truly did not matter if it was day or night when one was crawling through a cavern whose innards were black as pitch. Many of Michael's students found cave exploration unnerving and dropped out of training classes. Kaela and his brothers remained to the end.

No longer was the renovation of Father's house the angels' sole achievement. On this day, Autumn sat on Paint, the pony Michael gifted her with when she signed up for his classes. It was up to her to tame the red-and-white miniature horse; break it into a saddle, harness, and bit; teach it that she belonged on its back; and teach Paint to follow her instruction. She had grown to love Paint, and he loved her too. Standing next to Paint, she ran her small hand through the pony's full white mane.

"I can't believe He did it," she whispered close to Paint's ear. "I must be the only sane one in Heaven." She was talking about her surprise when, during last night's festival, Father rose from His seat at the stadium to announce that Archangel Lucifer had established Heaven's Council of Angels; and now, the archangel, Earth's future devil, was the prime director of God's panel of advisors.

Autumn snapped back to the present when she heard snorting from all sides. Patting her painted pony's neck, she slipped her foot into the stirrup and tossed her free leg over its back. Adjusting herself in the saddle, she pulled back slightly on the reins to stop her pony's dancing. Paint snorted and tossed his head a couple times before he calmed down. Turning slightly in her saddle, Autumn looked behind her to see that thousands of angels had gathered on the lawn. Some of her brothers were seated on the backs of powerful horses. Others were on foot. Autumn glanced at Kaela, who was right next to her. He sat on a beige steed with a long, luxurious white mane and tail. His horse danced sideways, anxious to feel the ground under his feet.

"Calm down, Champ," she heard Kaela say softly. The sound of his stern voice stopped the horse's head-tossing and hoofing momentarily.

"Everyone, listen up!" Michael called out, pointing toward the castle. "I want all eyes front." Autumn turned to see Israfel and his choir standing in the air, level with the castle's highest peak. They left their stations so they could honor Father for creating the globe's athletes. While they sang, they drifted like feathers on the wind toward the crowd gathered below. By the time they lighted on the ground, their song had ended. Standing before Michael, Gabriel, Uzziel, and Uriel,

Israfel broke into a song that noted the foursome's dedication to their apprentices and that they had changed not one but two eras in Heaven's history. The first era was the games, which Autumn was pretty sure she had missed completely. The second era, the exploration of Heaven's uncharted regions, was the journey on which she and Heaven's athletes were about to embark.

While Israfel sang his melodious tribute to the sport angels, Archangel Lucifer, Scribe Excelsa, Effiel, Evangeline, and the seven silver Goddesses descended from the castle's highest peak to its courtyard to stand before their adventurous brothers. On the final note of Israfel's song, Love stepped forward. In her a hands she held a scroll that she opened with great care.

"My brothers," the sweet Goddess said in a voice that was heard by all, even those who stood farthest from her, "our Father writes: 'My sons, at long last you are setting out on your historic journey. My heart bursts with admiration and love for each of you. Know that I am always with you and that I will keep you safe throughout your travels. Your choice to leave your homeland to explore your globe brings many new opportunities. While you are gone, I will check my altar daily for personal messages from you to me. Go with my blessings and my sincere and grateful love. Eternally yours, Father.'" The Goddess blew the sojourners a sweet kiss before she rejoined her sisters.

Wisdom took one step forward. She, too, held an open scroll. "The decree that I am about to read is written by God in agreement with the wishes of His almighty Word. Michael's team is permitted to explore the globe's eastern quadrant. Gabriel and his company of athletes will travel westward. Uriel's team will explore the globe's Southern region. Uzziel's company will fly northward.

"In compliance to the desires of God's almighty Word, who is the Creator of this universe and all universes throughout deep space, members of this expedition will gather plants and animals native to their assigned regions and bring them to the castle. You, as explorers, are required to catalog each find, fill vials with water from your assigned region, tag those vials, and store them for safekeeping until you return home. You will do the same with soil specimens using the leather pouches your team leaders have provided.

"When the exploration is complete and you have returned, you will take your findings to Father's laboratory, where research will begin. Go, and do God's bidding."

Cheers filled the Sacred Region as brothers on horseback broke into a full gallop, and the angels on foot shot into the air where they divided into four flocks that flew their separate ways.

Autumn's little horse raced across the grassy lawn toward the forest, its white mane flying and its hooves breaking ground. They were far from the castle when the pony began to fall behind the others.

"Wait!" Autumn called to Kaela, but in his excitement, he spurred his horse and galloped out of sight. "Which way am I supposed to go?" Autumn asked no one there. "Who is my team leader?"

She kicked her pony's sides with her heels. Paint, in his frantic effort to catch up to the larger steeds, stumbled, tossing Autumn from his saddle, sending her flying through the air. A brief moment later, horse and owner lay face-down in the high grass that swayed hypnotically in Heaven's gentle breeze.

"Well, isn't this just what I always wanted?" Autumn snorted, staggering to her feet, checking her knees, elbows, and hands for cuts. "Sometimes I could just kill Kaela!"

She searched the grassy field for her pony. "Here, Paint!" she called. The horse popped its head up, looking in her direction. "Paint, come here now." She walked to where the pony lay on its side, gasping for air. "Are you all right, baby-boy?" The pony struggled to stand. "Oh no … Tell me this isn't happening."

Certain Paint had broken a leg or two; Autumn rested her head on his side and wept in wild abandon. "I'm so sorry. I'm so sorry. Oh, Paint, I'm so sorry."

"What are you sorry for?" Kaela asked as he dismounted his steed.

"I'm sorry you bunch of *macholetes* couldn't wait up, and now, Paint's lying here with all his legs broken," Autumn scolded between sobs. "This was supposed to be one of the happiest days of our lives." She glared at her beloved angel through tear-filled eyes.

Kaela pulled his knife from its sheath and walked toward the pony. He knelt and cut the vine that had tangled itself around the small animal's left front and right hind legs. "Paint's fine, but he's too small for this journey. I should have insisted you ride with me, and this never would have happened." He helped the pony to its feet, relieved it of its saddle and harness, and sent it out to graze in the pasture. "Come on, we will ride together on my horse. Champ's a brute. He could probably carry half the expedition team on his back."

Kaela hoisted Autumn onto the huge horse, her feet hardly reached passed its thick neck. "You'd better ride sidesaddle," he mused as he mounted the steed. Autumn threw her leg over the horse's neck and leaned against Kaela. "Are you ready?" He smiled at the nod of her head. "Off we go!"

Autumn felt the movement of her angel's body as he spurred his horse. She screamed as the beast lunged forward in full gallop. "Hang on! We got a lot of ground to burn before we reach Michael and our brothers." So she was on Michael's team.

They were galloping across flowered fields and emerald hills when Citadel, a youngster created of the Lord's sixth flock, joined them. He was one of the sojourners on foot, but now, he flew on outstretched wings beside their horse. He was smiling, relieved that he found the missing pair so quickly.

"Michael sent me out scouting for you and Autumn. Are you both well?" Kaela assured him they were fine. "Shall I fly alongside you, or can you find Michael on your own?" Autumn looked back for Kaela's response. He shouted something, but his words were lost to the thundering of Champ's hooves. "Michael and our brothers have set up camp by a still crystal lake. They are awaiting our return. I will fly ahead and tell them you and Autumn will arrive shortly."

Citadel moved closer, positioning his body in diagonal flight. "Continue on this route. When you reach the grassy knoll where a tall shapely tree with pure-white bark stands, turn left. Follow the beaten path made by our captain. That path will take you to where the others await your return." That said Citadel lifted into the air.

The weight of the journey thus far tired Autumn. Weary, she leaned her head against Kaela's muscular chest and closed her eyes. A fearful, unfamiliar region lay ahead of them, but Father promised before they left the Sacred Region that no harm would come to His sons while they explored His globe. Champ's galloping seemed smoother, less aggressive. His snorting grew quieter too. Autumn dozed in her angel's arms, glad to know that she would not be left behind.

While she slept, her dreams introduced her to the beasts, birds, fish, and insects she encountered during her exploration of Heaven's eastern region. Images of the mountains she explored, the woodlands she walked through, the valleys she crossed, and the lakes she swam in presented themselves behind her closed eyes. And when she awakened, she knew somehow that seven wonderful months had past, and she and her brothers were returning home to Father's kingdom.

In the pasture where they left Paint, Kaela helped Autumn from Champ's back.

"Paint, here, boy!" Autumn called. "Come to me, Paint!" The little horse galloped to where she stood and nuzzled her cheek. "I missed you too. Let's get you saddled up and back home where you will be cared for properly."

She slipped the saddle on Paint's back and strapped it under his belly. Then she slipped the harness over his head and strapped it in place. "Come on, my precious darling," Autumn said softly as she mounted up, "we are going home." At full gallop, Paint took Autumn across the valley's grassy floor while Champ, with Kaela on his back, trotted close behind.

In the field outside Father's house, the four teams came together as one. Michael took his place at the head of the procession, accompanied by Gabriel, Uzziel, and Uriel. Led by their team captains, the sojourners approached the walls that surrounded Father's courtyard. When Michael's horse stepped through one of the wall's twelve ungated arched doorways, Israfel's choir broke into song accompanied by Zephon's orchestra, trumpets blared, and Zophiel flew high into the air announcing to one and all that God's adventurous sons had returned home.

Autumn, still far off in the distance, used her angelic vision to see cheering angels standing on the high walls that surrounded Father's lawn. She turned in her saddle. Behind her, brothers who were charioteers in the games guided their horse-drawn wagons across the landscape. The wagons carried fruit and vegetables that were native to the sojourners' assigned regions. Some of the carts had been transformed into cages that held beasts and birds, exotic and familiar, large and small. Walking on foot on either side of the wagons, athletes balanced baskets filled with seeds and roots on their heads while colorful birds they had captured perched on their shoulders. Growls, snarls, hisses, and squawks echoed through the wide-open pasture to the tree-lined border of a dense forest that encompassed the Holy Mount. It had been a good expedition, producing many good experiences, but as exciting as it was, Autumn was anxious to return to her cottage in the village.

As the explorers approached the castle's walls, Israfel sang a song of praise, crediting them for their sense of adventure and commending their wonderful messages of love and faith that crossed Father's altar every day. Wagons and cages rolled through the walls' wide, inviting entrances and did not stop until Michael galloped ahead, turned his steed in their direction, and shouted, "Halt!"

The wagons and explorers stopped in their tracks, awaiting their leader's next order. "So that an accurate account can be made of the specimens, plants, and animals we have gathered, all who participated in this expedition are responsible to replace or repair identity tags that may have been damaged during our travels. When your inspections ends and the imports can be easily identified, you will report to Archangel Lucifer for further instructions."

Archangel Lucifer was suddenly at Michael's side. The conqueror of Heaven's unknown regions to the east turned to his eldest brother and boldly said, "Archangel, since you agreed to head the research project, you will assign a team of volunteers to help you care for the animals. You will appoint another team to plant the trees, seeds, and roots that God's adventurous sons have imported from all over the globe."

Lucifer called out in his musical voice, "The soil specimens and water samples will be stored in Father's laboratory where they will be tested." He smiled at Michael. "I suppose I will have the pleasant task of telling Scribe Excelsa, Effiel, and Evangeline, they must catalog the names of the imported wildlife and foliage, and identify the lands they came from." Michael acknowledged Lucifer's comment with a slight nod of his head. "I was afraid of that. But for now, you and the other leaders of this great mission must report to Father."

While Autumn worked with the members of her team to remove damaged tags and replace them with new ones, Sonnet approached. "Can I talk to you?"

"Not now." Autumn said. "I'm busy."

"I really need to talk to someone." Sonnet whispered.

"So talk to Father." Autumn suggested.

"I would, but what I know … I need to talk to someone about what I know." Sonnet said desperately.

Autumn straightened, studying Sonnet's weary face. She could see that he needed to talk with her. She called to Lucifer for a time-out and received his permission to take a break. But when she turned to where Sonnet had been standing, he was gone. Autumn made a visual search of the area for her friend to no avail. Without explaining to the archangel why she did not leave her station, she returned to her work.

Throughout the day, Autumn rose to her full height, stood on her toes, and surveyed the courtyard's landscape for signs of Sonnet. Her curiosity about what her brother knew and why he needed to talk to her grew stronger by the hour. As clouds swept down from above the Holy Castle to create Heaven's pale night, Autumn hurried through God's house to Sonnet's apartment with Kaela at her side.

Chapter 12

The Deceitful Son

Autumn and Kaela stood outside the door of Sonnet's apartment. It was beyond their comprehension why Sonnet would choose to live on the first floor when the majority of Israfel's choir lived on the second floor. "I guess he is exercising his freedom of choice," Abdiel told his curious brothers when the singer's living arrangement came into question during dinner one night. Kaela left it at that, but Autumn was always after Sonnet to move the castle's second floor where he would live among angels who shared his interests. She worried that Sonnet might encounter Nesroc, Mammon, or Thummuz, members of Lucifer's inner circle who set up residency on the first floor to be close to him.

Kaela knocked at the door. Sonnet answered, "Come in. Please come in." While the pair made their way to the living room, Sonnet checked the hallway for prying eyes.

"I was hoping you would stop by before going home, Autumn," Sonnet said in a hushed voice. "Please sit down, Kaela, Autumn."

Kaela was dirty, and he knew it. Before Autumn could be seated, her angel grabbed her arm, forcing her to remain standing. "We don't want to soil your sofa." Kaela offered.

"Nonsense," Sonnet whispered. "Please sit so we can talk."

Autumn raised her brows, turning slightly to look at Kaela, who proved even more unwavering about his decision.

"All right, have it your way, stand." Sonnet moved closer to them. "Did Nemryd, Baneful, Flagitious, or Azazel go with you on your expedition?" The singer grew anxious when he learned they had not. "What I am about to tell you is quite disturbing. You may not even believe me, I don't know, but I do know this: Father's heart would be broken if He knew what Lucifer hoped to accomplish."

The singer sighed, motioning the pair to join him at the dining room table. "We can sit here," Sonnet said. Taking a chair, he encouraged his guests to do the same. Kaela and Autumn sat down, their eyes never leaving Sonnet's face. "After Michael, Gabriel, Uzziel, and Uriel led their teams from the castle to Heaven's uncharted lands, Israfel held a practice in the castle's small auditorium. Archangel Lucifer was present. When the practice ended, the archangel approached and asked me to join him in his suite. I was flattered since I thought he liked the song I sang during our rehearsal. I was wrong." Sonnet went on to describe a scenario only Lucifer could have thought of.

"I went with the archangel to his apartment where he showed me to his living room and asked me to be seated. He said he needed to speak with a trusted friend. I hardly know Lucifer," Sonnet said, his large eyes moving from Kaela's face to Autumn's. "At one time, I admired him, and respected his title, but now … Anyway, I listened in disbelief when he spoke about Father's inability to perform miracles or create more flocks. He said, and I quote, 'Father's powers have dwindled so that He rules Heaven in a diminished capacity.' Then he took my hands in his and asked, 'Are you among those who believe the sojourners are exploring this globe's distant shores?' I indicated I was, and he said, 'Of course you are. Let us suppose that you knew the expedition was a ruse to trick Heaven's citizens into believing in something that does not exist. To whom would you turn for solace, Sonnet?' I told him I would turn to Father. Hearing that, the archangel rose from his chair, weeping.

"Lucifer wiped his tears from eyes and hugged me close. All the while, he said, 'This is what I mean when I speak of God's deception. He has everyone, even you, believing He is the sole reason for angelic happiness. Now listen while I tell you of our Lord's hateful lie.'" Sonnet blinked back tears. "The archangel told me the athletes were sleeping in the wooded area just outside the Holy City beyond the lumber-yard. He said Father cast a spell on Prince Michael's athletes, and he went on to say that he and I had to do something about it. Once more, Lucifer buried his face in hands and wept. When I questioned why the athletes slept, he told me the air in Heaven's uncharted regions is toxic. I never heard that word before. Lucifer explained that toxic, or poisonous, gases rise up from the plants growing in the Heaven's uncharted territories, thus rendering the air impure."

"Surely you knew the story was fabricated?" Autumn asked.

"Yes, I knew it was a fabrication," Sonnet said, his eyes huge with worry. "I read Father's book *Angelic Creation*. On the first chapter's opening page, it is written that we are created compatible to our globe's environment. So I told Lucifer I had to go home and that I would see him in the morning."

"Good for you," Kaela said with a nod of his head.

"Yes, but not good for Bernella," Sonnet said solemnly. He saw the questioning expressions on his friends' faces as they looked at each other, then back at him. "Lucifer saw he could not sway my faith in Father, so he sought after others he felt might be naive enough to believe his lies. Bernella is one of the most trusting brothers I know. And, I am afraid, one of the most gullible."

"So what did Lucifer tell Bernella?" Kaela asked.

"We should go to Bernella to find that out," Sonnet said. He opened his door, checking the hallway before leaving his suite. "Come, he lives just a few doors down from me," Sonnet whispered. "We must walk softly so as not to be discovered."

Autumn and Kaela followed Sonnet down the hallway to Bernella's apartment. They waited while the singer tapped out a code on their brother's door. It opened slowly.

"Come in," a frightened voice whispered. "Please hurry."

When they were inside the apartment, Bernella leaned out the door to check the hallway. It was clear. Without a sound, the angel closed the door. "Please have a seat in the living room. Would you like something to eat or to drink?"

"We aren't here on a social call," Autumn stated. "We want to know what the archangel did that has you and Sonnet afraid to talk above a whisper."

Bernella motioned for them to sit at the dining room table.

"Please tell us why you are so frightened," Autumn urged.

Bernella pulled out a chair and sat down. With hands clasped before him on the tabletop, he said, "I was invited to Lucifer's suite. I arrived as he was preparing to leave. He apologized, saying that his concern for the welfare of Heaven's sojourners caused him to forget about our meeting. I was confused, and I must have looked it because he asked me to join him on his mission. I followed him down the stairs. The castle was dimly lighted since Father had long since retired to His inner sanctum. The archangel motioned for me to be silent, not to speak, and to walk lightly so as not to be heard."

Bernella lowered his voice. "Under cover of Heaven's pale night, Lucifer and I made our way down God's hill to the village. There, we stopped at Buer's house. The archangel had been hoarding supplies he gathered from all over the castle. From Chynella's kitchen, he had taken dried fruit rolls, candied fruit, spiced vegetable, and herbs. From the rooms that lay vacant, he took sheets, blankets, and pillows. We left Buer's house in the village, walking through the city, past the lumberyard to the forest that lay beyond our Lord's kingdom. It was Heaven's darkest hour when we arrived. A thick fog rolled through the valley in our direction. The fog found its way to the forest where it dampened our hair, our garments, and the packs we carried. Shrouded by the mist, Lucifer signaled me to follow him to a mossy clearing. Before we ventured deeper into the forest, the archangel reached into one of the packs and took from it two strange-looking devices."

"What sort of strange-looking devices?" Kaela asked.

Bernella frowned. "The strangest strange-looking devices I ever saw." He closed his eyes for a second, and when he opened them, he said, "Lucifer told me if we were going to go any further, each of us had to use what he called a breathing apparatus."

"He gave you a breathing apparatus," Autumn echoed, "for what reason?"

"So we could breathe without inhaling the toxins," Bernella replied. "The archangel wrapped a heavy cloth over my nose and the bottom half of my face. A slit in the cloth was fitted over my mouth. When the cloth was in place, Lucifer produced two reeds. One was long. The other was short. They snapped together. The short reed fit through the hole in the cloth and was inserted between my lips. The long reed was braced against my forehead with a leather strap. Then I did the same for him. Together, we checked each apparatus to see if it worked. It did." He sighed, rose from his seat, and leaned out the open dining-room window. Assured no eavesdropper lingered there, he took his seat and continued his story.

"We walked a short time before we saw another clearing in the distance," Bernella told his visitors. "Darkness, the likes of which I had never known, spread out across the forest's floor. I realized the trees that canopied the woodlands were blocking the night's pale light. Their branches and leaves were painted black against the white glow of the fog that swirled above them. And then, the fog began to filter downward through the limbs of the trees. The mist did not touch the ground at once. Instead, tall pillars of fog rose up throughout the forest, and suddenly, I had the eerie feeling that Lucifer and I were not alone.

"As we made our way through the shrubs, my eyes adjusted to the woodland's darkened rooms. Up ahead, I saw what looked to be uneven ground. Signing, I suggested that we find a new route to wherever it was we were going. At Lucifer's insistence, we remained on course. The fog that siphoned downward through the trees had spread itself across the ground and was rising around us. I waved my hands as though my gesture might clear the air. Annoyed at the mist that blocked my view, I relied on my angelic vision to show me where I was going. Focusing on a clearing ahead, I tested my sight to learn how far I could see. I felt my eyes widen in terror. My senses reeled. The forest's floor was littered with bodies.

"I tore through the bushes until I reached Nemryd's side. He was breathing. I looked to where Lucifer stood seconds ago. He was gone. A hand touched my shoulder. My flesh crawled. I turned to face the archangel. He offered me a wooden bucket that he had filled with water from a nearby stream. Throughout the long night, Lucifer and I cleansed the poisons from our brothers' skin.

"Before the landscape brightened, we gathered our cloths and set the bucket near the last brother we washed. We took the fruit rolls from our pockets and tore them into even pieces and we placed them on the athletes' chests. This offering was made in case our brothers woke up hungry. Tomorrow, we would return to this place and resume our task. For now, however, we had to get back to the castle. 'Where are the team leaders?' I asked during our ascent to the Holy Mount. Lucifer disclosed that our Lord had sequestered His favored sons in a secret place inside the castle. Without saying, I assumed that Michael, Gabriel, Uriel, and Uzziel had taken refuge in the center rooms of Father's house. The median chamber, Scribe Excelsa calls them."

"Did you reveal what you saw to Father?" Autumn asked.

"No, I was warned not to do that," Bernella said. "The archangel told me to push all thoughts of that night's events from my mind. He said if word of Father's deception reached the public, His popularity would suffer. Lucifer told me when I felt troubled I should turn to him and no one else. The archangel revealed that Father made the breathing apparatuses we used so we could serve Him well. So there was no excuse not to return to the forest every night thereafter."

Kaela rose to his feet. "Do you still believe the air in the forest is toxic?"

"I believe all the air outside the Sacred Region is toxic," Bernella said, trembling. "I believe that we cannot leave this region and that you, Kaela, and you, Autumn, were hypnotized into thinking you just returned from a rewarding journey to the east when, in fact, Lucifer cared for your sleeping bodies in the forest every night until this one, when you supposedly returned home."

Sonnet turned his weary eyes from Bernella's face to study the faces of his two astonished friends.

"Do you see how easily someone with a title can deceive a common citizen?" Autumn asked Kaela. "This is why I say no one in Heaven but Father, Scribe Excelsa, and our sisters should hold titles. Lucifer holds the titles of archangel and prime director of God's Council of Advisors, so he feels he is equal to the royal family when, in fact, he is one of us. He lacks Father's wisdom, and unlike us, he is disobedient and deceitful."

Kaela ran his hands through his hair. How could he convince Bernella the air in Heaven was as pure as God's precious heart? He stared out the window for a long moment, his mind refusing to work past the story Bernella just told. Then without even knowing himself what he was about to say, he turned to the defeated angel. "I want you to come with me. Trust that no one will place blame on you if we are seen. I want to take you on an expedition of your own. This journey will be short, and as you can see, it will be done under cover of night to protect us from prying eyes. Do you agree to my proposal?"

Bernella shook his head. "I am so frightened, Kaela. What proof do you have that we will not be uncreated by the toxins in the air?"

Autumn assured Bernella that there were no toxins, that Lucifer had made up a senseless story to defame Father. When asked about the bodies, she explained that those who lay in the forest, pretending to be asleep, were angels rejected by Michael because they could not take instruction.

"But Archangel Lucifer said he was caring for you, Autumn, and for Kaela! How do you explain that?"

Autumn drew her brows together, glaring at Bernella. "Let me explain to you what a lie is."

"Lie? What is this word? *Lie?*" Bernella grabbed the sides of his head with his hands. "I am so confused and hurt by all this. I know what I saw. I know what I had to do to work safely to save the athletes from uncreation. What is happening? If Lucifer's story was false, why were those athletes unconscious? Why did Father allow it to continue?"

Kaela took Bernella's arm, encouraging him to stand. "Father allowed it to continue because sometimes we have to work out problems, such as this one, on our own." That said, Kaela wrapped his arms tightly around his brother's chest and leaped out the window into the foggy night with Autumn and Sonnet following after him.

The foursome flew close to the treetops to avoid being seen by Lucifer. When they reached the forest, Kaela lighted on the ground, releasing his grip on Bernella. "Show us where the bodies were," he demanded.

Bernella, trembling with fear, his heart racing, fell to his knees clutching Kaela's legs in his desperate hands. He raised his face, fully prepared to beg his brother to take him back to the castle, but his frightened gaze was met with calm, assuring eyes. Gently, strong hands encouraged him to stand. A comforting arm steadied him while he wept and soft words were spoken.

"Father knows the reason for your dread," Kaela assured Bernella. "He will protect you from harm. Show us the place where Lucifer practiced his deception, and I promise I will prove to you that Heaven's air is as pure as our Lord's love for us and as breathable as the air on the Holy Mount."

Bernella walked with a brother at his side as he entered the forest where the athletes had lain unconscious on the ground. Relying on Kaela's trust in Father, he breathed in deeply. The air was pure.

"How can this be? In this very place, I was required to wear a device that purified the air I breathed. But how is it that now, I can breathe without effort, without the fear of uncreation? I can breathe as freely here as I can in my apartment."

Bernella lifted from the ground and disappeared above the treetops. Kaela, Autumn, and Sonnet followed him over the mountains that separated east from west, then north, then south, then back again.

"How dare Lucifer! What was that word you used, Autumn?"

"*Lie.*"

"Lucifer lied to me! He made Father appear to be weak. He took away my joy of greeting my brothers as they returned home from their journeys." Bernella turned to Kaela. "You freed me from my fears. If not for you, I would never dare to leave God's kingdom. I will never again accept Lucifer's word above the truth of our Lord's miracles."

The flight from the forest to the castle was a race fired by anger. Bernella entered God's house through its front door, stormed through the main entrance hall, shouting Lucifer's name while avoiding Kaela's reaching hands. He turned a deaf ear to Autumn's plea for patience. He ignored Sonnet's wise advice that the Lord should handle this matter.

"I am going to teach the archangel that if he cannot speak the truth to me, he should remain quiet!" Bernella shouted, not caring that he made a scene. Kaela spread his wings and lifted his angry brother off his feet. "Put me down! Let me go! This is between Lucifer and me!"

"Be quiet," Kaela growled in Bernella's ear. "I am taking you to your apartment, and I will remain there with you until you calm down enough to listen to me."

At the apartment, Bernella continued to fume over the lies his eldest brother told him. "It makes me feel as though I did something wrong," he said in hollow tones. "I willingly took part in Lucifer's deception. I even encouraged poor Israfel to help us. He wept so bitterly when he saw the bodies, and he promised to keep God's secret. And oh! Roman! He, too, was deceived by me." Bernella's tears flowed in rivulets down his cheeks. "I am as bad as Lucifer, if not worse, because I was the source of spreading this falsehood. Every member in the choir trusted me. Now I am nothing. I am worse than Lucifer."

Bernella cringed at the thought that he, not the archangel, had to face the choir today, knowing that his choral brothers helped cleanse and cover the false athletes because they trusted him. "Oh! Oh! Why was I so easily deceived?"

Suddenly, Heaven knew hypocrisy, deceit, anger, guilt, shame, and suspicion. The globe had lost its innocence through Lucifer's devious act against God.

"Why would the archangel do this? Was he testing my belief in Father's miracles and strength?" The miserable angel groaned. "Why would Lucifer do this to Father, to our brothers, to our athletes, to our sisters, and to me?"

"Envy," Autumn said quietly. "Lucifer envies Father's power in Heaven. He doesn't care who he deceives or how he does it, so long as our Lord appears weak to our brothers, and our athletes appear as frauds to their admirers."

She rose from her seat and stretched. Stifling a yawn with the back of her hand, she said, "Envy is a horrible emotion. When practiced privately, envy reveals itself as criticism, sarcasm, suspicion, and displeasure. Practiced openly, envy disguises itself as kindness, love, understanding, friendship, and brotherhood. The envious brother always leaves his target confused and feeling worthless or guilty because of something he had no control over. Be wary of Lucifer because he is envious of his productive, talented brothers. He is envious of our powerful King and our virtuous sisters. In time, Lucifer will use his envy to possess gullible souls."

Bernella stared slack-jawed at Autumn. "This is incredible! How do you know this?"

Autumn shrugged. "I don't know. This knowledge just comes to me." She turned to Kaela. "Are we going to the lumber-yard today?" He wasn't sure. "Good. I need some rest. I'll be showered by the time you come home. Your bed will be turned down."

She walked to where her weeping brother stood. "No one blames you, dear Bernella. You thought Lucifer was caring for our sleeping brothers to protect Father from public ridicule. You trusted Lucifer because he is the only one of our kind who owns a title."

When Kaela arrived home, he found Autumn sitting at the kitchen table in her bed-clothes. "I thought you would be asleep." He sounded disappointed to find her awake. After pouring himself a chalice of lukewarm nectar, he said, "Bernella is calmer now. He is reasoning out what happened, and he is becoming more aware with each passing moment that he was not the one who betrayed Father. Our fears always fade in God's light." He covered her small hand with his. "Are you all right?"

"I'm fine." Autumn sighed. "But I think Heaven, its angels, and our Lord are in for a trying time. Lucifer has revealed his secret heart to us. We should make our decisions wisely. We should consider everything the archangel tells us and turn to Father for guidance. We should not allow our thoughts to become clouded with the possibility that Lucifer can be anything but evil."

The Righteous Son

The months following the exploration of Heaven's uncharted regions were almost as exciting as the exploration itself. Brothers left their shops and put their dreams behind them to care for animals that they hoped to domesticate. They built corrals for the wild horses that were imported from far-off lands and stables for the ones that were winged. They cared for birds of all species, ensuring that the most beautiful birds, such as peacocks, parrots, and cockatiels, found homes close to Father's house. Autumn obtained God's permission to put beasts of a more independent nature on a vast expanse of land that she called a reserve. Meanwhile, the choir members tested their horticultural skills by planting the seeds and bulbs, which grew into magnificent trees, shrubs, and flowers.

In the laboratory, Archangel Lucifer and his associates ran tests on the soil, water, and minerals that were brought back to the Sacred Region from foreign lands. They learned that the composition found in one region of Heaven was found in all regions of Heaven. They put their findings on record and presented them to the scribe, who added his seal and signature to each page, but not before he read the results put before him. Then he carried the pages to Father, who added them to His public library on the castle's ground floor.

When their work ended, the angels were invited to attend a Festival of Light in the castle's main auditorium.

"I feel like I've been waiting for this forever," Autumn said, her eyes shining with joy. She had been working with Kaela and his carpenters on some furniture that they hoped to trade at the market. "I hope Father recognizes our team leaders for their accomplishments."

She slid her tape measure into her apron's pocket. She was especially pleased that seconds after Zophiel delivered God's invitation to His sons, Kaela excused her from her work so that she could prepare for this evening's celebration. "I'll be ready when you come home and I will have your clothes laid out for you," Autumn promised. Smiling, she left the lumber-yard.

At the cottage, Autumn went straight to the bedroom where she searched Kaela's closet for an attire suited for this evening's festival. For him, she chose an aqua cloak and white robe with a golden sash. She set his new sandals on the floor next to his nightstand. For her, she chose yellow sandals, her pale-yellow robe with a matching sash, and a white cloak trimmed at the sleeves, hem, and lapels with yellow daisies. Autumn placed her clothing neatly on her bed before she retired to the bathroom. Two hours later, she emerged from her bedroom fully dressed and ready to go.

Autumn estimated that if she were on Earth, it would have been about four o'clock in the afternoon when she sat down at the table to wait for Kaela. She expected him to burst through the door any minute. When an hour passed and he did not come home, she left the house to wait on the porch. She estimated she waited there for a good thirty minutes. Autumn left the porch to stand on the sidewalk where she watched with great expectation the path that led from the forest to their cottage. When still another hour passed, Autumn strolled up the sidewalk to the path she took every morning on her way to the lumber-yard.

Should she go to the castle without Kaela or to the lumber-yard, where she last saw him? Autumn pulled her long ash-blond hair over her left shoulder and twirled the ends of it around her fingers as though that would help her think of what course she should take. Surely Kaela would not miss Father's festival to work on something at the shop? If she went to the lumber-yard she worried that he would find her intrusion annoying. But, what if something happened and he needed her help? What if–Oh! What the heck! Spreading her wings, she lifted off the ground and flew through the air to Kaela's shop. She would have gone inside, but the sound of Archangel Lucifer's voice stopped her cold. Tiptoeing to a side window, Autumn listened to the archangel's conversation with Kaela.

"All I am saying, Kaela, is Father is not as powerful as He once was. It will not be long until our Lord seeks an heir to fill His throne. Keep in mind that no one in Heaven is as prepared for the task as I am. So it would be to your better good if you showed me more respect and obeyed whatever command I might find fit to give you.

"I have with me a book I took from God's private library on the castle's third floor. It reveals that other worlds exist—maybe not in this universe, but far off in deepest space. These alien worlds house creatures that are not so different from us. Our Lord allowed these lesser beings to create what He calls a government, where a few reign over many. In time, they no longer revered Him. They put Father aside so they could worship the leaders of their government. I intend to start a government. And I want you to reign with me. We will be worshipped by Heaven's citizens as God is worshipped now."

"I have no desire to be worshipped by my brothers," Kaela said. "And I have no idea what a government is, but if Father was rejected after these so-called alien beings set it up, then it must be wrong." Kaela glanced toward the window. It was getting late, and he had promised Autumn he would be home early on festival nights. "You will never rule Heaven, Archangel. Father will never relinquish His throne or His scepter to you."

"You do not know Father's thoughts," Lucifer hissed. "I am as God in Heaven. I am aware of our Lord's thoughts. I know the minds of all angels in Heaven. That is why we are having this talk now because I know, in your heart, you doubt God. You, like so many others, long for me to rule this globe from Heaven's throne. You are reluctant because, though you doubt Father's powers, you likewise doubt mine. Know this: through my power of persuasion, I will create an eighth flock. They will admire me, make me their king, and call me blessed." Lucifer's eyes narrowed. Was this fool laughing at him? "What did I say that you find so amusing, Kaela?"

"I find your words amusing, Lucifer." Kaela straightened to his full height. He studied the archangel's face as intently as the archangel studied his. Crossing his arms over his ribs, Kaela asked, "What am I thinking right now."

Archangel Lucifer groped for words that might have some meaning to his brother.

"All right, I'll tell you what I am thinking," Kaela said, peering into Lucifer's eyes. "Each of Father's created flocks is a representation of our sisters' virtues. My flock was created to honor our precious sister Inspiration. Being created full-grown and wise, most of us memorize the lessons of the sister for whom our flock was created. I learned Inspiration's lesson well, and I think she is quite proud of me and the accomplishments I made in this region since I left Father's laboratory.

"But Inspiration taught me something else," Kaela told his awful brother. "She taught me to turn to each of my sisters for guidance. I turn to Charity when I am commissioned by a brother who longs to have the furniture or gazebos that I build. I refer to Faith's lessons when I pray to Father. I heed Love's lesson when I am with Father, my virtuous sisters, and my brothers." He wet his lips with the tip of his tongue. "Wisdom's lesson taught me that challenges can be resolved through patience and understanding. Truth's lesson taught me to reject any brother who is as lowly as I am when he offers me a throne next to his in Heaven, for God's law reads 'angel shall not rule angel.'

"Presently, I am leaning on Mercy's lesson that encourages me to use angelic grace when rebuking anyone who demeans Father in Heaven. All my sisters' lessons combined reveal that we should give our Lord the respect He deserves." Kaela studied Lucifer's face with leveled eyes. "Who do you honor, Lucifer? Not Truth. Not Wisdom. Not Faith. Not Mercy. Not Charity. Not Love. Not Inspiration. By which virtue are you influenced?"

"These qualities are inborn in me," the archangel said boldly. "I am as God in Heaven."

Kaela shook his head in disbelief. Was he really hearing this? "I truly doubt that Father will make you Heaven's king, Lucifer," he said with a chuckle in his voice. "Our Lord's law concerning such matters clearly states that you will never rule Heaven from His throne. Father created us equal, full-grown, and wise. We know the difference between right and wrong, and we are aware that our obedience to God is the sole source of our happiness."

"But He has grown weak, Kaela," Lucifer snarled, "and there is no other God in the region to take Father's place. I am more like God than anyone else in Heaven."

"You compare yourself to God," Kaela scoffed. "I cannot recall an instant where Father ever discredited His sons. Our Lord practices all seven virtues when He deals with us. He does not seek out gullible sons to instill doubts in them about their skilled and courageous brothers. But you—you deliberately set out to defame our Lord to our brothers, and you hoped to convince them that Michael, Gabriel, Uzziel, Uriel, and their teams of sojourners are frauds. You knew it would do no good to threaten them to assure their silence, so you told them Father would look bad if word leaked out that He was losing His powers."

"Who told you these falsehoods?"

"Brothers who shall remain nameless," Kaela stated firmly. "Oh, I forgot, you can read my mind. These poor confused brothers told me how you lied to them while the athletes were absent from this region." Lucifer lifted his hand in anger. "Do not threaten me, Archangel. I will go directly to Father with your secret, and I will give Him the names of the brothers you deceived, and the King will deal with you accordingly."

Autumn felt this was a good time to interrupt. "Excuse me, Archangel," she said with a smile, "I must speak with Kaela." Lucifer turned his back as though that would give the couple the privacy they needed. "Kaela, the hour has grown late, and the celebration at the castle has certainly begun by now. Should I attend the ceremony alone, or should I go home and wait for you?"

"Neither," Kaela said. "The archangel and I are done here." He walked to where Lucifer stood and peered fearlessly into his eyes. "I am sure when Father asks why you were absent from His table this evening, you will use your powerful imagination to fabricate a convincing story." Kaela motioned to Autumn, who hurried to his side. Draping his arm over her shoulder, he told the archangel, "Shop's closed."

More fearful of what Kaela might tell Father than angry now, Lucifer hurried from the carpentry shop to stand in the lumber-yard, his eyes fixed on the castle's highest peak. From here, that was all he could see of the mansion. The rest of the house was hidden from view by the tall trees that separated this place from the Holy City. He turned slightly to throw a hateful glance over his shoulder at Kaela, who had just left the shop with Autumn in tow.

"Remember this," Archangel Lucifer told the pair, his voice trembling, "God chose me above all of you to be His archangel. He chose me to supervise His counsel. No one else holds my titles or carries as much responsibility as I do. Therefore, all the rest of you are nothing. I am the most powerful angel in Heaven. Do you understand?"

Kaela, whose obedience to God instilled dread in the archangel's heart, walked past without so much as a glance in Lucifer's direction. Autumn, who seemed out of place in Heaven but was loved by everyone, cast Lucifer a quick discouraging look, then turned her face away from him. It was not her glance or the expression that accompanied it, but the way she drew her robe close to her body so its hem did not touch his robe as she passed by that infuriated Lucifer.

At the cottage, Kaela washed up and threw on the clothes Autumn handed him. He tied his sash as he hurried out the door, his cloak thrown over his shoulder. The pair lifted from the ground and flew to Father's house in haste. Kaela finished dressing in the castle's lobby, where he slipped on the sandals Autumn brought for him to wear. They were running down the corridor toward the auditorium when they saw the doors closing.

"Wait!" they shouted in unison. "Wait!"

Their voices echoed through the lobby, down the corridor to the ears of a young brother named Sammael. He smiled when he saw the desperate couple coming his way. When they were inside the theater, he closed the door. Reaching out a gentle hand, he touched Autumn's shoulder. "Good to see you made it," he whispered in her ear.

While Israfel sang the evening's opening song, welcoming his brothers and sisters to God's house, Autumn leaned close to her angel. "I've been meaning to ask," she said, resting her hand on his arm, "what prompted Lucifer to visit the shop?"

"He worries that Father will give titles to the leaders of Heaven's exploration," Kaela replied in a whisper. "He asked what I would do if Father offered me the position of archangel."

"Would you accept if asked?" Autumn questioned.

"No," Kaela answered. "I have no desire to be tied to the throne room as a counselor to the King." He nodded toward the stage. "The concert is beginning. Let's listen."

Following the concert, God rose from His seat, saying, "My children, welcome to my home. Before I bestow honors upon my accomplished sons, I have a few things to say. When I created your race, I gave each of you freedom of choice and self-expression. Be forewarned, however, that even freedom has its price. Many of you know that through careful deliberation, any situation can be approached with dignity and confidence. But even then, you must be careful about the decisions you make because your decision may determine the price of your freedom. The definition of *decision* is 'choice.' The definition of *freedom* is 'free will.'

"The price of freedom of choice and freedom of self-expression is determined by how you accept responsibility for the decisions you make. Any one of you can make a wrong choice. Simply exercising dignity when one makes a choice does not make it right. So you stand accountable for every choice you make and every word that falls from your lips. That is why I created your race full-grown and wise and instilled within you the knowledge of good and evil.

"Responsibility means that you are accountable for your choices. Your choices create new experiences. Experience brings independence, the rewards of which are intellectual growth and emotional stability. Use your wisdom daily, and know that my laws are written on each of your hearts. When you break Heaven's laws, you have made a willful choice, and you will be held accountable."

Autumn nudged Kaela. "It sounds like Father is wise to Lucifer and is discouraging anyone from following him." Kaela patted her hand to hush her. God had projected His image as well as the images of the scribe, the Goddesses, Effiel, Evangeline, and Lucifer onto the stage before them.

"This is better than the big screens in the conventions halls on Earth." Autumn listened as God introduced His holy scribe before taking His seat.

Scribe Excelsa unrolled a thick scroll, and began to read. "Tonight, as we embrace the future, we must reach back into the past to honor one whose existence made a marked change in Heaven's present. Without this brother, we would have lived in a diminished capacity. His sense of adventure, his inspiration, and his willingness to establish the games we enjoy began a new era in our lives that will live on forever." He looked away from the scroll as though taking in the faces of everyone in the audience. "Our Lord requests Michael's presence on stage before His towering image."

Autumn was oblivious to the ceremony. By the description he gave, she thought Scribe Excelsa was about to introduce Kaela to the audience. "When did you become archangel?" she asked. "I mean, without your skills, the Holy Castle would still be a zoo, and Lucifer would still be sleeping in a box of straw in that dirty, smelly room of his."

Kaela shushed her. "Listen to what Excelsa is saying." He pointed toward the stage.

"Michael toured the east, thus bringing home young saplings of cypress, hemlock, bamboo, lotus, cryptomeria, subtropical evergreens, and camphor. Birds included the beautiful peacock and the impressive crowned eagle. Beasts from the east included pandas, wild boars, pangolins, tapirs, gibbons, tree shrews, white lions, and camels."

Gabriel was called to the stage where took his place beside Michael.

"The expedition headed by Gabriel toured the west, bringing home with them such beasts as coyotes, cougars, big-horn sheep, and skunks; the dried carcasses of dog fish, salmon, and shellfish; such trees as conifer, yellow pine, sequoia, fir, and cedar; and such ores as granite, uranium, mercury, and potash."

Scribe Excelsa gazed out into the audience. "Would Uzziel please present himself before our Lord God's towering image?" Uzziel ran to the stage from the back of the room to stand with his brothers.

"The expedition led by Uzziel toured the North, bringing home with them baskets filled with mushrooms, tomatoes, and wild corn; trees such as oak, ash, conifer, elm, and sycamore pine; birds such as turkey, geese, pheasants, quail, and pleasant meadowlarks; beasts such as black bears, raccoons, woodchucks, deer, elk, penguins, white bears, and beavers. In their backpacks, they carried such rocks as limestone, sandstone, and shale."

Uriel was the last of the exploration team leaders to be called to the stage.

"The expedition led by Uriel toured the south, bringing home with them exotic trees such as mangrove, palms, and cypress; exotic plants such as cactus and moss that lives on air; animals such as foxes, raccoons, otters, and alligators; and birds such as egrets, flamingos, herons, pelicans, and cranes." Excelsa turned to where Father sat in the family booth. "My Lord, I have the honor and the privilege of presenting our four courageous explorers to You."

Father rose from His seat. "Everything I do is deliberate. By the power of my almighty Word, this globe is formed from space dust and cosmic dew. On its surface, trees and grasses grow, various animals wander over hills and through woodlands; fresh-water streams, lakes, rivers, and salty oceans are filled with aquatic life. This world houses flying, creeping, and crawling insects and reptiles. I name this globe Heaven, meaning "paradise," and my angels—my beloved sons—were created to enjoy everything I put here. All this was done by the power of my almighty Word.

"Michael," our Lord said, calling on the source of Heaven's exploration, "our lives have not been the same since you were created. Your brothers regard you as a role model. By your example, they sought to become athletes. Through your careful instruction, they learned to ride horses, winged horses, and unicorn. You encouraged them to leave my kingdom to explore their world. Therefore, I christen you archangel."

That night the leaders of the expedition, who led their curious brothers from God's kingdom to Heaven's uncharted regions, received titles.

"My sons of light," Father said, extending His hand toward the angels kneeling on the polished floor of the auditorium's massive stage, "I present to you, your brothers—Archangel Michael, Archangel Gabriel, Archangel Uzziel, and Archangel Uriel."

Thundering applause rocked the auditorium. Brothers rose to their feet in admiration and respect for their mentors, who opened their hearts to adventure and showed them the wonders of their world. Many of God's sons hoped to live in the regions they explored. Their dream, to make the new vast expanses they discovered as productive as the Sacred Region. While the body of the auditorium celebrated their brave brothers' promotion from common citizens to archangels, Lucifer remained seated. He did not applaud. He did not acknowledge the new archangels' accomplishments. And, when asked by Father to say a few words of encouragement to Heaven's titled sons, Archangel Lucifer refused to speak.

Autumn turned in her seat, peering into the family booth; she focused on Lucifer. Using her angelic vision, she marveled that the archangel's facial muscles were so tense that his skin resembled plastic. She knew it was hard for her ancient brother to be glad the athletes received titled promotions. Now, there were five archangels in Heaven. Autumn smiled. She almost expected to Lucifer to leave his seat in a huff, but he wisely chose to stay put. She turned and gazed up at Kaela. Would she see this wonderful honor bestowed on him? Would she wake up one morning knowing that she shared a cottage with a titled brother? Father's voice caught her attention.

"Arise, my son," Heaven's King requested. "Bernella, you have expressed your desire to know your globe more personally. Suddenly, it is not enough for you to breathe the air on this mount. You long to breathe the scented air of the tropics, the piney air of the northern region, and the sandy air of the western shores. When you return home from your travels, promise me that you will teach your brothers what you learned. Tomorrow, with my blessings, you shall join Archangel Uriel and his crew on their mission to map all the newly discovered regions in Heaven.

"There are those among you who question my powers. Believe me when I say, I know your every thought. I hear your every prayer.

And I see your every move. Whatever you do, wherever you go, I love each of you as much as I did on the day of your creation. If we must disagree with one another, let us never surrender our status of Father and sons to ill feelings. If in the future, you choose another over me, know that I am where you left me, and I will rejoice when you return home. I will never begrudge you a room in my house. I will keep you safe from harm. I will offer you water when you thirst and bread when you are hungry. I will never neglect your needs for you are my precious children, my sons." When Jehovah God finished His speech, He turned to Lucifer, who sat fidgeting in his seat. "Arise, Archangel Lucifer, and accept your promotion from the station you now hold to that of Heaven's first prince."

Autumn had to bite her tongue to keep from screaming, "Father, this angel is an abomination! His body is Sin's vessel, and his mind does her bidding! Your eldest son is Your enemy!" Her heart sank when she saw God set a prince's crown on Archangel Lucifer's head.

The haughty angel grinned at his beloved Father. Then he turned to face his cheering public. "Thank you!" he shouted, sounding very much like a politician. "Thank you, one and all, so very much!" Prince Lucifer turned away from his admiring brothers to face God. "You made me Your prince, but what is a prince without a throne? He is no more than a titled son who is deprived of his high seat in Heaven. Must I stand before my siblings with tears streaming from my eyes while I plead with You to provide me with the throne that sits closest to Your sacred heart?"

"From this day forward," Heaven's King announced, "Prince Lucifer will occupy a high seat that will sit to the left of my throne in the outdoor throne room and my inner sanctum."

A seat nearest to God's heart! Autumn's stomach knotted. Nausea dampened her skin. Too weary to move, she rested her head against Kaela's arm. Instinctively, he reached for her.

"I think I should have eaten something back at the cottage," she whispered. Gulping hard, Autumn struggled to stand. When she found her footing, she stumbled into the aisle. The thought of Lucifer gaining more power over her brothers caused her to gag. Suddenly, Kaela was at her side, squiring her through the theater's doors to the fresh air outside.

Autumn did not get sick as she first thought she might; instead, she developed a severe case of noisy hiccups.

The walk home was dreadful. Autumn's loud hiccups followed by her miserable groans brought laughter from anyone who passed by. Kaela walked with his arm draped over her shoulder, smiling down at her. He stepped from the path near Zadkiel's cottage and picked a sprig of mint from the garden.

"Chew this," he said softly, "maybe it will settle your stomach."

Autumn took the mint sprig and chewed it slowly. Sure enough, the hiccups subsided. But the mint did not settle her weary mind. How could Father set a prince's crown on Lucifer's head? Father began His speech that led to His eldest son's promotion by acknowledging He knew that there are those among us who questioned his powers. His revelation was followed by a warning to His sons: "I know your every thought. I hear your every prayer. And I see your every move." Was Father warning Lucifer and his supporters that they could not hide their conspiracy to seize Heaven's throne?

Autumn puzzled over God's promise, "If in the future, you choose another over me, know that I am where you left me, and I will rejoice when you return home." Did Father know that, like Bernella, good angels would succumb to Lucifer's lies? Did He know that His righteous sons would need Him more than ever if they chose to follow His false prince? She had so many questions. But then, she knew the ending of the book Father commissioned her to write. So was it fear she felt that turned her stomach and robbed her peace of mind? Turning on her heel, she studied the brothers who walked behind her, beside her, and now, ahead of her. They were laughing and talking as though nothing terrible had just happened in Heaven.

Chapter 14

A Royal Request

The night of Lucifer's promotion from first archangel to first prince was a long one for Autumn. She tossed and turned, moving from feelings of dread to comforting prayer and back again. Her heart was broken. No, it was sick. Sick with worry about how far Lucifer would take his new title. Never before had she longed to leave her bed to walk the streets of her village at night. But now, she rose to her feet, slipped her sandals on, and tiptoed from the room, hoping not to awaken Kaela. She was on the porch when she heard a noise behind her.

"You can't sleep either," Kaela said, patting the wooden seat of the swing he sat on. "Come and sit with me a while. Let's talk."

Autumn lowered herself to the seat. Like a child, she leaned her head against his arm. Taking her angel's hand, she said, "I listened to your conversation with Lucifer when he visited your shop yesterday evening. I am so proud of the way you stood up to him. But I heard him mention that he hopes to start a government in Heaven." She rolled her eyes up to study her angel's face. "Father was wrong to promote Lucifer to prince. Now, our eldest brother not only has a royal title but a throne nearest to our Lord's heart, which he will use to convince unsuspecting sons that he is Heaven's best-loved angel."

Kaela leaned toward her. "There is already a government in Heaven. There has always been a government in Heaven, with God serving as its only King. Father is good, kind, and loving, but He is the head of Heaven's government and His Word is law. Only He can choose who will inherit His throne." He sat back on the swing, wrapping his arm around Autumn, holding her close to his beating heart. "According to Zophiel, Belial told him that Lucifer's plans to establish a new government were going nowhere since the other council members refuse to break God's laws. Since Lucifer could not sway Father's board of advisors to his side, he had to go another route."

"He had to convince Father to raise him to royalty," Autumn interjected. "Now he will move about the village and town, swaying everyone's beliefs to suit his agenda. The more he shows himself, the more endeared he will become, and the easier it will be for him to set himself up as a leader." She frowned so fiercely her face hurt. If only she could tell her brothers the truth about Lucifer.

"When you write of Lucifer's promotion to royalty, do not capitalize the first letter in the word, *prince,* unless it serves as a prelude to his name—Prince Lucifer," Kaela said. "How Lucifer became prince is known only to those who serve in God's throne room. Perhaps, Lucifer convinced Father to promote him by lending his wisdom to his brothers to solve their problems. Or maybe he excelled as a council member and earned a promotion that way. The truth of Lucifer's promotion will make itself known in time.

"What you must remember is, not all our brothers who chose to follow Lucifer were bad. In fact, even after Lucifer separated himself from God, the majority of his followers never broke Father's laws."

He noticed that Autumn was strangely silent. Glancing down at her, he saw she had fallen asleep. "This talk made me feel better too," he whispered. Lifting his beloved Autumn in his arms, he carried her to her bed, slipped her sandals off her feet, and covered her with a downy blanket. "Sleep in peace, precious angel," he whispered before leaving the room.

Weeks after Lucifer was crowned prince, Zophiel arrived at the lumber-yard where he spoke privately to Kaela. In his hand, the messenger carried an invitation signed by Scribe Excelsa. The invitation the scribe sent requested the carpenter's presence at a luncheon that would be held in his suite on the third floor of God's house. Autumn's name was not mentioned in the invitation or during the conversation between Zophiel and Kaela, but when she learned of the luncheon,

Autumn made it very clear that she would be present at the scribe's table for any talks that may follow the mid-day meal. It was when they were making their way down the hall toward the scribe's apartment that Autumn spoke her mind. "It was wrong of Excelsa to invite you and leave me out. I noticed that, don't think I didn't. Wherever you go, I go. It's only right that I know what is happening behind the scenes since I am the one Father chose to write His book."

She turned her attention from what she was saying to try the doors on the median rooms they passed. After turning several door-knobs with no luck, Autumn let out a long loud sigh. "I cannot understand why these empty rooms are locked," she grumbled. "Do you know how annoying it is to turn every knob on every door of the median rooms, on any one of these three floors, only to learn that you can't gain entrance to any of them? What a waste of time."

She turned to Kaela. Her tortured expression made him smile. "What?" Autumn asked sharply. "I want to know why these rooms are so secretive that they are off-limits to the general public."

"Why do you care?" her angel asked as he knocked at the door of the scribe's apartment. Before Autumn could answer Kaela's question, Scribe Excelsa was in the hallway, inviting them inside.

The lunch was not one of those noisy, festive affairs where everyone talked at once while bowls of delicious food were passed around the table. No. Instead, the guests—who included Effiel, Evangeline, and God's daughters—ate their meal in silence. When the table was cleared, everyone settled in the living room where Excelsa opened the conversation with an explanation.

"I took the liberty of inviting our sisters, my associate, and Evangeline to help me convince you to accept the mission I am offering." The scribe smiled in Autumn's direction. Her gray eyes were wide with anticipation. He could almost hear this small brother's thoughts. *Ah, a mission!* "As you know, our eldest brother, Lucifer, holds the distinction of being many *firsts* in Heaven—first created son, first archangel, first director to our Lord's advisors, and recently, he was promoted to the position of first prince." Excelsa paused for a moment. "Last night, Lucifer had a dream that disturbed Father. The dream not only revealed his desire to rule Heaven from our Lord's throne but that he intends to make Sin his queen."

"Why would he do that?" Autumn asked. "Sin cannot live in Heaven. God's pure light is like poison to her." As though to prove her point, Autumn told the scribe, her sisters, and Effiel what she saw after Father released the witch's evil cells from the vial. "I was in that cave with her. She stayed there until Father retired to His inner sanctum, and then Sin set out on her mission to infect my brothers with her foul venom."

"As disturbing as it is that Prince Lucifer wants to rule with Sin as his queen, I find it more disturbing that he wants to turn righteous sons against Father," Scribe Excelsa told his listeners. "Our dreams are private. They help us deal with our daily problems. More often than not, my dreams told me how I should respond to a situation in the throne room. But Lucifer's dream was so troubled that our Lord took it upon Himself to 'take a little peek,' as Autumn would say. What He saw broke His heart. In the dream, Lucifer was with Sin. They were plotting ways that he could establish himself as Heaven's king. The prince and his witch were trying to decide if he should use flattery or fraud to deceive God."

"What is this word *fraud?*" Kaela asked. "And how will it help Lucifer seize Father's throne?"

"Fraud is not new to Heaven," Autumn told Scribe Excelsa and his guests. "Lucifer committed fraud during Heaven's exploration when he convinced several of his unsuspecting brothers to assist him in caring for brothers who were disqualified from the expedition. Fraud is deception. Deception means to tell falsehoods, preferably laced with facts to encourage others to believe what they are being told. If you recall, the fraud that was perpetrated against the athletes who explored our globe was not as severe as the fraud Lucifer commits against Father when he tells us our Lord's powers are failing."

"What our small brother tells us is correct," the scribe said. "Lucifer commissioned his supporters to lie in the forest dressed in clothing similar to what Michael's athletes wore when they left Father's kingdom. That scene convinced some of our trusting brothers that Father could not protect His adventurous sons. Brothers like Bernella, Roman, and

Israfel were tricked by Lucifer into believing our Lord's powers had diminished."

"So how will Sin leave Lucifer's body to rule in Heaven with him?" Effiel asked.

"That's a very good question," Excelsa said, rising from the chair he occupied. "I am sure Father knows how Sin can break free to walk among us. Maybe she will make her appearance when Lucifer is sleeping soundly, something he rarely does. But on occasion, I'm sure he closes his eyes and his dreams fill his head with comforting thoughts. How else is he able to face each new day?"

The scribe walked to the dining room window, reminding Autumn of Bernella the night she and Kaela visited his apartment with Sonnet. "This morning, Lucifer petitioned Father to promote him to the position of God's ambassador to the northern region of Heaven." Excelsa returned to his chair, crossed his legs, and studied the faces that were turned in his direction. "According to what our Lord learned from Lucifer's dream, the prince intends to use his title to amass a following that will, in time, enable him to build an army powerful enough to seize Heaven's throne."

Kaela gasped. "Surely Father will stop this betrayal before it happens."

"No," Scribe Excelsa sniffed. "Father hopes to separate Heaven's doubters and disbelievers from His faithful sons. Since Lucifer acquired his princely title, he has become more popular. His visits to the city and village have only added to his prestige. Presently, Lucifer has been pleading with Father to build starter colonies in the North that will supply a safe place for his supporters."

"A safe place from what?" Kaela asked.

"Lucifer wants to stop any interference that might hinder his progress," Excelsa replied. "He mistakenly thinks he will hide behind a cloak of tolerance, turning his supporters against their Creator and the brothers who love them. He is planning to set himself up as the king of Heaven's northern region where he will make his own laws. He will try to convince his supporters that Father's laws are too rigid and too ancient to be obeyed. He will rewrite them to suit his own agenda."

Autumn was haunted by memories of how the political parties on Earth worked against each other. It did not matter that they were bought and paid for by the taxpayers, each party carried its hatred for the sitting president and his administration to their supporters. Liberals called names, put horrid labels on every common-sense value, and upheld everything that was illegal or defied nature. They encouraged their supporters to riot, destroy property, and attack people who did not think like their leaders. The conservatives held fast to the laws of the land, but to enforce what was already in the books, they made laws that restrained law-abiding citizens more severely than the criminal element that threatened society. Surely Heaven's citizens would never know the chaos and destruction of being separated by two ruling parties: God and Earth's future devil.

Truth leaned toward her brothers. "Father informed us that He will not stop Lucifer. He wants to see for Himself how influential His eldest son has become. Father says His angels should make wise choices about who they want as their king because whatever they get themselves into, they must get themselves out of."

"What brothers have joined forces with Lucifer thus far?" Kaela asked.

"Some of the globe's most talented sons have fallen in league with Lucifer," Excelsa answered, his weariness apparent in his tone of voice. "Origen, Azazel, Belial, just to name a few. I need your assistance, Kaela. It will take time to resolve this problem and I am so sorry that I cannot go into more detail. If you agree to accept the mission I am offering, we will succeed in stopping Lucifer's attempt to seize God's throne and keep him from ruling in Heaven."

"I came at your request," Kaela reminded the scribe. "I will do whatever I must to aid Father, you, and our sisters, but you must act as my guide during this troubled time since I have never had to deal with a problem that threatened Heaven's peace."

"I need you to befriend Lucifer and his courtiers," Excelsa told Kaela. "If you gain their trust by attending their secret conclaves, you could keep tabs on their comings and goings and report to Father in prayer. No one in Heaven can hear your prayers but Father. So wherever you are, whoever you are with, you can speak with Him in private."

The scribe left his chair in the living room to peer out the dining room window a second time. With his back turned to his guests, he asked Kaela, "Were you aware that Abdiel joined Lucifer's supporters?"

"No, I was not," Kaela said softly.

"You are now." Scribe Excelsa motioned for his guests to stand. "I know that Autumn will love this. I want both of you to observe Lucifer and his crew throughout the day. Knowing their habits will put us on the path to ending this problem. Do you agree to do this for God?"

"Yes," Kaela and Autumn said in unison.

The scribe led his guests to the door. "I must return to the outdoor throne room. Oh, I almost forgot. Kaela, Father wants to meet with you late tonight, after He takes His throne in the castle's inner sanctum." Scribe Excelsa glanced at Autumn. To Kaela, he said, "Come alone."

Late that evening, after God's sons were fast asleep, Kaela arrived at the Holy Castle with Autumn in tow.

"How am I going to know what to write if I have to wait in the lobby?" she asked. She was obviously upset. Her eyes were moist. The tip of her nose was red, as were her cheeks, and her voice waivered when she spoke. "Are you going to tell me what Father says?" Autumn asked, but her angel ignored her. She sat down on the sofa closest to the inner sanctum's closed door. She heard Kaela's knock. She heard the door open. And then she was alone.

It was almost morning when Kaela shook Autumn awake. "Come on, we have to go home," he whispered. "Let's go."

He helped his sleepy beloved Earth angel to her feet and together, they left God's house. The pair walked in silence through the mist that nourished the globe's lush landscape. It wasn't that Autumn didn't have questions, but Kaela was walking toward their cottage so fast that she could barely keep up with him. When they arrived home Kaela told her, "Father assured me He will guide us in everything we do."

"Well, that's good to know," Autumn whispered. "What's our mission? I mean, in addition to what Excelsa wants us to do."

"Father wants Lucifer to amass a following that includes sons who doubt Him, who doubt His Word's creative powers, and who feels Heaven's laws are obsolete," Kaela replied.

The evening of the following day, Zophiel announced from on high that Heaven's sons were invited to attend God's Festival of Light. Autumn and Kaela arrived at the dining room late. Executing the first leg of their mission, they sat at a table with Moloch, Nesroc, Thummuz, Mammon, Azazel, and Apollyon. Autumn wished with all her heart that she didn't have to sit with these awful brothers. The brashness of their harsh words made it hard for her to look into their eyes when they addressed her. She sat quietly in their presence, for she knew that Father would put His words in her mouth when He had something for her to say. In the meantime, Kaela had become someone Autumn hardly knew. He whispered doubts about Father's capacity to maintain stability in His kingdom; he expressed his desire to join Lucifer's forces and indicated he would work to make the North attractive to God's sons so that they would leave the Sacred Region.

"We hoped you would come around, Kaela," Moloch said in his low guttural voice.

"Abdiel assured us that if we gained your acceptance, Autumn would follow suit," Apollyon said, smiling down at the small brother who had not spoken a word since he arrived.

"You are going to join Lucifer's forces, are you not?" Mammon asked, directing his question to Autumn, who seemed to loathe making eye contact with him.

"Yes, of course," Autumn replied. If she had not known that Lucifer was Earth's future devil and that faithful mankind would consider these brothers equally evil, she may have felt more comfortable in their presence. But she saw things that made her uneasy. She saw the influence Satan had over Eve and how he devoured the witch during her nocturnal visit to his room. A chill ran down Autumn's spine. Until a brother sat at a table with his most feared enemies, he could hardly know how frightened she was at this moment.

The twenty-third Psalm suddenly came to mind. Knowing that only Father could hear her, Autumn prayed, "The Lord is my Shepherd [Father, You are my Guide and my Protector], I shall not want [You love me without question]. You make me lie down in green pastures [You comfort me]. You lead me beside the still waters [when turmoil threatens, You give me peace]. You restore my soul [You nourish and cleanse me of sin]. You lead me in the path of righteousness for Your name's sake [You guide me with the wisdom and grace that only You have]. Yea, though I walk through the valley of the shadow of death [I am embarking on a treacherous journey], I will fear no evil [my faith in You will keep me safe], for Your rod [Your power] and Your staff [Your Laws] comfort me. You prepare a table before me in the presence of my enemies [Lucifer and his followers]. You anoint my head with oil [I am blessed by Your love]. My cup runs over [Your eternal love for me is overwhelming]. Surely goodness and mercy shall follow me all the days of my life [You are always with me, guiding me and forgiving my shortcomings], and I will dwell in the house of the Lord forever [Now and always, I am welcome to sit in Your presence]. Amen."

Like King David, Autumn invited Father to look into her heart to witness the love she had for Him. "Look into my soul," Autumn prayed. "I would not be sitting at this table reserved for idolaters, sinners, hypocrites, or evildoers if it was not done but to please You."

At the main theater, Kaela sat with Moloch and Nesroc. He was glad when Abdiel took the seat behind him. Autumn sat with Apollyon and Beelzebub. Sick at heart, aware that the task she accepted was dangerous and bordered on treason, Autumn turned her weary eyes to the stage where the choir sang praises to God. The voices, the music, the concert that excelled any she ever attended on Earth added to her burden. Unshed tears blurred her eyes; the entire auditorium became a blur. Autumn sniffed and dabbed her eyes with the soft material of her robe's sleeve.

"Help me, Father," her weary heart cried. "Make me brave. Make me strong. Let my faith in You overpower my fear so that I can better serve You."

The songs ended long enough to allow Father to speak with His sons. God rose from His seat, saying, "Children, I have an announcement to make that will thrill each of you who long for adventure. My son, Heaven's prince, has requested that I permit him and his followers to leave the Sacred Region to live in the North."

Applause thundered and cheers roared through the auditorium. Father waited until the theater grew quiet. "We will need skilled carpenters, metallurgists, plumbers, and laborers who can take instruction. Later, we will commission our weavers to lend us their skills. At Lucifer's request, all skilled craftsmen will remain in the auditorium following the concert. The prince would like to meet with you."

Father was about to sit again when Prince Lucifer leaped to his feet. "Are we forgetting something?" He asked his Lord. "You promised me a new title. Have you forgotten?" Throwing his brothers a sly smile, the false prince said apologetically, "Father's memory is not what it should be."

"Prince Lucifer, I christen you ambassador to the northern region of Heaven," Father said, waving His hand over Lucifer's head. "Sons and daughters arise and join me in applauding our new ambassador."

When the concert ended, Autumn stood at her seat, watching brothers who had not yet realized their skills and crafts leave the theater. Kaela motioned for her to follow him to the front of the room where he took a seat next to Abdiel in the third row from the stage. No one spoke. Everyone sat facing forward, eyes fixed on the portion of the stage where Heaven's prince was standing. "I am in need of thousands of skilled craftsmen to build starter cottages and my bungalow in the northern region of Heaven."

Hours later, Kaela escorted a weary and distraught Autumn home. "I can't believe that of all the skilled workers, Lucifer did not choose me. I worked in the castle with you, Kaela. I remodeled the pig-sty that Lucifer called his apartment. My talents can be seen all over Father's house, and I am denied my chance to make history by building Lucifer's ridiculous starter colony in the North." She left the sidewalk, taking a right turn onto the walk that led to her cottage. "How am I going to know what is happening in the North while you are away? I can't believe that Lucifer would put you in charge of thousands of carpenters and not see me sitting right there beside you."

"Maybe Father has need of you here," Kaela told Autumn, turning the door-knob to let her inside. In the living room, he added, "If my memory serves me correctly, the craftsmen labored all day without stop when we worked in Father's house. Our conversations were in jest. We shouted our plans to each other. There was no real personal communication among us. I mean, we didn't sit down and talk like craftsmen. We shouted our thoughts to each other while we worked."

"But I should be there, shouldn't I?" Autumn asked. "What about God's book?"

"Father will see that a paragraph or two describing the work in the North will be written on one of the pages in you book," Kaela assured her. "Stop your worrying. Go to bed. Everything will seem so much better in the light of day."

Chapter 15

Heaven's First Politician

The dreaded day for Kaela to leave for the North came too soon. Autumn stood on their porch, weeping in her hands, too broken-hearted to say good-bye.

"It won't be long," Kaela told her. "You will be busy. I put you in charge of running our shop in the lumber-yard, and more importantly, you have the chore of acquainting yourself with Lucifer's supporters." He smiled when Autumn flung her arms around his waist, sobbing. "Time will pass quickly for you. You will have our brothers and our sisters to talk to when you are lonely. You will find ways to amuse yourself. There will be concerts to attend and the games at the stadium. Father promised more contests for His sons to compete in." He gently freed himself from Autumn's desperate grip. "I will be back soon. I promise."

Six months passed since Kaela left Autumn standing on the porch of their cottage. She had done as he said. She made friends with Prince Lucifer and his clan of haters. Oh, they presented themselves as being compassionate and loving toward their brothers, but they were the opposite. The pleasantries they exchanged when they met their righteous brothers on the streets or in the castle's courtyard was an act to encourage others to join Lucifer in his betrayal of God.

During Kaela's absence, Autumn taught carpentry to his apprentices. Together, they built bridges over the creeks that ran through the back-yards of those who lived closest to the forest. They built gazeboes, tables and benches, and even swing sets, which they transported to grassy areas bordering the Sacred Region's mirroring lakes. Under Autumn's watchful eye, the apprentices cleared ground in the city where they built a large gazebo with a bandstand big enough to accommodate Zephon's musicians and Israfel's choir. Though Autumn did all the finish work herself, she found it necessary to ask for assistance from Caim, Azazel's former apprentice.

In her spare time, Autumn improved Kaela's cottage by adding a deck that wrapped all the way around it. She built furniture for the deck so that when her angel came home, they could enjoy the scenery that stretched from their property to the forest. When she wasn't in the shop or the lumber-yard, she was Moloch's student. Over the past months, Autumn became proficient in the martial arts, earning praise from Moloch and Thummuz. Even Nesroc admired her as her skills improved. Autumn grew to know Caim quite well too. As a result, she learned to forge metal, bending it into decorative shapes, which she used with some of her wood creations. Her days were full, but her nights were lonely.

When she wasn't attending one of Lucifer's ridiculous clandestine meetings in the forest, she sat on her deck, gazing into the pale sky, praying that Kaela would come home soon. Times like these, she wished she hadn't obligated herself to Excelsa's mission. But it was either accept the mission and acquaint herself with Lucifer's supporters, or dishonor Father by refusing the mission. Autumn could never dishonor Father, and anyway, someone had to break the ice with these foul spirits so that when he returned, Kaela would be more readily accepted.

It was the night of one of Lucifer's meetings. Non-believers and doubtful citizens who lived in God's kingdom would meet in the middle of a forest located far from the Holy Castle, far from Father's prying eyes. The meeting would be held during Heaven's darkest hours while righteous brothers slept and Father was confined to His inner sanctum. Autumn left her cottage, heading in the direction of the forest where she would team up with Moloch and Nesroc. But as she passed the lumber-yard, she got a familiar yearning. Turning around, she went to the shop where she slipped on her carpenter's apron, picked up her saw, her tape measure, her level, and her square.

Moloch was on his way to Lucifer's meeting when he saw the lanterns were lit in Kaela's shop. Curious, he stopped in for a visit and found Autumn alone, working cypress wood to a hard shine.

"Have you forgotten that on this night, Lucifer will hold a meeting in the woods just outside the lumber-yard?"

"No, I have not forgotten," Autumn said as she buffed the piece she had just finished setting in place. "If I had, the pounding of my brothers' wings would have reminded me." She glanced upward as a flock of angels glided on the air current toward the forest.

Moloch simply grinned. "At the last meeting, Lucifer encouraged his supporters to think of ways that we could overthrow Father before He can retaliate. None of us truly know how powerful Heaven's King is. I mean, if He created us, can He uncreate us? No one knows, and we certainly do not intend to find out." God's disobedient son rested one huge hand Autumn's shoulder. "I will save a seat for you. You may change your mind and decide to attend the meeting. I will give Lucifer your apologies, brother." Then, he was gone.

"Brother!" Autumn grumbled. All of Heaven's citizens save for Father, the Goddesses, and Kaela, saw her as a male angel. "If I had my choice, I would not be your brother."

She put Moloch's visit behind her and returned to her work. The hours passed quickly. Her project was showing signs of promise. Autumn ran her hands over the smoothly sanded surface of the cypress wood and smiled broadly. The wood was ready to be sealed and buffed some more. Morning was not far off, but she was too involved in her work to notice, and since there was no one waiting for her at home, she really did not care about the time. She was so busy, so immersed in her task that she did not hear the lithe feet that set down outside the shop's open door.

"We missed you," the prince said. "I noticed you were absent from my meeting, even from the stage where I stood, and so I took time to ask about you." He walked to where Autumn worked and extended his hand to her shoulder, but before his fingertips touched her robe, he withdrew his hand. "I hope you have not lost interest in our cause." The false prince leaned toward her, smiling graciously into her face. "I hope you have not sided with our enemy."

Autumn shook her head and back stepped once, then again. "I have no enemies in Heaven, honorable prince. I simply felt the need to work. Kaela will be home soon, and I am preparing a few surprises for him."

"You are preparing a surprise for Kaela?" Lucifer echoed. Again, he reached out as though he desired to touch her, but his hand fell short. "You should forget about Kaela while he is away. He's safe. The golden horn on God's altar is filled with his prayers for you. He prays that you will be looked after by your friends, that you will fill your time with projects that give you joy, and that your time will speed by so you will not be lonely." He smiled at Autumn's cocked head. "Yes, I am privy to all your prayers too." His words nearly stopped Autumn's heart.

"Why, your cheeks are glowing," Prince Lucifer asked. "Are you pleased that I know your thoughts?" She did not answer. "Well, no matter. I need for you to concentrate on how we will rule Heaven from God's throne."

A third time, Lucifer extended his hand. This time, his fingertips touched her cheek so slightly that she could barely feel them against her flesh. "Maybe you have grown tired of hearing me speak? Maybe my voice annoys you? Perhaps you think I lack Father's charm when, in fact, I am God incarnate." Lucifer saw Autumn's eyes widen. She was impressed. "That is correct. I am the physical personage of God. Does that frighten you?"

Autumn shook her head. What irony! Could she go to hell for lying to Earth's future devil? She fought the urge to laugh aloud. "I am in awe of you, Prince Lucifer."

She truly was in awe of anyone who proclaimed himself to be God's incarnate when he was nothing more than a common angel with a title. Something told her that tonight he made his proclamation publicly. She felt weary. How many more times would he repeat this lie to convince innocent brothers to believe him? "How do you know you are God incarnate?" Autumn asked. The pounding in her chest made her voice tremble.

"Father told me so," Lucifer lied. "But I was warned that I could never reveal my true nature to anyone, not even the scribe. Our sisters, who are Goddesses, could never understand why Father favored me over them, but soon, they will know why Heaven's King adores me." He moved closer to Autumn. "I need your trust ... I have heard your prayers, and I am aware that you are doubtful of me. Put your faith in me, Autumn, and I will give you power that others only dream of." Lucifer studied this little angel with his bright blue eyes. She was considering what he said, but she was not professing her faith to him. "If you need for me to stay here, to convince you, I have stories that will awaken your senses, and you will know who I am, and you will never doubt me again."

"Oh, I know who you are, Prince Lucifer," Autumn said quietly. "I just cannot fathom how you are going to pull off all these fantastic deeds and make good on your artfully expressed promises when Father, the Holy Spirit, has so many followers who believe in Him. It's rather like you are fighting a war with yourself that you cannot win alone." She saw the prince's eyebrows raise high on his forehead. "I have to finish up here and catch some sleep before I open the shop. Maybe we can talk over lunch or continue this conversation when I'm more awake."

"Are you mocking me?" Lucifer demanded. Strangely enough, he felt as though he had been mocked by another brother who boldly defended Father on this very site not so long ago. Lucifer frowned when this little angel, who seemed to fear no one, turned away from him. "You should be more respectful toward me since I am Heaven's only prince."

Lucifer followed her to her work area and watched anxiously as she put her engraving tools in their proper place. "Now, I am the curious one? Are you for me or against me?" The object of his growing concern wiped her hands on her apron before she removed it to hang it on a hook outside the door to Kaela's office. "Well, answer me! Are you for me or against me?"

"That depends on who wins the throne." Autumn sniffed. "You or yourself?"

"What?"

"You say that you are God incarnate," Autumn mused. "I would think if you are God, you would be too busy ruling Heaven to worry about who is for you or against you." She walked to the door, motioning

Lucifer to follow. That he obeyed her instruction made her smile. "I think you and Beelzebub had better sit down and go over the speech you made tonight and do some damage control." Autumn turned and gazed up at Lucifer's beautiful face. "What am I thinking right now?"

"You are thinking about how sleepy you are," Lucifer said with a smug nod of his head.

"Wrong," Autumn said. She closed the shop door and walked toward the path that led to the cottage. "I am thinking that you have a major task ahead of you. You must convince our brothers that you are more powerful than Father, and then you must amass a following of loyal supporters that will fight your battle as fiercely as God's followers will fight His. Father has innumerable sons who will do His bidding at His command. Who do you have, Prince Lucifer, that obeys you without question?

"I am not talking about me, Kaela, or your close associates. I am talking about brothers who do not attend your meetings, brothers who never heard your speeches. I'm talking about brothers who will accept you as Heaven's future king and who will do your bidding even though you do not wear God's crown. You have a long, hard, and tedious task ahead of you. I would suggest you work to reach your goal without presenting fantasies to the crowd about being God incarnate. I suggest you convince the crowd to believe in you by making your own reputation and allowing Father to keep His identity to Himself."

"You do not believe that I am God!" Lucifer shouted.

"Nope," Autumn called over her shoulder to the angel who stood stock-still just steps from the path she took.

"You have no idea who it is that you have defied!" Lucifer called out angrily.

"Yes, I do. Go home and try to think of a different way to win followers!" Autumn shouted. "I need to get some sleep."

"How will I do that? I already opened my mouth and told them I am God," Lucifer called after her.

Autumn was surprised that the prince remained rooted to his spot in the lumber-yard and did not follow or insist on walking her home. She turned on her heel, walking backward and keeping her eyes on the prince, she replied, "You can always tell them they misunderstood what they thought they heard you say. Tell them you are feeling contrite about what you said. Tell them you misspoke, you acted inappropriately. But don't admit you told a bold-faced lie." That's the way the politicians on Earth did it.

Autumn turned her back to Lucifer and continued walking down the path until she was out of his sight, then she half ran half flew until she reached the cottage. Never in her life had she felt so intimidated. Never had anything frightened her as much as this visit from Lucifer. Deep inside, she feared that Lucifer really could read her mind, that he was privy to Kaela's prayers, that somehow he knew she and Kaela worked for Scribe Excelsa and their sisters to expose his plan to overthrow God in Heaven.

"Father, I need Your strength. I need Your protection. I need Your understanding. I need Your love. I am so afraid of Lucifer and his cohorts. Please be with Kaela too. And send him home soon. I miss my angel, and I need him with me. Amen."

Chapter 16

The Home Coming

Autumn's days dragged on until, at last, God's messenger sounded his trumpet and announced in a voice that could be heard from the highest peak of the Holy Castle to the farthest shores of Heaven that the skilled workers and their laborers who had journeyed to the North were returning home. Autumn gained permission from God to sit on the balustrade that encompassed the floor of the outdoor throne room to watch for Kaela's arrival. From this high perch, she had a magnificent view of Heaven's glorious landscape. Using her angelic vision, she scoped the emerald expanse, fervently hoping that she would be among the first to see the carpenters returning home and that Kaela would be among the first of those to arrive at the Holy Castle. For hours, she saw only birds and beasts in the fields below the castle's walls. Then when she least expected it, in the far-off distance, she saw angels in the air, on foot, and on horseback.

"They're here!" she shouted. With a happy yelp, she dived from the banister.

Autumn directed her flight to the field beyond the castle's northern wall. She scanned the returning carpenters. Kaela was nowhere in sight. He had to be here among the first to return because he promised her he would come back; he said nothing about remaining in any of the newly mapped regions. Her heart sank. Kaela never let work go undone. He was probably finishing something that no one else wanted to do. She saw Archangel Uzziel and directed her flight to where he sat on a huge steed, awaiting the carpenters on foot to file into formation.

"Where's Kaela?" Autumn asked. "I've looked, and I don't see him anywhere."

"He will return home later," Uzziel told her. "Kaela remained in the North. He is putting the finishing touches on the cabin where Prince Lucifer and his cabinet members will live." Seeing Autumn's disappointment, the archangel suggested, "Ride with me. We will go back to the castle together, and enjoy the festival Father planned for His returning sons."

Without acknowledging the archangel's offer, Autumn lifted high in the air above her returning brothers, her glistening eyes fixed on the northern border. Her gaze never faltered, not even when the last angel had long since left the field. The reality that Kaela had not returned home as he promised numbed her to her bones. She hated that he felt obligated to oversee projects that were wrought with detail and responsibility. She hated that Kaela could never step aside and let someone else finish what he started.

Barely moving her wings, Autumn glided on air currents that lifted her high and then dropped her almost as low as her spirits. As she approached the Holy Castle, she heard sounds of jubilation. Heaven citizens were celebrating the craftsmen's home-coming. She would have joined them if Kaela had come home, but now, she had no reason to celebrate. Tears that streamed down her cheeks dripped off her chin during her flight to the cottage she shared with her angel. Their homestead was beautiful from the air with its wrap-around porch, so spacious and new. She descended on the walk that led to the porch, went inside, and closed the door. Alone and heartbroken, Autumn dropped onto the sofa and wept until she fell asleep.

It was Heaven's darkest hour, the time when the thickest clouds descended from above the Holy Castle to spread across the valley, blocking God's light so affectively that everyone referred to this time as the best hour for sleeping. During this calm, peaceful time, gentle dews nourish the globe's lush landscape and fragrant breezes filled cottages, town houses, and all the rooms in Father's mansion with the sweet scents of amaranth and lavender. Autumn lay on the sofa in the living room, absorbed in a dark, dreamless sleep, when a noise startled her to wakefulness. She opened her eyes but narrowed them when she saw a figure sitting in the chair directly across the room from where she slept.

Hoping the intruder thought she slept undisturbed, she closed her exposed eye and opened the one closest to the pillow a bit wider. Try as she would, she could not make out the face of the one who, without request or invitation, had boldly entered her cottage. Across the room, the window above the chair where the intruder sat revealed the night fog, though still thick, had taken on the glow of Father's light. Soon, she and her trespasser would see and know each other. As the fog cleared, the dew stopped forming on the plant life, and the birds of Heaven began to sing. Just enough light filtered into the room now to gently lighten the face of the one who sat motionless before her.

"Kaela, you're home!" Autumn squealed. She was off the couch and in his arms before he could smile. "I missed you so much. I was afraid I'd never see you again!" She dampened his face with kisses and tears of joy. She hugged his neck. "I have so much to tell you. Wait! I'll fix breakfast for you, we can talk then."

Autumn leaped to her feet and ran to the bedroom. She was gone for a second. When she returned to the living room, she invited her angel to join her in the kitchen.

Kaela spent one full week at home with Autumn before Zophiel arrived at his door to invite him to join Father in His inner sanctum. "Come tonight at Heaven's darkest hour, and come alone."

Chapter 17

A Meeting of Righteous Sons

The night after his private audience with Father, Kaela opened his shop to his most trusted brothers in the hope that they would join Scribe Excelsa's quest to halt Lucifer's desire to rule Heaven from God's own throne. The warehouse, cloaked in thick, white billowing clouds, was packed with righteous citizens, mostly those ancient angels created of the first four flocks. Joniel sat on the floor next to Autumn and Octaviel; Sonnet, Bernella, and Kamyel sat with them. Chairs were provided for the seven Goddesses, Scribe Excelsa, Effiel, and Evangeline. The chairs formed a semi-circle and faced the numerous attendees that stood waiting to learn what the meeting was about. Archangels Michael, Gabriel, Uzziel, and Uriel stood inside the door that opened to shop. Seeing that no one else was coming, Kaela walked to the center of the room.

"Thank you all for coming tonight," Kaela told his brothers. "You are here because you are Father's most faithful sons. When we leave this place we will not speak of what we said here since this meeting is being held in secret. Tonight, we will discuss Lucifer and his desire to rule our globe from Father's throne." Kaela glanced over his shoulder at Scribe Excelsa, who motioned for him to continue.

"Lucifer has been exhibiting bad behavior in the throne room because he hopes to take from Father that which is rightfully His. As I speak, Prince Lucifer is holding his own clandestine meeting in the forest where he seeks to convince unsuspecting citizens that he, not Father, is the God of the universe. By doing this, our eldest brother hopes to rob our Lord of His power and prestige. Lucifer is amassing followers who have pledged to do whatever they must to help him win access to Father's throne." Kaela studied the faces of those closest to where he stood. "If you find what I just said hard to believe, you will be even more doubtful when I call on Autumn, Scribe Excelsa, Sonnet, Bernella, and our sisters to reveal their dealings with Lucifer."

Kaela turned to Autumn and invited her take the floor. "Tell our brothers what you saw the night Father released Sin into the air." He saw the astonished expressions on his brothers' faces. "Feel free to ask questions anytime."

When Autumn finished her account about Sin's release into Heaven and how she invaded the body of each of God's sleeping sons, Octaviel rose to his feet. "Are we to believe we have an eighth sister who is prepared to destroy our globe with her less-than-virtuous ways?" His eyes were wide with doubt, his expression incredulous. "Kaela, why have none of us seen Sin? Why has Father remained silent about her existence?" He glanced at Autumn, unable to make eye contact with her. "It is hard for me to believe this story of a questionable spirit who lived in a vial until our Lord released her to infect our minds with negative thoughts and desires."

Wisdom spoke next. "My brothers, you all know me. Each of you spent time with me when you needed advice. I am aware that you trust my guidance without question. Believe me when I say, Sin does exist. She is formed of the cells my sisters and I shed during our creation. Father put the cells in a vial and set them on a shelf in the laboratory. Autumn's revelation about Sin is true. A witch walked Heaven's streets in search of a decaying mind. She found that mind in God's mansion. Prince Lucifer, who always envied Father, whose greed and conceit made him lazy and hostile, was the perfect one to house Sin's corruption."

Atella raised his hand and called out for recognition. Kaela pointed to him. Atella stepped forward. "If Lucifer is corrupt—which in my mind, he is extremely questionable—but if he is corrupt, why did Father make Lucifer Heaven's first prince?"

Scribe Excelsa rose from his seat. "While Lucifer was archangel, Michael started the games, the stadium was built, and the athletes entertained us with their physical skills. Then Michael, Gabriel, Uriel, and Uzziel gained Father's permission to explore Heaven. When they returned, our Lord rewarded them by promoting them to the position of archangel. Lucifer was incensed. Now there were five archangels in Heaven. He demanded a higher promotion … a promotion that set him above his athletic brothers. Father sought to keep peace in His kingdom and so He made Lucifer a prince in title only. Then Lucifer demanded a throne," the scribe sneered. "Prince Lucifer knows his promotion is dishonorable. He is well aware that his high title resulted from flattering, fawning over, and threatening our King."

"Threatening our King?" Chynella asked incredulously. "How does one threaten Heaven's King to the point of earning a promotion?"

Angry voices filled the room.

"How about some silence!" Scribe Excelsa demanded. Everyone stopped talking. "There, that's better." He paced before the crowd. "After Lucifer became the prime director of God's High Council of Angels, he had access to our Lord's most classified scrolls. He read them in-depth, so he is well aware of events that Father chose to secret away from prying eyes and angelic minds. Following the athletes' promotion to archangel, Lucifer demanded a new title. When Father refused, Lucifer promised to reveal the contents of the scrolls to Heaven's citizens. After making further demands and leveling more complicated threats, Lucifer forced Father to agree to make him Heaven's first prince, with one stipulation, our eldest brother had to promise to keep what he knows about the scrolls' contents to himself. Lucifer agreed to our Lord's requirement, and you know the rest."

Truth left her seat and took her place at Excelsa's side. "Do not think Father is a weak ruler. The promotion Lucifer received is a test put upon him by our Lord's Word. Until Lucifer became prince, he interrupted our work in Heaven. He had become a distraction, a hindrance, and his bad behavior had to end. Father's council members witnessed Lucifer's tantrums and threats, but they took an oath to remain silent about all that happens in the throne room, and they cannot comment on what they see or hear there."

Truth turned to Kaela. "Scribe Excelsa and I will sit so Bernella and Sonnet can tell us of their dealings with Lucifer."

Sonnet, believing what he had to say was hardly important, relinquished the floor to his brother, who spoke in-depth of how Lucifer tricked him into believing the air beyond the Holy City was toxic. The angels sat awestruck when Bernella produced the breathing apparatus he was forced to wear while walking among sleeping angels in the forest.

"None of them were athletes," Bernella revealed. "They were misfits who could not take orders and who were rejected by Michael long before the expedition began. But Archangel Lucifer led me to believe that what I saw should be kept secret—that he, out of concern and pity, was trying to hide the fact that Father's powers had failed Him."

Bernella turned his face from the audience and pointed to where Kaela stood. "It was he who gave me the courage to return to the forest. Kaela and Autumn came to my suite on the very night they returned home from exploring the North. They were accompanied by Sonnet. They listened with the same stricken expression on their faces as is on each of yours now. That night, Kaela lifted me from the floor and carried me out the window through the fog to the forest where I learned two important facts. First, the air throughout all of Heaven is pure. Second, Lucifer is a fraud."

Bernella bit his lower lip as he considered what to say next. A thought sprang into his head and he said, "Beware of God's false prince. He has many followers who will joyfully do his bidding. Some of them work with you. Some of them live next door to you. Some live down the hall from you, and their numbers are increasing."

"Why? How is Lucifer amassing this following?" Citadel asked angrily.

"He promises to change Heaven by doing away with Father's laws and replacing them with new ones," Bernella said. "I learned this when Moloch came to me, asking me to join Lucifer's cause against our Lord." He took his place next to Sonnet. "I intend to join Scribe Excelsa's quest to stifle Lucifer. And I hope each of you will consider joining me. Unlike Father, Lucifer does not use his power to aid and assist us. He uses it to deceive us. That's all I have to say."

Kaela took the floor. "You've heard much tonight. Most of what you heard is disturbing and unbelievable, I know, but I would not have involved my brothers if I could stop Lucifer on my own. I need your help. Through a conversation with Abdiel I learned that Lucifer wants to seize our Lord's throne, imprison Him, and start a government."

"What is a government?" Sammael asked.

Autumn rose to her feet. "Presently, Father's laws are the foundation for our government. Our Lord rules with love and understanding, asking only that we trust in Him and recognize that He is the sole reason for our happiness. Lucifer wants to establish a government of corrupt brothers who will chisel away at our freedom of choice and our freedom of self-expression until we have none. Unlike Father's government—which is comprised of our sisters, His council members, and our worthy brother, Excelsa—Lucifer's governing body will be made up of his hand-chosen aides. They want nothing less than to increase Lucifer's wealth, prestige, and authority in Heaven. They will gladly uphold Lucifer's harsh laws and unreasonable demands that will force saints and righteous sons into servitude."

She paused for moment, giving her brothers a chance to ask questions if they wished. When no one raised his hand to speak or make inquiries about what she said, she continued speaking. "We believe that Lucifer is influenced by Sin. Sin wants us to work for her. She wants to make us her servants. Both our eldest brother and his witch want to overthrow Father. But for Lucifer to become a ruler, he must amass a large following. If he does that, he will promote his most loyal followers to high offices that will give them the power they need to rule over us. In time, we won't be governed by just one arrogant ruler, but by many."

Raphael, the youngest child of God's seventh flock of angels, asked. "Autumn, how could anyone ever take Father's place in Heaven?"

"Lucifer's governing officials will do it by raising our hopes and earning our respect with empty promises and blatant falsehoods," Autumn replied. "When they do not fulfill the promises they made to earn higher positions in Lucifer's government, they will accuse us of fabricating tales to make them look bad. In time, we will become indifferent to the lies being told to us, and we will close our eyes to the corruption that explodes around us. We will accept that our lot in life is to labor to keep our government officials happy and content, and we will reach the conclusion that we can expect nothing of substance from our leaders."

"We can stop Lucifer's government from becoming corrupt, can't we?" A brother in the back of the room shouted.

"The corruption of which I speak will start slowly at first. Most of us won't notice that our rights are being violated. The government will tell us our loss of freedom will keep us safe. When in truth, our loss of freedom will give the government a way to manipulate us so that we will do its bidding. To overcome this impending threat, we must infiltrate Lucifer's camp."

Someone asked if Autumn knew the identities of the brothers Lucifer chose to rule with him. "His courtiers will rule with him—Moloch, Mammon, Nesroc, Thummuz, Apollyon, and possibly, Beelzebub."

Kaela stepped forward. "Did you listen well to what speakers like Bernella, Autumn, and our sisters told you tonight? If you truly heard what was being said, think on it when you leave this building and as you walk home. We must stop what Lucifer is doing. If Lucifer succeeds in his plan to seize Heaven's throne, then we fail Father miserably." He studied the faces of those closest to where he stood. "To form a government in Heaven, Lucifer must overthrow our Lord, thus seizing His throne by force. Lucifer is heir to nothing on this globe. He is an angel, not a God. According to Father's law, 'Angel shall not rule angel.' This is why Lucifer must be stopped now. If he overthrows God's rule in Heaven, he will become a—"

"Dictator," Autumn interjected.

"I am curious about Autumn's knowledge of unfamiliar terms that define various forms of corruption," Abelson shouted from the back of the room. "Father never familiarized us the description of a government or words like *dictator*."

"I meet with Autumn often," Scribe Excelsa said quickly. He hoped to draw the crowd's attention from Autumn to himself. His ploy worked. "I sit in Father's presence day and night. So I am privy to much of what has transpired over the past several millennia. At my insistence, Autumn has become familiar with terms and words the rest of you have never heard until now." He smiled; his brothers were bobbing their heads in acceptance of his explanation. "And before you get too curious about how I can spend sleepless nights with our Lord, let me tell you that it is through the magnificence of His power that I can assist Him day and night."

The scribe paced before his audience for a moment, and then he said, "If you wish to help us but cannot do so at this time, please keep this meeting and what you have learned here to yourselves. If you speak out of turn, you will have defeated our purpose. On the other hand, if you wish to help us and you can, please come forward, and I will let you know how we plan to stop our eldest brother from disrupting Heaven's peace."

It seemed that everyone stepped forward at once.

"Kaela, we have one hundred brothers anxious to join our cause," the scribe said when the shop cleared. Autumn, Sonnet, Bernella, and Joniel gave their sisters quick thankful hugs. "The Goddesses and I must return to the castle. I have shirked my duties long enough, and anyway, I have to be at my desk when Lucifer arrives to take his throne, or questions will be asked, and Father being Father will answer them in His own provocative way."

From his hiding place under a bush below the shop's open window, a lone brother rose to his feet. Through narrowed eyes, he watched the Lord's faithful sons make their way through the lifting haze to their homes in the village and to the castle on the mount. Abdiel had heard the entire meeting and was grieved that he had not been invited to attend. But his reward would come in time, and it would not come from the scribe or Lucifer. His reward would come from perseverance and patience. It would come from using his wit. Maybe he could convince his wayward brother to give him a high seat in this so-called government Autumn accused him of hoping to establish.

Abdiel was about to spread his wings in flight when he felt a hand on his shoulder. He turned to look into Kaela's angry eyes. Lowering his wings, he glared back at his former friend with like ferocity.

"So you would damage your place in God's heart to warn a fraud of our intentions," Kaela said. "Come with me. We must talk."

Abdiel followed Kaela to his office.

“Sit,” Kaela ordered. He took his seat behind the desk Autumn built for him and glared over its polished surface at Abdiel. “I need you. I need you on my side. I need to trust you like I did not so long ago.”

“If you need me so badly,” Abdiel questioned, “why was I not asked to attend your meeting last night?”

Joniel entered the room. Frowning, Kaela glanced up at him. “This is a private meeting, Joniel. Please leave us.” He could tell by Joniel’s expression that his words made him curious, but his brother nodded and left the pair to settle their differences alone. “You were left out of the meeting because I did not want to jeopardize our Lord’s throne by telling you what I had planned. And I see my decision was a sound one. If I had not caught you before you took flight, you would be kneeling before Lucifer, telling him what you heard.”

“I kneel before no one,” Abdiel snorted. “I am a free spirit. I can do as I please, when I please. I can be on your side, as you call it, this morning and be on Lucifer’s side this afternoon. By evening, I can go to God with what I know about both of you.” Abdiel narrowed his eyes and studied Kaela’s face. “What?”

“Scribe Excelsa warned of brothers like you when he asked me to do God’s work,” Kaela said through closed teeth. “You are a hypocrite, a fraud just like Lucifer. You would use your freedom to disrupt Heaven’s peace by breaking Father’s heart.” Kaela stood and said, “Get out of my sight. Don’t come back here or bother me again with your views on freedom. You haven’t a clue about what freedom is. What you defined was disobedience and arrogance. You, Abdiel, are no longer my brother. Leave me. Go to Lucifer, but do not tell him what you heard, or I will—”

“You will what, Kaela? Uncreate me? Can an angel uncreate another angel? Our Lord says we cannot procreate, so can we uncreate?” Abdiel glared at his angry brother. “I will do as I see fit. Now, however, I will give you an alternative that may ease your worries. I will keep quiet for a fortnight, and then I will decide if I wish to be on your side or Lucifer’s. It just depends on who I think might be more helpful to me in Heaven.” That being said, Abdiel turned and storm out the door that closed behind him with a thunderous slam.

Chapter 18

Evil Finds a Place in Heaven

A day shy of a fortnight, Father held a festival that was different from previous festivals. The concert that usually followed dinner was held early in the afternoon, during which awards were presented to productive angels who used their skills to improve Heaven. And rather than give His usual speech from the royal family's viewing box when the concert or the games ended, Father expressed His gratitude for His sons' love and respect there in the dining hall.

"Something's up," Autumn whispered to Kaela.

Nesroc, suspicious by nature, demanded that she repeat her statement so everyone could hear what she said. "I was telling Kaela that something is up," she told Lucifer's courtiers. Moloch leaned toward her to hear what she had to say. "Where's Zophiel? Why didn't he announce this festival? Kaela and I received paper invitations inviting us here; did you guys get paper invitations?" They had. "Everyone received paper invitations to a festival that is held a day early, in the afternoon rather than in the evening—very strange. Stranger still, our King presented awards to His chosen few before dinner was served."

She lifted a slip of paper from where her table settings had been. "And now, here's another written note—the games will be held immediately following our meal. Never has a concert been pre-empted for the games since the building of the stadium. And if the concert does not precede the games, will it be held late in the evening?" She leaned toward Nesroc. "Something's up."

"Something's up," Nesroc repeated, his eyes fixed on Autumn's face.

"Prince Lucifer says God's powers are failing Him, so maybe He has to do everything in one day now," Mammon said, directing his statement to Moloch. "I notice the athletes are seated at the table, but they are not eating." He gazed across the table at Kaela. "Why is it that you are not eating, Kaela?"

"I am in the games," Kaela answered. "During practice today, we made a pact. We would go onto the field with no other nourishment to sustain us but Father's healing light. I have decided that since I am not eating, I can enjoy my brothers' company all the more."

Moloch reached out, giving Kaela's arm a friendly squeeze. Mammon smiled, nodding in agreement with Moloch affection toward their talented brother. Seeing that he was well accepted by Lucifer's courtiers, Kaela excused himself. "I must go. The athletes are filing out. I hope you enjoy the show tonight."

"The show?" Autumn echoed, glancing questioningly at her table guests. Why hadn't Kaela told her that he was taking part in the games?

At the stadium, the angels enjoyed an extravaganza of sporting events. Autumn nudged Moloch in the ribs when Kaela took the field with several others. They were dressed in short white tunics topped with blue vests that were girded at the waist by wide leather belts from which hung a quiver filled with arrows. In their hands, they carried long bows. On their feet, they wore sandals that sported leather straps that crisscrossed up the front of their lower legs and tied at the knee. Autumn remembered when she met Michael in the garden after man's first disobedience to God; the outfit he wore then was similar to those worn by his athletes this evening. She frowned, knowing the sport angels' attire could serve as military uniforms by simply adding helmets, breastplates, and swords.

Jacobus walked onto the field to stand before his athletic brothers. On his mark, they set their arrows and drew their bowstring taunt into firing position. That done, Atuniel and Nathaniel stepped onto the field. When they were ready to perform, Jacobus ordered his archers to shoot their arrows into the air toward the opposite side of the playing field. As the arrows reached their maximum height, Atuniel and Nathaniel stretched out their hands; fire shot from their palms, igniting the arrows so that they resembled a fireworks display. The audience stood, cheering, as more and more arrows were ignited. Autumn's eyes glowed with excitement. Kaela had kept this skill from her so he could surprise her by being part of this spectacular event.

Following the games, Prince Lucifer rose from his seat. "Father wishes to extend His heartfelt thanks to each of you for attending this special Festival of Light. Join me in giving your Lord, your King the attention He deserves."

The prince turned to his Creator. "Father, I relinquish the floor of this stadium to You." Lucifer took his seat amid thunderous applause, but the ovation was not for him; it was for God.

"My sons," Father began, "I am so proud of each of you. Your existence has made my world a wonderful place in which to live. I watched you from the time of your creation and marveled as you developed and honed your individual skills. To say my sons are wise is an understatement. You have excelled in ways I never thought possible. And you never cease to amaze me." Father paused for a moment. The stadium was completely silent, even the horses and unicorns were still.

"For many seasons, Prince Lucifer approached me with questions about the North," Father revealed. "For eons, he stood on the balustrade that embraces the throne room, his eyes fixed on the northern region. I was certain that, one day, he would fly off and discover the North and its many wonders for himself. But he remained at my side." Father turned to Lucifer and asked him to stand. "When my sons returned from the exploration of Heaven, Prince Lucifer approached my throne to suggest we build starter colonies in the newly discovered regions. I sent the leaders of the exploration with several thousand skilled craftsmen to the North. The colonies are finished. There is no reason why anyone must remain in the Sacred Region if he desires to make his own way in Heaven. Soon, construction will begin in the south, east, and west. I ask my precious children to consider which region you might choose to live in, and within another month, we will meet here to say farewell."

"Farewell, but not good-bye," Lucifer interjected. "Anyone who chooses to join me in the North will return with me every fortnight to the Sacred Region where you will bask in your Lord's pure light. You will enjoy the concerts and the games every fortnight, just as we do now, and anyone who wishes to remain in the Sacred Region may stay here without question. I shall draft committee members from those who plan to join me. Only the best skilled will serve since they will oversee the progress in the North. When we return for our visits, they will stand before their Lord's throne and report on the work being done in the northern region. The information our craftsmen give Father will aid Him in setting up starter colonies in Heaven's unpopulated regions."

The prince smiled and stretched his arms toward the spectators. "Our journey to the North from this region will be an enjoyable one. I need your help to make this mission a successful one. Please join me in making the North a productive place to live." Lucifer took his seat, smiling at Father, who had risen from His throne to speak once more to His sons.

"Children," Father said. His voice filled with love for His innumerable sons, "you have a month to make your decision. There are other regions that must be populated, not just the North. Confer with the archangels, my council members, or your precious sisters. Deliberate long and make the choice you feel is best for you. It was always my intention that, in time, all of Heaven would be populated with angels, but whether you remain here or settle in a new region is your decision. Choose wisely."

Days later, Archangel Uzziel led the globe's first pilgrims from the God's kingdom to Heaven's lush northern region. It was a day of joy and adventure for most; but Kaela, Autumn, and their trusted friends were on a mission. With Archangel Uzziel in the lead, Prince Lucifer at his side, the flock enjoyed a quiet flight, their eyes brimming with the beauty of the landscape below. Lucifer's wings never knew such heights; he had never seen majestic splendor as was here, in the North.

He called to anyone listening, "I cannot wait to make this region my permanent home." The prince flew in silence for a moment. Then he posed a question to the archangel. "Where is my cabin? Is it near a lake? Is it higher than the other adobes in the area so that it proclaims my authority over all?"

"You cabin is magnificent," Archangel Uzziel called as he prepared to climb in flight to avoid having to fly around a high mountain. "It is located in a peaceful valley, and it is the largest dwelling in the North."

While the globe's first pilgrims hastened to their destination, Lucifer hovered in the air above the mount. With eyes narrowed, bottom lip puckered, he examined the hill's magnitude. It was high and wide covered with tall leafy trees. Surely no one could see beyond the mountain's towering crest. When Lucifer asked Uzziel

"Since I will live in a dwelling in a valley, I will be free of God's prying eyes," Prince Lucifer mused. "I shall rule in the North, and my will, not Father's, will be done. This region with its hills, forests, lakes, rivers, and caves will guard my secrets well."

CHAPTER 19

The North

Archangel Uzziel led Lucifer and his supporters to the heart of the northern region of Heaven where they lighted in a valley that was filled with trees, shrubs, and bushes that blossomed and bore fruit at the same time. In this peaceful place, colorful wildflowers lifted their petals to the sky, lending their fragrances to the cool, gentle breeze that, as it passed by, tenderly caressed the sweet emerald grasses carpeting the ground. Bird-song filled the region. Yellow canaries warbled love songs to their mates, who tended to their young. Brilliant red cardinals and bright blue jays called to each other from the branches of nearby trees. Butterflies, hummingbirds, and honeybees busied themselves gathering pollen while caterpillars dined on the dried leaves of rooted plants.

On distant hillsides whose mounds were saturated in God's nourishing light, animals, large and small, assembled in herds and packs to watch the angels enter their domain. According to Nature, these winged creatures, God's sons of light, would improve the North with their presence. The birds and beasts of this region had seen angels several times before, but the work they did here was not important to the woodland animals; it was simply a curiosity, something to watch while passing idle time. Heaven's wildlife, being pure, almost holy in its innocence, was not familiar with the complex desires that lived deep within the heart of those infected by Sin; and so, they were comforted by their inherent belief that darkness could not live in light.

Prince Lucifer walked with his jaw dropped, his hand pressed against his chest in awe of the beauty that stretched out before him. How he wished he could have seen this place before the carpenters arrived and built these cottages made of logs. Archangel Uzziel accompanied the prince, pointing out plant life, describing its fragrance and its taste.

"I can eat the plants growing in the region?" Lucifer asked. Before the hour passed, Uzziel introduced the prince to edible flowers as well as tasty herbs. "These plants are delicious. We will use them to flavor our food," Lucifer told his guide.

Now it was time for Lucifer and his followers to acquaint themselves with the cabins that had been built to house them while they lived in the North. Archangel Uzziel walked God's false prince to the cabin built especially for him and his handpicked courtiers. The structure stretched half the length of one of Earth's football fields and was two stories high. Every ten feet or so, huge trees extended their mighty branches high over the sprawling cabin's second story, giving the impression that their broad canopy of leaves were hiding it from God's sacred light.

"May we enter?" Prince Lucifer asked. Graciously, the prince invited his followers to join him inside his new home. Excited angels assembled on the grassy lawn, sandals in hand, awaiting a grand tour of their leader's woodland mansion. As brothers of all generations filed through the door, their eyes drank in the beauty of polished oak floors and walls. Their jaws dropped in awe of the expertly designed furnishings that were set in place throughout the structure.

"Kaela installed the wooden shutters that you see at the windows of each room of the grand cabin," Uzziel told the prince and his supporters. "He designed and fitted the shutters to all the cabins he built to keep the cool, moist night air out of your homes while you sleep. The shutters have slats that allow the residents of each cabin to determine the amount of lighting they awaken to the next morning."

Chandeliers, whose lanterns were filled with an eternal store of fuel, burned day and night and were sized to fit each room. The main lobby sported a great lamp that hung in the entranceway, lighting the lobby and the staircase leading to the second floor. A smaller lamp hung over the conference table in the adjacent sitting room.

The tour ended at the front door where it began. Lucifer stood motionless, his fingertips pressed against his breastbone, tears brimming in his eyes.

"This house is beautiful. I am honored to call it my home," he said, his voice filled with emotion. "I want to thank the carpenters, the weavers, anyone who used their workmanship to turn this rugged land into the perfect dwelling place for me and my courtiers. I hope with all my heart that you will join me in taming the rest of the North so that this region rivals the one we just left."

Kaela and Autumn exited the prince's cabin, passing Abdiel, who lounged in a chair on the porch, his feet propped against the decorative wooden banister. They nodded their heads in recognition of him, but no words of greeting passed among themselves and this questionable brother.

Holding Autumn's hand, Kaela led her to their cabin.

"Well, this is more like it," Autumn laughed as they walked across the lawn to a large front porch. She loved porches. Autumn ran her hand over the swing that had been built for her by her angel. She flopped down on its curved seat. "Oh, Kaela, let's just sit here awhile and daydream of how we will beautify our lawn with lovely fragrant flowers and lush green plants like those growing in Father's yard."

They sat on the swing for several minutes, planning their flower beds, hanging gardens, herb gardens, and where they would put their gazebo.

"We had better go inside," she suggested. "I probably need to acquaint myself with the bathroom."

Smiling, Kaela held the door for her as he always did and waited until she was inside before entering the cabin himself.

Autumn's mouth dropped open. Now she knew how Lucifer felt. Every room in the cabin was appropriately furnished. The living room was cozy with oak furniture topped with over-stuffed cushions that invited her to try them.

"And there is a fireplace." Autumn gasped. "Oh, I can't wait to burn logs in it." At Kaela's urging, she inspected the rest of the house.

The eat-in kitchen was very much like the one in their cottage in the Sacred Region. It was a tad bigger but hardly as exciting as the living room.

"Take a look at the bedrooms," Kaela urged. "Each cottage we built has two bedrooms, a master bedroom, and another one for guests. This should please you—each bedroom has its own bathroom." He laughed at her excitement. "Go on; check out the bedrooms, but hurry. We have a meeting to attend."

Late that evening, under cover of darkness and heavy fog, Kaela met with his associates.

"Thank you for coming," he said, acknowledging the inconvenience of having flown from the Sacred Region to the North to find that there was one more thing that had to be done before they could rest. "I know you all would rather be familiarizing yourselves with your cabins before going to sleep, but I think we need to make a plan and see it through."

"What kind of plan?" Autumn asked.

"We need to infiltrate the committee Prince Lucifer is going to form. I need a volunteer to approach Lucifer with the request to become a member." Joniel raised his hand. "Good. Joniel is volunteering."

"I am not volunteering me," Joniel said. "I am volunteering you." Muffled laughter ran through the sixty or so angels present. "It was your idea that we come here to keep an eye on Lucifer. Therefore, I think that you should be the one to sit on his committee." The others were in agreement. "I also think you should be in that oversized cabin with him, day and night. If you want someone else to back you, I will be glad to be of whatever help I can be, but—"

"But you fear Lucifer, as well you should," Abdiel said, stepping onto the path. "You are careless, Kaela. Soon I will reveal all I know to Lucifer, and he will make me his head courtier. Where will you be then, my brother? You will be exposed, and so will your followers. I, on the other hand, will be rewarded. I will sit in the presence of Heaven's new king, helping him expand our kingdom to the east, south, and west. All this globe will be ours and you will be our prisoner."

Joniel gasped. "What is this word *prisoner*?"

Autumn turned to Abdiel and, sneering, she said, "Abdiel wishes to take Kaela from us because Kaela is not in agreement with Lucifer's plan to rule Heaven from God's throne. If he has his way, Kaela will be caged, hidden away from society, and punished for worshipping Father as his God."

She turned to those gathered. "Kaela will become Lucifer's prisoner. Prisoners are convicts, meaning they committed a crime, such as the one Lucifer hopes to commit against Father. Prisoners are called convicts, perpetrators, criminals, because they are unlawful. Prison, whether it is a room that is separated from others by bars or a cage used to house animals or a hole in the ground, is where criminals are kept until they are safe to be release into society."

"Who decides when a brother is a criminal?"

"God will decide if His son has committed a crime or not and how long he will be locked up. Our Lord is our Judge, no one else can truly judge us, but in Kaela's case, Lucifer—corrupt and false—will set himself above Father to judge Kaela for worshipping as he pleases. Kaela will be caged and possibly forgotten by society."

Abdiel tilted his head and studied Autumn for a moment. "You know too much, little one. Everything Lucifer knows, you know. How is that?"

"Maybe Lucifer is dumber than he looks," Autumn quipped.

"I will be sure to tell him you said that," Abdiel said with a shallow laugh. "Please don't let me keep you from your plans. I intend to keep quiet about your conspiracy to overthrow Lucifer until I am assured that my reward will be great." He turned and vanished into the bushes.

Autumn followed after him. When she returned to her waiting brothers, she announced, "Abdiel is gone. We can talk freely, now."

"I would rather not give our ambitious brother any more information." Kaela sighed. "We will find a new meeting place when we are more aware of our surroundings. That will be all for tonight."

He watched the crowd leave. Joniel walked with Kaela and Autumn until they reached their cabin. It was the darkest hour in Heaven when the pair lay down in their beds. Tired and somewhat weary, Autumn drew the covers to her chin.

"Do you like the bed?" Kaela asked. "Is it comfortable?" She nodded. "You're home-sick?" Autumn shook her head. She got up and peeked out the window. "You feel like someone is listening in on our conversation?" He smiled when he saw her nod. "You can't remain mute. You must talk, sing, yell, and do whatever makes you look normal to everyone involved in this plan. Do you understand?" She nodded. Kaela laughed at her determination to remain silent.

Chapter 20

First Visit Home

Prince Lucifer had lived in the North for only seven days, and already, Autumn could see signs of a rebellion in the making. Though no cabinet had yet been formed, his courtiers no longer called themselves God's sons, nor did they refer to themselves as brothers of the angels who lived in Father's kingdom. They were northern angels, and soon, they would force the settlers to follow their example.

"We are starting over," Moloch told Autumn when she boldly complained that it was wrong to remove Father from the equation since it was He who encouraged them to populate the North. And it was at His request that carpenters and other skilled craftsmen journeyed to the region to build structures that would accommodate the needs of Prince Lucifer and his followers when they arrived in the North.

"True," Moloch said, smiling down at Autumn. "But we have a leader now, not a father, not a creator, not a failed king. We have a leader whom we must respect and obey if we wish to maintain our happiness and enjoy our comforts."

Fourteen days after they arrived in the North, Prince Lucifer and his supporters set out in the early morning hours for God's kingdom. The prince's courtiers breakfasted together, barely speaking to anyone who was not a member of their inner circle. Craftsmen who left the Sacred Region to build shops in the North showed no interest in their former students. Lucifer's unskilled loyal supporters were content to spend idle hours in their cottages in the village or their apartments in

Holy City, where they stayed until Zophiel sounded his trumpet as a signal that the festivities were about to begin. Only Kaela visited his apprentices in the lumber-yard to see how they were progressing in their work.

At the sound of the trump's blare, Kaela left the lumber-yard, satisfied that his students were proficient in all that he taught them before he left for the North. Now he had to find Autumn. She was not at the cottage, where he expected to find her, primping for the gala this evening. She was not with Excelsa or their sisters. Sonnet and Bernella had not seen her all day. When he ran out of righteous brothers she may have visited, he went to Abdiel's cottage. He had not seen Autumn since they breakfasted together early in the morning. Moloch, Nesroc, and Mammon claimed to have seen their small brother walking through the field that lay just beyond the stadium.

Passing the arena without a glance, Kaela walked swiftly to the stable. There, he found Autumn in the stall that housed Paint. He smiled when he saw her brushing her pony's thick pure-white mane while she whispered future promises in his ear.

"Are you going to the festival?' Kaela asked. Autumn indicated that she was. "Then, we should go to the cottage and freshen up."

"Go ahead," Autumn said. "I will be along soon."

"Are my ears deceiving me?" Kaela asked. He could hardly believe Autumn was allowing him to have the entire cottage to himself, especially their coveted bathroom. He thought about it a moment. His heart quickened at the comforting thought of a long, relaxing bath followed by a nap before dinner without any interference from Autumn.

He assessed the situation. Paint had to be groomed, put back in his stall, and fed before Autumn left the stable. Of course, she could always ask Hadriel, or one of his stable hands, to care for Paint so that she would have more time to primp before going to dinner. Kaela called Autumn's name. She was oblivious to him as she continued whispering sweet nothings in her pony's ear while he nuzzled her neck.

Kaela licked his lips and looked away. He knew it was wrong, but he was anxious to enjoy the privacy of the bathroom he hardly saw since Autumn moved in with him. Without another word to her, Kaela spread his wings, directing his flight to his cottage.

Time had passed more swiftly than Autumn realized. She was late getting home from the stables and began undressing the moment the cottage door closed behind her. In the bathroom, she stepped under the shower before the water warmed. In a mad rush, she showered, washed her hair, and toweled it dry. Wrapping her bathrobe around her, she hurried into the bedroom where she found her clothes had been placed neatly on her bed, and her sandals sat, nearby, on the floor. A sigh escaped her throat. Dropping the bathrobe, she slipped on underwear and pulled on her robe. Kaela would help her with her sash.

No sooner had the thought crossed her mind than he was there, wrapping the material around her waist, pulling the loose ends through the girded clothe so they lay flat and neat against the front of her long, full skirt.

"I'm sorry, I'm late," Autumn said as her angel brushed her long pale-blonde hair. "I just couldn't tear myself away from Paint. When we are settled in the North, I'm coming to get him. I'm going to take him back with me, and from that moment on, he will be wherever I am."

Autumn reminded Kaela that before they agreed to go on this mission for God, she had moved her pony to the stable she built for him in their yard. When they left for the North, she had moved Paint to the stable where Michael and Gabriel housed their wingless mounts.

"After breakfast, I went to the stable to see Paint," she told her angel, her eyes welling with tears. "I found him standing in an oversized stall. He was surrounded by hulking muscular steeds. He looked so small and meek that I threw my arms around his neck, and I cried." She wiped her nose on her sleeve. "I spent the entire day making garlands for Paint's neck and promising him that when the time was right, I would take him to the North."

Kaela smiled. Autumn treasured this one little horse, a sweet painted creature whose reddish-brown markings decorated his white coat in symbolic strokes. Paint was unlike any horse in Heaven. Reddish-brown hair shaded his ears, moving down the sides of his face to his cheeks, leaving the white fur that highlighted his nose and forehead and his long, white bangs untouched. The balance of color gave the pony the appearance of wearing a helmet on his head. Reddish-brown hair spread from under Paint's neck, across his chest to just above his thighs, covering his entire belly and shading his flanks to his lower back. His lower legs and exterior hips were pure white, as were his thick mane and tail. On Paint's feet, thick long, white hair reached from above his ankles almost to his hooves. On his shoulders, he wore a reddish-brown patch, the centers of which carried the symbolic image of God's crest highlighted in pure-white. To Kaela, Paint resembled a little war-horse; to Autumn, he was the most beautiful horse in Heaven.

The pair was late to the castle. Autumn led Kaela through the dining room to the table occupied by Lucifer's courtiers. Two chairs had been saved, probably for her and Kaela. The thought of being so accepted by these criminal types left her cold, but she was doing God's work, so she took the vacant chair next to Beelzebub. Kaela took the chair across the table from her, the one between Moloch and Mammon. From this seat, he had a delightful view of the entire dining hall.

"I am so sorry we're late," Autumn said, spreading her napkin in her lap. She leaned slightly to the side so the cherub attending their table could set a plate of food before her. "I spent too much time with Paint. I would love to take him back to the North with me. I would like to ride him through the region's plush foliage and walk him by the lake in the evening." Her cheeks glowed pearl pink, the precious sign of heavenly love.

When Autumn grew quiet, Kaela asked, "Where is Abdiel?"

Moloch answered, "He took a table with Sammael, Belial, Nathaniel, Atuniel, Gabriel, and Uriel. He says he hopes to convince them to join us in the North." He saw Kaela's contented smile. "Do not be so quick to accept them, my brother. They are not worthy to sit with Prince Lucifer in the North. Abdiel says that we should keep our enemies in sight."

"Why would Abdiel refer to our brothers as his enemies?" Kaela asked.

"God and His supporters are the enemies of everyone living in the North, especially Prince Lucifer," Moloch replied. "And whosoever associates with the King and His royal family is an enemy to Prince Lucifer and his supporters."

"Then Lucifer is his own worst enemy," Autumn quipped, leaning across Beelzebub toward Moloch. "The prince is dining with Father as we speak."

"Prince Lucifer wisely hopes to learn God's plans for us," Beelzebub said, a haughty air in his voice. "If anyone can convince Father to reveal His plans, it is Prince Lucifer. After all, God trusts and loves him best in Heaven."

"So says Lucifer." Kaela laughed.

"Who do you think God loves best?" Thummuz asked.

Kaela held up his goblet of freshly poured nectar. "I think God loves you best, Thummuz." He sipped his nectar amid the laughter of the others seated with him. While they talked, Kaela's eyes searched out and found his traitorous brother seated at a table across the room. Their eyes met. Abdiel stretched out his arms to his sides, draping them over the backs of Gabriel and Uriel's chairs so that it seemed he was embracing them. His face haughty with delight, Abdiel settled back in his own chair, his eyes riveted to Kaela's face.

"Come, Autumn, let us take this time to say hello to our brothers who are seated with Abdiel."

"Let Autumn eat," Mammon argued. "Too soon we will leave this place and go to the auditorium. "Stay with us, child. Kaela needs no help delivering his greeting."

But when Kaela left his place at the table, Autumn followed.

"Those two do everything together," Mammon complained, "and to the delight of whom?"

"Good evening," Kaela said as he approached his brothers' table. "I saw you from across the room, Abdiel, and I had to come over to say hello. Good to see you again, my brothers." Kaela nodded his greetings to God's council members, Belial, Archangel Uriel, and Archangel Gabriel. "I hope we can sit together during the concert."

"What is it you really want, Kaela?" Abdiel asked.

Kaela's face grew hot. He hadn't believed Abdiel would be so bold in the presence of God's archangels. "I want to speak with Belial. I hope to convince him to join us in the North. When our city starts growing, we will need some expert advice."

Abdiel sipped his nectar. "You and I must be of like minds, Kaela. We need the advice of God's council members when Lucifer pens new laws for his northern citizens." He saw the shock on Kaela's face when he heard Lucifer's plan. "You weren't aware of that? Yes, after we are settled in the North and the town is more productive, the prince hopes to fashion laws similar to Father's that you and I must obey." Without taking his eyes off his former friend, Abdiel lifted his goblet to his lips and sipped from it.

Autumn approached Belial. "I thought there was a law in place that firmly states, *Angel cannot rule angel.* Is that true?" Belial indicated that what she said was correct and conveyed his doubts that Father would allow Lucifer to amend Heaven's ancient laws. "Then I guess we don't have to worry about Prince Lucifer drawing up any laws that we must obey," Autumn said, casting Abdiel a leveled glare.

"Ah, little one," Abdiel sighed. "Alas! You don't know Lucifer. He will not amend Father's laws. They will remain in place. But he will create new laws, and they will change Heaven for the better."

It was time for the concert. The angels had begun filing out of the dining room. Many stopped to greet Kaela and Autumn as they left for the auditorium. Archangels Uriel and Gabriel joined their departing brothers, as did Atuniel and Nathaniel.

Abdiel rose from his chair. "You may sit with me if you wish. We can enjoy the concert together and discuss northern business later."

"I think that would be nice," Autumn said, smiling up at Kaela.

"Yes," Kaela agreed, "it would be like old times."

He motioned for Abdiel to lead the way. He and Autumn followed close behind. The threesome entered the theater together and took their seats in the same section as Lucifer's courtiers. Kaela sat Autumn between him and his former assistant. They were there hardly a moment when Israfel stepped onto the stage to lead his attending brothers in songs praising God. When all the songs were sung, Love rose from her seat and invited her brothers to walk with her to the arena where they would see a spectacle she was certain they would find unbelievable.

Kaela filed out of the theater behind Abdiel. "After seeing Atuniel and Nathaniel deliver their fire from the hands display, I can believe anything," Kaela said.

Abdiel laughed aloud, agreeing with his comment. Both tall angels smiled down at Autumn, who walked between them. Yes, it was almost like old times again.

Trumpets blared and choral voices sang praises to Father as the stadium's seats filled with happy, eager spectators. Autumn took her place between Kaela and Abdiel in the highest row of seats in the bleachers. She could see everything from here. Turning in her seat, she marveled at Heaven's beauty. Tall trees, green and leafy, waved their branches in time with the music; birds sang loudly, mingling their voices with the angels' songs. The air was fragrant with the perfumes of native and imported flowers. Autumn sighed. Silently she prayed that God would never ask her to leave this serene and gentle place to return to the chaos on Earth that robbed society of its peace. Her thoughts were interrupted when the stadium's wide doors opened and Archangel Michael's athletes marched into the arena on foot, followed by Archangel Gabriel's equestrians. A trumpet blared. The games were about to begin.

Competitions were held first. Two newly trained unicorn stallions and one winged mare won trophies for best disciplined and best groomed among their kind. A chariot race was held; the performance did not test the speed of the vehicles, but the skills of the horses and the drivers. Daniel, a shy, quiet brother, won the trophy for that event. Then Muriel, a fifth-generation son, took the field. So far as anyone knew, Muriel had mastered no craft. He was not a carpenter. He knew nothing about science. He did not sing or play a musical instrument. He was a terrible dancer, had no interest in sports, had never participated in the explorations, and had no artistic skills. He was an angel of average height, average build, and average looks. There was nothing special about him from his outward appearance. Yet here he was, the center of everyone's attention, handing large barrels to two of Michael's muscular athletes, instructing them to set the barrels at the opposite end of the playing field. A trumpet blast signaled the spectators to lend their attention to the feat Muriel was about to perform.

Everyone's eyes focused on the trembling angel. Nervously, he rubbed the palms of his hands down the sides of his cloak. Muriel stretched his arms out before him; the fingertips of each hand pointed upward, palms toward the playing field. *Swish!* As quickly as that, ice pellets exploded from the child's hands and in an instant both barrels were filled to overflowing.

The spectators were dumb-struck. What had happened? The performance was so swift that no one applauded. Now a rider on a large steed appeared on the opposite side of the playing field. The rider held a small tree above his head. Muriel assumed his position and pelted the tree with ice chips. The tree froze solid. To prove how frozen the tree was, the rider snapped its trunk in half.

"That's amazing!" Autumn shouted over the crowds' loud cheers. "That is absolutely amazing!" A power such as Muriel's had never been known to exist in Heaven—until now. Muriel's talent proved what Kaela believed; Father never created a worthless son.

When the applause subsided and the arena grew quiet, Father, shrouded in a cloak of thick clouds, rose from His seat in the family booth. "Muriel, your performance, though short and to the point, was unlike any seen in Heaven before. I am proud to call you my son. Your skill, though displayed for entertainment tonight, may be of great use in Heaven's future. I have the pleasure of giving you my Medallion of Achievement. Wisdom will present it to you."

The stadium was so quiet that Autumn could hear Muriel's footsteps as he walked to where Wisdom stood holding the medal Father designed for His productive sons. After the award was presented, Muriel walked arm in arm with the Goddess to the family booth where he stayed for the remainder of the festival.

Chapter 21

Lucifer's Council of Advisors

Several months drifted serenely by. The northern angels, as they called themselves now, visited the Sacred Region whenever they wished, attending festivals every fortnight and polishing their skills so that when they returned to their new region, they could build a town as modern and productive as the Holy City. When it was finished, Lucifer's town encompassed the base of the high mountain that shadowed the valley where the starter cabins were constructed. Weavers, candle-makers, tailors, cobblers, and merchants filled the shops with their wares; and trading began. Autumn traded her skills as a carpenter for tapestries or clothing she found too beautiful to pass by. Kaela did the same, but he traded skill for skill. Just recently, he taught one of Azazel's apprentices the art of fashioning a divan for his cabin, and in turn, the apprentice taught him metallurgy.

It was a cool morning in the North when Zophiel arrived at Lucifer's cabin. In his hand, he carried an invitation from God. The invitation read, "To the residents of the North, with its majestic mountains, verdant forests, lawns of lush greenery and sweet fragrant flowers, I, your loving Father, request that you attend my festival, which will be held out of time. This evening, as a follow-up to the events you will enjoy during your visit to the Sacred Region, I will present my Medallion of Achievement to one of your productive brothers."

"I will not disappoint Him," Prince Lucifer said with a nod. "My citizens and I will arrive long before the evening meal is served. Would you like to come inside?"

Zophiel's reply made Lucifer question what he heard. "What? What did you say?" The prince walked swiftly to where the messenger stood. "I don't think I heard you right. Did you say that you must be on your way to deliver God's invitation to his sons in the east?"

"Yes," Zophiel replied. "You heard what I said. Several of our brothers, led by Bernella, have settled in the east. Others have relocated to the southern and western regions. Our globe is growing. God's kingdom is very quiet. I think that only a fourth of our brothers live in the Sacred Region now." Zophiel spread his wings, lifting slightly from the ground. "Our Father says there will a mid-day council meeting. He would like to discuss some of His plans with you and His advisors before the dinner meal is served."

"Tell your Lord that I will be there," Lucifer said as Zophiel prepared to leave.

That evening, Autumn chose not to sit with Kaela in the castle's main dining hall. Seated with her righteous brothers, far from the criminal element she had been courting these past several months, she carried on a conversation with Balthioul that was meant for their ears only.

"You know, the North is as beautiful as Father's kingdom," she said softly. "I think you would like it there. We welcome brothers who are staunch believers in God's laws." She studied his face with anxious eyes. "Say that you will come to the North to work with Kaela and me. We need brothers who are obedient to Father."

"I would love to go to the North with you, Autumn, but I am needed here," Balthioul told her truthfully. "I have taken on the responsibility of counseling my brothers when they are disheartened by their lack of abilities. I have guided several of our unskilled brothers to study the arts, and I am pleased to say that some of them are being considered to receive Father's Medallion of Achievement." He patted Autumn's hand. "But I agree with you. More of us who adhere to Father's laws and who are obedient to Him should go to the North. I think righteous presence is needed there more than most of God's citizens know."

Baradiel, a brother who, like Muriel, could expel hail from the palms of his hands; Kutiel, a brother who had the ability to find water where none existed; and Zaphkiel, who was as wise as Wisdom, turned down Autumn's request to live in the North. As Zaphkiel told her, "We all know that nothing good comes from Lucifer. He is immature and irresponsible. Soon, there will be an exodus from the North to God's kingdom, and we, God's righteous sons who never waiver from His laws will welcome our prodigal brothers back home with open arms."

Autumn felt her heart melt while she listened to her wise brother's words. "I hope you will welcome me home," she said softly. "The mission I am on in the North has taken me far from everything and everyone I love here." Suddenly, her heart broke into a million pieces.

"And we love you, Autumn," Balthioul said, hugging his small weeping brother to his breast. "You will always be welcome in Father's kingdom." Those at the table backed Balthioul's statement by lifting Autumn's sinking spirits with words of encouragement.

From across the room, Kaela watched his beloved Earth angel, knowing by the expression on her face that she could not convince even one righteous brother seated at her table to join them in the North.

"So what's that all about?" Abdiel asked, breaking into Kaela's thoughts. "Your brother is seeking acceptance from others and ignoring you?"

"No, Autumn is trying to convince others to join us in the North," Kaela said, turning to glare into Abdiel's face.

"Oh, I see," Abdiel said with a nod. "If I could not convince God's so-called sons to follow after Prince Lucifer, why would a tiny creature like Autumn think he could?"

Zophiel's trumpet blared. Effiel rose from his seat, inviting his brothers to join him and the royal family in the grand theater. Kaela rose to his feet as did Abdiel.

"Should we wait for Autumn?"

"No." Kaela left the table without a backward glance at Abdiel, the brother he disowned.

The concert was a short one. When it ended, Father rose from His seat to speak with His sons. "Children," the gracious King said in a loud, but loving voice, "I am so proud of each of you. Some of you have yet to discover your skills, but I know that when your talents are needed, they will surface."

He turned to where Lucifer sat. "Please join me." Prince Lucifer left his seat and took his place nearest to God's heart.

The King turned to Michael. "Please join us." Archangel Michael rose to his feet, positioning himself nearest to God's power.

"My precious sons of light," Father said, "after much deliberation I have concluded that Prince Lucifer will no longer hold a seat on my board of advisors. It is apparent to me, and to the members of my council, that our prince is very busy making the North a productive region. As a result of Prince Lucifer's dedication to the northern region, he is serving the council in a diminished capacity. Therefore, Prince Lucifer, who founded my High Council of Angels, has resigned from his position as the board's director."

Scattered-applause was heard throughout the auditorium.

"Prince Lucifer will be kept informed of all my plans, even to the point that he may attend the meetings if he so desires. I am not relieving him of his position to alienate him from my kingdom. I am giving him time to accomplish his goals in the North. Therefore, I am pleased to announce that Archangel Michael will hold the position as director of God's High Council of Angels."

The theater roared with applause and cheers. When the room grew quiet, Father asked, "Prince Lucifer, it is my decision for Archangel Michael to preside on the council in your place favorable to you?"

"Yes, it is," Prince Lucifer replied. "I am certain that Archangel Michael and I will work well together."

"Very good," Father said. "Archangel Michael, I christen you prime director of God's Council of Angels. When I deem necessary, you will inform Prince Lucifer of impending council meetings, and if he cannot attend, you will provide him with a written report the following day."

Heaven's King gifted the Archangel with a golden notebook, a quill, and a medallion to wear around his neck that bore the name his newest title. "My sons of light, I bid each of you a blessed good night." Father's image faded from view.

"Is that it?" Autumn asked Kaela.

"I guess so, the royal family is leaving." Angels from all over Heaven rose from their seats in preparation to return to their regions. Kaela smiled at Autumn's disappointment. "Come on, we have a long flight ahead of us."

When the northern angels arrived in their region, Lucifer called his most faithful supporters to his cabin; Kaela, Autumn, and Abdiel were among them.

"Autumn, take notes," God's false prince ordered when everyone was seated at the conference table. "The archangel Michael may have replaced me as director of God's advisory board, but I am still recognized as the one who founded it. Also, I have access to all God's meetings, and when I cannot attend, Michael must report to me." Lucifer glanced from one brother to the next. "I intend to delay any and all of God's plans by instilling doubt in the other board members when I attend His council meetings."

"Tonight, we will found a new advisory board in the North," Lucifer told his trusted few. "My council members will be hand-picked to assure that brothers faithful to God are excluded." He paused, annoyed to see that Autumn was leaning against Kaela, her eyes closed tight. "Excuse me, Autumn, but are you hearing what I'm saying?" When she didn't answer, Prince Lucifer repeated his question.

"I don't think half of us are hearing what you are saying, brother," Kaela yawned. "I cannot even concentrate on what you are telling us. This has been a long day, we are tired. I make a motion that we adjourn this meeting to get some sleep."

Moloch nodded. "I agree."

The following day, Lucifer called a meeting at his cabin. "My brothers, I long to walk in the footsteps of Heaven's King, so I have decided that the sooner I establish my council of northern angels, the better," he said pleasantly. "I have appointed Moloch, Mammon, Apollyon, Nesroc, Beelzebub, and Thummuz as my permanent advisors." He smiled across the table at Kaela, Autumn, and Abdiel. "I need two more members to complete my cabinet."

"I would be honored to take a position as one of your council members," Abdiel said, his eyes searching Lucifer's face for signs of acceptance.

The prince ignored Abdiel's bid, turning to Kaela instead. "I would like you to consider being on my council. Unlike Heaven's King, I will not attempt to bribe you by offering you a ridiculously high position. I am simply hoping to establish a base that reports to me on the progress being made by my citizens in this region." Lucifer studied Kaela's face as intently as Abdiel had studied his. "Say you will do it. If you change your mind, you may step down, and I will find someone to replace you."

"I will gladly accept whatever position you have in mind for me, sire, with one stipulation," Kaela said. He cast Autumn a side-eyed glance. To Lucifer, he said, "Our small brother, Autumn, must be given a position on your board or as my aide. Scribe Excelsa tutored Autumn in the technique he uses for keeping God's journals."

Prince Lucifer leaned back in his chair, gazing at Autumn. "So if I get Kaela, I get you too." Peering into her eyes, he said, "Your responsibility as my scribe will require you to keep an accurate record of our council meetings, meet with me at a moment's notice to discuss and record actions I will take to encourage our citizens to become more productive, and it will be your responsibility to make apologies to Heaven's King for meetings and festivals that I and my supporters cannot attend. Do you accept the responsibilities of your office?"

"Yes, I do," Autumn said without hesitation. How simple was this? Now she had complete access to Lucifer's every thought and he was demanding that she put everything he told her in writing. "Sire, my reports will require not only my signature, but yours too. Otherwise, every note I take will be null and void."

"Of course, I will sign your reports to make them legal," Prince Lucifer agreed.

"I want Sonnet to assist me," Autumn said. "He is still in God's kingdom, but he told me that he would be more than pleased to assist to me if I need his help while I live in the North. My office makes it necessary for me to have an assistant whom I can trust."

Lucifer smiled. "Then Sonnet may assist you."

Kaela breathed a sigh of relief. He and Autumn would attend Lucifer's meetings. They would know his plans for the North, and how he might retaliate against Father or the citizens of the Sacred Region. With Sonnet as Autumn's assistant, two reports could be penned. One report would be presented to Lucifer; the other report would be given to Archangel Michael when they returned home for the festivals. Michael could keep Excelsa, Father, and the Goddesses aware of Lucifer's activities. With Sonnet's help, Autumn could keep brothers who worked for God abreast of Lucifer's plans for the North.

Kaela sat thoughtful for a moment. There was one more task he had to accomplish. "Prince Lucifer, I noticed that there is a vacant room on the second floor of your cabin. With your permission I would like to make it mine. If you accept my request to live here, I will relinquish my share of my cabin to Sonnet so that he and Autumn will have the privacy they need while they work on the minutes of our meetings."

Lucifer expressed his profound delight in having Kaela under his roof.

Autumn smiled. They were in.

CHAPTER 22

Unrest Begins

"Life in the North is moving at an astonishing pace," Prince Lucifer told his council members during a recent meeting. "Craftsmen from all over the globe are coming to our region. We have admitted thousands, allowing them to settle in our city and our village, adding to the population here." With one brow perched high on his forehead, God's false son added, "Our brothers from the Sacred Region are building a cathedral where they plan to worship their fading Deity with prayers and songs of praise." Lucifer scanned the room with narrowed eyes. "As long as these brothers are lending their skills and talents to our region, they will be permitted to praise their so-called Creator however they wish, but if I find their work is inadequate and if they become disobedient to my laws—well, we shall see what we shall see!"

Before the meeting ended, Prince Lucifer rose at his seat. "Listen to me, Autumn," he said, glaring down at her, "and write what I say word for word, for it is a proclamation that will be obeyed by all. Citizens throughout Heaven will add the word *great* before my name and my title. When speaking of me, others shall call me great Lucifer, great prince, or great sire. When my name or my title is written, the word *Great* will be capitalized. My cabin shall be referred to as the grand cabin the first letters of both words must be capitalized."

During one of Kaela's secret meetings, Autumn told her brothers, "Lucifer put himself above us by adding the word *great* to his name and title. I fear that that our eldest brother plans to set himself up as a tyrant. Tyrants believe they are far better than their citizens, and they have little compassion for anyone but their chosen few."

"How do you know this?" one brother asked.

"Quiet," another brother scolded, "Autumn studied with Scribe Excelsa."

"Lucifer founded his northern advisory board to level laws against his citizens that will not apply to himself or his council members," Autumn told her listening brothers. "This is how tyrants operate—a handful of brothers pass laws that thousands are expected to obey. Lucifer is talking about applying penalties when his laws are broken. We are in jeopardy of losing all we have if we so much as mistakenly break a law made in the North."

Autumn sincerely doubted that Prince Lucifer could rob his supporters or visitors to the North of their freedom of choice or their freedom of self-expression since these gifts came from God, but as a punishment could he confiscate the belongings of those brothers who were not aware that unfair laws had been leveled against them?

A fort-night had passed and another of Father's festivals was about to be held in the main theater of the Holy Castle. Northern citizens arrived early in the region since Father changed the time and date of His festival so that Prince Lucifer could be in attendance. Seated in the dining hall at a table with the members of the northern delegation, Kaela had full view of the royal family. They were unusually quiet. They, clearly, were not themselves this evening. He glanced across the dining hall at Autumn, who sat with Chayyliel, Evangeline, Balthioul, Eae, and Zophiel. The messenger rose to his feet, lifted his trumpet to his lips as a signal for his brothers to retire to the concert hall.

Inside the theater, faithful sons joined Israfel in singing Father's praises and they applauded themselves when the songs ended. The angels were so jubilant that they did not notice the argument raging in the family booth between God and Heaven's first angel. When the show on stage ended, Father rose from His seat to praise the singers, musicians, song-writers, and those who worked behind the scenes whose skills He admired. "I wish to welcome my sons of light to my home," Father said to a rousing applause.

"Children," Father said when the room grew quiet. "I am so pleased that we could spend this time together. I am always delighted when my sons return home. Please know that each of you has a special place in my heart and that I will never forsake you." Heaven's King paused for a moment. "I love Heaven. I love my precious angelic sons. After much deliberation, I have decided to create a world very much like this one. My new world will house beings second only to Heaven's angels. My creative force will fashion these beings in my image, as He did each of you, and they, too, will receive my gifts of self-expression and freedom of choice." Again, our Lord paused. "These living beings will be made of clay. They will procreate and give birth to live young. I will bless each female with the gift to produce life, and I will know their babes before they are conceived in their mothers' wombs."

Prince Lucifer rose to his feet. "Father, I beg You, stop talking this nonsense," he scolded. "We have discussed this subject more times than I have fingers on both of my hands. I am opposed to creatures being created on new worlds. I am opposed to procreation. I am opposed to these beings receiving a soul." He walked to where Father's image stood at the balustrade that encircled the family booth. "You threaten to give beings that You hope to create more rights and privileges than You gave angels at the moment of our creation."

Father spoke, His voice filled with sorrow. "Lucifer, you are envious of a species of beings that I have not yet created." To the audience, our dear Lord said, "I plan to appoint my archangels as mentors to these beings. My faithful sons will teach them what they must know to live on their world, and they will instill these beings with angelic grace."

"Tell Your sons about the soul that You intend to give each of these creatures," Prince Lucifer hissed. He heard the mutterings rising up from below him. "Quiet!" God's false prince shouted. "Let Father describe this immortal soul He plans to give each of these beings, a gift that we were denied."

"My future race will possess an immortal soul," our Lord told His sons. "From the day of their conception in the womb to the day of their expiration, their soul will record their thoughts, their desires, their hopes, their dreams, their attitude toward others, and their faith in me." Father paused to allow His sons time to consider what they had been told. "Their soul will be their reward or their curse. If my clay beings are obedient to my laws and faithful to me, they will be rewarded. If they are disobedient or if they lack faith in their Holy Father, they will be cursed. I will see their past, their present, and even their unlived future simply by scanning their soul through the power of my Word."

The auditorium was dead silent. "These beings, like my sons of light, will be responsible for what they say and do. They will love and care for, even name, the lowly beasts that I shall put on the surface of their world. All that I ask of them is that they recognize me as their God, that they obey my laws, that they are kind to each other, that they never waiver from the truth of my existence, that they never put any God before me, and that they praise my name when they awaken in the morning and before they go to sleep at night."

"Father, that is so unrealistic," Prince Lucifer growled.

"Not so," our Lord told his wayward child. "It only requires faith, love, and obedience."

"Faith, love, and obedience," Lucifer hissed so that all present could hear him. "And I suppose that Your beloved angelic race will teach Your new race those virtues." He waited for God to speak, but heard nothing. "First, these clay beings will be mentored by Your sons of light. We will serve them though they are unwinged and beneath us. Second, Father intends for their immortal souls to rise up to Heaven when the mortal part of these creatures expires. Do you know what that means? That means, not only will we serve these lowly beings while they live, but we will be their servants when they intrude on us in our world. I object to Heaven being invaded by alien creatures who are not Gods, or angels."

"Prince Lucifer, by opposing me, you have put your high title in jeopardy," Father told his eldest son. "For too long you have caused unrest in my throne room. Tonight, I am proclaiming that you shall no longer be heard as my advisor. As supervisor of the North, you will report all progress made in that region to Archangel Michael. I will no longer tolerate your bickering, your senseless demands, and your fawning to achieve titles that you do not deserve. I will create a new world and fill it with clay beings that never stop learning about themselves and their planet. I will accomplish my goal simply because I am the Universal King and my word is law."

Prince Lucifer turned to the spectators. With his arms outstretched, he shouted, "His word is law! Did you hear Him say that? He will create new sons, and we will be their servants. These clay creatures shall be rewarded with a soul that lives within them while they are on their world and that lives outside their bodies when they expire. But as usual there is an element of the old King in that promise. These creatures must kneel before Him and praise Him without question. If they are obedient to Him, they will live in Heaven. Our globe will become a haven for misfits and malcontents." Lucifer glared at his Lord, his pursed lips trembling in anger. "What if these creatures are more faithful than Your sons of light? Will we lose Heaven to the likes of them?"

Father said nothing.

The false prince stepped onto the balustrade that encircled the royal family's booth. "I appeal to any-one of you who is of a free will and is not satisfied with your existence in the Sacred Region to join me in the North. You will be afforded the freedom to express yourselves, and you will be rewarded for your good works." Without a glance in our Lord's direction, Prince Lucifer stormed up the stairs that opened to the outdoor throne room.

That evening, a quarter of Heaven's sons chose Lucifer over God, bringing the total amount of those who left the Sacred Region to nearly half of all created angels. They foolishly based their decision on the lie Lucifer told when he said they would be free to express themselves.

Changes were coming. Autumn could sense it. She lifted off the castle's grounds to join her brothers in the air, her eyes shining with tears. How would Father react to the heartbreak of losing so many sons of light to a lying hypocrite?

Far ahead, she could see Prince Lucifer flying with Moloch to his left and Beelzebub on his right. Mammon, Nesroc, Apollyon, Abdiel, and Kaela brought up the rear. But Autumn flew far behind them. She was hoping to hide her tears and the fact that she had not stopped talking to Father since she rose up in flight. Now the North lay below her. She almost hated returning to this region.

Ramiel lighted on the ground outside Lucifer's grand cabin. Lifting his trumpet to his lips, he sounded a call that signaled a public meeting was about to be held. Brothers from all over the region who had just returned from God's festival hurried to the grand cabin to hear what Prince Lucifer would tell them. Autumn couldn't find Kaela anywhere.

Lucifer stood on the porch of his massive cabin. "I brought you here because this is a sad night for me. I have been defrocked, robbed of my position on God's council. Worse still, a world will be created where creatures resembling us will move in spirit-form across the surface of Heaven. I cannot abide this atrocity by our self-proclaimed King."

From somewhere deep within his head, the same sinister being that convinced Lucifer to think he was greater than his brothers reawakened with a new plot against God. "Gather close, my beloved brothers, and listen to what I am going to tell you. Long before Heaven was created, long before God or angels lived here—"

Autumn was standing on her toes, straining to see Lucifer to no avail. If the area around the cabin had not been so crowded she would have unfurled her wings and rose above her tall brothers. But the crowd was thick and she worried that she would poke someone's eye out with the tip of her wing. A hand on her shoulder caused her to turn. Looking up, she smiled. Kaela had finally arrived. "He's about to tell us something he knew before Heaven was created."

Kaela lifted Autumn in his arms. Before setting her on his shoulder, he whispered in her ear, "Well, then, maybe we should hear what he has to tell us." Now his beloved Earth angel could see God's enemy while he spoke.

"My poor, dear brothers," Lucifer said, faking a horrible sob. "I fear that I must break my vow of silence to God and reveal why it is we live in Heaven and not on our beloved home world." Gasps ran through the crowd. Moloch called for silence. "One hundred million billion trillion millennia ago, our ancestors lived on a beautiful globe that was not so unlike this one. We were a happy and productive race until we welcomed the Gods, who were also known as deities, to live among us. These Gods were disrespectful to our ancestors and depleted our world's natural resources."

Chatter rose up from where the angels gathered to hear Lucifer's false account of how Father and Gods like Him extracted cells from their ancestors that were used in experiments that led to angelic cloning.

"Did you hear what I said?" Lucifer asked, his eyes scanning the crowd for a show of acknowledgment. "Then let me repeat what I just told you. There was our world, and there was their world. The deities came in a fraudulent show of peace, and they befriended our race. In time, they depleted our natural resources and mistreated our ancestors." The prince paced the porch from one end to the other while he thought of what next to say. "The world in which we lived became overcrowded. Angels, native to our world and their clones, were forced to build structures whose peaks touched the sky. Tens of us shared one small room. As a result, our globe's resources dwindled. Waterways became polluted. Fish were poisoned. Birds perished. Insects perished. The members of our race hungered for food and thirsted for water. Desperate to survive, our brave ancestors fled the city's bounds and fought the deities to regain control of our globe."

Kaela stifled a yawn. He wondered where this story was going. And what it would prove? Surely his brothers knew that Lucifer was devious, and being so, he could not be trusted.

"Explosive devices were launched into the air," Lucifer was saying. His words seemed measured, but in truth, a vile Goddess who lived deep within his brain instructed him on what to say next. "Deadly chemicals were locked within the devices' warheads. When the warheads crashed against the ground, their poisons were released, thus killing angels and Gods alike.

"I am the sole survivor of our world," Prince Lucifer falsely revealed. "The One you call Father carried me to this realm. With Him, He brought the cells that provided Him with enough angelic clones that He succeeded in establishing a new kingdom."

"Father created this world for us!" Octaviel shouted, his voice trembling with anger.

"No, He did not," Lucifer argued. "This world developed when the gases ignited and burned white-hot. Debris from deep space containing opposing magnetic charges clung to one another, forming a solid world. Heaven! Moisture rose up to form a firmament. Canopied by chemical substances, Heaven warmed and expanded. Its trapped water flowed to its surface. Life began to stir. Your King played no part in creating any birds or beasts that dwell here."

"I do not believe you!" Hagith shouted furiously. "Father created Heaven. He created every living thing in Heaven, including us. God is the Father of us all. He is the universal Creator. He is the universal King. You are the nothing."

"Yes, he is something," Joniel shouted. "Prince Lucifer is the Father of Fraud!"

Moloch left the porch, his plan for Joniel and Hagith was as evident as the club he carried.

"Do not harm those brothers," Prince Lucifer ordered. "They have been hypnotized by God's lies." The crowd quieted. "You see," the false prince told the onlookers, "I am compassionate."

Weeping angels listened, spell-bound, while the prince continued his colorful story that falsely described God's deception, making Him seem cruel and secretive. Though Lucifer dishonored all that Heaven's citizens held dear, most of them believed that he had done well by them. He led them to a new land. He gave them their northern homes. He offered them a promising future in the North. When they yearned to return to the Sacred Region to attend the festivals held there, Lucifer led the way. The prince provided for his followers almost as well as Father did. And though Father was powerful, Lucifer was beautiful.

Prince Lucifer's handsome face, his height, his attractive physique appealed to brothers who held physical beauty in high regard. And Lucifer's self-assurance made him alluring to those who doubted their worth. The most frightening ability Heaven's eldest angel possessed, however, was his power of persuasion. Scribe Excelsa often said the prince was so persuasive that given the opportunity, he could corrupt God's most righteous son.

With his fingertips pressed against his lips, the prince continued pacing the cabin's porch. "I am the only true angel in Heaven. The rest of you are the residue of the cells your so-called Creator scraped from your ancestors' skin. He carried those cells with Him from our world to this one." Prince Lucifer grew quiet. Did he run out of lies to tell?

"Think on all that I told you. If there is one intellect among you, he will agree that we are safer here than we would be if we were in God's Sacred Region. Let us build our empire in the North where we will hold our own festivals. While you nourish me with your love, I will reward you with powerful titles."

With his council members standing before him, the prince made them responsible to enforce the laws he would make. "Before you return to your homes, you need to know that you will no longer leave this region to visit your brothers in God's kingdom without obtaining a permit from me first. And further—"

Kaela was joined by Octaviel and Hagith. Both brothers were angry. Both had planned to return to God's kingdom as soon as Lucifer's speech ended. Autumn tried to hush the three who spoke openly before Abdiel, who was listening more intently to what they were saying than to what Lucifer said. When Heaven's first angel finished speaking, he turned with his courtiers and went inside his grand cabin. Kaela circulated among his stricken brothers, who stood unmoving on Lucifer's lawn.

"Leave now," he told them. "Exercise your freedom of choice. Return to the safety of Father's kingdom."

Several brothers lifted in silent flight to return to the Sacred Region. Chemosh, Thummuz, Nesroc, and Moloch rose into the air, hoping to stop them before they reached Father's Throne.

Heaven's false prince returned to his porch. The sound of Ramiel's trumpet quieted the chaos. "Listen to my verbal proclamation: Anyone who lives in the North must obtain my written permission to visit God's kingdom, except when God holds any of His so-called festivals, the likes of which all of us will attend. But it is forbidden for my supporters to converse with any of God's citizens or His council members while we are there unless one of my council members is present to hear the subject being discussed."

Autumn snorted. "Every time I think something is about to work out in Father's favor, it gets turned around." She stepped on a pebble. "Ouch!" Had she just been assaulted by pain? This was the first time she felt pain since she left Earth to live in Heaven.

After saying good night to Kaela, who had taken a room in Lucifer's grand cabin, Autumn returned to the cottage that she now shared with Sonnet. In her bedroom, she removed her sandals, sat down on her bed, and rubbed the painful area of her foot with both hands. She wondered if she should have mentioned the sensation to Kaela before he left for the grand cabin.

CHAPTER 23

The Accuser

Bam! Bam! Bam! A series of loud raps and angry voices sent Autumn bolting upright in bed.

"All right, I'm coming!" she called. She pulled her bathrobe on over her nightclothes and stumbled down the hallway toward the living room. Sonnet grabbed her arm. He was terrified, begging her to ignore the intruders. Strong raps sounded at the door again. "All right, I'm coming!" Her head spinning, Autumn clung to the wall, the door frame, and the nearby furniture. "What's wrong with me? I've never felt like this before."

Reaching one trembling hand toward the knob, she opened the door to be blinded by Archangel Uzziel's lantern. Pain—shot through her pupils to the back of her head. Covering her eyes with her hands, she turned away to avoid the lantern's light.

"Why are you here? Is Father all right?" Autumn stepped back, motioning her brother inside. Uzziel entered, followed by five of his athletes. "Come in. Come in, but don't let Lucifer see you. He's not happy that Father gave Archangel Michael his old seat." She was fully awake now. So was Sonnet. "It is a pleasure to see you, my brothers, but why have you awakened us in the middle of the night?"

"This is not a social visit, Autumn," Archangel Uzziel informed. "Several of our northern brothers met with Father last night. They revealed that Prince Lucifer is bent on dividing Heaven by removing

God from all creation. Will you repeat the story Lucifer told his followers?"

"I sure will," Autumn replied, motioning for the archangel and his athletes to be seated. When Uzziel remained standing, she said, "Lucifer made up a story about some alien world that became so overcrowded that its natural resources diminished to the point where angels perished. Supposedly, Father carried Lucifer and angelic skin scrapings to Heaven, which, by the way, Lucifer claims existed long before God set up a kingdom of cloned citizens. Don't ask me where the prince got that nonsense. He seems able to pull dumb stories like that one out of his hat at a moment's notice."

"Come with us," Archangel Uzziel said. "You are expected at Father's house. He is waiting to hear your account of Prince Lucifer's story."

At the Holy Castle, Archangel Uzziel led Kaela, Autumn, and Sonnet down the third-floor hallway to where Prince Lucifer sat. He was smiling, calm, as though nothing out of the norm was happening. As the threesome passed, their eldest brother instructed, "Say nothing. I will take care of this problem."

Autumn turned in time to see Archangel Uriel leading Nesroc, Chemosh, and Dagon into a room, separate from where she would be kept. Up the hall from the room she occupied, Archangel Gabriel opened a door, motioning for Thummuz, Apollyon, and Abdiel to go inside.

"What's happening?" Autumn asked. "Why are Lucifer's cabinet members being led to separate rooms?"

"You will be asked to describe what happened after you returned to the North with Lucifer," Archangel Uzziel told her. "After you tell what happened, you will write it down and sign your written account."

"Will Lucifer be made aware of our betrayal when we tell Father the truth about what happened last night?' Autumn asked. She worried about what Lucifer might do. Knowing her eldest brother was Earth's devil and being aware of the division his meddling caused between God and mankind, Autumn feared that Lucifer would wreak havoc on anyone who did not agree with him. She was relieved to hear that her written report would be kept confidential. "Will Father remove Lucifer's princely title as a result of the lie he told about angelic creation?"

"That's a possibility," the archangel told her, though he spoke softly, the matter-of-act tone he used told Autumn that Father was genuinely upset with Lucifer.

Uzziel opened the door to a room, instructing Kaela, Autumn, and Sonnet to go inside. "We will call on you after Father hears Lucifer side of the story. Lucifer will stand before Father alone. You, Kaela, Abdiel, and Sonnet will be present at the inquiry that will take place in the castle's inner sanctum. Archangel Michael will preside over the inquiry. Until then, you can wait here. Make yourself comfortable and have some refreshments."

When the door to the room closed, the Goddesses made their presence known.

"We haven't long to talk, so let me get to the point," Wisdom said, sounding very much like Scribe Excelsa. "No one in the northern council will be questioned about the slanderous lie Lucifer told about God last night. Your written reports will serve as your testimony for or against Heaven's first son. However, you must look as guilty as our false brother. There will be eyes on you during the inquiry so you must mimic the appearance and behavior of Lucifer and his haughty cabinet members. Open your minds to Father so that He can see into your hearts and know your true feelings for Him."

Footsteps in the hall caused the Goddesses to turn their attention to the room's closed door.

"We must leave. Prescience, a brother of the second flock, God's faithful son, is about to escort Prince Lucifer to the inner sanctum where he will stand before our Lord's throne. That is where justice shall be served. It is imperative that we take our thrones immediately so we can cast our ballot against our awful brother."

As her sisters vanished from sight, Wisdom's fading image turned to face Kaela, her eyes bright with the glow of God's sacred light, her voice soft and sounding far away. "Refuse to speak on Prince Lucifer's behalf. Say nothing to convict him of his crime, but think with your heart. My prayer for each of you is that your heart is one with Father's."

"Always," Kaela, Autumn, and Sonnet said in unison.

Minutes that seemed like small eons passed before Archangel Uzziel returned to escort the threesome to the castle's inner sanctum. Archangel Michael stood before Father's throne. He faced toward the back of the room where rows of chairs had been set out for the comfort of the northern council members. Lucifer sat on the side of the room occupied by Holy Scribe Excelsa, who shared his desk with his apprentice, the common angel Effiel. The seven Goddesses sat upon thrones that were position on either side of Father's high seat. Wisdom, Truth, and Faith sat closest to Excelsa's desk, while Inspiration, Mercy, Love, and Charity were seated on the opposite side of the room. Father sat on His great white throne, shrouded in clouds so that His sons could see Him without having to shield their eyes with their wings.

Prince Lucifer rose to his feet, walking to where his sisters sat, and he hissed, "You heard me tell our Father why I could not have made up a story that removed Him from creation, but I will repeat it for our Lord's advisory board since they have chosen to be seated in our midst."

Heaven's false prince gazed across the room to where his cabinet members sat, and that was when Autumn realized that Father's advisors had taken the chairs that were stationed in front of where the northern council members sat.

"When I left the Sacred Region, I was dismayed at the thought that my Creator removed my title from me. I founded God's High Council of Angelic Advisors. But because I do not agree with Him about a world that has not yet been created, I was denied my right to speak openly about my opposition to Father's plan—"

"Prince Lucifer," Archangel Michael interrupted. "Please tell us why you fabricated a hateful story that removed our Lord from the creation of Heaven and His angels."

"I told Father that I never lied about Him." Lucifer almost growled. "I have my idea of who did." He scoured the room, his face tight and arrogant, head tilted back on his neck. "I blame the historian Evangeline."

"How dare you?" Evangeline shouted, rising to his feet. "I was here last night. I was at the Holy Castle, working with God's scribe on a book defining Heaven's historic events."

"Well, then, if it was not you, it was the scribe's apprentice," Lucifer accused. Before Effiel could protest, his hateful brother said, "I am accusing those brothers who work with words. They have the kind of minds that would develop stories, true or false, about God." Prince Lucifer saw a successful brother seated with Father's advisors. "Maybe it was Bernella. His active mind designed a farce during Heaven's exploration that convinced me our Lord's powers were failing."

He turned, glaring at Father. "When will You learn that my siblings envy me? The sons that You created without giving me fair warning blame me for everything that is wrong in Heaven," Lucifer accused. He was speaking now of Father's creation of His first flock. "Now they have come to You with a story that is unfamiliar to me, but I am the one who stands accused."

A brother named Flagitious rose from his seat. "Archangel Michael, what Lucifer did is not in question here. What is in question today is why everyone in the Sacred Region believes Lucifer is guilty of a crime he says he didn't commit? He is Heaven's prince. Like God, he has no reason to spread falsehoods—or as it is now being called, lies. What proof does God have that Prince Lucifer told a horrendous tale that removed Him from all creation?"

Flagitious walked through the room to where Archangel Michael sat. "I demand access to written accounts of Lucifer's supporters who were taken hostage by you and your athletes and who were dragged here to suffer the degradation of your insulting accusations."

"That is not possible," Archangel Michael told Flagitious. "Father has decided that He, and only He, will have access to the written accounts—all of which tell the same story."

"Exactly," Flagitious said. "They all tell the same *story*. There is no factual evidence against Lucifer that has him telling the story of which he is accused."

Flagitious turned to the members of the northern delegation, then to the few supporters who were permitted to hear God's case against their leader. "Someone, anyone, stand and tell Archangel Michael exactly what happened. Do it in your own words so that you can express yourself freely."

In the midst of God's High Council of Angels sat Belial, God's confidant and legal advisor. He had been listening with great interest to what Flagitious was saying. Walking to the center of the room, Belial said, "If anyone wishes to make a statement that will conclude this inquiry, please speak now."

No one had the courage to expose Prince Lucifer as the fraud he was.

"Since no one will stand before God and repeat the story so many here submitted in writing, I declare this inquiry closed, and I declare Prince Lucifer innocent of the accusations made about him."

Turning to Prince Lucifer, Belial said, "You and council members are free to return to your homes in the North."

At the grand cabin, Prince Lucifer called a special meeting. Autumn sat at the council table with the other members of the delegation, listening in disbelief as Lucifer invoked a law that defined how his supporters would perceive their righteous brothers.

"Write this down, Autumn," her eldest brother ordered. He waited while she dipped her quill's tip into the ink-well and straightened her parchment on the glossy table top. He did not speak until he saw her nod, a sign that she was prepared to record his every spoken word.

"Supporters of the Great Lucifer shall no longer recognize members of our race who reside in God's kingdom as their brothers. Supporters of the Great Lucifer will claim no fraternal bond to anyone, except those over whom I govern. To disobey my law will result in penalties and severe punishment."

Apollyon questioned what God's faithful sons should be called.

Autumn suggested the word *friends*. "That word reveals our closeness to the ones we are addressing but with the understanding that, even though the person is accepted with affection, he is not a family member."

"My supporters shall call God's sons *friends*," the false prince told his cabinet. "But as long as they live in God's kingdom and pledge their loyalty to Him, the citizens living in the Sacred Region are not our brothers. Are there questions?"

Prince Lucifer looked from one council member's face to the next, allowing them the time they might need to put their questions to him. His eyes fell on Autumn whose hand was raised. "What's your question?"

Autumn scooted her chair away from the table. Rising to her feet, she said, "Great prince, it is impossible for us to tell our northern brothers how they should think. Father gave all members of our race the right to self-expression and the freedom to do what we wish." She glanced at Flagitious who, just this day, had been appointed to serve as Lucifer's counselor. Why was he letting this farce get out of hand?

"And you are saying what?" Prince Lucifer asked, leaning toward her.

"I mean, regardless of how you may feel about them, great sire, I still consider all of God's sons my brothers," Autumn told the prince, more boldly than she had planned. "I can't shut off my love for them. And no matter what you demand of your supporters, most have brothers in the Sacred Region that they admire and care about. The craftsmen who are here, who are helping us build up the North, will abandon us if we try to tell them what they can say and how to think. We need all the talented and skilled citizens we can get, so, my suggestion to you is, forget your animosity toward Father and His sons and allow things to return to normal."

Before Prince Lucifer could express his anger toward his small arrogant scribe, Moloch abandoned his chair. "Great and honored sire, I agree with Autumn," he said. "We don't really know how powerful God is. He says He created Heaven, which I believe He did. And He says He created us, so how do we know He can't uncreate us? God may be able to uncreate this globe, this universe, and whatever lies beyond it—we just can't be sure." He grew quiet for a moment. "I say we forget about what happened and try to make amends by giving God what God wants."

Nesroc spoke next. "Great Lucifer, I am intimidated by God's powers as well. For a while, I thought maybe He was losing His touch. But after being escorted from my room by His council members during Heaven's darkest hour and being taken to another region where I am guarded until I am ordered to speak, defines God's power over me. What if He decides to take us prisoner? What if He puts us in a hole in the ground or in a cage, like Autumn implied when she spoke to Abdiel the night he interrupted Kaela's outing with his crew of carpenters? No. I say, let us forget this plan and make amends with our brothers in God's kingdom."

Autumn glared at Abdiel, who winked across the table at her. Here was the proof she needed to openly call her former associate a traitor. Abdiel interrupted only one meeting Kaela held in the North. It happened on the first night they arrived. Kaela had called a meeting in a wooded area, and before it could begin, Abdiel stepped out of the bushes into their midst. He had obviously overheard her explanation to God's trusted spies defining the terms *criminal* and *imprisonment*. Then, he hurried to tell Nesroc what he heard.

"Well, here's another thought," she grumbled aloud. "God could remove His protective powers from us. Making us vulnerable to the elements and nothing says He can't make the weather change."

"You give God more credit than He deserves," Counselor Flagitious said arrogantly. "Without the help of His council members, this travesty never could have happened." He left the table to pace before the prince and his council. "Think about it. God would never have known a story existed had it not been for His loyal sons carrying the information back to Him. He never could have forced us to return to the Sacred Region against our will had it not been for Archangel Michael's athletes obeying His orders." He turned to where Prince Lucifer sat. With a haughty smile, he added, "It is as you have so often said, great sire, God's powers are diminishing, and He cannot rule without the help of His sons."

Autumn played with her quill, wondering if indeed she should even mention the pain she felt in her foot the evening Lucifer told his story. "I say we take a vote." She looked around the table for approval and found it in the faces of those who feared God as much as she loved

Him. "I vote we don't do this thing against our brothers. Let us never distance ourselves from our family."

"You are already distanced from your family," Lucifer scoffed. "I made the law that anyone who pledges loyalty to me shall never speak in private to anyone in God's kingdom."

Autumn glanced at Sonnet, who sat at her side. He was wide-eyed with fear. Turning her attention back to Lucifer, she said, "Great prince, I feel the law you set in place forbidding us to speak freely to anyone in God's kingdom is wrong and should be repealed." The coldness in her eldest brother's eyes sent a shiver down her spine. "To ignore the citizens of the Sacred Region will make us look suspicious."

"I agree," Abdiel said, realizing he had forgotten to address Lucifer in the proper manner. "I apologize for my abruptness, great prince. But I do agree with Autumn. To enforce this mandate on the heels of being held hostage by God and forced to testify at His tribunal about a story that, in my opinion, is at least partially accurate, would draw attention to everything we do and say." He couldn't believe Lucifer was hearing him out. "I believe we should play this thing 'by ear', as Autumn so often says." He walked to where Autumn stood and, in a gesture of acceptance, placed his hands on her shoulders. "Should God do something rash, something unexplainable that affects your followers in some negative way, then I say put a law into effect stating we are a region unto ourselves and that we will have nothing more to do with God and His citizens."

Prince Lucifer was quiet for a long moment. When he spoke, it was in gratitude to Autumn and Abdiel for their thought-provoking suggestions. "This is what I need," he told the others who were seated at the table, "two such thinkers, much like my scribe and Abdiel, who are not willing to draw suspicion to me and what I do. Though I am loath to say I am related to God's citizens, I am. We are all brothers on this globe. I will handle this situation more carefully. I will see to it that no one knows how upset I am with Father's decision to make my rival the director of His council.

"Only those of you in this room know how anxious I am about having been taken hostage and questioned like a common citizen." Lucifer took his seat at the table. "Speaking of common citizens, should anyone ask about the inquiry, tell them that I was warned to keep the meeting at the Holy Castle confidential, or God will uncreate me and possibly everyone living in the North. Let our curious brothers believe that I fear their Lord." He rose to his feet. "You are dismissed."

To Autumn, he said, "Thank you, little one. You know that I will be expecting your notes on my desk no later than this evening."

Autumn nodded. "Come on, Sonnet, we have work to do." She smiled at Lucifer as she left the room with her friend. In the conference room down the hall, she took her seat at a small table with Sonnet at her side. "We have three hours to get these notes done. I am going to write each report accurately."

This became Autumn's practice. She wanted the prince to trust her to write exactly what he said in his meetings with the understanding that, someday, she would publish his journals. What the so-called great Lucifer did not know was, after each meeting, three reports were written. One report was for her records. A second report was presented to Lucifer, along with the hand-written notes she scribbled. A third report was given to Kaela who, undercover of Heaven's veiled night, took it to Father.

Throughout the following days, Lucifer sent presents to God with notes attached revealing his love and admiration for the Holy Father. "I am so far removed from the Sacred Region," the prince whispered seemingly to himself, "that God cannot see me. He does not know that, someday, I will storm His unguarded castle and seize His throne. I have all the time I need or want to make this plan work without failure. Soon enough, I will be king, and all of Heaven's citizens will bow before me."

Fourteen days after the tribunal was held to determined Lucifer's guilt or innocence, Heaven's false prince stood before his followers. "My brothers, my true brothers, we must meet with God once again. It is His will that must be done in Heaven, and since we are merely His servants, we must obey. When we arrive in the Sacred Region, enjoy the company of God's citizens. Accept their greetings, exchange gifts with them if you wish, treasure the moments we spend there, for it will be another two weeks before we return. Here is the plan: we will leave the North immediately, and we will arrive at the Holy Castle around mid-day. We will spend time with God's citizens and enjoy their hospitality. We will dine in the great dining room before leaving for the theater. When the events of the evening are over, we will remain in the Sacred Region. In the morning, we will breakfast with God's citizens. After breakfast, we will return to the North." Lucifer nodded as though he agreed with his plan. "Now go and make yourselves presentable for your King."

Chapter 24

The Birth of Sin

On outstretched wings, Zophiel lifted high above the Holy Castle's outdoor throne room. Using his angelic vision, he scanned the northern horizon for signs of Prince Lucifer's approach. He spied the brothers he feared he would never see again drifting over the tallest trees just beyond Archangel Michael's sports arena. In a loud voice that penetrated the depths of the Sacred Region, Zophiel stated, "Rejoice, all you citizens of Heaven, for Prince Lucifer and our skilled brothers have returned home today!"

Bells tolled, trumpets blared, music lilted in the breeze, and sweet angelic songs filled the area. Lucifer, with his head held high, his eyes peering straight ahead, and his shoulders squared, led his followers on foot through the wide-open gates into the castle's courtyard. Flagitious walked at the false prince's side, a smile on his lips, his bright eyes moist with tears. Zophiel trumpeted again. Lowering the horn to his side, he called, "Come! Join our Lord in welcoming our northern brothers!" While the messenger heralded the good news from high above the castle's peak, the seven Goddesses, Scribe Excelsa, Effiel, and Evangeline drifted to the courtyard to greet their northern brothers with smiles and hugs.

Anxious to avoid the pomp and circumstance surrounding their return, Kaela, Autumn, Sonnet, and Joniel made their way to the buffet tables set up in the castle's courtyard. Autumn helped herself to the honeyed fruit and the creamy vegetable soup. Setting a roll on her plate, she commented that it was worth missing breakfast in the North to enjoy a delicious brunch at Father's house. Kaela accepted a goblet of cherry nectar from one of Altacia's apprentices. This was all he needed for now, just some juice to wet his lips. While his companions helped themselves to the feast before them, he circulated among his righteous brothers. Everyone was looking forward to the upcoming luncheon, the afternoon of games, the dinner, and the concert that would be held in the auditorium.

"Kaela," Effiel said, resting his hand on his brother's shoulder, "you and Autumn are requested to join Excelsa, Evangeline, and me in the Goddesses' suite for lunch."

"We appreciate the invitation," Kaela told Effiel, "and we will be there."

The pair arrived for lunch as planned but apologized for being late when Evangeline opened the door to them.

"We are so sorry," Kaela said. "We were at the shop in the lumberyard, re-acquainting ourselves with our carpentry skills when our apprentices showed us a new woodworking technique they are trying to perfect. One thing led to another, and well—"

"It is about time!" Excelsa snorted playfully when Evangeline escorted Kaela and his beloved Autumn to the table where everyone was seated. "I told your sisters you were either at the shop or exercising your ponies. And as usual, I was correct." He laughed at his own arrogance. "Please, sit. We will talk while we enjoy our lunch."

The scribe waited until the pair was seated, then he asked, "So, Kaela, what would you compare Lucifer to? Would you say he is a companion or a master?"

"Prince Lucifer is very hard to please," Kaela replied, "very demanding." He grew thoughtful for a moment. "And he is very strange. Last evening, I observed him talking to himself." The scribe's expression change from amused to concerned. "Yes, the prince sits in his study at night, and he talks to himself. It is as though one-half of the conversation goes on inside his head while the other half is spoken aloud. There are times when he sounds as though he is arguing with someone. Other times, he speaks in soft, gentle tones—the way you speak to Wisdom and our sisters, you know, half-teasing, half-scolding."

Kaela lifted his goblet from the table and sipped his nectar. He was delighted to find his chalice was filled to the brim with cherry juice. "The only explanation I can give concerning Lucifer's one-sided conversations is the witch that possesses him has moved from his innards to his brain."

"So then, while Sin is invisible to us, she is very aware of everything we are doing when we are with Lucifer?" Scribe Excelsa questioned.

"In my opinion," Kaela replied, "Sin hears what we say when we are with Lucifer and she probably discusses our conversations with him when Lucifer is at rest." Kaela took another sip from his goblet. "I doubt that the prince has ever seen the witch." He looked around the table at the trusting eyes focused on him. "I want you all to know this: the brothers who joined me in this venture have never faltered. Father's faithful sons will not disappoint Him. However, there is very little news to report since Lucifer has been on his best behavior since we were escorted from the North by Archangel Michael's athletes."

A cherub arrived at the table. He carried a tray burdened with steaming plates of food. Kaela remained silent while he and the others were being served. The moment the little angel left the suite, Autumn said, "I've been shooting down a lot of Lucifer's plans by appealing to the council members' fear of God. Lucifer is still angry that Archangel Michael holds his previous titles, but for the time being, I think he has put his desire to rule from Father's throne on hold."

Wisdom leaned forward, her wrists resting on the table's ledge. She studied Kaela's face. "Nature is curious. She longs to know if the North has changed in any way." Though her question was directed to her handsome brother, it was Autumn who answered.

"Yes, it has," Autumn said, resting her fork in her plate. "The North is the same in appearance and climate, the animals are the same, but I felt a pressure in my foot the night Lucifer related his false story to us. It happened when I stepped on a pebble while going to the cottage that I now share with Sonnet. And I feel weary. Not like when I was waiting for Kaela to return home from the North, but in my body. When we left the North this morning, I was so weary I had to struggle to stay aloft in flight. The moment we reached Father's kingdom, I felt happy and energetic. I felt as though I had been revived."

"Many of us suffer from these symptoms," Kaela said. "The carpenters complain when they hit their fingers with hammers or if they drop a board or piece of furniture on their foot. Even Joniel, who takes joy in building furniture, gazebos, swings, and gliders for northern brothers, complains that work is not as pleasant as it was when we lived here."

Autumn studied her brothers' and sisters' faces. "The strange thing about the entire situation is when Sonnet and I do our notes we become so tired that we can hardly hold our eyes open. Sometimes we find it hard to concentrate. More than once, we have gone home, gone to bed, and awakened early so that we can report to Lucifer on time."

Excelsa's expression changed from sadness to anger. "A hypocrite has awakened emotions that slept until now. These emotions infect the body with what our sisters call sensation. Sensation caused the pressure in your foot, Autumn. Let us pray that no one experiences the full depth of that sensation. So far, no one else has reported this phenomenon. As for the weariness that you are experiencing, it is caused by your emotions. Emotions will affect the way one thinks, interfere with plans that one makes, and impact one's daily routine. The most affective cure for troubling emotions is to be cleansed by Father's pure light and nourished by His love."

The scribe leaned back in his chair and closed his eyes for a moment. "Sin must remain imprisoned in Lucifer's body. If she breaks free of her bonds, she will become powerful, and she will infect doubtful and unbelieving brothers with her venom, and then, we will have a real problem on our hands."

Excelsa opened his eyes to see everyone was focused on him. Smiling, he said, "This has been a good and informative conversation. Let us keep it between us. We are working for Father, but mostly, we are working to acquire enough evidence against Lucifer to encourage our brothers to ignore his lies and false promises."

God's scribe rose from his chair. "Come, we must be off to the stadium, after which we will be entertained in the auditorium. One of our brothers will be honored tonight." He studied those who stood before him. "I wonder who that special someone might be?"

When the games at the stadium ended the angels filed into the dining room to enjoy a fabulous feast, after which, they retired to the auditorium. Seated in the theater, God's sons of light listened to the choir sing songs praising Father. Sonnet sang a solo praising Father for creating Heaven, for the love He showered on His sons, and for the common-sense laws Father wrote that, when obeyed, enhanced angelic grace. When the music ceased and the voices were still, God rose from His seat.

In a loud voice, the Father of all living things said, "I created your race full-grown and wise. I seeded your minds with my conscience so that you might recognize the difference between right and wrong. Do not stray from the path of righteousness if you wish to rise up to glory. Do not break my laws or ignore the Goddesses' virtuous lessons if you wish to bask in my presence and know the comfort of my love. Your obedience to me is your sole source of eternal happiness."

"Do you hear what You are saying?" Prince Lucifer gasped, leaping to his feet. "You are threatening Your sons. First, You praise us for our wisdom. Then You tell us if we wish to achieve wealth and splendor, or glory as You call it, we must obey Your laws. And, Father, our obedience to You and Your ancient laws is not our sole source of happiness. Through Your false claims, You have blackmailed my brothers into obeying Your every demand."

Father patiently, but sternly, addressed His angry son. "No false claims have been made. My statements are constructed of the common sense values I instilled in your sisters."

To those in the audience, our Lord said, "I gifted you with freedom of self-expression, but be aware that freedom, when practiced irresponsibly, has its price. I gave each of you a curious nature so that you may carry out your innate sense of adventure. Some of you have dedicated your lives to me. In you, I find my greatest pleasure. You work for the good of Heaven, and honor me through the wonderful work you do here. I am amazed every day by your intellectual growth and your independence. But I ask each of you, my sons, whether you reside in my kingdom, or elsewhere on this globe, to work for Heaven's well-being. Through your accomplishments, you will earn the respect of your brothers, and I will adorn your neck with my Medallion of

Achievement, a jewel that is formed from Infinity's purest gold, which reflects my appreciation of your skills."

"Your so-called Lord who professes to be your Creator is rewarding your servitude to Him with bribes," Prince Lucifer called aloud, his scorn for God evident in his voice. "He bribes you with gifts so that you will do His bidding. He wants you to forget that He is your Master, not your Father."

"To be free," Father continued as though Lucifer had not spoken, "you must revere my name, make sound decisions so as not to shame yourselves, and admit your mistakes. To be truly free, you must be willing to accept responsibility for your actions and work for the betterment of society. The price of freedom is your responsibility to God, for one day, you will answer to me for all you've done throughout your lives. I came here today to issue no decrees, but to speak to my sons as a father who adores them and wants only the best for them. I have been fair with each of you, allowing you to evolve in your own way. Therefore, anyone who cannot uphold my fundamental laws is not suited for this region."

Father grew quiet. Had He run out of things to say? Or, was He giving His sons time to grasp what He told them? In conclusion to His speech, Heaven's King added, "My laws were written by my daughters, your beloved sisters, long before I created my first angel, and my laws must be obeyed."

Love joined her Father at the balustrade. "My brothers, Wisdom wrote, 'Angel shall not rule angel' since you all are created equal. God, the Father, is Heaven's eternal King, and no other king shall rule here, with the exception of the One Father makes His heir. Truth's law discourages angels from bearing false witness against their brothers and to be forthright in their daily lives. Faith wrote the law that states, 'Reverence belongs to the Lord, your God. Pray to Father morning, noon, and night, for He is your Comforter and your Guide.' Charity's law reminds us to turn to Father in times of need for He is the giver of joyful things and that we should be Godlike toward our brothers who have less than we have. Mercy's law reminds us that we should respect one another's opinions by abstaining from judgement, for God is the Judge of all things. And her law teaches us that a willfully disobedient son shall be judged in accordance to God's almighty Word. Disciples of a corrupt or treasonous brother will share his penalty. Inspiration's law encourages brothers to test their knowledge of their skill, to improve every day, and to share their talents with others so that, one day, every angel in Heaven will be a master craftsman."

Love studied the faces before her. The reverent faces belonged to believers; they were proud to be Father's righteous sons. The expressionless faces belong to the sons who chose to believe in nothing. But the arrogant, haughty faces belonged to those who willfully chose to break God's laws.

"Now for the law I wrote: 'Angels shall not procreate.' God, our Father, is the giver and taker of life. He determines the time of our creation, and only He can revoke His gift of life to us." Love paused. "My brothers, to be forever loved by God, you must pledge your obedience to Him. Worship Father as your King, and revere Him as your Creator. Accept Father's gifts with joy and gratitude. Your greatest reward will come when you do not expect more than He offers. Love each other as He loves each of you.

"The laws I was so honored to read to you are the great heart of Heaven. They were passed, not to stifle your progress or to confound your life, but to enhance your true angelic grace." Love kissed Father's cheek when she finished speaking and returned to her seat.

"Now," Father said as He resumed His speech. "I will define the difference between a titled angel and a common angel." He asked the titled angels to stand at their seats. Hearing His request, all but Prince Lucifer stood. "My titled sons are bound to me by duty. They were promoted to obey my commands without question and to be of service to my citizens. These who stand before you must gain my permission to carry out their individual plans, no matter how great or small. While the Goddesses, the scribe, his assistant, the council members, the archangels, and the messenger are essential to God, their titles are not important since their titles can be removed if these sons and daughters cannot properly perform their duties, which are so essential to our globe's continued productivity and peace.

"Common angels are so very important. Though they have no titles, they are the source of my joy." Applause filled the auditorium.

Father voice was soft and filled with love when He spoke. "My sons of light—that is what each of you are. Heart of my heart! Common angels are the core of my world, and I cannot express how deeply I care for each of you. I cannot describe the happiness I feel watching you grow wiser with each passing day. I created you to explore this globe, to research your environment. Some of you are unaware of your powers, but soon enough, you will come to terms with your inborn skills." A moment's pause allowed the listeners to ingest what was being said, then Father stated, "It is true that Heaven's laws apply to everyone and that everyone is bound to obey me, but that does not deter the love and appreciation I feel for my children. Now let's get on with the ceremony. I think you will be pleased with the one receiving his promotion tonight."

Seated in the auditorium with Kaela at her side, Autumn wiped tears of joy from her cheeks. Effiel, whose interest in Heaven's growth and well-being made him precious to all, had been asked to kneel before God. The apprentice knelt before his King, his eyes closed, his head lowered, and the palms of his hands touching together as though in prayer. Father motioned Scribe Excelsa to stand next to Him and gave him the lacey multicolored rainbow intended for Effiel's head. Holy Scribe Excelsa glowed soft pink as he set the bow in place and bid his beloved brother to stand, facing his admirers.

"Archangel Effiel, my wonderful brother, my dear apprentice, you have earned this titled position through your constant and earnest desire to keep our Lord's books accurately. You have proven yourself wise beyond your years, becoming affluent in our King's ancient languages, staying aware of your surroundings, and by helping anyone and everyone you know, especially me."

The scribe's humble statement was met with light applause and soft laughter.

"I truly hope you will continue working with me. Perhaps someday, you will take on an apprentice of your own, and the three of us can work together. Please know that I would welcome anyone you chose since your heart is pure and you are just."

To the audience who stood at their seats facing the family booth, Excelsa announced, "My brothers, I am pleased and honored to have the privilege of presenting to you Archangel Effiel!"

Autumn sobbed and blew kisses that floated invisible through the air to where Father and His family sat. The auditorium roared with cheers and applause. Only one son remained seated and silent. While everyone rejoiced Effiel's new position as archangel, Prince Lucifer sat rigid in his seat, the palms of his hands pressing down on his knees, his brows lowered. Was he thinking of what he told his supporters earlier today? "I would not return to the Sacred Region if I were free to indulge my own wishes, but I am curious to learn which special brother in God's kingdom deserves a promotion."

Seated in the family booth at Father's request, Prince Lucifer displayed his boredom with yawns and exaggerated squirming. He glanced over his right shoulder, past Heaven's King, at Archangel Michael, who applauded Effiel's new title. When the applause died and everyone was seated, Michael left the family booth and was nowhere to be seen. Lucifer leaned toward the scribe, mumbling, "I see God's pet is absent from the festivities. Has God tired of him?"

Before Scribe Excelsa could answer, Prince Lucifer turned to the universal Creator and asked, "Where is your beloved archangel? Have You banished him from our sight to save Yourself the embarrassment of knowing You mistakenly believed Michael could replace me as director of Your High Council?"

Overhearing the prince's disrespectful question, one that was aimed like a knife at Father's heart, Excelsa leaned and whispered in the prince's ear, "How do you know Michael is absent from the theater? Maybe he is dangling from the chandelier, watching you, Lucifer." The scribe smiled when God's false son turned his face upward to study the auditorium's high-arched ceiling.

The night was drawing to a close when God rose from His seat to address His sons. "Children, my beloved sons, I am honored to stand before an assembly as great as this one. I am even more honored to present to you your noble brother, Archangel Michael."

Many trumpets sounded to announce Michael's arrival. Truth and Wisdom escorted their righteous brother to where Father stood. Without instruction, the archangel knelt before His King.

"Michael, you are one of Heaven's most gracious sons," the Lord announced. "You are faithful to me and obedient to my laws. You apply your sisters' virtuous lessons to your life. You are a wise instructor. You are a trustworthy and merciful. Your athletic skills, your patience with your apprentices, and your desire to explore our globe earned you the title of archangel. This evening, I wish to honor your unshaken sense of justice by christening you; Most Honorable Prince of Righteousness." Having finished His speech, Father sat a haloed golden crown atop the His new prince's head.

Lucifer rose to his feet and shouted, "Do you see why I would not have come here if I had not been coerced to do so by the power that lives within me!" The false prince leaped onto the balustrade. "My faithful citizens, on my mark, we will leave this auditorium and return to the North. But I have something to say first."

He turned to God. "I did not come here to learn that Michael is far better than I am. I did not come here to have my heart broken by You." He pointed his finger at Michael. "If you cherish your life, never show your face in the North, for I will find a way to uncreate you."

Lucifer's angry voice was so loud that had a trumpet blown, it would have been drowned out. His envy of the realm's new prince, his hatred of Father's power, his shame at knowing he did not earn his titles, roused to wakefulness the ancient entity that lived within his rotting mind. Inside Lucifer's head, the thin veil that separated discontentment from horror, ripped. He heard it tear, and without a word to his waiting citizens, he stormed from the family booth and up the stairs to the outdoor throne room.

Autumn and Kaela stood at their seats, jaws dropped in horror at the sight of their brother raging like a maniac while standing in God's presence. They watched until Lucifer was out of sight and did not move until they heard Moloch order the northern citizens to assemble in the castle's courtyard. With a backward glance in Father's direction, Autumn raced behind Kaela, who walked swiftly toward the theater's doors with the other council members.

In the courtyard, Moloch called out, "Prince Lucifer, we are assembled and awaiting your order to return to the North." His eyes scanned the area for a sign of his eldest brother. Minutes passed like small eternities. The northern angels were becoming restless. "By order of Prince Lucifer, all but his council members will return to the North, now. The council members will remain with me in the courtyard."

Brothers whose choice it was to follow Lucifer to the North long before his discontent was realized lifted upward, directing their flight toward the region where Michael's athletes and Kaela's carpenters built a colony for them. While Lucifer's followers took their leave, a group of merchants assembled on the porch outside the theater. They had been living in the North, not to support Lucifer's grandiose dreams, but to add their skills to a newly discovered land in the hope of making it as productive as God's own kingdom. The merchants on the porch were joined by teachers and weavers of cloth who also lent their skills to the North. A discussion was held.

At last, all the brothers who gathered on the porch that night turned away from the North, returning to the auditorium to join the celebration of Michael's promotion from archangel to prince.

"What makes Moloch think Lucifer went back to the North?" Autumn asked. "The last time I saw our eldest brother, he fled up the stairs toward the outdoor throne room."

As though to put a period at the end of her sentence, a loud, pained cry resembling an injured wolf's forlorn howl echoed through Heaven's pale night. All faces turned upward. The shriek drifted down from the roof of Father's house. Without a word to one another, Autumn, Kaela, and Moloch lifted from the ground to rise up, lighting on the balustrade that encircled the outdoor throne room. From their perch, they beheld a horrid sight. In the throes of a temper tantrum, Prince Lucifer beat Father's great white throne with a narrow board he had ripped from the back of the scribe's desk.

"You are nothing! You are nothing!" Lucifer was shouting at the top of his voice. Then he would bellow pitifully, the sound of his cries sickened Autumn. "You are not my Father. I curse the day I opened my eyes and looked upon Your cloud-shrouded face. How dare You? How dare You assign Michael my position on Your council, and then make him equal to me in princely stature!" He continued to beat God's throne with the board he held in his hands.

Moloch left the balustrade. Racing to Lucifer's side, he placed himself between God's throne and the broadside of the board. Grasping his eldest brother's wrist, he wrestled him to the ground.

"Great prince," Moloch gasped, "we should return to the North as you so ordered when God committed this crime against you. We will make our plans there. And we will return when the dictator of this region reconsiders Michael's promotion and reduces his title to that of archangel. But if you continue this destruction, I fear our followers will be banned from the Sacred Region forever."

The prince staggered to his feet. "I am this globe's sole prince." He grasped his head with both his hands. "Shut up! Stop it!" Lucifer sobbed like a child. "She is in my head. I hear her voice. She says openly and without shame, God set His haloed crown on an athlete's head and draws him nearer to His heart because Michael is more loved than you." Lucifer tore at his hair, ripping it from his scalp, tossing it to the floor at his feet.

"Who says this?" Moloch asked. "What are you talking about? I hear no voice?"

"Sin," Lucifer replied, "our eighth sister, the Goddess who longs to rule Heaven with me." Blood dripped from the prince's nose, draining faster with each word he spoke. Blood clots forced their way from his nostrils, sliding downward over his lips and chin, dotting his robe and cloak with their gooey warmth. "She keeps telling me that I am nothing," he sobbed. "She is telling me God hates me. Everyone on this globe despises me."

He clasped his hands to his ears, but it was impossible to hush the vile spirit who droned on and on inside his head, delivering one insult after another. He fell to his knees, and then he fell into a sitting position. "She says I must uncreate Michael! She says only then will I be Heaven's sole prince again."

Moloch pushed Lucifer gently to the floor.

"Do not touch me!" he shouted in his courtier's face, the blood that drained into his mouth sprayed the council member's face, cloak, and robe various shades of red with each word he spoke.

"Master, we must leave the region," Moloch whispered. "You are in no condition to be seen."

While he spoke, he noticed a thin crack in Lucifer's forehead. It formed above the bridge of the prince's nose, and judging by the blood that stained the prince's blond hair, the crack ran in straight line to the base of his skull.

"Someone help us!" Moloch screamed, but no one came to their rescue. Slowly, regretfully, Lucifer's loyal servant left his side. "This is something that I cannot be a part of," he whispered as he cowered behind Father's throne.

Still perched on the balustrade, Autumn watched in horror as her eldest brother writhed and screamed in pain. She knew what was happening. She had read, and re-read, John Milton's *Paradise Lost* as many times as she had read the Bible. Hadn't she always believed that John Milton was God's righteous prophet who, in the hope of saving mankind, revealed Lucifer's fall from grace? And now, here she was, witnessing everything her favorite poet wrote in his book. But if John Milton had covered all the facts concerning Sin's birth, then why did she have to see this atrocity take place?

"Why am I here?" she whispered so softly that her question could not be heard over Lucifer's screams.

The answer to Autumn's inquiry came, not as a spoken voice, but as a realization, since this is the method our Heavenly Father uses when He advises His children. "There is more to see than what lies before your eyes. You must know how Lucifer's sin against God's laws affects his brothers, how Sin's birth affects Heaven, the suffering and heartbreak that led to Lucifer's incarceration, Heaven's first criminal trial, the verdict that led to Heaven's bloody three-day war, and you must be here to celebrate with my citizens when my victorious saints will be hailed as heroes."

Across the room from Autumn, Lucifer crawled on his hands and knees, crumbling at the base of Father's throne.

"Help me! I AM BEING UNCREATED!" he screamed. Weak from shock and loss of blood, the false prince pounded his head with his fists, shrieking madly. Nausea washed over him. Then darkness swallowed him, and he was still.

In the quiet darkness that became his new condition, Lucifer sensed he would survive. But even in his altered state, the pain that tore through his skull like a dagger was more than he could bear. Unable to open his eyes, he begged for someone, anyone, to remove the blade from his head.

"My brain," he sobbed miserably. "The dagger's blade is dividing my brain into two separate spheres."

Then it happened.

Lucifer's eyes opened wide, bulging from their sockets. His skull split in half, exposing the wide tear in his brain to the moist night air. Immediately, a warm, red, sticky fluid gushed like a small fountain from the wound in his head. Blood spread across the floor, pooling around the base of God's throne.

"Look!" Kaela gasped. "Lucifer's blood is moving. Do not let it congeal."

Autumn tore off her cloak, raced to where Lucifer laid quivering and groaning, and dropped to her knees. Throwing her cloak over the blood, she attempted to wipe the floor clean. But try as she would, she could not get the blood to soak into the material of her cloak. Instead, as the sticky red fluid dropped like beads to the floor, the cells sought each other out as though being driven by an unseen force. While the cells pooled, their nucleuses ignited, and a common bond was formed. Bones, internal organs, arteries, and veins—the same sickening mess Autumn saw during Lucifer's creation—took shape. Strands of connective tissue, sheaths of muscles, and at last, skin and hair formed. Trembling with fear, Autumn watched Sin rise up before her.

At the moment of her physical birth, the witch took on the appearance of a radiant Goddess. Her disheveled golden hair flowed over her shoulders to rest against her full bare breasts. She turned to survey her surroundings; Lucifer's courtiers had arrived and were moving toward her, their eyes drinking in her curves and feminine graces. Sin walked among her brothers, her long hair swaying in layers of curls that reached down her back to embrace her slender waist.

Hypnotized by his sister's beauty, Nesroc offered her his vest. Apollyon offered her his cloak. With a smile, the creature lifted her long hair from her shoulders and allowed her brothers to clothe her. No innocent, this one. Clad in a vest that scarcely covered her naked differences, and with Apollyon's cloak tied low on her hips, its lapels poorly covering her bare legs, Sin demanded passage to the North.

Autumn ignored the new-born Goddess's request. Instead, she helped Kaela minister to Lucifer, whose bandage, once red and wet, was now free of the blood that soiled it. The tear in his brain healed. His skull knitted. His scalp stretched its hairy growth over the wound that had been the terror of this night.

Moloch lifted his sleeping brother in his arms and ascended into the night sky. Autumn watched her comrades direct their flight northward.

"If you want to see the North, you had better go with them," she told Sin without as much as a backward glance. "I have yet to master the art of pretending that you are not evil."

The witch smiled at the fearless little angel. Then with her eyes fixed on Kaela's handsome face, Sin tore off her borrowed clothing and drifted upward through the moist night air.

Autumn was obviously shaken by what she witnessed in Heaven. Trembling and shivering, she clung to Kaela's hand like a frightened child. Tears drained from her eyes and ran like rivulets over her colorless cheeks. Even her lips were white. Standing on the polished floor of the outdoor throne room, she listened while Kaela expressed his amazement that there was no sign that anything horrendous had happened here.

The blood was gone. The throne seemed fine, its white and golden surface shining as though God's light had penetrated its every grain.

"Did this horror really happen?" Autumn asked, pressing her forehead against Kaela's arm. Unable to stand on legs that could no longer support her, she slumped and began a short descent to the floor. A large hand reached for her and gently lifted her into a pair of strong arms. Kaela gazed into her face, his eyes tender with love. Autumn leaned her cheek against her angel's broad shoulder. Heaven's pale night grew darker. Her vision failed, her ears grew deaf, she could no longer smell the ambrosial scent that rose up from her angel's wings, and she could not ward off the dismal gloom that covered her like a blanket.

When Autumn awoke, she was on a sofa in the scribe's study. Voices filtered into the room where she lay. On unsteady legs, she made her way to the living room where Kaela conferred with Heaven's royal family.

Chapter 25

Lucifer's Empire

On the night of Sin's physical birth in Heaven, Kaela and Autumn remained in God's kingdom where they met with Prince Michael, Archangel Effiel, the scribe, and their sisters. No one in the North missed them or wondered where they were, except Sonnet. Being alone, he hid under his bed all night, and that is where he stayed until morning. The small angel was about to leave his cottage to report to the grand cabin when Joniel arrived with a message: Kaela and Autumn were back in town. They were at the grand cabin, briefing the members of the northern delegation about what happened in the Sacred Region after Prince Lucifer's supporters returned to the North.

"Is the great Lucifer all right?" Kaela asked when his report ended. "I must see him to be sure that he is well."

Apollyon led Autumn and her angel through the grand cabin, up its sturdy oak staircase, to Lucifer's private chamber. Before they entered the room, darkness—made possible by several layers of heavy fabric that had been draped over the windows' drawn shutters—and a familiar stench announced the witch's presence.

Inside the room, Heaven's false prince slept soundly in his bed while his courtiers doted on his perverse daughter. Sin, clad in a black gown, its material as thin as a spider's web, enjoyed the royal treatment she received from brothers who had never seen a scantily clothed woman before.

Autumn glanced up at Kaela. His eyes were fixed on the witch. His heart was pounding so hard that she could see it beating in his neck. He was as affected by Sin's vulgar display as his brothers.

"We've seen enough," Autumn told her angel. Tugging at his cloak, she whispered, "Look at me."

When Kaela continued to stare at Sin, Autumn kicked his ankle. He turned, glaring down at her.

"I said look at me." She pulled her angel to her level. "Sin is the gauge by which Father measures our obedience to His laws. She is evil." Autumn saw Kaela's face soften. "We need to pray that you will be immune to her perversions so that we can continue to do God's work together." She glared at him. "I need you to be clear-minded so that you can give me an accurate account of what happens during Sin's little frolic in the North."

That morning, in the privacy of his room in the grand cabin, Kaela and Autumn prayed that Father would save them from Sin.

"Dearest Father, reason for our joy," Autumn whispered, "we are about to encounter emotions that we have never known before, and we ask that You guide us in our daily lives. Please, Father, touch our hearts so that we love no one but You. Clear our minds of evil and cleanse our souls. Make us one with You so that we will never go astray. While we do Your work in the North, Father, we will have good experiences and bad. We ask that You lend us Your wisdom, Your understanding, and Your patience during this trying time in our lives. Walk with us, Father, so that when our work is done, we can walk with You. Amen."

"I prayed," Kaela told her. "I prayed that Father would save me from the weakness I had for Sin. The emotion has subsided, but the feeling that emotion infected me with has lodged itself in my memory so that I will recognize it as being evil."

"Just remember," Autumn mused, "when you find yourself being tempted by Sin, Father is only a prayer away."

That night, Autumn left the grand cabin, her heart heavy, her mind sore with worry. As she walked to her cottage, she talked with Father.

"I'm concerned about the safety of my righteous brothers who live in the North. So far, Lucifer has not hurt them, but he has grown more emotionally unstable since You relieved him of his duties by transferring his titles to Michael. Last night, Father, my eldest brother gave birth to an abomination at the base of Your throne. And though we tried to stop the blood from congealing, we couldn't. Now Your eighth daughter is living in the North, and all ready, I see that she is a threat to Kaela. He experienced the dreaded emotion called lust. He didn't act on the emotion, but You need to protect him from his desires." She paused outside the cottage. "Well, I'm home. Thank You for escorting me safely here. I'll talk to You again when I know more. I love You. Amen."

She stood on the cabin's porch with questions pouring through her mind. What affect would Sin's presence in the North have on Heaven's angels? Would she prevail in turning her brothers from the sons of God they are now to the demons in Hell that Lucifer's supporters were destined to become? Autumn paused at the door of her cottage to wipe sad tears from her cheeks. Drawing in a deep breath, she opened the door to receive hugs and kisses from her beloved brother, Sonnet. She closed the door. Inside her cottage, she felt safe, but she could not shake the uneasy feeling that Sin's birth would change Heaven forever.

For over a month, Lucifer kept to himself. The only one he shared his days and nights with was his daughter, who proved to be a remarkably perfect companion to him. When they were not in bed, comforting each other, they were seated on the bed, eating fruit. Their conversations were private and carried out in close proximity so that their lips touched while they talked.

Then one day, Moloch stepped onto the front lawn of Lucifer's grand cabin and blew into the trumpet he pressed against his lips. Immediately a crowd gathered. When the lawn was carpeted from front to back with angels, Lucifer made his appearance.

Graciously, he accepted the applause and cheers he received from the spectators. He smiled when some called his name and others held up banners declaring their love for him. He had, after all, given them their homes in the North, He had allowed them to worship Father freely; he allowed his supporters to visit the Sacred Region knowing the stories they told of their adventures in their new homeland encouraged God's curious sons to visit the North. When the applause, cheers, and verbal declarations of unending love died down, Prince Lucifer held out his arms as though embracing all his supporters at once.

"My brothers," Lucifer began, "we have succeeded in building the North into a prosperous region. Look how far we've come since we arrived here.

"A while back, our Enemy committed a travesty of justice that robbed me of my birth-right." Lucifer's voice was no longer sweet and gracious. Now he spoke in hateful tones. "He set a prince's crown on another son's head. Just as Heaven can have but one King, it can have but one prince. I am that prince. Since that night, I have written several laws that will be strictly enforced, even under penalty of uncreation."

The foul emperor opened the rolled parchment he held in his hand and read decrees that robbed his brothers of their rights.

"Great Lucifer, what does *uncreation* mean?" Maximus, a fourth-generation angel, shouted.

"It means you shall cease to exist," the prince answered.

"How will you make me cease to exist if I disobey your law?" Maximus questioned. "Will I vanish into thin air? Will I turn to powder and be blown away on the breeze? Will I turn to water and nothing will be left of me but a puddle? Explain to me how a child created by God ceases to exist."

Lucifer glared at Maximus. "Your question shall be answered soon enough." Snapping the parchment so that it was opened before him, the false prince introduced a new law to his citizens. "Upon entering or departing from our region, visitors will be required to sign a registration book at the border. This law will be enforced by severe punishment."

"Who gave you the right to take away our sense of adventure?" Bethaniel shouted. "We were created free, full-grown, and wise, so where we go is none of your concern."

Lucifer ignored Bethaniel's question, all that mattered was the laws he penned that would enslave his citizens and alienate God's righteous sons from their brothers. "Whosoever sets up permanent residence in the North must sign a document denouncing God as his Creator, his Father, his King, and he must sign a second document pledging his loyalty and obedience to the Great Lucifer."

Autumn's weary eyes sought out Kaela. She saw him standing with Joniel and several of God's faithful sons. She watched as brothers who carried banners sporting Prince Lucifer's name tossed those banners to the ground, trampling them beneath their heels.

Lucifer was defining his third law. "I have declared myself emperor and high priest of the North, a ruler and a judge capable of determining the fate of anyone who dares to commit a crime against me or my cabinet members. My fourth law states anyone who commits a crime against me, even as minor as referring to God's citizens as brothers will be uncreated, and his followers will suffer their leader's fate."

"Are there any questions for the Great Lucifer?" Moloch asked.

"No," someone shouted, "but I would like to make a statement. I will not choose the prince over Father. I am not in the North to prove my obedience to Lucifer. I came here to donate my skills to improve this region. According to Father, we are free to make our own choices. Therefore, we are free to come and go as we please, and you cannot stop us."

The crowd turned hostile. Moloch, Nesroc, Azazel, Thummuz, and a guardian of Lucifer's estate named Odium bore down on their assembled brothers with clubs and whips.

Until as recently as a moment ago, an unseen entity named Pain had been content to nibble at the nerve endings of northern residents when they stubbed their toes or nicked their figures. Now, however, with angelic blood flowing from wounds inflicted by whips and clubs, the entity attacked. Pain's ravenous appetite was so fierce that his bite took the tallest, strongest brothers to their knees. Trembling in fear, God's sons did not defend themselves. Instead, they fled their attackers.

Kaela back-stepped as the crowd gathered around him. Some were angry; some were weeping. Lucifer's faithful followers had gathered close to the grand cabin to await their emperor's reappearance. The globe's false prince had retreated, inside, when the chaos broke out. Kaela reached out to his wounded brothers, motioning for them to listen to what he had to say.

Silence reigned; it was as though the birds, the insects, the foliage, and even the air itself paused to hear his advice. "If you cannot accept or obey Lucifer's laws," Kaela said softly as his brothers closed in to better hear him, "leave now." He took one brother's forearm in his hand and examined the knot on his elbow. "Those of you who care to stay, I beg you to remain. But know, too, that Lucifer's rules must be obeyed, or we will be food for the entity that sets its misery upon us, or worse, we could be uncreated."

Kaela lowered his whimpering brother's arm to his side. "Go to Father. He will heal you. Tell Him what happened here today." He grasped his injured brother's face in his hands and kissed his forehead. "Whatever you do, don't come back."

Hundreds of righteous souls lifted into the air, directing their flight toward the safety of God's kingdom. To Autumn, the sight was reminiscent of the day Lucifer told his awful story that removed Father from all creation. And though many brothers left the region, thousands upon thousands remained. Autumn wondered how many of them were working for God. Or were the angels who stayed so confused by what they heard that they simply lost their wits?

"Who here is for Lucifer, the great emperor of the North?" someone shouted. Applause and cheers rose up from the brothers who chose to remain, even from Kaela and Sonnet. Well, everyone was for Lucifer, or at least, that is how it seemed.

Suddenly, Leo was at her side. He was bloody, and Pain was feeding on his wounds.

"My brother," Autumn gasped, catching the injured angel in her arms, breaking his fall to the ground. Kneeling over Leo's unconscious form, Autumn called for help. She turned away from where Leo lay unmoving on the lawn's lush carpet of tender grass in time to see a club that seemed to hesitate in the air above her for the briefest moment before it came crashing down hard on the crown of her head and the back of her skull.

Autumn lay on the sofa in the grand cabin's main foyer, her eyes closed, praying to Father to save her from becoming evil. It was a fervent, fearful prayer, like the prayers of one who learns he is terminally ill. Mingled with her faith was the dread that even Father could not spare her from a fate that frightened her more than death itself. If she became evil, she would suffer the torments of hate, prejudice, and the inability to do what she knew was right. If she became evil, she would commit crimes against her brothers and sisters, she would break Father's laws, and she would be haughty in her wrong-doings. She prayed desperately that if she became evil, Father would send her back to the gazebo and that He would ban her from Heaven forever. Then she fell asleep.

Autumn awakened from her dreamless sleep to find Kaela leaning over her.

"How do you feel?" he asked. She nodded, smiled, and sat up, rubbing the knot on her head. Before she could answer his question, Kaela said, "While you slept, Lucifer leveled a new mandate that will separate us in appearance from God's sons. Tomorrow, we must visit Darkion's fabric shop so that we can be fitted with clothing that is nothing like the clothing we are wearing now. After we acquire our new wardrobe, we must visit Rive's grooming salon where we will have our hair cut short."

Autumn studied her angel's face with weary eyes but said nothing.

Chapter 26

Weapons, Underground Structures, and a Special Key

The streets of Lucifer's empire hummed with activity in the days following his mandates. Rive's grooming salon and Darkion's fabric shop were busier than they had ever been in days gone by. Northern citizens lined the streets, prepared to have their hair cropped short and their style of dress changed from the look they were given only moments after their first awakening in Heaven. So that their transformation moved swiftly, a warehouse was set up at the edge of the city. Weavers who migrated north were not pleased with their eldest brother's plan to separate his followers from Father's righteous sons. Master craftsmen came here to teach their skills to others, not to question if what the prince did was right or wrong. If, as Father said during His last festival, responsibility is the price of freedom of choice, then the angels' indifference to Lucifer's bogus laws was the key that closed and locked the door to their freedom of self-expression.

Unlike her brothers, Autumn adapted nicely to her new look. Her short ash-blonde hair curled around her face, hiding her small ears while emphasizing her large gray eyes, and called attention to her long, slender neck. While the others grumbled that the new attire was too dark in color and wearing the new shades of clothing made them feel out of sorts, Autumn pranced before the mirror in the warehouse, tugging at the ballooning sleeves and wide cuffs of the black blouse she tried on. After tucking her bulky shirt into her dark-gray riding britches, she topped the outfit with a dark-gray vest. Prancing again, she expressed aloud her sincere hope that the sandals she chose would "make this outfit rock."

"I'll take it and those sandals, for now," Autumn told Malpas, who was busy bagging up his brothers' goods. "Write this down. I would like to order this same outfit in different colors." She chose the material she liked in colors of olive-green midnight-blue, and jet-black. To complete her new wardrobe, Autumn ordered sandals with closed toes in black, gray, and olive-green.

When Autumn returned to the grand cabin she learned a meeting was about to be held in the conference room located on the second floor. Everyone, was present, but Kaela. "State the reason for your delay," the false emperor demanded when Autumn's angel finally arrived.

Kaela took his seat, propped his knee against the table's edge, and said, "Great sire, I was working in your name, and I still have much to do. So I would appreciate it very much if we could make this a short meeting."

Autumn filled one side of her parchment with notes regarding the border's status, and how well work was progressing in the small city that was located close to the village. Then moments before adjournment, Emperor Lucifer rose at his seat to make a stunning announcement. "I am considering leveling a law against our citizens, and those who visit our region, that states: no one is permitted to fly over the border whether they are coming to the North, or leaving our area to visit God's kingdom."

"Great Sire," Autumn said, rising at her seat. "No one has entered our region in winged flight since you enacted a law that tells us we must sign a register at the guard house regardless of which direction we are going. And, no one flies in the North since the atmosphere is disagreeable to flight. Your supporters, craftsmen, and visitors to our region find it easier and less painful to walk where we are going, than to fly."

"I see," the emperor said, the fingertips of both his hands pressed together as though in prayer. "All right, then. This meeting is adjourned."

Kaela escorted Autumn down the staircase that led to the cabin's main foyer. Pausing at the door, he leaned close to her ear and said in a whisper, "Meet me in the forest outside of town. Joniel stopped me on my way here. He said one of our citizens made a startling discovery that needs to be looked into."

Autumn notified the members of Kaela's crew that a meeting would be held at the usual place during Heaven's darkest hour. Without question, righteous brothers who worked for God's scribe assembled in the wooded area far from Lucifer's grand cabin. Hidden from view by a curtain of pink dew that nourished the region's lush foliage, they watched for northern intrusion while Joniel escorted Kaela and Autumn to a structure secluded by tall trees and thick brush.

The trio paused outside the building, looking through its open windows.

Inside, Azazel worked at a glowing fire; its smoke and steam were concealed by fog that shrouded the entire globe. Kaela gasped when the metallurgist lifted the steel he molded to reveal a great sword. On the wall, beyond Azazel's work area, hung a large variety of metal *tools*.

"He's forging trophies," Kaela whispered. "We must learn the reason for this and tell Father." Joniel volunteered to confront the metallurgist. Kaela shook his head. "I will confront Azazel. I need you out here to guard the door."

That being said, Kaela pounded on the side of the structure with his fist.

"Who is there?" Azazel called out. "Show yourself."

Kaela motioned the others to stay down and entered the building. Autumn, fearful that he might be harmed, followed him inside.

"What is going on here?" Kaela asked sharply, catching Azazel by surprise. Before his startled brother could answer, Kaela tossed him another question. "Does the great Lucifer know what you are doing while he sleeps?" He reached out his hand and ran his fingers over the cold shaft of the sword that lay closest to him. "Why are you forging these … oddities? What are they called? Are you making them for our emperor or our Enemy?" Kaela's eyes drank in the vast number of arms Azazel had forged in secret. "Explain yourself."

"I am doing this at the great Lucifer's pleasure," Azazel said in a bold and arrogant manner. "The oddities, as you call them, Kaela, are swords, daggers, crossbows, and arrows." He motioned to the sword that lay on the table. "You were admiring it. Pick it up. Take a good look at it. Get the feel of it, and then tell me how you like it."

Azazel turned back to his work. "As we all know, after the stadium was built, Michael and Gabriel established what they called the games. They were always looking for ways to make competing in the games more exciting. They came to my shop with sketches that they had drawn up of crossbows, arrows, daggers, swords, and other tools they planned to train their athletes to use to entertain their audience."

With a long-handled clamp, Azazel lifted the red-hot metal from his furnace and placed it on the anvil. Kaela reached and touched his arm. He nodded and set the metal back into the roaring fire. "I designed the tools that Michael wanted. My apprentice and I took them to the Holy Castle where we gained Wisdom's permission to show our work to Father. At that time, Lucifer was the director of God's High Council. Michael was a council member, so it was a chance for him to see what I had done with the sketches he drew up.

"I presented the tools to God, who was very pleased with them. He called on Archangel Michael to inspect them. Michael was very satisfied with what he saw, saying they were forged above and beyond his specifications. Prince Lucifer left his throne to inspect the tools I forged. He studied them with great interest, and as he did, he whispered the word *weapons*.

"Weapons," Kaela echoed.

"Weapons," Azazel repeated. "Immediately, God found fault with my work and banned my forged instruments from Heaven." The metallurgist shook his head as though defeated.

"Excuse me," Autumn interrupted. "Father and Michael found the tools you forged acceptable. Your work was not banned from Heaven because it was marred or subpar. Your forged instruments were banned from Heaven because of Lucifer's description of them. When Lucifer called your crafted devices weapons, he put a violent slant on their purpose. The great Lucifer did not see them as gaming devices. He saw them as tools of destruction or uncreation."

It suddenly became clear to Azazel that Heaven's prince tainted his workmanship with a single word. "I never thought of it like that," Azazel mused aloud. "I guess God felt it was best to ban the devices from being used in the games if they could be used to harm or destroy others."

"Did Lucifer order you to forge these crossbows, swords, and daggers for a purpose?" Autumn asked. At the sight of Azazel's nod, her mouth became so dry that she could barely swallow.

"We can get to that later," Kaela said. "What happened to all the gaming devices you presented to Father?"

"Nature rose up a steel building from under the ground," Azazel said. "My work was stashed there for safe-keeping. When the devices were securely sheltered, the building went underground."

"The entire steel building went back underground, and it did not make a sound as it sank into the soil?" Kaela asked—his brows raised high on his forehead. He studied Azazel through narrowed eyes. "I'm sorry. But it is hard to believe that an entire steel building—are you sure you didn't dream this? I mean, maybe you were so upset by God's rejection of your forged tools that you dreamed a steel—"

"It happened, Kaela!" Azazel growled. "Let me tell you, since you find the steel building so unbelievable, the building was above-ground for three days. No one saw it, though it was not hidden from view. During its appearance in Heaven, Scribe Excelsa came to my shop with a lock. He told me he needed a key forged that would fit the lock. Under the scribe's watchful eye, I forged one single key to fit the lock. The instruments I forged were set within the steel building, the door was closed, and it was locked with the key I made. When I reached for the key, the scribe told me God planned to present it to someone special."

He grabbed Kaela's sleeve. "Everything I did was done under the scrutiny of God, the scribe, and the high council members, so there was nothing illegal about my work in the Sacred Region."

"I believe you." On the way to the door, Kaela ran his finger down the blade of the sword he admired earlier. "I apologize for taking so much of your time. But we must be careful of who we trust these days. If you become curious about what I do, please question me as I questioned you this evening. And if you need someone to confide in, besides the great Lucifer, know that I am a very good listener."

Once outside, Kaela ordered Autumn and Joniel to inform the others of his conversation with Azazel and to let them know he had left the North for the Sacred Region.

The next morning, Autumn crossed the porch of Lucifer's grand cabin. She was a little earlier than usual since she was curious about what Kaela told Father and what, if anything, her Lord planned to do about the changes being made in the North. She waved to Apollyon, who sat at a huge desk in the foyer. It was here brothers from the Sacred Region were brought by Nesroc to sign Lucifer's register. Since the mandate began, thousands of righteous citizens signed in to either visit brothers they missed seeing at the concerts and festivals or to teach Lucifer's citizens new skills.

Autumn made her way down the hall to Kaela's office. Even before she reached the room, she was aware that he was not alone. Cracking the door, she peeked inside. Kaela was at his desk, going over some papers with Belial. Curious, Autumn leaned against the wall, listening intently to what was being said inside the room.

"Be sure to give these papers to Lucifer," Belial sniffed. "Father is upset that His sons who live in the North are absent from His festivals and concerts. His only wish is to coax them back to the Sacred Region where they can be nourished by His light. You are aware, are you not, that Father is responsible for the comforts you enjoy?" Belial studied Kaela's appearance. He shook his head in disgust. "I won't ask whose idea it was that encouraged you to change your appearance or why I must sign a register at the border and here, and then do the same before I leave, but this must end. Our righteous brothers are returning home less than happy with Lucifer."

"I will be sure to give the emperor the papers you brought with you today," Kaela promised as he walked God's counselor to the door. "Flagitious will sift through some of the wording too. I'm sure. Of course, I don't know how well the northern delegation members will take the King's proclamation, but whatever He wants is fine with me. I would like to spend more time in Father's kingdom. I would like to work as a carpenter with my former apprentices and, I miss my sisters. How are Inspiration and Wisdom? They used to visit me every day."

Belial stepped through the office door into the hallway. "Inspiration and Wisdom are fine. I will tell them that you asked about them." God's counselor was so pre-occupied with Kaela that he did not see Autumn sprint into the room he just left. "You don't have to escort me to the desk. I will sign the register under Apollyon's sharp eye and be on my way. Take care. I will see you at the festival."

Kaela returned to his office to find Autumn leafing through God's new proclamation. "I see you found the mandate ordering northern citizens to attend Father's festivals. According to Belial, our physical and emotional health will suffer if we continue to avoid Father's healing powers." He took the chair Belial had previously occupied. "I doubt that Lucifer is as concerned about his supporters' well-being as our Lord is."

"Lucifer wants us to believe that he is our provider," Autumn mumbled. "Dressing differently or wearing our hair shorter than our righteous brothers does not change what we are inside. The fact that we don't resemble our brothers who faithfully worship Father as their Creator and King serves only to point out who we are if, or when open war is waged in Heaven." She reminded Kaela of the many ways Lucifer set himself apart from his brothers. "He claimed that he was far more intelligent that we are. He had us believing that Father sat in unapproachable light to avoid us and that only he could look on God's face without having to shield his eyes with his wings."

"I am not concerned about Lucifer's past," Kaela said. "Azazel is developing these tools that Lucifer calls weapons for a reason. I doubt that they are being fabricated to defend us against God's peace-loving sons. I fear the weapons are being constructed so that they can be used in an attempt to seize Father's throne."

Kaela reached his huge hand across the desk and retrieved the papers Belial delivered that morning. "Let's go. I need to get this over with. I have much to do. According to a note I found tacked on my door, immigrants, as we now call our righteous brothers, are disobeying some of Lucifer's laws, and I have been appointed to put the trouble to rest."

Chemosh stood guard outside the door of Lucifer's office. When asked to state the nature of his business, Kaela said, "I have papers signed by God and His high council members that require the emperor's immediate attention."

Chemosh knocked at the door.

"Come in," Lucifer called.

Without bowing or greeting Lucifer, Kaela made his way to the false emperor's desk. After the papers were presented, Kaela asked, "Is there anything else I can do? If not, I am needed at the border. Nesroc sent word that immigrants from the Sacred Region are being disobedient." Seeing the wave of Lucifer's hand, Kaela turned to leave.

"Uh, Security Officer Kaela," Lucifer called. He smiled when his servant turned to face him. "What you did last night was courageous." The emperor left his desk. "Azazel came to me this morning. He told me about your visit to his shop last night. Your concern for my life and your obedience to my laws impresses me. You are due for a promotion. Keep up the good work." Lucifer returned to his desk and took his seat. "You are dismissed."

Opinions in the North changed as quickly as a blink of an eye. Whosoever Lucifer praised in the morning could easily find himself under the false emperor's scrutiny when night fell. Unfortunately, tonight, Kaela was the unfortunate brother who was forced to speak out in his own defense. In the conference room, members of the northern delegation made accusations against him. The worst of all charges brought forward was his failure to enforce Lucifer's travel law.

Flagitious arose from his seat at the table. "We are here to learn if there is just cause to remove Kaela from our counsel and if we should take action to induce suffering upon him as punishment for his insubordination. This hearing is about to begin."

Everyone stood when Lucifer swept into the room, and they remained standing until the false emperor was seated.

"You purposely disobeyed my law that states all immigrants from all regions must sign the appropriate registers," Emperor Lucifer accused.

"Great emperor, today's visitors to your region were not immigrants," Kaela soothed. "They are our brothers. They are choir members and we know each of them well. They feel no malice toward you, great sire."

Lucifer narrowed his eyes. "They were in my region, were they not?"

"Yes," Kaela answered, rising from his chair. "I almost—"

"You *almost*!" Lucifer shrieked. "Let me tell you about the word *almost* and why it does not exist in this region." He paced before Kaela. "The word *almost* is as negative a word as the word *never*."

Kaela turned his head from one side to the other. He glanced at Nesroc, who sat smirking at him from across the room. Now he knew who turned him in for not forcing Bernella, Israfel, and Zephon to sign the register at the guard shack. Instead, he escorted them to the cottage he built for Autumn, where they visited with Sonnet for several minutes. When their visit ended, Kaela escorted them back to the border and saw them off.

Turning back to Lucifer, he said, "I don't understand."

"He does not understand," Lucifer told the northern delegation. "Kaela does not understand how *almost* is as negative as the word *never*. Well, then, let me explain. You say 'I almost obeyed your law,' tells me that you chose not to obey it. Do you see? 'I almost obeyed your law; I never obeyed your law. I almost signed the register, I never signed the register. Do you get it now?" He studied Kaela's face. "A criminal is a criminal. A disbeliever is a disbeliever. A loser is a loser no matter how delicately one puts it. So there you have it. *Almost* is a fickle, empty little word."

"So what do you plan to do with me?" Kaela asked.

Emperor Lucifer pressed the palm of his hand against his forehead. "Why should I do anything with you?" he asked.

Kaela shrugged.

"What's that?" Lucifer snarled, imitating Kaela's gesture. "What is that?"

The emperor turned to his council members. "What would you have me do with Kaela?"

Suggestions were heard. Nesroc wanted him bound to a tree and made to shout all day in a loud clear voice why no one in Heaven should break Lucifer's laws. Moloch wanted Kaela put to work at hard labor so that Pain could feed freely on his physical wounds. Apollyon suggested sending Kaela back to God.

"Send him back to God?" Lucifer snarled. "What lunacy! I would rather have him uncreated. If Kaela returns to God's kingdom, he would encourage our Enemy to hate us more than He does now." Lucifer turned to Kaela. "How would you handle this situation?"

Kaela's brows rose high on his forehead. He *almost* burst out laughing. He hung his head to hide his smile. When he got a grip on his emotions, he said, "I really don't see how I committed a crime or why I am being chastised. I escorted the choir members to Sonnet's cabin where I listened to their conversation. Nothing of importance was said."

"How unimportant was their visit?" Nesroc asked.

Kaela turned to face his gruff brother. He smiled when he saw Autumn sitting with Sonnet at the same table as his accuser. "Their visit had to do with a song they hoped to sing to God at the next festival that will be held in three days, which - if I may interject my thoughts on that matter - I think we should attend. Anyway, I heard the song. It's beautiful. I had some nectar with them, and then I escorted the choir members back to the border where I stayed until I was certain they would not return." He shrugged. "That's it. That's what happened."

The emperor glanced at the table where the council members sat. "'That's it. That's what happened,'" he echoed. "How do I punish my council member for doing his duty to me?"

He walked to where Kaela stood. "This brother chose not to make a spectacle of himself or God's citizens, so he used his most gracious nature to obtain the information he needed to decide if action should be taken or if their visit was innocent. It was innocent, and it ended after they sang their song and had a drink of nectar. Then he escorted the choir members back to the border. He stayed there to make sure they did not circle back to re-enter our region unlawfully."

The council members applauded their brother's wisdom. Lucifer motioned Kaela to take his seat at the council table. "I am promoting Kaela to the position of—"

"Excuse me, great Lucifer," Kaela said. "You know that I am happiest working alone and untitled. I will keep my current position, if you don't mind."

Sin burst out laughing. "Father, forget your dreams of ever having Kaela rule with us in the North. He is a wonderfully loyal brother, but he simply is not interested in being your prince."

Her admiration for Kaela was evidenced by the glow in her eyes. "The rest of you could take a lesson from Kaela. Instead of seeking prominence, admire Emperor Lucifer's greatness and uphold his laws by applying wisdom when you are on duty. Otherwise, our Enemy will defeat our purpose in the North."

She glared at Autumn, who sat taking notes. "You don't have to write that down. What I am saying must be kept off the record."

"Yes, of course," Autumn said as she blotted the ink on the parchment with the hem of her robe. "I will draw a line through your statement so that it will not be entered into the minutes."

Lucifer stood at the head of the table. "I have decided to pen a new law." He waved his hand in Autumn's direction. "Write this down: After much deliberation, the Great Lucifer has determined that his supporters, meaning the residents of the North, will no longer visit the Sacred Region unless they"—he glanced at Kaela—"need healing due to injuries sustained at the work sites. Their injuries must be so severe that they cannot be healed in this region." He paused and had Autumn read back what he said. "Also, songs of praise to God are forbidden. Anyone found writing or heard singing songs of praise to God will be severely punished."

Autumn read that law back to Lucifer. The emperor smiled. "Very good, Autumn, I want my laws written separately from your minutes. I will sign them into effect tonight."

Kaela spoke up. "Excuse me, Great Lucifer, but what makes you think God will heal anyone from our region who refuses to praise Him?"

"I thought about what you said earlier." Lucifer beamed as he took his seat at the head of the table. "Just basking in God's light heals our bodies and our minds. Perhaps all we need do is transport our injured citizens to the northern-most parameter of the Sacred Region, and they will be healed. If not, you will speak to God for us, since your tongue is made of silk. He would do anything for you, Kaela."

Heaven's false emperor glanced at the others seated at the table. "Is there anything else we should discuss?"

His question led Heaven into a new hostile era.

Chapter 27

Queen of the North

Autumn had often wondered how Sin's physical arrival in Heaven would change the lives of those living in the North. Now she sat at a table with the witch to her right and Lucifer to her left. And even though she was not directly sandwiched between the evil twins, from where she sat, she could smell Sin's stench and the musty scent that rose up from Lucifer's unwashed skin. The meeting had been called tonight was held to learn what sort of punishment, if any, should be doled out to her angel.

Kaela was guilty of uniting brothers from the Sacred Region with the poet, Sonnet. A song that Sonnet had written some years before had been discovered in Israfel's loft. With the choir leader's encouragement, Zephon added the instrumental touch that put the final period to the poet's words. The reunion between the brothers had gone so well that a light luncheon was enjoyed before Kaela escorted the choir members back to the border to see them off. Nesroc, who was envious of everything Kaela did, had gone directly to the grand cabin. After checking the register and seeing no new signatures were added, he told Lucifer that Kaela had broken one of the North's strictest laws. So this meeting was called out of time. Kaela was exonerated. And now Lucifer wanted to know if there was anything else to be discussed.

Sin rose from her seat at the opposite end of the table from where Lucifer sat. "Tonight, I shall have the palace I so longed for since my birth."

With arms spread wide, Sin uttered words unlike any words heard in Heaven before. The grand cabin trembled violently and Lucifer's council members were tossed from their seats to the floor. As Kaela stumbled toward Autumn to move her away from the table, he noticed Sin's feet hovered inches above the floor. With his angry eyes fixed on the witch, he reached for Autumn, pulling her to his chest and away from the table as it toppled over onto her empty chair, pinning Nesroc and Moloch beneath it. While council members screamed in fear and pain, the witch continued her incantations.

Outside Lucifer's estate, the great mountain that divided God's region from the North shed its wildlife. Deer, elk, mountain goats, wild-cats, wolves, and lions—all species of four-legged beast, large and small, blind with fear, raced through the area where the cabins sat, knocking over wooden lawn ornaments, and leaping through open doors and windows trapping themselves inside cabins and gazeboes. Stumbling, falling, making a dreadful noise, the terrified beasts ran for their lives. Snakes and insects that lived underground burrowed furiously in the direction of God's kingdom. Trapped in their aquatic homes, fish hugged the muddy bottoms of crystal northern lakes. Birds abandoned their nests and unhatched eggs, directing their flight to the safety of the Sacred Region.

A thunderous roar that echoed with great intensity disturbed Heaven's peaceful landscape, sending God's citizens into the streets of the village and the Holy City. Those who lived in Father's home and the Archangels who served on His Counsel of Advisors left the castle to gather in the courtyard below. All eyes were fixed north. Righteous angels watched and listened hoping that through their unwavering vigilance they could learn the cause for this racket. Questions were asked by many, though no answers could be given by anyone living in God's kingdom.

In the north, dreadful tremors shook the region; tossing Lucifer's citizens on their backs as they ran for cover from falling debris. Giant boulders as large as small hills shot high into the moist night air from the mount's torn plateau, crushing cottages and destroying the shops they fell on. In the forest, tall trees with thick trunks bent just short of breaking, combing the ground with their limbs before snapping into their former upright positions. From somewhere in the territory, a scream that grew louder by the second rose up. Fearful angels pressed their hands against their ears to mute the deafening shrieks that traveled from the bowels of the mountain that shadowed the northern village to escape through a tremendous tear that formed from one end of the mount's jagged plateau to the other.

The North was devastated—trees were felled, cabins were leveled, and brothers were buried under debris, screaming for help as Pain feasted on their newly torn wounds and broken limbs. The only cabin left undisturbed was the one Kaela built for Lucifer.

In the upstairs conference room, Sin levitated in the air; her mutterings filled the room, almost deafening every ear in the region. Her words churned on, sounding like the unbearable rumble of an earthquake or a volcano.

Atop the mountain's highest peak, a black rock appeared. Its height and width devoured half the grand hill's wide range. The rock had risen from the depths of Heaven's deep-seated core to crown the great mountain's trembling head in onyx splendor. Visible to the entire North, the rock reached upward to a horrific height, blocking God's light, turning the landscape below jet-black. While brothers sought to help brothers and Pain feasted freely, Fear invaded the region. Uncertainty was next to join the mounting emotions. Confusion and Worry made their presence known as soil, rocks, boulders, and oil rained down on northern citizens, complicating their search for their wounded brothers.

Kaela leaped from the upstairs window, followed by Abdiel, Autumn, and Sonnet. Joniel and his apprentices joined the three council members. Together since Heaven's youth, Kaela and God's faithful sons made their way through the destruction, dodging the fireballs that shot into the air from the injured mountain's peak.

"Down there!" Kaela shouted over the chaotic roar. "I see Rive." The rescuers descended to the ground. While the others sought out more injured souls, Kaela stretched himself across the tumbled logs of a fallen cabin determined to save Rive's life.

"Hurry, take my hand!"

The noise from the eruption was so loud that the urge to forget Kaela's outstretched hand overwhelmed Rive, and he covered his ears. Like everyone in the region, he felt as if his head would explode. The unbearable noise and the pain in his limbs dulled his senses.

"Take my hand! Take it now!" Kaela shouted over the chaos. He motioned Sonnet and Autumn to drop the logs they struggled to move and cover their ears with their hands.

The small angels fell to their knees, and breaking Lucifer's new law, they screamed for relief. "Father, help us!"

The noise ceased. Kaela thought he was deaf until he heard Rive's groaning. Stretching himself over the logs a second time, he drew his brother to him.

"Are you all right?"

"No," Rive groaned.

"What's wrong? Where do you hurt?"

"Everywhere," the injured angel sobbed.

"Lie back. You are safe. I have you." Kaela knelt at Rive's side.

"Thank you, precious Father, for the strength you have given me. Help me raise more brothers from this awful destruction." Kaela repeated his prayer many times as he pulled brother after brother from the debris that imprisoned them. By morning, hundreds of injured northern angels owed their lives to Kaela, Abdiel, Joniel, and their apprentice carpenters.

Inside the onyx palace high above the destruction below, while the witch slept, Kaela argued violently with Lucifer and his council members. "Your newly written law states that if we find our brothers injured so badly that we cannot heal them ourselves, we may take them to the Sacred Region where we will let God do His work. Uphold your law and do it now, for the sake of your citizens."

"Who are you to tell me, the great Lucifer, what to do?"

"I am one of your advisors!" Kaela shouted.

"You will not raise your voice to me," Lucifer scolded. "I am your emperor."

"Yours is a self-appointed title, it was not earned." Kaela snorted. "Either I do this with your permission, or I do it without your permission. But know this, great Lucifer, if I take the injured to God without your permission, I will pledge my loyalty to Him—and you do not want me for an enemy."

Moloch rose from his seat and attack Kaela with a force that sent both angels rolling across the floor. Nesroc was next to leap, followed by Apollyon. Kaela kicked Moloch in the face, sending him sliding across the black polished floor toward Lucifer's throne. Before the other two could pounce on Kaela, Lucifer intervened.

"Stop it!" Lucifer shouted. "He is right in what he said. I do not want Kaela for my enemy." The false emperor took his throne. "This very evening, I made a law that stated our severely injured citizens would be carried just over the border where they might be healed by God's light, after which they would be returned to their work sites. If I disobey the laws I make, why would I expect anyone else to obey them?" He turned his hateful eyes on Kaela. "You are favored by God. Take the injured to the Holy Castle with the understanding that those who cannot be faithful to me must remain in the Sacred Region. I do not want them here.

"And, Kaela, while you and your apprentices—as you call them—are in the Sacred Region, you had best not speak ill of me. I have my spies established in the Holy Castle, and they will tell me if you are disloyal to me. Disloyal subjects will receive a stunning reprimand when they return to the North—a reprimand that will be remembered until the end of time."

At the Holy Castle, Kaela remained with his injured brothers, escorting each one to the outdoor throne room where they were healed by Father. While he waited in the hallway of the third floor for the last wave of his brother to be healed, he was joined by Belial.

"It was awful," Kaela told God's counselor, "cabins fell on unsuspecting brothers, the wildlife fled the area, and this huge structure rose up from underground. Joniel, Abdiel, and our apprentices worked throughout the night to save our brothers." He motioned to the line that formed down the hallway. Many of those who waited to be healed were too injured to stand on their own. They were either being bolstered by their brothers or lying groaning on the floor.

Belial patted Kaela's shoulder with his hand. Sighing, he said, "I am here to deliver the scribe's invitation for you to join him in a late dinner. All the council members will be present as will the prince. We are all curious about what happened in the North." He rose to his feet. "Zophiel is directing our healed brothers to the median rooms where they will freshen up and rest awhile. Father has prepared a feast for them to enjoy before they return to Lucifer's so-called empire." He gave Kaela a quick hug. "I will see you this evening. Right now, I am going to visit with my poor brothers. I want to hear their stories. I want to hear their thoughts."

The counselor turned away as his weary brother lifted still another injured angel into his arms to deliver him safely at the base of God's golden throne.

Chapter 28

Enter Evil

It was late evening in the Sacred Region when Father healed the last of His sons that Kaela brought to Him from the North. Each heavenly sojourner was given a room in God's house where he bathed and slipped into fresh garments before going to the theater to relate to Belial what he thought happened in Lucifer's region. Some brothers believed that Nature had performed a cataclysmic event that caused the mountain to erupt, thus spewing debris into the air, destroying all the homes located at the mountain's base. Others were confused. They had no opinion on the eruption. They were too distraught over being injured or losing precious belongings to talk in depth about anything. When the inquiry ended, the sons Father healed feasted in the castle's dining room after which God's righteous sons saw them safely to the border.

In the scribe's apartment, Kaela paced before his beloved sisters and Father's high council members. Archangel Gabriel and his apprentice, Anael, were absent from the meeting. They and their crew of athletes were patrolling the streets in the village and the city to ensure the safety of God's citizens. Prince Michael would brief the absentees on what was learned during this meeting when he saw them in the morning.

"I worry for the safety of Father's faithful sons who live in the North," Kaela was saying. "Contrary to the laws our false emperor makes, righteous brothers have been escorting injured workers to the Holy Castle. During meetings at the grand cabin, Lucifer and Sin used words like *uncreation, imprisonment, pits and pens.* If these words are given definition, they could prove harmful to God's citizens. So far, I have tried to be the voice of reason, but every day tests my ability to out-think our rebellious brother. And I must admit that, lately, Lucifer seems to be increasingly bored with my advice."

Scribe Excelsa leaned back on the sofa. He studied Kaela for a long moment. "You are more than willing to risk your life to save your injured brothers." He smiled at Kaela's nod. "I know you. You are God's fine son. You would put yourself in danger to do what is right. I admire you and your crew. Through the information they have given you and what you have brought back to Father, we can see a dastardly trend emerging. The deception began when Lucifer studied Father's journals that clearly described the strife other-worldly beings brought on themselves through their loss of faith in God. What he read taught him about governments and dictatorships and how to use regimes to gain notoriety and amass a following. Lucifer seeks to make Heaven like the worlds whose children are spiritually destitute."

"What does it mean to be 'spiritually destitute'?" Belial asked.

"When one is described as being spiritually destitute, it means that he is perverse, greedy, self-seeking, and deceitful. It means that he has lost faith in God," Scribe Excelsa told his listeners. "And without Father, there is nothing."

No one spoke for a while. The scribe broke the silence, asking, "Kaela, how powerful do you estimate the witch is now that she is flesh?"

"I would say anyone who can raise a palace from the furthest depth of a mountain is very powerful," Kaela replied. "I doubt that Sin is as powerful as Father, but she had no problem completing her hideous task." He sighed, glancing at each of the faces that were turned in his direction. "During the meeting last night, Sin rose to her feet, spread her arms, and began chanting. While she chanted, she rose from the floor and began turning slowly in the air. It was during this time that the ground began to shake and the furniture in the grand cabin overturned, and we could plainly hear the screams of the animals as they fled our region. Moments later, fire shot into the air. I didn't see this, you understand, but brothers I helped rescue did. Rocks shot upward and fiery mud oozed from mountain's wound. The damage to the village we built is horrendous."

"Why would Sin build her house on a mountain's peak?" Belial asked.

"Sin put her house on a high hill so that she could see her enemies' approach," Prince Michael told his concerned brother. "You entered the dark palace, what was it like, Kaela?"

"It is polished onyx," Kaela said. "Unlike Father's house, the dark palace has several stories, and it is gloomy inside. Even a torch's flame cannot brighten its interior. Walking through Sin's palace is menacing. It's like walking through a closed mind or an empty heart." He lowered his gaze to the floor for a moment. When he looked up, he said, "Keep what I tell you among yourselves. Lucifer is abusing his power and is becoming more violent as time goes on. He has threatened to violently reprimand anyone who is disloyal to him. He says he has spies living in the Sacred Region, living in the Holy Castle."

While the council members discussed Sin's growing powers and the threat she could present to the Sacred Region, Kaela's thoughts strayed to the underground building and the keeper of its key.

"As we speak, Azazel is forging devices for Lucifer in a shop that lies deep within the wooded area beyond the grand cabin. Joniel discovered the building. He reported his find to me. Autumn and I paid a surprise visit to Azazel's shop. It is filled with swords, daggers, crossbows, longbows, and slingshots. These tools are unlike anything your athletes ever used. I fear they are being forged for use against our Lord and His faithful followers." He paused for a moment. "Autumn took it upon himself to visit the shop while Azazel was out. With Sonnet's help, he made a record of the numerous tools that can be found there."

Belial left his chair. "It has been a long night and an even longer day. I must be on my way, but Kaela, it is always good seeing you. I hope we will enjoy each other's company again soon." God's counselor thanked his host for the fine meal he enjoyed and spoke briefly with Prince Michael before leaving Father's house for his apartment in the city.

The conversation, though off the record and casual, continued a short time longer. Questions that could not be answered were asked about the building that, presumably, was lodged somewhere underground in the Sacred Region. Kaela marveled that while the structure sat in the open, it was invisible to every eye in Heaven but Father's. The scribe admitted that he had delivered Father's request to Azazel to forge a key for Him, but He did not state the purpose the key would serve. Excelsa confirmed, however, that Father trusted His key to someone for safekeeping, but he could not say who that someone was.

"I gave Father the key the same day it was forged, and I have never seen it since."

Kaela, who had been pacing all evening, turned away from Excelsa to face God's council members. "It is well-past time that I left. I want to check on Autumn and Sonnet to assure myself of their safety before I retire to my room in the grand cabin. I have no doubt that Lucifer will hold a meeting in the morning. If anything of importance is said, I will return to Father's kingdom with the information you need to make a case against Lucifer."

He lifted his cape from the back of the chair he had been sitting in. "May our Lord bless each of us while we are separate from one another."

The scribe rose from his seat. "Kaela, you have revealed so much to us. Tonight, I will report to the inner sanctum with Prince Michael at my side, and we will deliver all that we learned to Father." He walked to where Kaela stood. "Allow me to walk you to the door."

"No!" Michael said swiftly. He was already standing. "I will walk him to the door. I would like to escort Kaela to the main foyer. I will be waiting for you, Scribe Excelsa, just within the closed doors of Father's nocturnal throne room."

The brothers walked down the hallway to the stairs that led to the second story of Father's house without saying a word. The same was not true for their walk together to the stairs that led to the first story.

"This is the first time I heard of a key and a building underground that is filled with sporting tools," Michael whispered. "A couple of years before Lucifer left to supervise the North to make the region more productive, Gabriel and I approached Father to gain His permission to have the tools I sketched used in our games." The brothers descended the stairs that led to the main foyer on the castle's ground floor. "Father saw the sketches and approved of my athletes using them in the stadium. When Azazel presented the finished tools to Father, Lucifer called them weapons."

"And that is when Father banned them from being used?" Kaela asked.

"Yes. He banned the tools from ever being used in Heaven." Prince Michael sighed.

"I would suggest that when you meet with Father," Kaela said, glancing toward the door of God's inner sanctum, "you explain that Lucifer has every intention of using the tools you designed as weapons against his brothers in the Sacred Region."

"Did Azazel say that?" Michael asked.

"No, but we know Lucifer, and we must be prepared for whatever he does," Kaela answered. "So gain Father's permission to open the building, remove the tools, and secretly train your athletes in the skills they will need to defend the Sacred Region when the time comes. I would suggest training your athletes at night, when prying eyes are sleeping." Kaela rested his hand on Prince Michael's shoulder. "I will see myself out. Excelsa is at the door of the inner sanctum, waiting for you."

Kaela was in north-bound flight when someone came streaking out of nowhere in his direction. Startled, God's righteous son dropped several feet lower so as not to collide with whoever it was that seemed so hurried. It was obvious to Kaela by the steady rustle of the traveler's wings that he had gone undetected. Using his powerful vision, he scoped the mysterious sojourner. Kaela's visual inspection revealed the traveler wore a blue-and-white banner emblematic of a council member's regal yoke. The banner ascribed to a council member's oath that he would be forever loyal to God and eternally just to Heaven's citizens. Curious to learn the sojourner's identity, Kaela turned in flight following his unsuspecting brother through the damp night air to the Holy City.

Of those who were absent from the meeting, only one resided in this part of the city. Anael lived in an apartment above Duma's trinket shop. The two began working together when Anael developed a substance that was unlike anything previously known to Heaven. The substance was hard like rock but transparent like water. Some called it ice, but Anael called it glass. The glass Anael produced through the palms of his hands formed the shop's home decor and the colorful beads God's sons loved so much. Gliding high above the rooftops, Kaela followed his night-loving brother as he hurried through the dimly lit tree-lined streets toward the city's residential sector.

A ray of pure white light penetrated the globe's pale darkness, catching the eye of both the hunter and the hunted. In unison, they glanced toward Father's house. It was apparent that God had left His inner sanctum and was fast approaching the castle's highest peak. A new day was dawning in Heaven. Soon, righteousness brothers would awaken, rested and refreshed, ready to be nourished physically, spiritually, and emotionally by Father's healing glow.

Kaela turned his attention back to his subject. The unknown traveler was gone. Using his angelic vision, he combed the sidewalks for a trace of the elusive night-flyer. The sky grew brighter. Time was of the essence. Kaela had to return to the North where he would take his place at Lucifer's council table. As he turned in the air, directing his flight northward, a new thought entered his mind. Did the night-flyer sign Lucifer's register, or had he entered the North undetected? Today, at his leisure, Kaela would check both registers, the one at the guardhouse on the border and the registry at the front desk in the grand cabin's foyer.

Flying high over the Sacred Region, Kaela used his angelic vision to study the landscape below. Behind the Holy Castle's great stadium, a stately forest stretched out for miles. The forest dipped several feet down the side of the Holy Mount before opening to a peaceful valley where unicorn and horses, winged and unwinged, grazed with Heaven's common beasts on tender, nourishing grasses.

Still using his angelic vision, he focused on the lake. Beneath its crystal waters, he saw the shadow of bass, walleye, trout, and perch. It was feeding time, and the fish hoped to capture and devour insects that lighted on the water's glistening surface. Fish and amphibians were the only carnivores here. Four-legged beasts, the types that would attack a man on Earth, fed on plant life in Heaven.

Kaela ascended in flight, leaving the open field that separated Father's kingdom from Lucifer's false empire far below him. The first hour of the morning was Heaven's most beautiful time of day. Now, as when he explored Heaven's uncharted region with Michael's team of athletes, he was awed by the sight of glistening pink dews, haloed by rainbows, lifting upward, rising higher than the angelic eye could see. Flying through the nourishing moisture that fed Heaven's verdant landscape, he tasted its sweetness on his lips, but all was not so sweet.

At this hour, birds throughout the globe should have been lifting their voices in praise of the new day God created for them. Instead, birds of all species were flying toward Kaela. Their terrified screeches echoed through the valley below as they passed overhead, desperately winging their way toward the Sacred Region. Birds perched on the limbs of the trees that bordered the forest stopped their warbling. One by one, they rose in silence on weary wings to follow the birds that seemed to be fleeing the North. Was this the result Sin's conjuring wrought? Or was the region under a new threat?

On the ground below, four-legged beasts, large and small, swift and slow, burst out of the forest. Stampeding across the meadow they frightened grazing herds that joined them in their race toward God's kingdom. Only the fish of the northern lakes, rivers, and streams were destined to remain behind, and they, to assure their safety, buried themselves under the muddy floors of their aquatic homes.

Beyond the chaos that erupted in the valley below, a thick veil of what could only be described as black smoke billowed and churned unceasing at the North's outer parameters.

Kaela was upon the border now. Fearful to enter the murky climate, he reached out his hand, shoving his palm into the wall of black smoke.

"Black mist," he whispered. He smelled his fingertips. The mist carried no scent. Glancing over his shoulder, he considered returning to the Sacred Region to gather Father's archangels so that they could see for themselves how Sin's presence affected the North, but he was too worried about Autumn, Sonnet, and his crew to delay entering the region much longer. Streaking across the border, Kaela disobeyed Lucifer's law that stated anyone entering the North, regardless of their status, must register first at the border, then at the grand cabin.

Lighting outside the cottage he had built in the center of the village, Kaela studied the damage that had been done by something other than Sin's conjuring. From where he stood, he could plainly see, even through the thick, smoky black fog, that the cabin's door had been torn from its hinges. It lay in pieces on the lawn just beyond the front porch. The swing Autumn loved was gone. Kaela suspected it had been used to knock out the porch rails that blocked his path from the porch steps to the cabin's front door. Tossing the debris aside, he stepped over the threshold. The sight he saw inside the cabin robbed his lungs of air so quickly that he could not inhale or exhale.

Splintered wood that had once been living room furniture lay everywhere, from the hallway to the kitchen to where he stood. Kaela stared, unbelieving, at the destruction that happened in the short time he was absent from Autumn's side. It wasn't the scattered furniture or the missing swing that made him scream out her name; it was the dried blood that made its path across the floor from the hallway to just about a foot away from where he stood.

Kaela tossed broken furniture from his path, picking his way through the shattered wood to check the kitchen. Dishes were broken and drinking cups were strewn everywhere. The table was over-turned. And on the floors and walls, he saw more blood.

"Autumn! Sonnet! Sonnet! Autumn!"

He was gasping now. Stumbling through the house, Kaela made his way to the hallway that led to the bedrooms. In Autumn's bedroom, Kaela spied a porch rail under a broken chair. It was covered with dried blood. Tears spilled down his cheeks unchecked as he traced the tiny red handprints on the walls with his fingertips. Pressing his forehead against what appeared to be a partial imprint inscribed in blood, he wept unashamed.

The broken furniture, the bloody fingerprints on the shutters that were torn away from the window, the furnishings that lay in pieces on the floor, revealed that a life-or-death struggle took place here.

Kaela left the cottage. Standing on the lawn, he turned in a circle. It was lighter now. He could see the destruction done to the gazebo, the lawn ornaments, and the cabin's porch.

"Autumn! Sonnet!" he shouted, terrified of what might have happened to his small brothers.

"Father, help me," he sobbed, falling to his knees in the mud that carpeted the ground. "I am Your loyal son. I am Your faithful servant. Have mercy on me, for in my desire to serve You, I neglected to protect Autumn. And now, I fear I have failed her miserably."

Kaela stretched out face-down in the mud, just as he did when he knelt before Father's throne in the Sacred Region. No words were spoken; no messenger appeared—only a whisper-soft thought as gentle and comforting as a fragrant breeze caused the sobbing angel to rise to his feet.

"I haven't searched the grounds around this cabin."

Using his angelic vision, Kaela checked every upturned clump of mud and under every toppled tree. He tossed aside the gazebo's splintered wood, clearing the ground beneath it. Blond hair mixed with the mire that covered the area lay at his feet in curly wisps. Kaela knelt to inspect his find. Lifting strands of hair from the ground, he realized that he had found Autumn.

"Oh, Father, help me!" Kaela shouted, not caring if he was heard by Lucifer's supporters. Digging with his hands, he unearthed the top of Autumn's head. "No!" Panicked now, he clawed at the dirt, digging deeper, removing welling water in his cupped hands.

"Someone—help me!" he shouted at the top of his voice. But no one came. His labor continued throughout the misty morning until, at last, he had Autumn half removed from her grave. Tugging and pulling at her beaten body did not dislodge the part of her that remained buried underground.

"Here, I'll help you," someone said.

Kaela turned to see Martyr standing behind him. He dropped to the ground, digging madly, until Autumn's entire upper torso was exposed.

"We have been recovering brothers all night. Many were stuck in the mud but were uninjured. Autumn and Sonnet were helping in the rescue. At one point, Autumn wanted to see if his cottage had been as severely damaged as some of the others." Martyr leaned into the grave, talking while he worked to free his small brother. "We had agreed that no one should do anything alone until we were certain that there would be no more eruptions. I accompanied Sonnet and Autumn to their cottage. It was fine, just minor damage, unlike the cottages that lay closer to the base of the mount. I encouraged the pair to bathe and get some rest. What happened to Autumn is not the result of the mountain's eruption—this was the result of an attack."

He wrapped his arms around Autumn's legs, just behind her knees. "Pull Autumn toward you. Grab him under his arms and jerk hard."

Kaela did as he was told. He pulled until Autumn was completely unearthed. As he sat her up against his chest, he heard her welcome coughing. "You will be all right. I'm taking you back to Father. He will heal you. And you will remain there with Him until I know it's safe to bring you back."

"Sonnet," Autumn gasped. "He tried to save me … Help Sonnet."

Kaela lifted his beloved Earth angel in his arms. To Martyr, he said, "I will be back. I have to find Sonnet and my crew."

"Your crew is working at Shadow's base," Martyr told Kaela. "They are saving brothers, just like we saved Autumn. Go, ask Father to extend His blessing to those of us who are doing His work in the North. Tell Him what happened here, and let Prince Michael know that Lucifer is putting on an aggressive show of power."

Chapter 29

Uncreation Realized

Father was preparing to leave His outdoor throne room to retire to His inner sanctum when He heard His daughters' horrified screams and mournful sobs. He turned His attention to the area that lay before His throne to see a son walking in His direction. In his arms, he carried the object of his deep affection. The closer to the throne he came, the louder and more heartbreaking were his sobs.

"Father, forgive me," a familiar voice pleaded. "Heal my child or transfer his injuries to me so that when he awakens, he will be whole and healthy."

These words, though spoken through Kaela's trembling lips, came from the creative force that lived deep within our Lord's sacred heart.

Father opened His arms to receive Autumn. Kaela rested her broken body across His lap. Our Lord reached out, touching Autumn's face lightly with His fingertips. His touch told Him that behind the cuts and bruises that discolored her cheeks and forehead, several bones had been broken. Teeth were missing, mostly in the front of her mouth, but a number of teeth had been broken in the back of her mouth, probably from biting down so very hard when the whip's braid cut through her flesh. Father lifted the bloody rags that did little to hide her wounds. Autumn had been whipped until the bones beneath her flesh were visible. Her ribs were broken, as were the bones in her fingers and knees.

Heaven's King peered down into the face of His beloved daughter. With tears welling in His eyes, He recalled Kaela's words when he placed her in His lap. "'Heal my child or transfer his injuries to me so that when he awakens, he will be whole and healthy.'"

What love! What selflessness!

Father placed His hand on Autumn's bloody face. "My child, hear my voice, you are healing, slowly but perfectly. My darling angel, you will sleep, dreaming only the most pleasant dreams, and when you awaken from your second creation, you will be whole. The realization of the attack will fade with time until you will wonder if it ever happened."

To Kaela, he said, "Take Autumn to Lucifer's former suite. Stay there until your small brother awakens."

"What about Sonnet? He is still missing," Kaela whispered as Father transferred Autumn's sleeping form into his arms.

"Stay with Autumn," Father repeated.

Autumn slept throughout the day into the night. Kaela sat in a chair beside her bed, holding her hand. Tears stained his cheeks. Agreeing to be Father's spy was a bad idea. He worried about Autumn every time he left the North for the Sacred Region. Now she was recuperating in the apartment that she remodeled for Lucifer. Sonnet was missing, and who knew what was happening in the North where Sin wove spells that changed its climate and sent its wildlife stampeding to the Sacred Region.

Kaela settled his back against the chair's soft belly. He slipped off his sandals, lifted his feet, and set them on the edge of the bed. Resting his head against the chair's wing, he closed his eyes for the first time in hours. The breeze that filtered through the window was gentle, its fragrance was sweet. In moments, Kaela was asleep.

Autumn woke to find her angel stretched out in the chair beside the bed she lay in. Quietly, so as not to disturb him, she slipped off the opposite side of the bed and made her way to the bathroom. There, she inspected her face in the mirror.

"I'm healed," she whispered to no one there. "Thank you, Father. But I must speak in private with You. I'll be seeing You soon."

Autumn found some of Lucifer's robes and cloaks, all of which she rejected because they were too long for her to wear comfortably. Leaping out the window, she made her way to her cottage where she rummaged her closet for a proper outfit. Dressed in fresh clothing, she flew to the Holy Castle. She did not stop until she set her feet down on the floor of Father's outdoor throne room. Shielding her eyes with the tips of her wings, she approached God's throne.

"Precious Father, my King, sole reason for my happiness," Autumn said as she knelt, "I come before You with a grateful heart and renewed faith in Your extraordinary powers. I humbly request permission to return with Kaela to the North to find my brother, Sonnet. He defended me when I could not defend myself, and because of my condition, I allowed him to be taken."

She lowered herself to the floor where she laid face-down before the throne. "Look deep into my heart and see that I am Your child, created by You, and saved through Your mercy. Sonnet is Your son too. He is in the North, afraid and alone. I simply hope to bring him back to the castle so that You can heal him and convince him to stay here with You until all danger has passed."

"Arise, my darling Autumn," Father said, His voice thick with love. "Your request is granted, but I cannot promise that you will find Sonnet in the same condition you were in when Kaela found you. Lucifer, under Sin's influence, sent his brutes to conduct an experiment on you and Sonnet when he learned that you betrayed him. In an attempt to uncreate what I created, Sin had both of you whipped, beaten, and buried alive to learn how much abuse your bodies could take and how long you could live without breathing air."

Autumn nodded. She knew what suffocation was.

"Father, I am going to Lucifer's apartment to awaken Kaela. After he freshens up and we get a bite to eat, we're leaving for the North to find Sonnet. Bless us so that we will be safe and know that no matter what condition Sonnet is in when I find him, I don't hold You responsible."

"My blessings are always upon you, Autumn," Father said with a loving smile. "Be aware that Sonnet sleeps not far from where you were found. He is closer to the stream than you were. Follow the footsteps in the mud. He will be there. Find your brother and return him to my kingdom."

In the suite on the castle's first floor, Autumn waited for Kaela to finish his shower. While he dressed, she amused herself by tossing a lot of Lucifer's stuff into the garbage.

"Hey, don't get rid of that," Kaela snapped as he reached into the pile of discarded trash to remove notes and penned blueprints. "Prince Michael should see some of this."

"Why?" Autumn sniffed. "This is all stuff that I drew up."

Kaela's face softened. He examined the prints he held in his hand. So they were Autumn's blueprints. Pressing them to his chest, he said, "I want to keep these." Without another word, he returned them to Lucifer's desk.

"We are burning morning hours," he told Autumn. "Sonnet is in need of our help, and we are standing here, talking."

Autumn and Kaela entered the northern region in flight. They did not stop until they reached the cottage where the assault took place.

"Father said to follow the footsteps in the mud," Autumn said, narrowing her eyes in an attempt to see more clearly through the fog that blanketed the ground and hung like a steel curtain in the air.

"What is that over there?" she asked, pointing to where the black mist teased her eyes by lifting its thick hems so that she glimpsed what appeared to be a bundle of rags. As quickly as she focused on the target of her curiosity, the mist dropped its thick skirts to the ground, successfully obstructing her vision.

Together, Autumn and Kaela cautiously approached the bundle of rags that lay in the mud.

"It's a body," Kaela whispered. Kneeling, he turned it so that he could see the face of the one who did not stir at his touch. "This brother has been badly beaten," he said softly, wiping the mud from the stricken one's face so that he could better see who it was he cradled in his arms.

"Martyr," Kaela whispered. At the sound of his name, Martyr opened his eyes. "He's alive."

Autumn fell to her knees at Martyr's side, taking his bloody hand in hers. She pressed it, palm side down, against her cheek. "Martyr. Who did this to you?" She wept at the atrocity that fatally injured her righteous brother.

Martyr swallowed hard. "Leave this place," he rasped. "Kaela, take Autumn, get out of here."

"What happened?" Kaela whispered as tears streamed from his eyes, dripping off his chin onto Martyr's face.

"After you left with Autumn," Martyr said, coughing, "our rescue team flew to Lucifer's cabin where Thummuz told us that the North is finally immune to Father's protective powers." He struggled to continue. "The dark fog that rose up around us grew thicker, and a female spirit appeared in its midst." Martyr coughed again. Blood bubbled from his mouth, spilling over his chin. The warm, thick dark-red fluid covered the hand Kaela used to cup Martyr's face. "We were told to fall to our knees and worship the Goddess." He grabbed Autumn's arm. "Her name is Sin." His voice grew hoarse and weak. "I fell to my knees, praising our Lord, our Creator. I was whipped, tossed to the side, and later dragged here to face uncreation alone."

"Where are the brothers who were on your rescue team?" Kaela whispered. Martyr's head lolled. "No. Listen to me. Where are Joniel and our Lord's faithful sons? Martyr, answer me, please." Kaela pressed his hand against his dying brother's cheek. "Please. I have to know."

Martyr could barely hold his eyes open now. He spoke in halted whispers. "Tell Father ... we refused to pledge ... our loyalty ... to the unfamiliar Goddess. Tell Him, the ground opened up ... and swallowed our brothers. I can still hear their screams."

Martyr's head lolled to the side again. He stopped speaking. He stopped breathing. His life ended.

For a long time after Martyr fell silent, Kaela sat on the ground, holding him in his arms, rocking him gently. Autumn's pitiful sobs shattered Kaela's already broken heart.

"We have to find Sonnet," Autumn whispered, still pressing the back of Martyr's hand to her cheek.

"Father, this was a bad idea," Kaela wept, his tears combining with the moisture wrought by the black fog. With a sigh, he glanced around him as though he expected to find God's Council of Angels standing by, ready to take Martyr from this region to where Father could prepare him for whatever followed uncreation.

Shifting his dead brother's body, Kaela laid it tenderly on the ground. "Sleep, precious Martyr," he whispered.

Assuming a reverent position, Kaela said, "Father, my brother, Martyr, was faithful to You always. Be gentle as You cleanse him. Heal his wounds and give him more rights than he had when he lived among us. Welcome him to Your table for his final feast, and until Heaven's peace is restored, let him sleep, never knowing the events that are to come."

He grew silent for a moment. During that time, he held Autumn in his arms. She sobbed against his chest. He let her weep. This child had never seen anyone die like this, not here or in the world she left behind.

"Come on, we have to find Sonnet, Joniel, and my apprentices."

"What about Martyr's body?" Autumn sniffed. She wiped her hands on her dripping wet cape. "What is this stuff?" She reached toward the sky as though she could catch the mist in her hands. "Why doesn't it stop?"

A bear tumbled from the forest into full view, running madly toward the border. "Will Martyr's body be safe here? Shouldn't we take it home? Or burn it? Or do something with it?"

"Martyr is with Father," Kaela said softly. "He no longer needs his body. Come. We have much work to do."

Autumn blew Martyr a kiss. "Farewell, dear brother."

Had Autumn glanced over her shoulder as she followed Kaela toward the stream whose muddy ground lay blanketed in black fog, she would have seen a flock of righteous brothers arrive to carry Martyr's body safely home. Autumn saw nothing but what lay before her. She wanted desperately to see Sonnet again. She needed to thank him for taking her part against Lucifer's sadistic ruffians.

"They think Father's influence in the North is hindered by this fog," Autumn heard herself say. "Sin called up the mist, hoping to block Father's view of this region so Lucifer could perform atrocities on righteous citizens. Little does Sin know that Father sees everything and knows about the awful experiments His faithful sons are forced to endure. Kaela, Father doesn't need to cast His light on us to see us. He knows our needs, and He provides for us. Soon, He will deliver Sonnet to us, and this nightmare will end for a little while."

Throughout the rest of the search, Autumn said nothing. Kaela knew in his heart she was praying Sonnet would be all right. As they searched, the landscape grew darker, making it necessary for them to use their angelic vision. Each mound of mud they came to offered them hope that they had found Sonnet. But each mound they dug out proved to be nothing more than an empty pile of soil. At last, they happened upon a mound that was heaped up higher and was longer than all the others. Footprints were embedded in the mire that surrounded the mound.

"I think we found Sonnet." Kaela's words were cut short by the sob that clogged his throat. Together, he and Autumn dug frantically until she felt the soft muscular structure of her brother's chest beneath her hands.

"Sonnet!" she cried.

Kaela tossed her away from the makeshift grave, digging hard and fast to unearth his brother even though he knew that what he found would not be good. After unearthing Sonnet from his head to his knees, Kaela reached into the hole and lifted him out. Holding him in his arms, he whispered against his quiet brother's ear. "You are safe now."

Using the moisture from the mist and his dripping wet robe, he wiped the thick, wet dirt from his beloved brother's head and chest. A scream sent Autumn reeling backward to the ground.

Sonnet's eyes and mouth were frozen open; his expression was one of pure horror. In an effort to revive him, Kaela turned him slightly and patted his back. A clump of mud fell from his mouth.

The poet remained quiet, unmoving. Kaela lifted him into his arms and carried him to the stream where its current ran swift and fast.

Gently, he lowered Sonnet's body into the fresh, cold water. Using the hems of his cloak, he washed the dirt from his brother's face. Peering into Sonnet's unblinking eyes, Kaela whispered, "He has been uncreated." With his fist pressed against his chest as if to calm his broken heart, he said over sobs that threatened to choke him, "We must take Sonnet back to Father. We will deal with Lucifer when we return."

Throughout the following day, God's sons and daughters labored over Sonnet's lifeless form. They washed the mud from his body, cleaned it from his mouth and teeth, and lovingly washed his curly blond hair. They washed away all traces of his ordeal in the North, even cleansing away the dirt from under the nails on his hands and feet. While grieving brothers wrapped yards of linens around the poet's body, Autumn knelt before Father's throne to request that Sonnet's remains be viewed by all of Heaven's angels. "So our brothers will at last know the severity of the word *uncreated*."

When she returned to the room where Sonnet lay, she draped the chair with the clothing she had chosen for his public viewing. "Ready the auditorium," she told her sisters. "Put flowers on the stage. Tell the carpenters and weavers that Sonnet will need a box to rest in while grieving brothers file by to pay their final respects."

Sonnet's coffin sat in the center of the main auditorium's spacious stage. He was beautiful. His expression was no longer frozen in horror. His cloudy, lifeless eyes were closed so tightly that his long blond lashes touched his cheeks. Large pots of flowers lined the theater's aisles. Israfel's choir members stood at the head and the foot of the coffin. Their voices, accompanied by Zephon's violin, echoed through the structure's open doors to the garden outside. While Israfel sang songs of love and truth that Sonnet wrote to honor Father and his sisters, righteous and rebellious sons paid their final respects to their fallen brother. Archangel Effiel stood at the top of the stairs, greeting all those who came to honor the poet with their presence. At the coffin mourners paused to look in at their beloved brother, Sonnet. As they left the stage, they stopped to offer their condolences to Kaela and Autumn.

The Goddesses were among the last to view the uncreated angel's body. They touched his cold hands, kissed his forehead, and arranged rose petals on his pillow so that they formed a fragrant halo around his head. While Kaela sat staring at the floor, hating himself, wishing it had been him who had died and not Sonnet, Heaven's royalty knelt before Autumn, wiping her tears with their long silver hair, whispering words of encouragement that comforted her wounded heart. Hearing their expressed reassurances, Kaela was flooded with guilt worse than any he had ever known.

It was time now. The coffin lid was closed. Autumn's gasp was heard by all. With her hand pressed to her heart, she collapsed into tears.

The six who carried the coffin to the auditorium lifted it from the pedestal on which it sat. Autumn and Kaela followed the procession from the stage to God's Garden of Meditation where Sonnet would be buried next to Martyr. Outside the castle, beyond the wide porch, the sky throughout the region turned lavender, the celestial sign of grief.

Moments before the globe's almighty Lord retired to His inner sanctum, Sonnet's coffin was lowered into its grave. Autumn's grief spilled out as one shovel of dirt after another fell onto the coffin's polished oak lid. The earth that rose up inside the grave would separate her from Sonnet forever, and that knowledge brought on a new onslaught of wrenching sobs. When the grave was closed, a stone was erected that read, "'This soul in flight from misery, abandoned Heaven's shores for eternity. Here sleeps the gentle angel Sonnet … Forever loved by Autumn and Kaela.'"

Throughout that night and the following day, Autumn sat like a sentinel at the head of Sonnet's grave. She did not hunger; she did not want for sleep. She was aware of nothing that went on around her. She knew only her grief.

On the third day, she rose to her feet, leaned and kissed the stone that carried Sonnet's name and the testimony of her love for him, and made her way to the cottage she once shared with Kaela. This was where her memories of Heaven began. She went inside. In the bedroom, she took off her robe and cloak, exchanging them for the uniform she wore in the North. With a sigh, she fell back onto the bed, and within minutes, she was asleep.

"Autumn, are you here?" It was Kaela.

"Yes," Autumn called. "Yes, I was sleeping." She sat up in bed. Her face was wet from the tears she shed while she slept.

"Go back to sleep if you are tired," her angel told her. "I just came to see if you were all right and to let you know that we will be leaving for the North later this afternoon."

Outside the Holy Castle, Kaela spoke with Prince Michael while Autumn said her farewells to Father, her sisters, Scribe Excelsa, and Archangel Effiel. When she reached her angel's side, she heard him say, "I will return with information concerning Lucifer's activities, but I will not speak of them before our Lord's Council of Advisors. One of His council members is Lucifer's spy. I will continue working in the North for Father, but I've seen the misery that speaking out of turn brings, and because of my ignorance, I will carry the guilt of Sonnet's uncreation with me forever."

Prince Michael whispered, "I have been training my athletes in what I call war games. They will carry their weapons on their bodies so that they will be prepared to defend themselves."

"Here," Autumn said, reaching into her tunic's pocket. "It's a blueprint for a weapons' belt. Kaela designed it after he visited Azazel's work-shop. He tossed the blueprint into the trash. He thought the idea was ridiculous, I thought it was ingenious. Take the blueprint to Origen."

Kaela placed one hand on Autumn's shoulder. "Are you ready to return to the North?"

"I am," she answered. "We must return. Our crew is missing. They will think we deserted them." With those words, the pair lifted from the ground, setting their sights on the North.

At the guardhouse on the northern parameter, they signed the register before hurrying on their way. Lucifer's empire had become a cold, dark place. Thick black fog rolled across the vicinity, blocking God's nourishing light. The air in the region was filled with the sickening scent of blood, with shrieks of agony, shouts of anger, and the horrifying sound of whips cutting flesh—*thwack, thwack, thwack!*

Trembling with fear and dreadfully weary, Autumn wept when she saw the gaping mouths of slave pits. Her angelic vision revealed their contents: half-naked mud-covered prisoners clung to one another as a last hope. Instinctively, she knew these were brothers who refused to reform to Lucifer's evil ways. Autumn gagged. Nausea gripped her so that she could not maintain her altitude. Too weak from grief, too worn by despair, she sank several feet toward the muddy ground below before she felt Kaela's strong arms tighten around her.

"I've got you," Kaela whispered against her temple. "I will not allow you to be harmed."

"My prayer is that Father stops His evil sons," Autumn told her angel. "I believe that when Lucifer's followers are imprisoned, they will miss their freedom simply because they tasted its sweetness when they lived in God's kingdom." She felt better now.

"Are we going to search for Joniel, or are we going to fly around all day?" Autumn asked. Her expression of determination, her willingness to risk her life, and her desire to do God's work moved Kaela. Her angel nodded, releasing her into the air. "Well, then, let's go. The day is half over, and this fog will grow thicker by the hour as night approaches."

Chapter 30

Black Palace Meeting

On the morning after they returned to the North, Kaela and Autumn glided cautiously through the air toward Lucifer's dark palace. The dark mist that rose up around them was denser now than it had ever been. Autumn noted that visibility was so poor even using angelic vision made the ground below looked surreal. Droplets of humidity that the black mist produced soaked the landscape, causing trees to rot and topple onto muddy soil that had once been carpeted with bushes, shrubs, and tender grasses. Autumn drew the collar of her tunic over the bottom of her face to block out the stench of rotting vegetation, which was made even more repulsive by the scent of her innocent brothers' blood.

Drifting closer to Kaela, Autumn asked, "What's the plan?" When Kaela did not answer, she said, "Surely word has reached him about the funeral in the Sacred Region. Lucifer is cold and calculating, but he is not brave. By now, he has most likely surrounded himself with guards. How do you suppose we will get into see him? I mean, we left his region without his per—"

"We will barge in," Kaela told her. When he accepted Scribe Excelsa's request to act as Father's spy, he had hoped the information he took to the Sacred Region from the North would cause Prince Michael's sainted peace-keepers to apprehend his eldest brother as they had when Lucifer circulated a false story that removed God from all creation. Like Prince Michael, Kaela believed that putting Lucifer under lock and key would cause his followers to disperse, and peace would reign in Heaven. Instead, his trespasses were overlooked. It was almost as though only a chosen few knew that Lucifer set up an empire in the North where he drew up insane laws denying his citizens the same rights Father's sons enjoyed every day. It almost seemed that Father loved Lucifer so much He could not bear to see him brought to justice for fear he might be harmed.

Kaela shook his head slowly. No. If that were the case, Father would be an accomplice in all the grief happening in the North.

Confused, weary, and riddled with guilt, Kaela drifted through frosty air that wet the feathers on his wings and drenched his hair and clothing. "Get ready," he told Autumn. "We are approaching the palace. We are in line with its highest, uppermost balconies. I see four guards. There may be more. Ignore the guards, don't stop. Just follow me. We are going to fly across the main balcony, through the wide arches that lead to the thrones. We will stop there."

"Oh, Father, please be with us," Autumn prayed.

God's unspoken voice whispered softly in her ear that regardless of what she suffered, He would not allow her to perish.

"Thank you."

Now, Autumn focused on the guards below. They had been spotted. "They are aiming their arrows at us!" Autumn shouted. Her heart was no longer pounding; it was rolling in her chest, and though she feared for her safety, she remained at Kaela's side.

"Halt!" the guards shouted, aiming their armed bows at the intruders. Arrows pierced the air. Kaela and Autumn instinctively curled their wings around their bodies. The arrows, whose steel tips would have met their marks, bounced off powerful wings and fell to the ground below. Spiraling like missiles, the pair crossed over the coal-black floor of the outdoor balcony, moving with great speed under the wide-open arches through the interior of the royal chamber. Kaela and Autumn slowed their approach, unfurling their wings, and set their feet down on the ebony floor that stretched out before the onyx thrones Lucifer and Sin occupied.

Lucifer rose from his seat, glaring menacingly at Kaela first, then at Autumn. "You left this region without my permission to return your uncreated brothers to the Sacred Region."

"You should thank us for returning the bodies of Martyr and Sonnet to the Sacred Region," Kaela replied. "When Autumn and I lay the bodies at the base of God's throne, it proved to Him that you have the power to uncreate what He created. But why did you uncreate Sonnet? He was our beloved brother, he was faithful to you, and readily did your bidding. Just the same, your heartless act proved to God that you are to be feared and respected."

Lucifer glared at Autumn. "What is your story? Tell me, before I have you both dragged out of here to face a worse punishment than either of you ever thought you could suffer."

"Don't blame Kaela," Autumn said, fixing her eyes on Lucifer's face. "It was my idea to take the bodies to the Sacred Region. Kaela wanted to tell you our plan, but I told him that you would never listen and that time was of the essence. He wanted to sign the registers before we left. I told him that I am not into such nonsense."

"You call my father's laws nonsense?" Sin shouted.

"With all due respect, Sin, shut up!" Autumn growled. "I am not talking to you." She glared at the astonished Goddess. "You are no more than an idea that fleets across someone's mind. Most of us choose to ignore your whispered annoyances since they are designed to suit your agenda and not ours."

Autumn turned to Lucifer. "Great Lucifer, I will not harken to the shouts of your guards or take commands from Sin because my time belongs to you and no one else. I respect only you, great sire. If you wish to uncreate me, then let this conversation end so that your will can be done in the North. I am your servant, and your every wish is my command."

"Kneel before me, Autumn," Lucifer demanded.

"No. I will not dishonor you by kneeling before you," she said, her heart pounding so wildly she could hear it beating in her ears. Didn't she just tell him his every wish was her command? And now, she was refusing to kneel before him. She sent a silent prayer to Father. Her only message to Heaven's King was "'help me'." Now, more words that were not hers fell from her lips. "I will not lower my great emperor to his Enemy's status by falling to my knees. The Great Lucifer is a leader of warriors, not a keeper of servants who must appease his ego by falling to their knees to worship him."

Lucifer glanced at Kaela, who stared at his small beloved brother with his brows drawn high on his forehead.

"Do you see how Autumn's mind works?" the false emperor asked. "Autumn studied with Scribe Excelsa and is as wise as God's holy scribe."

He reached to touch Autumn's shoulder but withdrew his hand. "I admire your brilliance, Autumn. I admire your ability to separate the great respect you have for me from the lowly respect you had for God." He turned and took his seat next to his daughter. "I command you to obey Sin while you live and breathe in my region. Now, why did you come to me in this disrespectful way? What is the purpose for your visit?" Kaela opened his mouth to speak. "Let Autumn explain your arrival to me."

"We need your permission, great sire, to search the region for our beloved crew members," Autumn told Lucifer. "That is why we are here. Now, it is up to you to make your decision by which Kaela will abide. As for me, I already know what I am going to do. I am going to search for our apprentice carpenters to assure that they did not betray you by leaving the region to serve your enemy. And then, I am going to celebrate our reunion."

"This child is truthful and courageous," Lucifer said, smiling affectionately at Autumn. "But know that someday I will tire of your boldness. On that day, the whipping you will receive from me will make you wish you had never left the Sacred Region." He waved the pair away. "Go, find your crew."

Without bowing or kneeling, Kaela and Autumn left the dark palace the same way they entered it.

Outside, Kaela asked, "What was that? I told you I would do the talking, didn't I?"

"Yes, you did," Autumn said with a nod of her head. "But the words I spoke to Lucifer and Sin weren't mine."

Throughout the remainder of the day and into the darkness of night, Kaela and Autumn searched for the members of their crew.

Weeks passed since they began their search, and so far, the leads they received from northern council members concerning the possible whereabouts of Joniel and their carpenters led them from one dead end to another.

The pair lighted simultaneously on the slick onyx floor of the dark palace's fore-hall. Crossing the dark foyer, they avoided making eye contact with the guards that lingered in the shadows. Without a word to each other, they took the many flights of stairs that led to Lucifer's throne room.

"Once again, you have come to me unannounced," Lucifer chastised, rising from his onyx throne to go out onto his balcony. At this height, the atrocities committed against the region's merchants and innocent citizens were hidden from his view. He could see nothing but the dense fog that darkened the northern landscape below. Behind him, the incessant sound of dew draining from the overhang that protected the thrones and the throne room's slick onyx floor from the elements all but stifled the screams of tormented slaves. "Why are you here?"

"We are searching the region for our apprentices," Kaela told his eldest brother.

"Have you checked the pits?" he asked. "Last I heard—they were clipped and pitted." He burst out laughing. "Look at your face. Your expression never changes. Are you not shocked to learn that your friends were not immune to my anger? How long do you think I will put up with you before I have you clipped and pitted? I could do it now. My law reads that no one shall approach the emperor's outdoor throne room unannounced. Another of my laws read that when in my presence, one must kneel."

"I don't kneel before God or angel, so have me clipped and pitted, uncreated, or whichever comes first," Kaela growled. Sin entered the throne room clad in a web that did little to hide her physical attributes. Kaela sneered; the sight of Lucifer's perverse daughter offended him. "Do you ever get cold?" He asked the witch.

Lucifer burst out laughing. "Come. Sit with us. We have some sad stories to share with you." He bid Kaela take the throne Sin would have occupied. "As you know, I have spies in God's kingdom. Something is up. I think you know what I mean. Something is happening that my

Enemy is keeping to Himself, and no one knows what it is but His chosen few. Are you one of His chosen few, Kaela? Has He revealed something to you that you are keeping from me?"

Sin offered Kaela a cup of warm nectar.

"I only know what I am told or what I overhear while I am creeping around the Holy Castle," Kaela hissed defiantly. "It would be so much easier for me to acquire more information about God and saints if I knew who all your so-called spies are. We could exchange information and make comparisons, but unfortunately—" He stopped talking for a moment, dumping the warm nectar from his cup to the floor. "I've answered your questions. Now answer mine: where are my brothers?"

Lucifer glared at Kaela. Then his eyes softened. "Yesterday, Flagitious told me they were escorted from a place of torment to Rive's shop where they were clipped and confined to a pit," the emperor draped his arm over his daughter's shoulder. "The counselor did not tell me the location of the pit, but then, I never asked, so I don't know where your associates are." He smiled, pausing to nuzzle Sin's ear and neck. "You should be more careful, Kaela," Lucifer said, his voice haughty, his eyes fixed on Kaela's face. "It seems that every time you leave the region without my permission, you lose more of your apprentices." Sin moved away from her father, positioning herself between him and Kaela.

"Here is what you lost, great Lucifer," Kaela hissed. "My crew is trained to protect you from your Enemy should He attack. You allowed Rive to clip my trained warriors' wings. Without the use of their wings, not only will they fall victim to your Enemy, but so will you and your witch. You had best know how to use a sword, great Lucifer, because I will be too busy fighting to save my worthless hide to worry about the likes of you." He shoved Sin aside as he made his way to where the emperor stood. "Let's hope that your order to maim my warriors will not end in your undoing."

"You are the most arrogant," Lucifer growled, tossing his nectar-filled cup across the room. "I command you to defend me if God's saints burst through those clouds, or I will—"

"Or you will what?" Kaela snarled. "Have me clipped and pitted? Or will you uncreate me? Do it. Don't hesitate to do whatever you will to me. I would be honored to die at your hand. But presently, I have to remove my warriors from your pit. Know this, if I don't find my crew members, I will uncreate the guards at your door, and then, I will come for you and the witch."

"Autumn will stay with us," Lucifer told Kaela. He motioned for guards to hold Autumn so that she could not free herself to join her angel in his search. "We have notes from meetings that we have held over the weeks while the two of you were absent from your duties. That alone is punishable by uncreation." He smiled at Autumn. "But for now, I need my scribe, so go, Kaela, find your apprentices. Take them to God, and let Him do His work. Then bring them back to my empire where they will protect me and my daughter from our Enemy."

Kaela lifted from the balcony, descending to the ground below. Autumn would distract Lucifer and Sin while he went about his business. She was really into this part of playing scribe.

Eons had passed since Kaela introduced Autumn to Heaven. During that time, she saw how important it was to Lucifer to set himself apart from his brothers. She played a major role in the exploration that led to Archangel Lucifer's betrayal of Michael's athletes. She watched Lucifer's climb from God's pampered pet to His vindictive prince. Autumn saw how through deceit and false promises, Prince Lucifer gained a following of supporters. She migrated north where she helped make the region productive. She witnessed Sin's birth. Autumn saw how envy brought Lucifer low in God's kingdom and how he became the globe's first dictator.

Presently, Autumn was living through Heaven's most dreadful era. She had lost a dear friend, one of the first of many to experience uncreation at the hands of Lucifer's cabinet members. She saw brothers being clipped and pitted, whipped, and enslaved simply because they chose to remain loyal to Father. These vicious crimes were routine now. Anyone who refused to recognize Emperor Lucifer as the rightful heir to Heaven's throne was beaten or buried alive, or both. Through it all, Kaela thought only of Autumn's safety. He was her guardian, and he was responsible to see to her well-being.

By evening, Kaela was exhausted. The search for his crew of Godly co-workers was becoming an obsession, but he had to know if they were all right. He crossed the landscape made muddy by incessant rains and heavy fog to enter still another pit—a new pit. He spoke briefly with the guard before making his way down the pit's slick sides.

"I am looking for Joniel and my former apprentices," he said, fixing his gaze on the rain-drenched warrior's face. "Are they in this pit?" He turned away from the warrior, focusing his angelic vision on the mud-covered prisoners who sat crumpled on the ground, exposed to the elements.

"Never mind, I see Joniel." He hurried to where his friend sat, muddy, half-naked, and covered in his own blood.

"Well, it's about time," Joniel grunted. He was clearly in pain since his wounds were fresh.

"What happened?" Kaela asked. Prisoners who recognized him moved closer to where he stood. Their eyes were filled with hope.

"Stand down and no one will get hurt," Kaela warned. During his search, he had seen hope turn to hate. Three members of his crew walked toward him. "I am here to help you," he told them. "I have been searching for you for days, for weeks."

"There is a rumor about you, Kaela," one sadly beaten brother said. "We are told you have become a flesh-eater. We are told that we should not trust you because you soften your calloused hands with our blood. There is a word that the warriors use when they speak of you—they call you *monster*."

"That rumor can work for us," Kaela motioned his crew closer to where he stood. "I might be able to use that story to free some of my brothers from this horrible existence. But you will be freed because I have convinced our false emperor that you will protect him if our Lord attacks. I have Lucifer's permission to escort you to God's kingdom, where you will be healed. If your heart is weary and you do not wish to return to the North, stay where you are safe. But I need eyes and ears here, and I would appreciate it very much if you would return with me."

Joniel groaned. Pain fed furiously on the stubs that had once been his wings. The injured angel cringed, bowed his back, and tried to feel his wounds with his muddy hands. "After the palace rose up from the bowels of the mountain, Lucifer called a special worship service in its courtyard. Martyr was seated with me. Sin appeared. Most of our brothers were unaware that she existed. She started dancing. The warriors were swaying from side to side, singing Lucifer's praises, and worshipping at the altar of the great Lucifer. Then our false brother quieted the room. He demanded that we stand. After we were all standing, he demanded that we fall to our knees and worship Sin as our queen. Those of us who refused were swallowed up in darkness. I think it was a spell woven by the witch that produced those results. We were dragged to a place—I don't know where. We were tortured for what seemed like forever. I don't know what happened to Martyr."

"He was uncreated, so was Sonnet," Kaela told his bruised and bloody brother. "I'm sorry."

"Yesterday, guards came in and dragged us from the place of our torment to Rive's shop. We were forced to extend our wings. Rive hacked them off with an axe. Now we are scattered. I have no idea where the others are." Tears welled in his eyes, spilling in rivulets down his cheeks. "Percible was clinging to me. They tore him away. They were beating him when they brought me here. Now, I'm one of them." He pointed to three angels trying to garner warmth from one another by huddling together, but regardless of what they did, the drizzling cold rain and thick fog sapped every fragment of warmth from their trembling bodies. "They are set for execution because they admitted that they were working for Father. Help them, Kaela."

"I can't leave you here like this," Kaela replied.

During his search, he had seen brothers being clipped. It was a gruesomely painful crime against angelic flesh. Perhaps that is when his reputation suffered and flesh-eater was added to his name. He jokingly referred to one newly clipped angel as lunch before spiriting him from the North to be healed by Father. Since his brother never returned, Lucifer's guards must have decided that Kaela ate him. He would have laughed, but seeing his best friend in this condition broke his heart. Once again, his absence from the North brought pain to those he loved. He never should have followed the night-flyer to the Holy City. He never should have stayed in the Sacred Region to see to Sonnet's burial. If only he had been here, this travesty against God's sons never would have happened. "Autumn thinks she knows who the spy is."

"Stop him, but help our brothers first," Joniel pleaded. "And, please, find Percible, and those whose skills we depend on."

Kaela turned away from Joniel, walking to where Celone, Japeth, and Ramael sat in the mud, clinging to each other, weeping. He examined the stripes on their backs. Though he did not do this to them, he felt as responsible for their wounds as if it were his whip that tasted their flesh and licked hungrily at the blood drawn by its braid. One day, he might be forced to obey the order that would strip the backs of the brothers he loved, and though what he did would result in their freedom, he would ask himself day and night, "'What kind of coward am I that I would assault what my Lord created?'" Turning away from the whimpering prisoners, he called to Artiff, the pit's hateful guard.

"They smell fresh," he said, referring to the blood scent. "I want these three."

"You must be especially hungry tonight, Kaela." Artiff said, tossing chains to him. "Be sure to bind them tightly. We don't want anyone to escape."

"Who cares if they escape?" Kaela said, encouraging the three slaves to stand. "I am going to uncreate them. It would be more exciting to have to chase after them, search for them, and then uncreate them."

He dragged God's righteous sons up the side of the pit, forcing them to stand on their own at the pit's sloppy rain-drenched brim.

He shoved Ramael. "Move it. I don't have all night. I have to report back to the great Lucifer by morning." Ramael, Celone, and Japeth refused to move. When they were Kaela's apprentices, they respected him but now, they questioned his loyalty to God.

Sooner than he thought was possible, Kaela did the unthinkable. He robbed Artiff of his whip and sent its braid flying through the air. The blood-starved braid did not stop until it sliced deep into Ramael's flesh. The angel screamed and fell to his knees. Kaela grabbed him by the arm, forcing him to stand. Tossing the whip aside, he grasped the chain that bound the three slaves. Turning Ramael to face him, Kaela hissed, "You will do as I say, or you will know uncreation."

Celone and Japeth struggled to free themselves, but they were weak, and easily overpowered. Their will gone, all hope extinguished, the three angels allowed their former mentor to lead them deep into the forest.

Hidden by the fog that drowned the trees and vegetation, the prisoners were ordered to stop walking. Ramael glared into Kaela's face as he extended his hands on command and waited while the chains were removed. "So what will you do with me now, Kaela? Feast on my flesh and bathe in my blood? That's the rumor—"

"If you know that my blood-lust is a rumor," Kaela said, his eyes fixed on Ramael's face, "then you know that what I did to you and the others had to be done so that Father's work could continue in the North."

He freed Japeth and Celone. "I am releasing you from your bonds so that you can more easily make your way through this forest to the safety of the Sacred Region." He smiled into their astonished faces. "I am not going to eat your flesh or drink your blood. And I want you to know that I never meant to harm you. But as Father's spy, as His emissary in the North, I must not only obey Him and do His bidding but I must also obey Lucifer's commands. I am no good to anyone if I am discovered."

"Come with us," Ramael urged. "Quit this facade. Save yourself."

Kaela shook his head. "I won't abandon my mission." He studied their faces. "Stay on this path. It will lead you to a forest that rises up at the base of Father's high hill. The leafy trees will hide you until you reach the open field behind the stadium. Be very careful when you cross it to the Holy Castle. When you reach Father's house, speak to no one but Prince Michael. He will take you to Father where you will be healed and cleansed. Tell Father the situation here is dire. Tell Him His saints should hone their skills in weaponry and martial arts. Ask Him to bless the plan I have that may lead to the liberation of over one million brothers."

Kaela hugged each of his former apprentices. "Go. Don't come back here. Discourage anyone who longs to be a hero to stay away from the North. Japeth, tell Father I love Him." Kaela's heart broke, and his voice trembled. He longed to live in Father's light again, but that was impossible.

A twig cracked. Kaela turned in the direction of the sound. Turning back to his brothers, he whispered, "You must go now. I will follow behind you for a short distance to assure you safety. Then I will return to this area. There is a fox den over there. I will stay in it until morning. Tell no one but Father that it was I who saved you. Give me your word."

"You've got my word," Celone said.

"And mine." Japeth nodded.

"You can count on me to keep your secret," Ramael promised.

"Go. Be careful," Kaela told them. "Do what I told you, and you will be safe."

"We will see you again," Japeth whispered.

"In God's kingdom, not here," Kaela said firmly.

The three brothers he trained in carpentry eons ago turned and walked away. Before the dark forest swallowed them, Celone looked over his shoulder. Kaela waved to him. True to his word, he followed behind them for a while, and then he made his way to the fox's den, where he stayed until morning.

Standing on the throne room's high, dark porch, Autumn used her angelic vision to break through the fog to search the muddy landscape for signs of Kaela's return. His outspoken disrespect for Lucifer and Sin since Sonnet's death made him a legend. Word on the streets in the North regarding Kaela's relentless appetite for blood and violence reached God's kingdom. Righteous souls cringed when they learned it was Kaela's whip that stripped the backs of captive slaves. Rumor rightfully had it that Kaela roamed the pits every night, searching for survivors of heinous crimes, but he did not make sport of them, nor did he lead them to obscure locations where he fed on their flesh and bathed in their blood. Instead, Kaela dragged his weeping brothers from the pits to spirit them, under cover of the North's dark, murky nights, to the safety of the Sacred Region.

Autumn turned to face Lucifer. Would he be as arrogant if he knew that a plan was in place to rob him of his slaves and reunite righteous souls with God? Recently, a pit that was deeper than most had been excavated at the base of the mountain that shadowed its southeastern slope. Following the false emperor's orders, Kaela and his apprentices worked to deepen the pit. While they dug, they found a shallow cavern. The cave was no deeper in depth than one of the rooms at the grand cottage, but the small cave would act as a cover until a tunnel was in place. The tunnel would run from the North to the Sacred Region, and it would serve as an escape route for millions of suffering and broken slaves. The only hold up: God's precious daughters labeled Kaela questionable, and until he re-earned their respect, his plan was going nowhere.

CHAPTER 31

Repeat After Me

In the days that followed the liberation of three of his apprentices, Kaela successfully led several more brothers to safety. But he could not convince Lucifer to keep his promise that Joniel would be transported to the Sacred Region where he would be healed. The injured angel suffered miserably in an upstairs bedroom at the grand cottage while Kaela and Autumn prepared to leave the North for God's castle. Together, in the dead of night, they crossed over an unguarded section of the border, keeping close to the treetops as they flew. It wasn't until they reached the open field that stretched out wide and flat behind the stadium on Father's lawn that they set their feet on the ground. As they approached the Holy Castle, Autumn turned to walk backward, her eyes scanning the sky for northern intruders.

Kaela made his way to the side door. He, too, paused to scan the open field and the area around the stadium for intruders. Seeing the grounds were clear, he opened the door. On his mark, Autumn ducked inside, where he joined her. Together, they walked in utmost silence through the Holy Castle's labyrinth of hallways and staircases until they arrived at the door of a suite that they opened without knocking.

"We've been waiting for you," Prince Michael said as they entered the room.

"We want to enlist in your army, Prince Michael," Kaela blurted out. "Autumn and I talked it over, and we concluded that after our induction into your service, we will return to the North, free as many of our captive brothers from their bonds as possible, then we will return here where we will make our loyalty known by openly pledging our allegiance to our King during one of His festivals."

Prince Michael shook his head. "You can't join my army." He saw Kaela's face flush. "I know that you are proficient in what you do and that you bring me the information I use to keep our borders safe, but your long-standing association with Father's enemy throws suspicion on you. My troops would never accept your presence in my service since you wisely insist on keeping your work in the North a secret."

Scribe Excelsa agreed with the prince. "The prince cannot have a bunch of suspicious soldiers concentrating their time trying to catch you two up in something. They need to concentrate on Lucifer and his followers. And besides, our sisters think you both went rogue."

"Then why not induct us into God's service secretly?" Autumn suggested. "No one needs to know."

Archangel Effiel entered the conversation, his faced masked with worry. "Kaela, Autumn, you both have changed so much since you left Father's region. Are you willing to put yourselves in further jeopardy by taking this oath to God and His citizens?" He fixed his eyes on Kaela. "There are some who say you both are as evil as Lucifer. We have heard stories, Kaela, of how you feast on angelic flesh, bathe in righteous blood, and it is a known fact that your whip scars the backs of Lucifer's slaves."

Excelsa nodded in agreement. "Prince Michael's soldiers would rejoice at your uncreation."

Kaela paced before Autumn and his three righteous brothers. "Have you forgotten that this was not my chosen occupation? I was commissioned by divine decree to give up everything I hold dear to maintain Heaven's peace." Scribe Excelsa looked away. He knew that what Kaela said was true, but he didn't want to hear the words he spoke. "This evil did not overpower the North in one fell swoop. It started here, in this house, and it spread unchecked throughout this entire region. We know its name: Lucifer. But we chose to believe he was better than us because he sat in God's presence. Did he? Did he really sit in Father's presence, day and night, like he said? Or did he sleep at night like the rest of us? We were so naive that we believed everything Lucifer told us without question."

Autumn nodded toward Excelsa. "Yes, we were ignorant in our innocence, but you always knew the answers to the questions Kaela asked. You knew Lucifer was a fraud. You saw what happened in the throne room day after day, and you were aware that Lucifer was not present in Father's inner sanctum at night, but you and our sisters kept quiet, allowing us to believe Lucifer's lies."

"We weren't wise enough to see the truth; therefore we are not the reason behind this awful situation." Kaela glanced at Autumn then back at the others. "Had it not been for Autumn's coaching, Joniel, Abdiel, and I would still be seated at my table, drinking nectar and waiting for word from Lucifer that Father had either finally accepted or finally denied my request to start a sawmill on Courage. Do you understand what I am saying? Maybe we, not Father, should put an end to Lucifer's false reign in the North by putting an end to Lucifer."

Autumn glanced around the room at her brothers who had grown silent. Speaking more to Excelsa than Effiel or Prince Michael, she said, "Looking back on all that's happened since we left the Sacred Region, it is hard to recall when Kaela and I were like you. We didn't know the meaning of uncreation, torture, atrocities, perversions, lies, lust, slavery, prisoners, spying, and hatred. We were innocent. We put ourselves in harm's way, faithful that Father would not allow us to perish. And here we are. Alive." She wet her lips and continued with what she had to say. "Evil dwells in Heaven because it gained strength through your indifference toward it. It established its voice in our society because you did nothing to stop it. God gave Heaven to His sons, so maybe He expects His sons to preserve all that is good and decent here."

Kaela spoke again. "You don't have a clue how it feels to wake up every morning and go to bed every night of your life asking yourself, If you had been in a certain place at a certain time, would your dear brother still be alive? My heart is heavy with guilt because while I followed a night-flyer through the sky to the Holy City, Autumn was being beaten and buried alive by Lucifer's courtiers, Sonnet was uncreated, and my entire crew disappeared. When I found Joniel, he had already been clipped and pitted."

Autumn took up the argument from there. "Have you ever seen the North? It's a dismal place. The vegetation there is almost gone. The grasses and trees are drowning in mud that was once solid ground rich in nutrients. And there are pits. The common punishment for anyone who poses a flight risk is to be clipped and pitted. Did you ever see what wings that have been freshly hacked off a brother's back with an axe look like? Did you know that our wings have tender nerves running through them so that when they are dislodged from our bodies, they flop on the ground for several minutes before they expire? It's a terrifying sight—and the scent of blood is sickening."

Her eyes welled with tears that spilled down her cheeks to drip off her chin. "Through it all, God's believers who act as His spies must square their shoulders and pretend not to hear the screams of the tormented. Worse than their screams is the laughter of Lucifer's perverse warriors. They aren't angels anymore. Lucifer and his followers are something else."

"Demons," Scribe Excelsa whispered. He rose from his chair. "What is not Godly is demonic. If God is inherently good, then Lucifer and his supporters who share his blood-lust are inherently evil."

"Why doesn't Father just destroy Lucifer?" Archangel Effiel asked desperately.

"If Father starts destroying everyone who crosses Him, He will be seen as a weak leader," Kaela said quietly. "This is our battle. An angel started it, angels must end it. But we cannot have brothers going North, who are not properly trained in combat. They could be captured, tortured, and uncreated."

"Then what do we do?" Effiel asked.

"Exactly what we are doing," Kaela replied. "We must secret our suffering brothers back to the safety of Father's kingdom."

"And we have a plan," Autumn added, her large gray eyes widened with excitement.

Kaela reached into his shirt and pulled out a rolled scroll. "I offer this to you, Prince Michael, for your inspection. If you think the plan is worthy of Father's attention, present it to Him." Kaela sank into the sofa beside Autumn and watched intently as Prince Michael pored over his blueprints.

After what seemed a short eternity, the prince glanced from the sketches to where his brothers sat. "Am I to understand that you intend to dig a tunnel through the mountain from the North to the Sacred Region? According to this sketch, you will enter through the southeastern side of the mountain, using a slave pit as your cover." Prince Michael's furrowed forehead revealed his doubt that Kaela's mission would succeed. "What if Lucifer's warriors stumble onto your work?"

"We will be uncreated," Autumn and Kaela said in unison.

Prince Michael's gaze moved from their faces to Excelsa's. He focused on the pair and asked, "Are you not concerned for your safety?"

"What safety?" Autumn asked, shrugging slightly. "If we get caught leaving Father's house today, we will be uncreated. So what do we care why, when, or where the end will come?"

"I am hoping Autumn is wrong about Belial being Lucifer's spy." Kaela sighed. "I ask you both to warn Father and to do all that you can to keep our Lord's legal matters from Belial. It will be hard since he is the royal family's counselor, but it must be done." He looked from Excelsa to Michael. "Now a question for you, Prince Michael: are you going to induct us into your service, or are we wasting our time here?"

"Induct them into your service, Prince Michael," Scribe Excelsa urged. "They are already saints."

Prince Michael rubbed his brow with his fingertips and leaned back in the chair he occupied. With a deep sigh and an expression of profound concern, he said, "You are two of the most courageous brothers I am honored to know. And, while I hesitate to do this, it must be done before I can accept your plan to tunnel through the mountain. Please rise and stand at attention." The prince stood with Kaela and Autumn. "Now, repeat after me —"

After Kaela and Autumn were inducted into God's army, Scribe Excelsa rose from his chair and paced before them.

"Listen closely to what I am about to tell you: this afternoon, Father met with me and our sisters. He told us that He will relinquish

His throne to His anointed Son. Presently, no such son exists which indicates to me that Father will surrender His crown and scepter to a newly created deity. Tomorrow, Father will inform His council members, including Belial, whom you distrust, of His plan to step down from His high position in Heaven."

Autumn stepped forward. "Is Father serious about relinquishing His rule to a new king? Or is this a plot to upset Lucifer's apple-cart?"

The scribe smiled. "You have quite a way with words, Autumn. In answer to both of your questions, Father is very serious about stepping down as Heaven's King. Be comforted knowing that meetings are being scheduled so our Lord can discuss His plans with His concerned citizens."

Excelsa took his seat at Prince Michael's desk. "Archangel Effiel, fetch Percible. He will be glad to know that he is returning to the North where he and Kaela will continue working for Heaven's greater good."

Chapter 32

Freedom Mountain

Autumn and Kaela were stunned but overjoyed to see their companion enter the room.

"I escaped," Percible told Kaela after a tearful reunion. "I fought off Moloch, Nesroc, and Rive. I flew through the fog and rain until I reached Father's house. He healed me, bathed me, clothed me, and prepared a meal for me. I ate from His table, and I slept here in His house. The next day, I joined Prince Michael's army. I am ready to report to you for duty. I am anxious to save my oppressed brothers from their torment." He studied Kaela's face, his emerald eyes glistening with unshed tears. "How are Joniel and the others?" The answer to his question revealed that his crew members had been found, and while they chose to remain in the pit, Joniel was safely recuperating in the grand cabin. "When are we leaving for North? I am anxious to see the expression on Lucifer's face when he sees that I am alive."

"You may go now," Prince Michael told his brothers. "There is nothing I can tell you about the North or how to deal with Lucifer and his thugs that you don't already know."

To Percible, he said, "You must understand that though Kaela is new to our armed services, he has been trained in the martial arts, dueling, and he knows our military tactics. He was easy to train. It is almost as though Father created Kaela to fight His enemies. You will obey his orders, and if you find yourself in a dilemma, you will do everything you can to escape your foes' clutches, and you will return home."

To Kaela, the prince said, "Should you become separated from your crew members, you must not tell your captors that I have begun an armed service that studies war tactics. Word has reached the North that God's sons are learning the art of self-defense, but so far, there are no council members who know where I train my troops or what sort of training they are receiving."

"What about me?" Autumn asked. "Does anyone care to brief me on what I should do if I become separated from my crew?"

"Pray that Father will rescue you," Prince Michael told her.

"That's it?" Autumn gasped. "So what should we tell Lucifer about our visit here tonight? I'm sure he knows by now that we are absent from his region."

"Tell him what you learned about our Lord's plans to pass His throne to His heir," Prince Michael said with a tender smile. "Go with our Father's blessings, and stay safe."

In the North, Emperor Lucifer circled Percible like a wolf circles its prey. His piercing eyes took in every part of the brother who wrested himself free of his bonds and overpowered three of the North's most combatant angels. Moving his gaze from Percible to Kaela, he asked, "Why is he still here? He was to be clipped and pitted like the others. When I learned he escaped, I put out word that he was to be uncreated. Why is he standing before me, seemingly unscathed?"

"Why would you order your guards to uncreate any member of my crew?" Kaela demanded his voice harsh and filled with hate. "I need my warriors," he spat. "I selected and trained my crew to protect you, just as I selected and trained them to build the looms, musical instruments, and refurbish God's house. They built the village around this mount, the city in this region, and the cabin you lived in before you moved into this pile of rocks," he said, referring to the onyx palace.

"Kaela and his crew were here before we ever saw the North," Autumn reminded the false emperor. "His warriors, and no one else, can protect you from your enemies."

"You can protect me from my enemies," Lucifer echoed. "I doubt that. One of my spies working in the Sacred Region told me that you sat with the imposter Michael, Scribe Excelsa and his fledgling, Archangel Effiel, and God's trusted legal advisor, Belial. While you met with them, you called my daughter a powerful witch and credited her with the rising of this structure."

"Yes, I did that," Kaela admitted. "What is so horrible about letting our enemy know that we have someone as powerful as God on our team?"

"You told God's trusted few about Azazel's work in the North," the haughty emperor said. "When I learned that Autumn and Sonnet had entered Azazel's shop unseen and made note of each weapon he forged, I was outraged. Do you realize that what you told God's council members on the night you transported your injured brothers to the Sacred Region to be healed is the reason Autumn and Sonnet were buried alive?" He studied Kaela's face for a moment. "I know how deeply you love Autumn. I knew your heart would break when you discovered his beaten and bruised body in a shallow grave. I know everything you did at the God's castle and I know what you told the thief who stole my princely title. So be wary of me."

Kaela chose to ignore what happened in the past. Let Lucifer dwell on events that could not be changed. Turning to Moloch and Nesroc, he said, "Release the remainder of my warriors you are holding captive into my care so that I can return them to the Sacred Region where they will be nourished and healed."

The North's self-appointed emperor had not finished with Kaela. "Abdiel came to me some time back. He voiced his suspicions about Joniel and the others, and he is suspicious of you too, Kaela. That worries me, his suspicions of you." Again, Lucifer studied Kaela's face. "Why are you so quiet? A moment ago, you were demanding freedom for your warriors. Now you have nothing to say. I notice that when Abdiel's name is mentioned, you grow quiet."

Kaela opened his mouth to take his part but was interrupted by Autumn. "I was in the Sacred Region this very night," she said, her heart pounding madly in her chest. Lucifer turned his attention from Kaela to his small brother. "I went there to visit Paint. Kaela was skulking around the region, trying to find out what he could before we returned home. Lucky me, I overheard a conversation between two of God's archangels. They were saying something about how God plans to turn His throne over to His chosen heir. They didn't say who the heir would be, but since God's law reads that 'angel cannot rule angel,' so I doubt that it will be Prince Michael."

"He's going to make an unknown son His heir?" Lucifer gasped.

"Not an unknown son, great sire," Autumn corrected, "a son who has never physically lived in Heaven. I am of the opinion that God plans to create a Son who is inherently obedient to Him. That Son will do all in His might to correct everything that is wrong with our globe."

"God's chosen heir will correct what has gone terribly wrong on our globe," Lucifer echoed. "And what has gone wrong that needs corrected, Autumn?"

"You broke the sovereign law that states 'Angel will never rule angel' in Heaven," Autumn replied. "Through your disobedience to God's laws you lost your titles and your high seat in Heaven. Soon, you will lose your place in Heaven, and with that loss shall go your small accomplishments and the rewards you could have earned if had you remained righteous." Once again, the words she spoke were not her own but were the unspoken thoughts of a much higher mind.

Lucifer was quiet for a long moment. Sin sat squirming in her seat, her eyes darting from Autumn's face to her father's.

"My spy didn't tell me about God's plan to leave His throne," the false emperor admitted. "I've learned more from both of you than I expected when you entered my chamber—unlawfully, I might add." He was referring to the fact that Kaela never used the stairs; instead, he chose to fly over the palace's highest balcony under the arched doorway, lighting just a feet away from the thrones.

"I will overlook that crime," Lucifer ensured. "Kaela, gather your crew members, train them to protect me, and when they are proficient enough they will train others in their skills. I will notify Azazel that he is to open his cache of weapons with you and your crew."

"Great sire," Kaela said, "I have a request. Relieve Artiff, Nashal, and Naral from their duties at the pit where I found Joniel. Make me its overseer. I will place my warriors around the rim of the pit. They will deal harshly with anyone who attempts to escape."

"Granted," Lucifer said. "Gather your warriors and go to the pit. Tell Artiff, Nashal, and Naral that they are no longer needed there. Tell them to report to me to learn where they will be stationed from now on."

Seventy-two hours after Kaela received his new assignment in the North, he, Percible, and Autumn stood before Heaven's almighty King, showing Him their sketches of the northern region and the area located at the mountain's southeastern base to its southwestern slope.

"Father, with the help of Prince Michael's saints, an escape tunnel can be built," Kaela told his Creator. "The passageway will start at the wall of the pit, and it will proceed through a hillside that adjoins the forbidden zone to the Sacred Region's abundant forest."

"Hopefully, the mountain's bedrock is not impenetrable," Percible said. When he learned he would join Kaela and Autumn on their journey to the Sacred Region, he was unaware that he would have the honor of speaking face-to-face with Heaven's powerful King. And now, here he was, standing before his Creator, the One he called Father. The fear that had encompassed him when he entered the Lord's inner sanctum was gone. His trembling heart was comforted by the wonderful sensation of peace and contentment that righteous sons feel when they are in God's presence. "If the rock is impenetrable, I can only pray that You will help us solve that problem. Otherwise, our labor of love will take forever to accomplish."

Kaela knelt on one knee, and lowering his eyes, he said, "Father, I ask You to bless our work. When our work seems too hard, I pray that You will lend us Your strength. We need wisdom, inspiration, and courage if we hope to accomplish this tedious mission. Help us to be patient and to understand one another while we work. This is going to be one of the most dangerous assignments Your saints may ever have to complete. I pray that You, Father, will help us see this enormous task to its end."

Kaela received God's blessing on his work; and when he, Autumn, and Percible returned to the North, they rushed to tell their crew the good news.

The following evening, Kaela summoned sixteen of his trained warriors to him and ordered them to guard the pit, allowing no one to descend its muddy slopes except those souls who worked for God. With his guards in place, he encouraged fifty righteous volunteers to follow him down the pit's steep slippery grade until they stood in the midst of their captive brothers.

"There is no time for tearful reunions," Kaela warned as he led them from the open pit to a wall that was packed with mud and rooting vines. He called out a name. "Hevron!" A small door opened. "Hurry, get inside quickly before we are seen!"

The volunteers had no choice but to pass through the door in single file. While they waited their turn, they crouched in the mud, clinging to the wall, eyes focused on the brim of the pit. Minutes that felt more like hours passed before the last volunteer was safely inside a room that was only big enough to hold the equipment Damian and Hevron used to fashion picks and shovels.

"Take up your tools and follow Joniel through this room to the tunnel. Now that you are here, this is where you will be until morning."

Kaela stood at the entrance to the tunnel, thanking each brother as he passed by for taking up Father's cause. His volunteers were not common angels whose skills needed honing. They were experts in their craft. They were familiar with hardship. Some had been beaten for breaking curfew when, in fact, they were closing their shops to go home for the night. Others had their shops destroyed for no reason at all, and they were not afforded the justice they deserved when the issue was made known to Lucifer. Most of the volunteers had received honors from Father while they lived in the Sacred Region. They could be trusted to do impeccable work without constant guidance.

"Father's blessings on you, my brother," Kaela told each one as they disappeared into the darkness and gloom that lay beyond the room. When the last brother was inside the tunnel, Kaela lifted his pick and shovel and followed behind him.

That same night, Joshanael, a tall golden angel who stood guard at the pit, summoned his brothers to him.

"Over there," he said, pointing to a pit that was located more than a mile from where he stood. "Atrocities are rampant in that pit. Use your vision and your heightened sense of hearing. The chaos rising up from that area is atrocious."

He glanced toward the wall that concealed the work going on behind it. "I am going to seek out Kaela's guidance on this matter. I think he should have the final word on what should, or should not, be done to save our brothers from this outrage."

Joshanael ordered the others keep an eye out for intruders before making his way down the pit's slick grade. When he returned to the pit's outer rim, Kaela was with him. Together, they made their way to the pit where righteous innocent souls were victimized by tortuous crimes.

Lying quietly on a muddy knoll that overlooked the questionable pit, Joshanael and Kaela cringed at the sight of screaming slaves being dragged from where they huddled to the center of the pit where they were stripped of their garments and beaten into unconsciousness. Several slaves were forced to leave the pit. Curious, Kaela crawled through the mud made treacherous by the North's turbulent climate. Joshanael followed close behind. They made their way to what would have been a wooded area if the trees and foliage had not suffered root rot, and there, the pair hid inside a deep gully that had been formed by the recent torrential rains. They watched in agony as Nashal's soldiers whipped frightened brothers into submission.

Esrochial, Stemon, and Arioc dragged a screaming fledgling through the muck and mire. Standing him on his feet, they stripped away his garment and forced him to lay face-down in the mud. Seconds later, Adramelec arrived.

Joshanael grasped Kaela's shoulder. "Destruction follows Adramelec everywhere he goes." Kaela gestured for silence.

Piece by piece, Adramelec's weapons and his uniform fell to the ground at his feet. God's righteous sons turned their faces from the perverse act that robbed a righteous child of his innocence.

"Adramelec is re-enacting Lucifer and Sin's foul behavior during worship at the dark palace. What are we to do about this, Kaela?"

Kaela ran his muddy hands through his hair. "Nothing— for now, we can do nothing."

With tears streaming down their cheeks, their hearts breaking in their chests, Kaela and Joshanael witnessed violent acts of the most unthinkable kind forced on more than one dozen frightened children that night. When the atrocities ended, Lucifer's perverse officers forced weeping fledglings to their feet and herded them through the dead forest until the mountain's arched back hid them from Kaela's view.

Trembling with anger and disgust wrought by the crimes they had witnessed, Kaela and Joshanael returned to their unit.

"Go to God's captive sons. See to their needs. If they hunger, feed them. If they thirst, give them water. Cleanse their wounds. Give them hope," Kaela said softly.

Long weeks passed. More crimes were committed against Father's faithful children by Lucifer's foul officers. Desperate to save their captive brothers from one more day of torture, Kaela and his crew of volunteers worked frantically on the tunnel. It seemed the further the work advanced, the more problems arose. While shoveling through the great mount's soft under belly, Kaela's team discovered her girdle of angled rock. The mountain's substructure wreaked havoc on their tools. Mallet handles snapped in half, picks lost their dowels, and chunks of boulders littered the floor so that walking through the tunnel became a chore. Suggestions were met with arguments that caused even more delays in the work. During the day, when he should have been sleeping, Kaela was sketching alternate routes that he might take if his original plan failed. At the pit, behind the muddy makeshift wall, carpenters built carts the workers would use to remove excess soil and rocks from their work area.

The carts presented a new problem. How would they be wheeled from the hidden room to the pit without notice? And where would the workers dump the boulders and dirt excavated from Shadow's depths? Certainly, the refuse could not be dumped in the slave pit, where its slick floor had been cleared of stones and rocks long ago. Kaela searched for a remote dumping ground, wary that a mound of dirt along the mount's barren slopes might make Lucifer's officers curious.

Joniel suggested the dirt be dumped into nearby gullies that were in need of repair.

Now, a new problem arose. The spell that made the North's climate so burdensome reduced angelic strength. Throughout the day, Pain fed on sore, overworked muscles and torn tendons. The entity's presence reduced angelic strength as powerfully as the region's environment.

Kaela watched in dismay as twelve of his strongest volunteers struggled without success to raise a loaded cart to the pit's brim. Pulleys were built. Secured by ropes, the carts were hoisted from the pit and unloaded in the dead of night without use of lanterns or torches. Angelic vision remedied that problem, but it did not reduce the strain of having to disassemble the pulleys before morning and rebuild them each evening so that the work going on inside the mountain remained a secret.

Within days of the excavation's start, civilian volunteers showed signs of fatigue. Unlike most soldiers who slept when they went off duty, the civilians had to carry out their daily routine. Complaints reached Lucifer's high council members. Teachers who were late for their morning classes had difficulty staying awake throughout the day, and their fatigue frustrated their eager students. Angry consumers claimed that trading with the town's shopkeepers was more of a hassle than a joy. How was one to barter with a sleeping merchant?

When Lucifer's soldiers were accused of sleeping while on duty, a meeting was called. Arguments broke out, and both sides made threats. At last, Chemosh rose from his seat and openly accused Father of casting a spell on the northern citizens. Lucifer's high council of advisors determined that Chemosh's suggestion was valid. While extra guards were stationed around the palace to protect Lucifer and Sin from God's wrath, Kaela's crew continued their excavation beneath the mountain's muddy slopes.

Through of this confusion and despair, Autumn kept in close contact with Kaela. He commissioned her to carry his project's progress to God and Excelsa.

"Be careful," he told her. "You were almost uncreated once. I can't bear the thought losing you."

In the small room at the Holy Castle, Autumn spoke with Scribe Excelsa and Prince Michael. "None of Kaela's crew, soldiers or civilians, is trained for this mammoth task. They suffer work-related injuries like blisters and muscle strains and tears. These are the common injuries and all are accompanied by Pain. Complaints have been received that Pain makes the injured workers miserable before a drop of their blood surfaces from their wounds."

Excelsa expressed his curiosity about Pain, calling the entity that fed on the wounds of the northern citizens, a phenomenon. "It seems that Pain is content to feast on the injuries of rebellious sons of God and the righteous sons of God without prejudice."

"Yesterday, we worried that we lost twenty-nine of our most trusted saints and at least twelve civilians when the tunnel's roof collapsed," Autumn told God's saintly sons. "I am relieved to report that though our volunteers were buried alive for a short time, they were rescued, and no one was badly hurt. But the cave-in has added weeks to our labor

"To guarantee an incident of this magnitude never happens again, Kaela's team members are setting sheets of wood against the tunnel's ceiling and shoring it up with strong timbers. You have to understand, they work at night because it's too dangerous to work during the day. Everyone is tired, and I see Kaela only when Lucifer calls a council meeting." She studied Prince Michael's face. "I think you and your saints had better get moving on this project, or Father will lose all his sons who are captive in the North, including Kaela."

Kaela and his crew were sixteen months into their work and still only one-quarter of the way through the mountain. Maybe if they could have worked more freely, they would have been further along with the tunnel's excavation. The safety precautions that they took had robbed them of valuable time, more so than outside interference. Kaela's volunteers were slowly losing faith in this plan. While they expressed their doubts to him, Kaela gave his concerns to Father.

"Please, dear Lord," Kaela prayed as he knelt in his cold, dark room, "help us. We are exhausted from our labors, and our accomplishments have been so small. We are not seeking praise for ourselves; we are seeking freedom for our brothers."

The following night, in the tunnel's lamp-lighted shaft, Kaela and his dwindling crew raised their picks to strike the stone that blocked their way. Voices far away and muffled paralyzed Kaela with fear.

"Listen." He reached for Percible's pick, hoping to stop it before it struck the rock. "I said stop digging and listen." Now the miners heard the voices. "We've been found out." He felt for his sword, but it was in gone. He left it with one of the slaves who he assigned to guard the door to this dismal place.

"You, civilians, snuff those lanterns and get behind us." At Kaela's command, the tunnel grew as dark as Lucifer's heart. "Warriors, prepare to do battle."

Armed with picks and shovels, Kaela's crew advanced mid-way through the tunnel toward its entrance. A bend in the wall was all that lay between them and their fate.

"Should evil prevail over righteousness, please know that I am honored to have perished with you."

Again, they heard the voices. Kaela's spirits sank. It was a soldier's sainted duty to die preserving God's honor, but what about the teachers, merchants, weavers of cloth, and construction workers who volunteered their time to dig an escape route to save their brothers' lives? He prayed that these good souls would not perish in the bowels of this mountain in this forbidden land.

Kerchunkita. Kerchunkita. Kerchunkita.

"What is that noise?" Percible asked. More curious than fearful, he turned to face the back wall of the cavern.

"Kaela," a merchant called in a loud whisper, "those voices are coming from behind the wall we are trying to break through. The voices are not coming from the tunnel's entrance as we first believed." A brief pause proved him right. "Someone come here now, I think you should see this."

Kaela hurried through the darkness to the merchant's side. He saw that his brother had not doused his lantern as ordered, but he had turned down the wick so that its flame was low and teetering. The merchant nodded toward the dank, jagged barrier that rose up before him. A pick's sharp point penetrated the mountain's firm foundation.

"Relight those lamps and resume your digging!" Kaela called, thrusting his pick deep within the mountain's thick shale wall. While volunteers lit their lamps, Kaela's crew ran to his side. Picks and shovels ripped through the dirt. Someone called out. It was Prince Michael.

"Dig!" Kaela shouted.

When the wall fell open, sainted brothers poured in to finish the work that had overwhelmed the fatigued craftsmen and slaves of the North. Kaela dropped his knees.

"Thank you, Father," he prayed aloud. "Thank you for lending us Your strength and sending Your saints to help us accomplish this mammoth task."

Within forty-eight hours of the tunnel's completion, Prince Michael's soldiers led more than two-thirds of their suffering brothers to freedom. Kaela gauged his crews' success by the ferocity of Lucifer's anger when he learned his slaves were missing.

"God is stealing my slaves!" the angry emperor raged as he paced the floor. "According to Flagitious, many pits lay empty. While I slept in my bed, God crept into my region and robbed me of my citizens. Will He stop at nothing?"

At Lucifer's command, dark-clothed warriors searched the town's shops, the vacant cottages in the village, and the sparsely occupied pits and pens and they combed the muddy hills, the mountain's treacherous slopes, and the North's barren valleys for signs of divine trespass. When none were found, they returned to the onyx palace to face Emperor Lucifer's fierce wrath.

Chapter 33

Northern Unrest

It was an exceedingly dreary day in northern Heaven. Dark clouds rolled up from the region's surface to the deepest space, releasing their store of moisture onto the soggy ground below. Thummuz and Dagon made their way from the pits, where they now worked, to the palace courtyard where Nephilim toiled over a cauldron that sat atop a roaring fire. In the cauldron, a bubbling brew boiled, its thick contents churning and rolling under its outer crust. Dagon pulled his foot from the mud and trudged across the courtyard to the cauldron. Holding out his clay cup, he allowed Nephilim to pour a ladle of oozing slop into it. Dagon sniffed the cup's contents. He couldn't identify what he was about to eat, but he was hungry, so what did it matter? Following Thummuz to the broken fountain, he cleared dirt away before making its base his seat.

"We were lured to this gray region by Lucifer's lies," Dagon complained. "Guard the slave pens? When did I become the emperor's warrior? When we lived in the Sacred Region, I was Lucifer's pampered courtier. When we came North, I was his exulted council member." Unable to contain his anger, he dipped his spoon into the yellow glop in his cup and dumped its contents into his mouth. "Ugh! Creamed corn." Cringing, Dagon spooned more of the golden scum into his mouth. "Did Lucifer promise you greatness when you became his courtier?"

"Yes, I was told I would receive a high title if I betrayed Heaven's fading deity," Thummuz answered, a daub of creamed corn oozing down his chin. "That was eons ago." He surveyed the premises. "Look at what God did to this place. This region was more beautiful than our homeland. Then God became envious of Lucifer for birthing Sin, and see what the North has become." Someone chuckled.

Thummuz turned his hateful eyes from Dagon's face to where he saw Kaela leaning against the wheel of a wagon that had been stuck in the mud for days. "Be careful what you say. There stands Kaela. I wonder who he is spying on today." He lifted another spoonful of food to his mouth.

Again, the subject changed. "I remember when we gathered in the Sacred Region's vibrant forest to hear Lucifer's promise of a more glorious future in Heaven. He led us to the North to build his city and populate his village. We upheld Lucifer's laws and uncreated anyone we suspected of working against him. And while Lucifer becomes more powerful, we are left to stagnate like still waters."

Dagon handed his food bowl to a passing slave. "If we could get our hands on God's journals, we could learn the truth about our existence." He glanced fearfully to where Kaela had been standing. He was gone. Still, as a precaution, Dagon lowered his voice, "I distrust Lucifer as much as I distrust God."

"Keep talking like that and your head will decorate the palace's dark foyer," Thummuz warned. "We are only a part of a team. We are trivial. God will never write my name in His journal unless I uncreate someone of importance. Then for a little while, my name will roll off every tongue. 'Thummuz uncreated one of God's favored angels,' they will cry, 'and he did it in a most gruesome way.' When my face is long forgotten, my name and my deed will be remembered."

"Perhaps we should follow Lucifer's perfect example." Dagon rose to his feet. "After God disowned him, Heaven's eldest son became the saints' most brutal enemy and the North's cruel dictator."

Thummuz set his bowl on the fountain's wall and followed his complaining brother through the courtyard.

"My warriors are assigned to the pen that teeters at the brink of collapse on the mountain's northern-most side," Dagon disclosed. "Where are you located?"

"Down and around the mountain's bend," Thummuz replied. He drew an invisible spiral in the air with his fingertip. "I will see you in the morning."

That evening, fog as thick as northern mud veiled the region. It was a good night for transporting sick and badly abused slaves through freedom's door to the Sacred Region. Hours before dawn, Sashel and Hevron entered the tunnel. Five, then ten, then twenty slaves arrived. Marcus, who carried one emaciated brother in his arms, leaned against the wall, fatigued by the North's heavy climate and the grief of seeing how terribly God's righteous children suffered.

"Put him down," Sashel said. "Kaela will check him over before we take him out of here."

Marcus set the slave on the ground, wrapped his trembling body in a borrowed blanket, and held him close.

"Kaela," Sashel called, "a few members of our crew saw your night-flyer enter the dark palace. He is robed and cloaked in the same garb worn by God's council members and his long golden hair falls freely around his face, hiding his identity."

Kaela, who had been kneeling beside his suffering brothers, cleansing their wounds and offering them fresh-water to hydrate them and food transported to the pit by God's saints, stood when he heard Sashel's message. With a motion of his hand, he called Percible to him.

"I must leave for a while. Please see to our injured brothers while I am gone." He was about to leave the safety of the tunnel to take his chances at the palace when Marcus asked him to examine Neptanel.

Kneeling beside his trembling brother, Kaela gently opened the blanket that covered him. "We will cleanse your wounds. We will feed you, clothe you, and prepare you for your journey home." Tears shimmered in Kaela's eyes. In Neptanel's case, going home might mean returning him to Father or preparing him for his burial. Either way, the trembling slave showed no sign of knowing what had been said.

Marcus stared in disbelief at the malnourished form that lay across his lap. Tears streamed down his face. He swallowed back a sob when he heard Kaela whisper, "You will be home soon, dear child of God."

Neptanel was bones, nothing but bones covered by scarred and bruised flesh. The blanket was removed and set aside while the mud was washed from the slave's leathery skin and matted hair. A ladle filled with water was set against Neptanel's lips, but he refused to drink.

"Dear son of light," Kaela whispered against his trembling brother's cheek, "soon Mercy will bless you, Love will comfort you, and when you hunger or thirst, Charity will see to your needs."

Neptanel swallowed, turned his head, and buried his face against Marcus's chest.

Kaela rose to his feet, his expression tortured. He had seen many brothers in poor condition, but not one who was as emaciated or as lifeless as this one. "Hevron, Marcus, find a clean blanket. Wrap Neptanel in it and carry him directly to God's house. Let nothing keep you from your mission. Delays are of no use to our brother now."

He turned to Sashel. "You are in command until I get back. I have business to tend to at the dark palace."

Creeping across the muddy field that had once been a verdant lawn, Kaela made his way to the onyx palace. Kneeling outside the window of the ground floor's conference room, he studied the chamber's interior. It was empty. He could enter the palace through this window without being seen. He was about to leap through it when the door to the room opened and a figure carrying a candle entered. One by one, lanterns were lit, their light dancing through the window to where Kaela stood. Crouching low, the left side of his body hugging the black stone that rose up from the mountain's depths to form Lucifer's mansion, he waited patiently for the slave to finish his duties and move on so that he could gain entrance to the palace through the conference room's open window

The sound of the door closing brought Kaela to his feet. His eyes widened and his jaw dropped. Just inside the room stood Lucifer and with him, God's council member. Kaela ducked down, hugging the onyx wall again. Now he was content to listen to what was being said.

"Please be seated." Lucifer's voice filtered through the window into the thick night air. "I know you must return to the Sacred Region before you are missed. Oh"—he laughed—"I forgot God's angels sleep at night. Would you like some nectar? Some water, perhaps? No? Fine, you say you have a message for me?"

"I come to the North as a bearer of great news," Lucifer's guest said. He spoke so softly that Kaela could hardly hear his voice. "At the dawning of the next millennium, Heaven will have a new king. When God sets His crown on His perfect son's head, all doubts will fade. Hearts will lean toward love or hate—there will be no in between. Traitors to the new king will loathe him. They will avoid his angry eyes and tremble when his name is mentioned. The mere sight of God's heir will turn his enemies' hearts to stone. For centuries after he takes God's throne, Heaven's future king will be known as the Divine Disturber. The description fits only one angel I know: the great Lucifer."

How could this be? Lucifer was Father's enemy? God would no more surrender His throne to Lucifer than He would surrender it to Sin. Kaela crawled along the palace wall until he was a safe distance from the conference room's window. He made his way through the courtyard toward the plateau's downward slope.

Asmadai called out to him. "Who goes there?"

"It is I, Kaela," God's righteous son replied. "I am leaving."

Without further delay, Kaela hurried to the pit. "Percible, remain at my station until I return from the Sacred Region. I have a matter of great importance to discuss with Prince Michael." Almost as an afterthought, he added, "Tell Autumn my plan and that I may be late coming home."

It was almost morning when Autumn went to her room. She had waited all night for Kaela to return from the Sacred Region where he was meeting with Prince Michael. After she was rescued from her shallow grave, she and Kaela abandoned their little cottage to move here to Lucifer's grand cabin. Glancing out the upstairs window toward the pits, she noticed the area was darker than any darkness she had ever seen before. On nights like this, when rain poured down on the region and the air was filled with that pungent scent that stung her nose, Autumn longed for home. She took off her northern uniform and slipped into the one robe she managed to salvage when Lucifer declared wearing sacred garb a crime. This rescued robe was, at one time, one of her favorites to wear when she attended Father's festivals. Now it was her nightgown.

Turning down Kaela's bed, she wondered if he would get any sleep tonight.

"Oh, Kaela," she whispered, "you take too much on yourself."

Autumn got into bed and doused the lamp. Drawing the comforter to her chin, she listened to the wind that howled outside her window; its forlorn cries winding their way across a dead landscape sent shivers down her spine. Pulling the comforter over her head, she fell asleep only to be awakened by *splat, splat, splat.*

The rain that had been falling straight down all day had taken a westerly slant, and like an uninvited guest whose visit is spurred by bad intentions, the rain came inside her room to wet her night-stand and soak the clothes she laid out for Kaela to wear tomorrow.

Autumn sat up in bed. She thought about moving the chair where the uniform hung. She thought about moving the nightstand to preserve its hard-wood beauty. Instead, she moved to opposite side of the bed, wrapped her feet tighter in her blanket, shut her eyes, and went back to sleep.

At the pit, Kaela stepped through the mud-covered door that hid the cavern's mouth from sight. Rain drained like a waterfall from an overhang of muddy ground that threatened to break loose if it was not bolstered by posts soon. Once inside, he met with the members of his crew.

"I overheard the night-flyer's description of the One our Lord will make Heaven's King," Kaela told them quietly. "It sounded as though Father had chosen Lucifer as His heir. That was the reason for my unscheduled meeting with Scribe Excelsa and Prince Michael. They assured me that Father has no intention of relinquishing His crown to any of member of His seven flocks. The Son who will rule Heaven in Father's place has yet to be created"

He turned to leave the tunnel. His crew walked with him to the door that was camouflaged to look like a wall of mud. "I need to rest. The meeting with Prince Michael and the transport of slaves from the

North to the Sacred Region has been so tiring that I can only think of showering this mud from my body and going to bed."

"Sire," someone called as Kaela stepped out from under the drooping overhang of ground. "You are needed at the palace. The great Lucifer demands your presence in his home."

"Tell him I'll be right there," Kaela called back. To Joniel, who stood behind him, hidden by the darkness of the overhang, he said, "Cover that door with more mud and add some dead vines to better hide it from view. I have to change this uniform and go to the palace to see what Lucifer wants."

The great cabin was black as pitch when Kaela entered it. He shivered. The fire-place in the main living room was dark and cold, which told him Autumn, spent the evening in their room. She had her own room, but for some reason, she insisted on moving her bed to his room. It didn't matter. The room could have held five beds; it was that large. Mounting the stairs, he yawned. This would be a long day. No sleep all night and now Lucifer found reason to keep him awake all day. In the bedroom, Kaela smiled at Autumn's sleeping form. He walked past her to the bathroom, where he showered the mud from his hair and body.

Autumn sat up in bed. Was that the shower running? She got out of bed, took a dry uniform from the closet, and placed it on the chair near the bathroom door. Kaela strode from the bathroom, lifted his uniform from the chair, and put it on. Smelling the sleeve of his shirt, he mumbled, "Everything in this region stinks."

At the onyx palace, Kaela was escorted by a guard to the conference room where Lucifer met with his spy. Entering the room, he took the chair closest to the door and watched Dagon act out his anger while voicing a very boisterous grievance.

"You told us to betray Heaven's all-powerful King!" the angry council member shouted. "You told us to follow you to the North where you would make us governors, principalities, dominions, and thrones. That was your promise to us when you still lived in God's house. After we moved here, you proclaimed yourself the great Lucifer, the emperor, the high priest, the general. While you live in splendor, your so-called courtiers have become your slave masters. We herd your slaves through the mud of this forsaken region, eating food that is not fit for pigs.

"In God's kingdom, we were common angels. In the North, we are equal to your slaves. Glory was, and always will be, reserved for the globe's prominent citizens." Dagon drew his sword and shouted, "Future king or not, prepare to die!"

Kaela pounced on Dagon. The tip of his own sword pressed against the soft flesh of Dagon's neck, drawing blood.

"Without releasing it, lower your weapon to your side," he said in a calming tone. Dagon did as he was told. "I know you are not as angry as you are confused by Lucifer's broken promises." He loosened his grip on his brother. "I'm going to let go of you. Do not try anything. Just calm down and sheathe your sword. No one is going uncreate anyone today," Kaela said. He extended his hand to Dagon, who took it and express his appreciation by dragging him into a hug. "Please be seated. I'd like to address the great Lucifer and my fellow council members."

When Dagon was seated, Kaela said, "Great Lucifer, each of us came here for different reasons. I volunteered my services as a carpenter. No promises of greatness were made to me, but had I not left the Sacred Region, I would still be kneeling before Heaven's King. Instead, I share this great region with the globe's most powerful sons."

Pleased with Kaela's statement, Lucifer lowered himself into his chair.

Kaela pointed the tip of his sword from the first of the twelve, who sat at the table with the false emperor, to the last of them. "Your courtiers," he said as though introducing evil to evil, "chose to serve you, hoping you would fulfill your promise to them. You promised Dagon, Nesroc, Moloch, Mammon, Thummuz, Apollyon, Flagitious, and, I would assume, Asmadai, Azazel, Chemosh, Baal, and Beelzebub that you would reward them with wealth, power, and the ability to control their righteous brethren. Eons have passed, and these promises have not been met. Your council members are understandably angry because their situation is worse in the North than it was in God's kingdom.

"Great Lucifer, nothing has changed. Your enemy still rules this globe and your servants are becoming impatient. They have been tested time and time again. They have proven themselves faithful to you, and in turn, you sent them into the elements to tend to your slaves. Can you doubt that they would demand satisfaction?"

Lucifer smiled. "You should have been a counselor, Kaela. Your case is well put, and I will consider acting on my promises when I become Heaven's rightful king." He glanced from Kaela to his perverse daughter. "I have it on good authority that I will own God's throne at the dawn of the new millennium."

"Surely you are not speaking of the millennium that is still over eight hundred and fifty light years away?" Chemosh asked his expression so very incredulous that it wrenched laughter from those who saw it.

Kaela slapped one of the council members with the broad side of his blade. "Quiet! All of you! Quiet! You are in the presence of the great Lucifer."

Turning to face the false emperor, he said, "For some time, I have been aware that you have a spy who visits you under cover of night. I often pass him in the air when he and I are returning to our homes after we've conducted business behind enemy lines. I am, also, aware great sire, that your night-flyer is a member of God's council of advisors. I've been close enough to him that I saw his saintly robes, but his long hair hides his face from sight. Tell me who he is, and I will bring him here. If he is not believable, he will undergo a brutal interrogation to learn who encouraged him to trick you into thinking you would receive a royal promotion at the start of the new millennium."

Lucifer glanced smugly at his courageous brother. "I will not reveal my source to you, Kaela. I will not reveal my source to anyone. He brings me more information from God and saints than all your fawning and deception extracts from the scribe. Understand, I am not calling you inadequate, but the one you call my spy is more trusted by our enemies than you are trusted by me. He sits in the very presence of God. He makes bold decisions to determine if God should move against the northern citizens or delay His desire to strike a fatal blow against us. He is the one who convinced Father to give me my titles. He is the reason Father assigned me to Heaven's northern region. And, he will be the one who convinces the saints to make me their king." Lucifer shook his head and leaned back in his chair. "I would be a fool to tell you the name of the one who works and achieves rewards that benefit me."

Kaela turned to those gathered in the room. "I followed this spy, not to God's house, but to the residential area of the city. I know of only two council members who chose not live in the Holy Castle. They are Anael and Belial. Anael made solid ice that never melts. He calls it glass. Belial is God's counselor. He helps God determine what steps will be taken to improve the Sacred Region."

"Is Belial your spy, Lucifer? Tell us." Dagon growled.

"No, I will not." Lucifer sniffed. "Think of this: I send Kaela on a mission. He is skulking around God's house, trying to gather information when he is captured by Michael and his saints. Kaela is captured, imprisoned, interrogated, and tortured. To save his life, he tells the saints my spy's name. Now, the book of knowledge is close to me forever. Not only I have lost Kaela, who is fairly good at gathering information, but also I have lost this other informer, who is excellent at gathering information and revealing God's plans to me. Who would I be more inclined to hate losing, Kaela or my righteous informant?"

"Well, now that really upsets me," Kaela said with a mocking grin. His eyes danced over the snickering council members. "Pain does not dwell in the Sacred Region," he reminded Lucifer. "How would the saints torture me if Pain did not come to feed on my wounds? Personally, I would rather be uncreated by a saint in the Sacred Region than suffer your wrath in the North."

"Enough of this pandering," Moloch growled. "Excelsa knows the truth. He and God are one in mind and spirit. Therefore, I will capture God's scribe and bring him here. I will torture him until I know your spy's name. I will learn if the spy speaks the truth or if he is just feeding you what God wants you to believe." Moloch looked around the room. "Who will join me on my journey to the Sacred Region?"

"Great Lucifer," Kaela said as he sheathed his sword. "Though I would like to be present when the scribe is abducted from his suite and dragged screaming to your empire, I am afraid that if I participated in Moloch's plan, my cover will be blown. Presently, Scribe Excelsa, Prince

Michael, Archangel Effiel, and our sisters believe that I am God's spy in the North."

"Yes, of course." Lucifer nodded in agreement. "Return to the pit. I would rather have you there than here when the scribe arrives at my door."

To the others in the room, the false emperor said, "Make your plans wisely, for if you are discovered during your covert visit, I will deny you re-entry into the North, and you will lose your future titles."

Chapter 34

A Bad Idea

Autumn slept through the meeting that Kaela had been called from pit to attend. She was aware that he had come home, showered, complained that everything smelled bad in the North, and left without telling her where he was going. Stretching, she turned in bed.

"Oh no," she groaned. The covers on the left side of the bed, the side where she would have gotten out, were soaked by the rain the wind had blown inside the room. Scooting to the foot of the bed, she struggled to free herself from the damp blankets she had been sleeping under. A streak of lightning crossed the sky, illuminating the room with its creepy glow, encouraging the furniture to cast their shadows dark and long against the walls. A crash of thunder rocked the cabin. It was so loud that it almost knocked Autumn off her feet. Her head was spinning, not so much from the thunder's assault, but from knowing that if she did not leave this evil place soon, she would go insane.

Nights like this one made her long to return to the Sacred Region and never come back to this part of Heaven with its cold climate, drizzling rain, mud, and stench. In the North, she, regretfully, was Lucifer's scribe. Her office in the onyx palace was a prison in itself. Every day that she was here, she watched more and more brothers become evil. And if that was not enough to unnerve her, she had to contend with the North's power-crazed self-appointed ruler and his dreadful daughter, Sin. Throughout the day, Lucifer and his witch tortured God's perfect sons. Autumn, being their scribe, had to be present when the atrocities were committed so that she could accurately record each episode in the emperor's private journals. At night, she would lie in her bed, staring at the ceiling. No one knew the torment she suffered when night arrived and her brothers' screams and pleas for mercy rang in her ears, robbing her of her sleep.

More disturbing to Autumn than the suffering she witnessed at the hands of Lucifer and Sin was the realization that she was losing respect for Kaela's crew. These dedicated brothers worked the pits and pens every day, risking their lives to care for the North's frightened, emaciated slaves. She felt no admiration for the righteous ones who dug the tunnel from the North to the Sacred Region, and she felt no sense of urgency for the safety of Prince Michael's saints who spirited their starved and beaten brothers to God's kingdom. Slowly but surely, Autumn was falling victim to the emperor's conviction that if God's righteous sons did not wish to feel the braid of the whip against their backs, they should not have ventured into the North.

Prince Michael's soldiers were the lucky ones. They weren't awakened from their fitful nightmare-ridden sleep to take notes on more advanced ways to torture unsuspecting citizens. Heaven's royalty was not called upon to attend services in the dark unholy place where Sin danced naked before her drooling brothers and committed insane acts of perversion with animals to feed her lustful nature.

Autumn desperately needed to return to the Sacred Region. She felt that she would go insane if she did not rest in God's sacred light and feel His healing powers renew her aching body.

"Father, I need Your warmth to comfort me," she whispered. "I need Your healing grace. I've seen things that would turn a mortal's hair white. Please, my Lord, find reason for me to return to Your kingdom so that You can cleanse and heal every cell in my body, so that You can mend my broken spirit. If I stay here much longer, I am going to become as evil as Lucifer and as perverse as Sin."

Voices that filtered up from the foyer below interrupted Autumn's prayer. With her narrowed eyes fixed on the door that opened to the hallway, she listened in a vain attempt to hear what was being said. Outside her window, the cold rain that pounded against the cabin's roof and fell in torrents to the ground made it impossible for her recognize the voices of those who spoke. She tip-toed to the window and closed the shutters. As she crept toward the door that led to the hallway, she lifted her sword from the chair it leaned against. Standing at the top of the stairs, she listened to hear what was being said to determine if she should be prepared to fight for her life or greet her uninvited guests.

"You say, Lucifer wants me to witness the scribe's demise," Kaela was saying. "I told him that I don't want to get involved in this!" He sounded so helpless. Autumn shrank against the wall she hid behind. Could Scribe Excelsa be uncreated?

"I feel no animosity toward God's scribe" Kaela told the warrior, "and I will not take part in his uncreation." He saw Moloch to the door, and then he went upstairs where he found Autumn standing in the upstairs hallway, dressed in her night-clothes, and leaning on her sword. "We are invited to the dark palace, but we will not be seen unless I determine that Scribe Excelsa is in extreme danger."

Autumn darted into the bedroom to change into her uniform.

"Listen to me," Kaela urged, "I don't want you being a hero. You stay with me in the shadows, and you keep your mouth shut regardless of what you see. Do you understand what I am saying?"

"Yes, I do."

At the dark palace, Moloch removed the sheet that covered Excelsa. Apollyon and Baal dragged the scribe to a chair that was set in the middle of the onyx palace's main foyer. Dagon tied Excelsa's hands at the wrists behind the chair's back and bound his ankles to the chair's legs.

Removing the gag from the scribe's mouth, Moloch leaned over his shoulder, hissing in his ear, "God cannot protect you from the great Lucifer's wrath." He pushed the gag back into Excelsa's mouth and stepped aside.

Kaela stood in the shadows with Autumn at his side. Using his powerful vision to cut through the gloom that filled the dark foyer, he saw and recognized the northern council members who lined the entranceway, awaiting their false emperor's arrival. A movement from the staircase caught his attention. Sin was cowering behind the onyx banisters that lined the staircase on both sides.

Kaela turned to Autumn. "Sin is crouching behind the banister. She is about halfway up the staircase. I wonder if she is hiding from God's all-seeing eyes. Or if she fears standing in the presence of Father's righteous scribe will reveal her true identity."

Dagon dragged a chair across the floor, which he set beside the chair Scribe Excelsa occupied. There was nothing to do now but wait for Emperor Lucifer to make his grand appearance. Dropping into the chair, the evil warrior unsheathed his dagger. Using the sharp tip of his blade, he cleaned away dirt that had accumulated under his nails after days of working at the pit. The scribe groaned. A glance in his direction revealed that Excelsa was in distress, he was shivering, and his eyes were rolling in his head. Dagon sprang from his chair and removed the rag from his prisoner's mouth.

"Stop scraping that knife under your nails!" Excelsa scolded in a loud and angry snarl. "The sound of it gives me chills. So help me, if you insist on making that noise, I will spit on you." The two enemies glared at each other for a long moment. "Did you hear what I said?" Before the scribe could repeat his threat, Dagon stuffed the rag back in his mouth.

Down the hall, a door opened. Footsteps, soft at first, grew louder by the second. As the footsteps drew nearer to the place where Excelsa sat bound and gagged, an image materialized in the dark onyx corridor. A distant torchlight sent its glow into the darkness where it glinted off a pure-white face before it flickered and dimmed. A breeze that entered through a window's unlatched shutter somewhere in the onyx palace circled the room, pausing just long enough to touch the failing flame, bringing it back to life.

The torch's flame, fed by the passing breeze, flared bright, lighting the way for Lucifer, who stepped out of the dark corridor to make his way to where Excelsa would be interrogated.

"Where is your God, Scribe?" the false emperor asked defiantly as he took the rag from Excelsa's mouth and dropped it on the floor. "Perhaps He is too busy creating more angels to replace those who deserted Him to join my cause in the North. Maybe He is too busy to save His scribe."

The evil general put his hands on Excelsa's shoulders and leaned close to his face. "I have it on good authority that I will become Heaven's future king. God stole my slaves and a fraction of my supporters, but I still own one-third of the globe's citizens, and soon, I shall add new residents to my flock. Your so-called righteous brothers are joining my forces as we speak. Uh … Yes, before the interrogation begins, think on this: the same source that told me of my impending kingship brought me four of God's treasured journals. Soon, everyone will know the secrets stored inside these books. God's horrendous crimes against His created children will be revealed, and His righteous sons will declare their loyalty to me."

At the emperor's command, Moloch began the scribe's interrogation. "Does Lucifer stand to inherit God's throne?"

"Never," Excelsa answered. As the word fell from his lips, a powerful blow was delivered to his face. The question was repeated. The same answer was given. Again, Moloch struck the scribe. Cringing, he rubbed his aching hand, marveling that Excelsa's expression never changed. Was the scribe so blessed by Father that he was immune to Pain's assault?

"Those of you, who are hiding in the shadows, listen to me," Excelsa called. "Lucifer has no future in Heaven. By choosing him over God, you have ruined your chances of holding a high position on this globe. And know this: Father is not creating angels to replace you. He is all-powerful. He does not need an army to destroy you. He can destroy this globe and everything on it quicker than your heart can take its next beat. Apologize to Father. Admit your mistake in coming here to support Lucifer. Leave the North and return to the Sacred Region. Heed my warning: a horrific prison named Hell exists, which will house Heaven's disobedient sons until the end of time.

"When Father speaks of Lucifer, Hell reaches its fiery arms toward Heaven. If you pledge your obedience to all that is wrong in the North, you are doomed to Hell."

Scribe Excelsa glared at the emperor. "Now let me warn you, Lucifer, Father will create this globe's next King. Heaven's future ruler will rise up from the Cradle of Conception, no angelic cells will taint

His Godly body, and when Father passes His scepter to Him, He will be more powerful than the Object of your unbridled envy."

"Your riddle does not amuse me, Scribe." Lucifer stormed across the foyer and threw open the doors to his house. A unit of warriors entered at the false emperor's command. "Take this worthless creature to the courtyard and bury him alive."

While Moloch and Nemryd prepared the scribe for uncreation, Lucifer raged, "The Cradle of Conception births daughters, not sons, so there is no created one who will rule Heaven. And since God created a so-called prison named Hell for me, I will make Heaven a hell for righteous souls."

Helpless, Autumn watched the dark soldiers drag Excelsa to the courtyard. His grave had been dug. They had no intention of returning the scribe to his homeland.

"Kaela," she sobbed. "Do something! Stop them!" She saw Kaela unsheathe his sword and make for the courtyard where the atrocity would be done. "Father, please, save Scribe Excelsa."

In answer to her prayer, Prince Michael appeared; his body glowed like a bright-blue flame, and his eyes burned white-hot with anger. Towering over the procession of evil-doers, God's sainted prince pursed his lips and blew air from between them. A blast of wind knocked Lucifer's dark warriors to the ground.

Excelsa was free. With one hand, Prince Michael lifted the scribe into his arms. On the ground below, warriors, all of whom had been so brave moments ago, lay in the mud, trembling with fear. Lucifer, who had spoken boldly to the scribe about his supposed new role in Heaven, and Moloch, who delivered the blows to Excelsa's face during his interrogation, lay on the ground, their mouths agape in disbelief and horror.

Kaela knelt beside Autumn, his arms wove tightly around her, and his head bowed in a prayer of thanksgiving. Autumn leaned her head on his shoulder. Kaela would have given his life, and hers, to save God's scribe.

"Lucifer, listen to me and be warned," Prince Michael thundered. "Before the end of the coming millennium, God's angry Son will separate believers from disbelievers. Driven by His love for His precious Father, Heaven's new King will herd the northern citizens screaming through the streets to the fragile brim of this wide world. While evil souls cringe before Him, He will give them a choice: eternal damnation in Hell or uncreation of mind and body forever."

Prince Michael's image faded, and with it, Excelsa.

Chapter 35

Northern Heaven Divided

The night of Prince Michael's eerie visitation to the courtyard, Lucifer, in a fit of rage, brutally punished his guards for cowering before the thief who stole his titles. To make a bad night even worse, Lucifer's council members rebelled against him. Seated in his private office, the false emperor listened to his courtiers' grievances. It was during this meeting that the old insecurities reintroduced themselves to the North's false emperor.

Dagon, who courageously expressed his unhappiness with his existence in the North, had attacked Lucifer in this same space days earlier. Now, he stood before his emperor, admitting his greatest fear: "to perish without ever having owned a throne in Heaven."

Apollyon worried aloud, "We will be powerless to protect our northern citizens from God's anger. You heard the scribe—before my heart can take its next beat, God can destroy this world and everything in it. That kind of destruction does not give us much warning."

Asmadai agreed with Apollyon, saying, "If God can extend His powers to Prince Michael to save His scribe from uncreation, how many others can He empower through His might to deny His throne to Lucifer?"

Moloch ran his hands through his hair, his eyes focused hard on Lucifer's face. "I fear war," he admitted. "These threats make me tremble. I want to live forever. I want to stand proud before my subjects and hear them call my name amid their cheers of admiration. But if God, the One we once called Father, can end this globe before my heart can take another beat, what can He do on a lesser scale that might cause us to suffer until He sees fit to end our torment?"

Nesroc rose to his feet. He was about to speak when Kaela, who remained seated, said, "We have over eight hundred years before this millennium ends. Isn't that what Michael said? Before the end of the next millennium, God will surrender His throne to a new King. If his calculation is correct, we have approximately eight hundred years to think about what we will do if God decides to send us to Hell—if indeed there is a prison named Hell.

"We should not concern ourselves about whether we will perish before or after the new King takes God's throne. We should be more concerned about what happens here and now. My instincts tell me that we must live for the present. Therefore, let us reconsider our priorities." Kaela's brilliant blue eyes studied each council member's face as he spoke. He had their attention. "What goals, what dreams, brought each of you to the North? Nesroc, what was your goal when you came here?"

"I dreamed of making history," the warrior admitted. "I hoped to be a great leader someday. Fool that I am, I chose to serve Lucifer."

Lucifer sprang to his feet, his face distorted with anger. "How dare you?"

"That is enough!" Kaela shouted over the emperor's tantrum. The fact that he had just scolded the northern ruler moved the council members' attention from Lucifer back to him. "Whether we are sentenced to Hell or uncreated by God's angry Son, our time in Heaven is limited."

Lucifer dropped into his chair and fixed his angry eyes on Kaela.

"All of us have been loyal to Lucifer, and we have received awards and promotions in return for our loyalty. We have served this region well, and we have accomplished all the tasks set before us by our emperor. Therefore, it is time for you, great Lucifer, to make good on your promise to share the North with your courtiers."

Thummuz rose from his chair, his jaw set, his burning eyes fixed on Lucifer's face. "I do not care to fawn over another fading deity. I came to the North to acquire the greatness I felt I deserved. For all these many years, we were forced to think only of our emperor and what he wanted. I agree with Kaela. It is time that we are rewarded for the loyalty we have given you. Divide the North now, or prepare to do war with your allies."

"I should speak with Sin in private," Lucifer suggested.

"Your promise was made long before Sin existed in Heaven," Dagon argued. "She has nothing to do with this facet of your life." The evil angel glared at the emperor. "Do as Kaela says, divide the North. You are the one who made God bitter with your lies. Now He considers each of us His enemy. Because you envied Heaven's almighty King, a prison named Hell awaits us. You have until tomorrow evening to determine which section of the North is yours and which is ours. Until then, this meeting is adjourned."

When the conference room was cleared, Lucifer pointed his finger at Kaela. "I should have you stripped naked and whipped until you beg for mercy." He sat down at the table and ran his hands through his hair. "Is this how Father felt when I grew defiant? Did He love me so much that even when I was at my worse, He wanted the best for me?"

Lucifer looked across the table at Autumn. He snorted and shook his head. "Get me the map of this region," he told his small brother. "We will get no sleep tonight. Kaela, you and Autumn will assist me. Together, we are going to divide the North among my officers. If they are not pleased, they can take their complaints to you."

Throughout the night, Kaela redefined the North's original map to meet Lucifer's specifications. Autumn pored over a copy of the map Uzziel sketched so long ago and noticed it contained discrepancies here and there. Knowing the North as she did, she could have corrected the mistakes, but she let them stand. She hoped with all her heart the errors she saw on the map would cause discord among Lucifer's officials.

"Sire," Autumn said, nudging the dozing general's arm. Lucifer's eyes popped open. He glared at her through sleep-reddened eyes. "Moloch is the governor of the North's eastern territory." She studied Lucifer's weary face. "He is a very influential force in the North. Therefore, Kaela suggested we should weaken his effectiveness by dividing his province into six separate sectors and leasing them to brothers who are opposed to his thoughts."

"Opposed to Moloch's thoughts?" Lucifer mused aloud. "The northeastern province would be filled with bickering brothers." The emperor glared at Autumn, shook his head, and looked away.

"We are thinking of your throne, sire." Autumn said, straightening her shoulders in an effort to relieve the stiffness in her neck. "By setting Moloch among titled angels who are opposed to his thoughts, we will eliminate his absolute rule in the northeast. Since the entire North is under your jurisdiction, you can level a mandate that restricts subordinate rulers from forming armies to seize their leader's throne."

Lucifer's jaw dropped open. "I never thought of that. I thought only of appeasing my officers' need for greatness. Am I so blind? Hours ago, Dagon stood before my high council members and threatened my security in the North, did he not?" Autumn nodded. "You are a good and loyal brother to me, child. You too, Kaela, you are a good brother. While your angry eyes and your scornful sneers annoy others, I know that you are one of my most faithful officers. I trust that you will do what is best for me." The emperor patted Kaela's shoulder. He reached out his hand, almost touching Autumn, but withdrew his friendly caress in a swift and flustered manner.

Kaela divided the North's eastern quadrant into seven sectors instead of six, as originally planned. "I set aside a parcel of land from each of the provinces for you, Lucifer. The smaller the divided sectors, the less powerful its ruler will be."

He scribbled the names of those who would serve under Moloch's supervision: Baalim, Benzata, Rimmon, Sammael, and Sarael. Sammael was to the North what Kaela was to the Sacred Region. The citizens on both ends of the spectrum distrusted and feared him. Sammael's ability to be good and evil at once made him a risk to be considered. Sarael was staunchly faithful to God. During the North's most stressful times, he reported to the pit at the mountain's base to help dig the tunnel that ran from Lucifer's dark empire to Father's sacred kingdom. He cared for ill and wounded slaves, and he was one of Prince Michael's most respected soldiers, second only to Uzziel. Sarael's opposition to wrong-doing would make him a thorn in Moloch's side.

Thummuz would supervise the entire northwestern province. His subordinates were the twins Astaroth and Ashtarothe. While Astaroth was muscular like Thummuz, Ashtarothe was lithe like Lucifer. The twin's differing temperaments greatly reduced their ability to rule in peaceful harmony.

Rive, the North's former barber, quit his practice of clipping wings when he was touched by Godly compassion for his suffering brothers. He dedicated his time to helping Sarael care for down-trodden slaves before they were transported to the Sacred Region. His anguish led him to despise the mistreatment of private citizens. Kaela knew Rive would oppose whatever harm Thummuz sought to do to the residents of his region.

Donniel was one of Kaela's boldest liberators. He exhibited an unbending faith in God from the first day of his creation, so he would add to the confusion of Thummuz's region. At Lucifer's insistence, Kaela gave Ire a cut of the northwestern province. Ire would serve Thummuz well. The two were almost identical in appearance, and as closely matched as they were in physical stature; their thoughts were exceedingly the same.

"What have you got so far," Lucifer asked as he stifled a yawn. Kaela read his list to him. "Very good, I see you chose Chemosh to supervise the northernmost quadrant of my empire. Subordinate rulers serving under Chemosh are Nefarious, Mammon, the warrior twins Asmadai and Adramelec, and—do I own two portions of Chemosh's region?"

"No," Kaela replied. "I simply forgot to add Octaviel's name to the list. He will serve under Chemosh." Octaviel was a youngster, but he was fearlessly faithful to God. His sense of justice would add mayhem to Chemosh's rule.

Lucifer pointed to an area on the map. "Who owns this section?"

"This section of the northern region is the fourth and last area on the map to be divided," Kaela replied. "You, and no one else, great sire, will supervise it since the onyx palace, the pits, and the pens are here."

The following day, Autumn distributed the revised maps to her comrades while Sin introduced them to their new titles. "You are powers, princes, governors, dominions, principalities, and provinces.

Your leadership in the North is secondary to your emperor's. You must secure permission from Lucifer if you wish to make any changes in your region. None of you may over-step his decisions or his decrees. Lucifer's word is final. You will accept your new positions with a pledge of everlasting loyalty to my father. Should you break your vow, you will be judged. If a hearing is held, a counselor will be chosen to represent you. If none is present, I shall assume the responsibility of defending you. Beelzebub is the North's new advisor. He will remain here with Father. If you need his advice, you will come here—he will not go to your region. You will be installed into your new positions without celebration. This is a solemn occasion."

"Kaela, where is your territory?" Asmadai asked as he studied the map.

"I will continue to occupy the cottage I built for Lucifer," Kaela told the false rulers of the North.

That night, at the grand cabin, Autumn struggled to close the shutter on the window that opened above the stand sitting between her bed and the one Kaela slept in. Yielding to her angel's help, she said, "I was thinking, all the upstairs rooms, except the corner rooms, have one window, and they are much warmer than ours. And since we gave the warmer rooms to our apprentices, it seems that we are forced to keep this one. However, we could take one of the rooms downstairs as our bedroom now."

Kaela sat at the foot of his bed, listening to what she was saying.

"Most of the rooms on the ground floor have built-in fire-places," Autumn pointed out. She could see he was interested. "The wind and rain comes through that window so forcefully that I don't want to leave the warmth of my bed in the morning." She studied Kaela's face. "You know a well as I do that this room is not right for sleeping."

That day, a choice was made. Kaela moved their belongings to a downstairs room in the middle of the house. While Autumn arranged their new room to her liking, her angel built a shutter of thick, heavy wood that would keep the rain and wind out, day or night. Above the top exterior of the window, Kaela built an overhang that guided the rain away from their room so that it drained to the ground below. Before he was done, every window in the cabin sported new shutters and overhangs. The improvements warmed the air so that the interior of the cabin dried out, putting an end to the musty scent Kaela hated. The room Autumn chose for their bedroom doubled as a study. It had one window, a large fire-place, and a new bathroom that Kaela had just finished installing.

Throwing himself onto his bed, Kaela pulled the sheet over his nude body; the scent of the soap Autumn made from lilacs lingered on his skin long after he left the shower. He closed his eyes and listened to logs crackling in the fireplace and the muffled sound of rain falling outside his shuttered window. Basking in the warm glow of gentle flames that fed his sleepiness, he drew the bedspread over his tired form from head to toe. Breathing in the material's clean fragrance, he yawned once, turned onto his side, and fell into a deep, soothing sleep.

Kaela awoke feeling refreshed and energized. He looked forward to starting his day, even if it meant reporting to the pit to spirit more of Lucifer's slaves to the safety of the Sacred Region. In the foyer, he strapped his weapons' belt around his waist and adjusted the strap on his thigh. He sheathed his sword and fastened his crossbow to the belt before walking to the door. Outside, he narrowed his eyes and studied the fog that burdened the air so much that it was impossible to see beyond the cabin's porch.

"Father, we brought this misery on ourselves through our indifference. Please help us end it."

At the palace, Botis escorted him to the conference room on the ground floor. Inside the room, a brother stood at the window. Though his back was to Kaela, the garb he wore identified him as one of God's council members. His blue-and-gold cloak revealed that he was God's advisor. Just as Autumn suspected, the night-flyer, the spy, was none other than Belial.

"I see you finally came to your senses and left Heaven's fading deity for one who will rule our globe with an iron hand," Kaela said, greeting his evil brother with false words that were not his own.

Belial turned at the sound of Kaela's voice. He had always like Kaela. The brothers shook hands while they exchanged greetings. Belial offered Kaela a cup of root tea. Both laughed at the tea's bitter taste, but its warmth was a welcomed relief against the cold, damp air in the onyx palace. They talked for over an hour with no mention of why God's counselor would leave the security and beauty of the Sacred Region to fly north, where everything was dead, rotted, and mud-covered.

Then without being questioned, Belial offered an explanation for why he was here. "I have come to the North to join Lucifer's forces." He studied Kaela's face. "No. I am not God's spy." He sipped his tea. "What you said about God being a fading deity will stay with me forever. In fact, that is why I left the Sacred Region. I see what is happening here in the North, and no action is being taken to stop it. If I were Heaven's King, Lucifer's bad behavior would have ended in the throne room. But our so-called Creator is weak. He loves each of us equally. I asked Him outright why He would not put creation in reverse and uncreate Lucifer and his rebellious followers. Do you know what God said to me?"

Kaela shook his head. "No, what did our Enemy say in answer to your question?"

"God told me that if He uncreated everyone He disagreed with, it would confirm the false narrative that He is a weak leader," Belial told Kaela. "I think what He was saying reveals His weaknesses." Belial sniffed, his nose was as cold as his feet and fingers were. "What do you think of that?" The traitor rubbed his hands together before wrapping them around the cup he drank from.

"I think God likes a challenge," Kaela half-whispered. "And, He really hasn't found one yet." He looked away for a brief moment, and then he turned his attention back to Belial.

"Anyway, while I was in God's kingdom, I had access to His holy journals," Belial confided. "I rewrote each of them, and soon, we will take our rewritten versions of the King's books to His region where Lucifer will read from them in the public square, thus turning God's loyal sons against Him."

Kaela nodded. "I hope I am present on that day."

"I have no doubt that you will be there to hear what our emperor has to say." Belial laughed. "I always enjoy talking with you, brother. I hope you will make me a guest in your cabin, but currently, Sin is enamored with me, and I must remain here until she loses interest. You know how that is."

Kaela smiled. No, he wasn't curious about how it felt to be the object of Sin's affections.

Chapter 36

God's Holy Books

"I called this council meeting out of time to inform each of you that Belial has joined our forces," Lucifer announced, a haughty smile curling the corners of his thin lips. Resting the palm of his hand on Flagitious' shoulder, he continued his speech. "My advisor has agreed to relinquish his duties to Belial, who assumed the obligation of counselor moments after he revealed he would not return to the Sacred Region. Now the fact that Flagitious is no longer my counselor does not mean he has lost his value in the North. No, indeed it means he is available to counsel my princes, governors, provinces, principalities, officers, and warriors. His duty has taken on massive proportions, and he will be regarded with respect by all of you at all times."

The evil emperor moved from where Flagitious sat to stand behind his own chair at the table. "Tomorrow, we shall embark on a new adventure. We are going to test our Enemy's powers. We will enter the Holy City with duplicates of God's journals in hand. We will use the false books to cast doubt on His so-called good works. We will encourage His citizens to ignore all warnings they received from Him about the alleged atrocities forced on their more-adventurous brothers by my warriors, and we will encourage them to join us in the North."

Lucifer's eyes glowed. "After our visit tomorrow, only a fool would believe God, even if the proof of what He said stood right before them. Our gullible brothers will learn that I am more than an angel, my pure essence is divine. And, to prove my power is greater than God's, I shall dim His light in Heaven. My miracle will occur when it is least expected." The insane emperor grew thoughtful. "I will perform my miraculous feat during Heaven's most restful hour. Yes. I will time it so that God's citizens will awaken to my light, not His."

Kaela sniffed and slumped in his chair. Scraping the blade of his knife under his fingernail, he asked nonchalantly, "How do you, great sire, expect to perform this spectacle of light?" He raised his eyes briefly, and then lowered them to his nails again. "Just curious," Kaela sniffed. His question sparked the interest of the region's newly seated rulers, and now they, too, demanded an explanation.

Sin rose from her seat. "Anchored in deep space, there is a gaseous planet. My darling father will rupture the globe's shell with a fiery dart, thus igniting its toxic vapors. According to my calculation, the planet's inferno will last forever. When the deed has been accomplished, one-half of Heaven will be drenched in light. God will no longer be needed here. Toppled from His throne, the arrogant Dictator will wander through deep space until He finds some forsaken globe to claim as His own. Heaven will be ours." The witch studied the shocked faces at her table. "Are there questions?"

"Yes, I have many questions," Kaela said, straightening in his chair. He shifted his bright-blue eyes from Sin to Lucifer. "Great sire, did anyone other than Sin counsel you about you decision to ignite a gaseous planet in deep space? Have you considered the possible results of your actions, good and bad? What if there is no good result? What if you destroy this world, and when God leaves Heaven, we have to follow after Him? Because, like it or not, great Lucifer, no matter how vehemently we deny our Enemy's power, we know that only God can breathe life into those barren globes rumored to be out there. Without Him, we will perish."

Whispers filled the room.

"Are you ready to bow down before our hateful King and beg His forgiveness?" Resting his knee against the edge of the council table, Kaela propped his chair on its back legs while studying Lucifer's blank expression. "Just curious." He shrugged.

Abdiel sat next to Autumn. Though he had no position or title, he attended every council meeting. Leaning in his seat, he glanced at Autumn's notes. How could she keep up with who was talking? The room had exploded into a heated argument between the North's newly appointed rulers, Lucifer, and Sin. Abdiel glanced across the table at Kaela, whose questions had ignited this riot. If he was not so worried about Heaven's safety, he would have smiled at the rascal who sat calmly, cleaning the day's mud from under his nails.

"Excuse me," Abdiel said. "Excuse me. I have a question." He leaned back in his chair, his face lined with disgust. Judging by the recognition his request received, Abdiel wondered if he had ceased to exist. "Could I have the floor, please?"

Kaela rose from his seat, and slicing his sword through the air, he yelled, "Silence! Abdiel has a question." He pointed the tip of his blade in his former brother's direction. "Go ahead. You have their attention."

In a slovenly manner, Kaela dropped back into his chair, set his knee against the table-top's rustic edge, and to the disgust of those seated closest to him, returned to the offensive task of scrapping his dagger under his nails.

Standing at his chair, Abdiel studied the faces of Lucifer's bold warriors. All eyes were trained on him. "I have a question," he said, clearing his throat. "For one moment, consider what Sin told us. She says there is a gaseous planet somewhere in deep space, and once it is ignited, one entire side of Heaven will be drenched in light. The other side, I assume, will be plunged into eternal darkness. I would like to hear an expert's opinion on how this unusual lighting condition might affect our globe, its environment, and its life forms." The Northern rulers agreed. "I believe Savantel lives in the palace. Could he be summoned to speak since he is one of the North's most prominent scientists?"

At Abdiel's request, Savantel joined the meeting. Seated in a chair next to Autumn, the scientist listened as Lucifer recapped his plan to ignite the newly discovered gaseous planet in the hope of extinguishing God's light in Heaven. Licking his dry lips with his equally dry tongue, Savantel rose to his feet to speak. "Abdiel is correct in his assumption that while one side of Heaven is drenched in light, the other side will be plunged into darkness. Unlike the universe's uninhabited globes, our world follows no course through the cosmos, nor does it rotate on its axis. Therefore, we should be more concerned about how our globe might suffer when one half of it is lighted and its other half is not. That brings us to a new challenge. Forget light and dark; let us think of hot and cold."

"Sin said the gaseous planet's inferno would last forever. Suppose the surface of Heaven's lighted side becomes scorched. Plants die. Lakes and oceans dry up. What of our brothers? How will our race survive without food or water?" Savantel studied the council members' concerned faces. "Forget scorched land and starving angels. What if the blast from the planet's ignition proves so forceful that it blows this world apart? What then? I suggest that we leave the gaseous planet as it is until we are certain that Heaven and its inhabitants will be safe. Maybe the great Lucifer can find another way to prove his super-powers."

"Savantel worries that my father's plan might have negative effects in Heaven," Sin informed the leaders. "Worry for globe is good. We must take precautions when we are faced with a project of this magnitude. However, the great Lucifer, who is a renowned scientist, believes that Heaven might suffer mild plant destruction. Since our region lacks vegetation, we will let God worry about Nature's trees and flowers."

Sin glanced around the table. "You are looking at me, Abdiel. Have you a question?" Abdiel shook his head and folded his hands on the table-top.

"God will not allow this globe to expire. He found it after He destroyed our home world." Sin sneered, repeating the lie she had Lucifer recite when she lived inside his brain. "God has a following here," she admitted. "But we can show Him our might, our power, so that He will reconsider who should be heir to His throne." She glared at the council members. "Disobey Lucifer, and you will deal with Sin."

"Yes, but—" Moloch's protest was cut short.

"I said, disobey Lucifer and you will answer to me," Sin reminded. "My powers changed this region from what it was to one that meets my needs. Need you more proof that I can sufficiently deal with my father's disloyal subjects?"

"This meeting is adjourned," Lucifer declared, casting a delighted glance in his evil daughter's direction. "We will meet in the morning in the palace court-yard, and we will leave from there for our mission in the Sacred Region."

The council members, including Autumn, Abdiel, and Kaela, left the room. They spoke not a word as they made their way through the dark palace to return to their homes. Council members who were governors, princes, principalities, dominions, and provinces returned to their regions in the North; each burdened with the fear that Lucifer's plan to ignite the gaseous planet might end Heaven's existence and theirs too.

Throughout the dark, dank night, Kaela awoke gasping, sweat seeping from every pore, his brain asking and answering questions about the effect Lucifer's plan to extinguish Father's light would have on Heaven. And what did the false emperor hope to achieve by reading Belial's fraudulent books to God's citizens in the Sacred Region? What reason would Lucifer have to deceive Father's faithful sons other than to lure them from the safety of their homeland to the North, where they would become slaves? Desperate thoughts continued to roll in his head until he sat up in his bed.

Without waking Autumn, who slept soundly across the room from where he lay, Kaela rose to his feet, walked to the window, and gazed out it for several seconds. Who would have thought Sin was so powerful? The fog she conjured not only blocked Father's healing light but it also enabled her, a creature of darkness, to live more comfortably in Heaven.

He pulled on his dark-gray britches, wrapped his feet in rags, and slipped on his boots. He hated leaving Autumn alone. Every time he left the North, he was detained, and each time he was detained, he lost another brother.

Kaela whispered a prayer to Father as he slipped a tunic over his head and fastened his weapons' belt around his waist. "Take care of Autumn while I am gone. She is in Your hands now. Be gentle with her."

In the foyer of his cabin, he sheathed his sword and dagger, strapped his quiver of arrows onto his back, and clipped his crossbow to his weapons' belt. After checking the progress at the pit, Kaela would go to the dark palace. There, he would meet with Lucifer and his fraudulent crew before leaving with them for the Sacred Region.

The briefing in the court-yard of the dark palace was quick and to the point. Nesroc, Moloch, Apollyon, and Kaela were given the dreadful task of keeping Lucifer safe … from what? God's righteous sons were gentle, warm, and compassionate. They would listen to Lucifer's false account in the hopes of being polite. Doubters who challenged Father's powers would disgrace themselves by acting out in public. Disbelievers who worshipped Lucifer would riot, harming innocent brothers and destroying property.

"Remember, our mission is to penetrate the minds of God's most righteous servants with fear and doubt," Lucifer ordered. "I will announce the coming destruction and possible annihilation of Heaven as we know it. This announcement will follow my reading of the passages from several journals rewritten by our counselor, Belial. The new journal thoroughly distorts the reason for God's laws and questions if He truly is the universal Creator." He smiled. "When God's citizens hear my words regarding their King's so-called miracles, they will weep and wail. Their grief will turn to doubt, and they will fly to my empire where they will pledge their loyalty to me."

With a wave of his hand, the North's insane leader lifted into the air, shouting, "Follow me! Follow me, my good and loyal warriors!"

Evangeline was the first to witness Lucifer's coming. He saw the emperor's arrival as a dark cloud rolling in from the North, so numerous was his minions. Zophiel, who perched on the highest peak of God's house, blew a trumpeted warning that trouble was approaching. Righteous sons raced from the outdoor markets and the city's shops in a desperate attempt to reach their homes before the invaders arrived. Disbelievers watched the sky, fully enjoying the excitement of the moment. They cheered when Lucifer and his dark warriors dropped from the firmament, filling the town square with their presence. Surrounded by his appointed bodyguards, the evil emperor took his stand inside the gazebo Autumn built before she left God's kingdom to live in the North.

"As you can see, I've taken precautions against Michael's heathens," Lucifer said with a horrid grin. He extended his arms as though honoring those who flanked him at his sides, front, and back. Walking to the lip of the gazebo's bandstand, he called in a loud voice, "Listen to me and learn the truth about your King." While some in the crowd focused their attention on the evil emperor, others continued to talk among themselves. Lucifer turned to his bodyguards. "Make them understand that they are to give me their undivided attention while I speak. Do it now."

Northern sentries, Kaela included, moved from the bandstand into the audience, pushing, shoving, and strong-arming their brothers until every tongue was silenced and every eye was fixed on Lucifer. With horrible gruffness and great disrespect for his brothers' dignity, the emperor's appointed guards took their positions on the bandstand next to him.

"Thank you for your courtesy." Lucifer laughed sarcastically. "Now I will read from a book that is closed to you as common citizens of Heaven but is open to the scribe, the Goddesses, and to all of God's advisors and saints. The words written herein are your King's own words describing His innermost feeling toward His sons of light, who He blatantly refers to page after page as His slaves or as His servants."

Lucifer opened the journal and read perverse passages so expertly written by Belial that they made God's sons weep.

When the false emperor finished reading, he shouted over the crowd's cries of protest, "Believe what you wish, but this journal holds God's thoughts about all of you and this world He calls Heaven. Soon, He will build a new world, one that rivals Heaven. He will fill it with clay beings, and we will be their slaves. These clay beings will procreate like the beasts of the field. The female creatures will birth infants who, in turn, will reproduce again and again, until they fill the globe with their offspring. They will possess souls, and whether they are good or bad, their souls will hold the key to their salvation." He shook the book he held in his hand in the air. "Yes, unlike us who, if we rebel, will be cast out of Heaven into a fiery pit, these creatures will be given a second chance before they perish.

"If they accept God as their Father, their Creator, and their King," Lucifer continued, "these creatures will come to Heaven where they will become our masters, and we will become their slaves."

Lucifer grew quiet for a long moment. Was he savoring the sobs of the brothers whose hearts he had just broken, or was he simply considering what he should say next?

"Clay beings will rule over us, and if you think the lies you hear about northern atrocities are frightening, wait until they fill our globe with their alien laws. We will never escape the slaughter. Greed for God's gold, envy of our beauty and wisdom, hatred of our kind, will drive them to uncreate us. That is why we must stop God in His tracks. We cannot allow another race to capture His throne and rule over us."

"How do we know what you are saying is true?" one righteous brother shouted boldly. "Truth calls you the father of fraud."

"Really, Truth has convinced you that I cannot be trusted?" Lucifer laughed, seemingly unmoved by the insult. "Listen to me!" the evil general shouted over the mayhem that erupted in the town square. "The alien world may be a long time in creation, but if I sit on God's throne, there will be no life-bearing alien worlds, no alien races to contend with, and slavery will not exist in Heaven." He paused while doubters and non-believers of God's power cheered his statement. "I will rule this globe justly. I will see to it that our race is the last race created, and I promise no race but ours will live in Heaven.

"Now listen to this!" Lucifer shouted, "Underground, behind God's stables, there is a locked building. It contains three mighty swords your Lord plans to use against you. The sword that would have been mine will most probably stay in the Dictator's hands. The other two weapons will be passed down to fools. Prince Michael and the Archangel Gabriel seem to fit that description perfectly. I promise a high and exalted title to whosoever finds the key that opens the door to God's armory. Bring me the key, and I will give you a copy of God's journals, copies of the ones I read from today that caused this mass hysteria. The journals I offer are reproductions of the journals that were removed from God's private study by an unidentified brother who is sympathetic to the North's plight. The finder of the key will not only receive a high title and books that contain the secrets to our universe but he will receive one of God's swords to hang on his castle's wall. That is correct—I said castle. I will have a castle built for whoever brings me the armory's coveted key."

Lucifer's offer excited many brothers who gathered to hear him speak.

"How do we know there is a key? Or that the journals are truthful?" the child Jubel asked. He, like Raphael, received a gift that Father had not yet revealed to him.

"My friend, the key is mine," Lucifer lied. "Before I left for the North, I placed it in my dresser's secret vault for safekeeping. While I was gone, the scribe and your sisters rummaged through my belongings. They found my treasured key and gave it to God to earn His favor." The foul general lifted one of the journals in his hand. "As for this journal, it is the true word of God. Written in His ancient language and translated by the scribe, it holds the secret of how we came to live on this world. Unlike the book that falsely describes Heaven's creation as a miraculous event, this book tells of our failed home world. It defines God's not-so-sacred globes and why they bear no life. If my speech seems harsh, it is because what I say exemplifies Truth's lesson."

Archangel Gabriel tired of Lucifer's lies, shouted, "How dare you mock Truth!" Storming through the crowd of on-lookers, he drew his sword. In unison, the dark warriors who guarded the evil emperor drew their weapons and prepared to battle the saint. Kaela placed himself between Gabriel and the North's self-appointed emperor.

"You, Lucifer, have never exemplified our sisters' virtuous lessons!" Archangel Gabriel shouted over Kaela's shoulder. The saint turned to face the crowd. "The northern emperor is evil. He defiles Truth's good name and mocks our Lord's words by reading passages from a false book. The key that Lucifer wants you to find belongs to Father, as does everything in this world."

The crowd rebelled. Faithful brothers demanded the emperor's departure from their city, while doubtful sons and disbelievers defended his right to stay.

Gabriel held his sword out before him. "Listen to me!" The archangel's voice was like thunder. The crowd grew quiet. "Belial was Father's counselor for eons. He was privy to where our Lord kept His holy journals, and he rewrote them. Do not believe that Father's journals are missing from His inner sanctum. Belial is missing from this region. He has turned against us for Lucifer's false promises of grandeur."

While Archangel Gabriel spoke, the northern emperor secured Moloch's sword from his belt, resting his hand on Kaela's shoulder, he lunged forward. The blade of his borrowed sword passed between Kaela's arm and ribs, slicing through Gabriel's body. Brothers, who stood close by gasped, horrified at what they witnessed. The righteous among them sprang into action. The angry crowd frightened Lucifer. He withdrew his blade from Gabriel flesh, tossing it to Moloch.

"I am not armed!" he shouted. "I am not armed. Do not harm me! I am not armed." His frantic eyes searched for Kaela, but he was busy fending off God's saints with his hands. Where was his sword?

"Retreat! Retreat!" Lucifer screamed.

Moloch, Nesroc, Apollyon, and the remainder of his minions spread their wings, directing their flight from God's kingdom to the North. The last sight Lucifer's eyes beheld when he glanced over his shoulder to assure himself that he was not being followed was six burly saints clasping irons on Kaela's wrists and ankles.

The clamor of the mob could be heard from the Holy City to the village that lay at the base of God's high hill. Their voices announced the impending arrival of a prisoner who fought against his shackles, who stumbled and fell, only to be dragged by the horse he was chained to whose speed he could not match. Prince Michael's saints slowed the steed, pausing long enough to help Kaela to his feet. And then, the procession began anew. Kaela, shackled at the ankles and wrists, a thick chain around his waist connecting him to the horse, jogged down center of the Holy City's wide golden streets leading to castle. He tripped, stumbled, fell face-down, and was dragged along as he struggled to right himself. A young soldier in Prince Michael's service urged him to rise to his feet and walk, but offered no help.

Lindsay, a child created of Father's seventh and last flock, pointed to the crowd who mocked Kaela. "Where is your courage now that you are unarmed and shackled?" Lindsay asked.

Tears streamed down Kaela's cheeks, though he had no pity for himself. It was his worry for his beloved Autumn that blurred his eyes and broke his heart. His every delay in Father's kingdom proved fatal in the North. A rock landed at his feet. Now more rocks were tossed in his direction. Lindsay attacked the mob that threatened the prisoner, dispersing them, watching them until they fell behind brothers who simply lined the sidewalks, shouting hatefully at Kaela while cheering Prince Michael's saints.

The scene continued through the village, up the mountain's staircase, across the field, through the wide-open gates of the Holy Castle, across the courtyard when, at last, relief came. Prince Michael, face stern and unsmiling, walked to where Kaela stood trembling.

"I am removing your irons," he said flatly. "Will I have a problem with you?" Kaela indicated that he would not. The prince unlocked the irons, removed them, and handed them to Archangel Uzziel, who was prepared to interrogate Kaela.

"I cannot do this," Kaela argued. "Our brother Autumn is in the North. Lucifer and Sin will uncreate him." He sobbed with abandon. "Please … please … this is not about me." He wept. "I fear for Autumn's life. Sin is envious of him." With each word he spoke, he was dragged farther from where Prince Michael and Archangel Uzziel stood to the center of the courtyard, where Lindsay tied him to a tree.

"What? This is it? You have no pits or pens where you put prisoners? No rooms or vaults or secure places to store captives, do you think that tying me to a tree will keep me here?"

"Shut up!" Lindsay shouted in Kaela's face.

"Now that really frightened me," Kaela growled. "Let me go, and I'll let you live."

"You should be very proud, Kaela," Lindsay hissed. "Father is considering putting a dungeon under His house where Nature originally put a cave. We thought of putting you there in the cave, but Father says that would be torture. Does the word sound familiar?" He glared at Kaela. "I heard what you did in North. You are worse than Lucifer or Sin. I doubt that Lucifer is thinking of you now. Are you thinking of him and his filthy daughter?" The righteous angel stormed off.

"I cannot believe that I am so hated for doing God's work," Kaela whispered. He sank down the trunk of the tree to the ground. Alone in the courtyard, he prayed. "Father, look after Autumn in the North. Sin sought to uncreate her, and I fear that in my absence, she will succeed in a second attempt on Autumn's life. Watch over your servant, Autumn."

When his prayer ended, he fell asleep.

"Well, this is another fine mess you've gotten us into."

Kaela opened his eyes. "Autumn?" He looked around. She was nowhere in sight.

"Yes, it's me." She snorted. "I'm over here, tied to the tree behind you, to your right."

"Oh, thank you, Father." Kaela wept. He rose to his feet. Tears streamed down his cheeks. He craned his neck in her direction. Drinking in Autumn's beauty, he said, "I thought … I was worried that—"

"It's all right." Autumn reached one hand toward him. "I think the experienced saints are being a bit dramatic about your capture so they can impress their new recruits." She glanced around the courtyard. "I was sitting at my desk at the grand cottage when Prince Michael's saints burst through the door, and I thought, *Uh-oh, here we go again.*" She drew on the memory of the night Lucifer's thugs broke down the door to the cottage she shared with Sonnet and attack them while they slept. "When I saw Uzziel, I almost ran to him. He motioned for me to stop, and I did. Then I was shackled, an experience I really didn't need. Anyway, I was brought here and mocked until I was slobbering and sobbing, and now I'm tied up to a tree next to you."

Kaela smiled. "I told you the fun never ends."

Autumn heard voices. She put one hand up. "Someone is coming. Act like you're asleep." She slid down the tree trunk, flopped onto the ground, and closed her eyes tight.

Kaela heard the voices too. He stood taller, straighter, with his shoulders squared. Lindsay approached. He was alone.

"I asked to see Father," Kaela said when the young soldier was a little more that arm's length away. "Has our Lord received my message?" He studied the soldier's face. "I asked you a question, sire."

"Be quiet," Lindsay told Kaela. "I have orders to take you to Prince Michael. It seems you and Autumn will not be interrogated here in Father's yard but, rather, in the prince's quarters, where each of you will bathe, change into proper attire, and partake of a dinner meal. You will be dining with the prince, our sisters, the scribe, and Archangel Effiel."

He removed the shackles from Kaela's wrists and ankles, and without taking precautions to keep his prisoner from escaping, he moved to where Autumn sat awaiting her release. "You both may go now if you wish, or you can wait, and I will escort you to Prince Michael's apartment." The pair chose to wait for Lindsay to escort them.

During dinner, Kaela announced, "I refuse to go back to the North." He said those words knowing full well that if Father told him to return, he would. "I worry for Autumn's safety each time I leave. Sin is envious of him for some reason. The witch tried to uncreate Autumn once, and I fear that Sin may succeed if we continue to be separated from each other." He glanced around the table. Inspiration reached for his hand. "I need to know that my decision to stay in the Sacred Region is acceptable to Father."

"So where do you plan on staying while you are in our region?" Prince Michael asked.

Before Kaela could reply, Autumn announced, "I'm going to live in our cottage again." Her cheeks were glowing pink. "I'd like for Kaela to come home with me. I think we should take up our lives where we left them. I'm hungry to do woodworking, and I know Kaela is anxious to—"

"I wish to become one of Prince Michael's saints," Kaela said. He cast Autumn a timid glance that brought smiles from his sisters. "I would like to become one of your saints, Michael. I didn't learn every new combative strategy so that I could spend the remainder of my life in a carpentry shop."

Autumn dropped her fork. Turning her weary eyes away from Kaela, she gazed at the contents of her plate. "We talked about this. I know we took an oath, but—"

"I was serious when I took my oath to uphold God's laws at the cost of my existence and to protect my righteous brothers with my life," Kaela said, reaching for her hand." I meant what I said when I promised not to falter from my duties." He studied Autumn's face. Her bottom lip trembled so that she gently bit it in an effort to compose herself. "I am so sorry, Autumn, but when we were inducted to God's sainted service, we made solemn promises to Prince Michael in the presence of the Father's scribe, promises that I will not take lightly." He leaned toward her, pressing her hand to his chest, he half-whispered, "This thing with Lucifer isn't over, it's just beginning."

"I know, but—"

Prince Michael interrupted. "I will not hold you to your word, Autumn. I know you were caught up in the moment. But, Kaela, I could use an officer like you. Of course, you will work your way through the ranks. That is, if I can find a way to tell my troops that you are not a criminal."

Scribe Excelsa reached for the pitcher of nectar that sat in the center of the table. "Since I cannot get the attention I need to be polite, I will get the pitcher myself," he said in a voice that revealed his annoyance at having been ignored. "May I interject? Father will have a festival out of time. Seems that happens a lot these days. He plans to speak to His citizens, tomorrow evening. Maybe someone will vouch before God and sons for Kaela and Autumn's trustworthiness after the concert or before—whichever comes first."

Chapter 37

Angelic Rights and a Grand Promotion

On the night of the festival, Father rose from His seat on the auditorium's third floor to address Heaven's angels. "My Sons, you are created equal, therefore no member of your race shall ever hold the title *King of Heaven's angels*. Recently, however, a great number of your brothers have gone to the North where they pledged their loyalty to a weak leader." Father studied the faces that turned upward to better see Him while He spoke. He smiled though His eyes were moist with tears. "I created you wise and gave each of you freedom of self-expression and freedom of choice. Who would have known the gifts I gave you would lead us to the events that have occurred these many centuries?" He paused for a brief moment, before continuing His urgent and heartfelt speech to His sons.

"To be truly wise you must be decisive," Father told His faithful children. "You must focus on what is right for society and for yourself. If you are uncertain about anything that you are doing, you should take time to deliberate on what you have done so far and where you will go from there. When you make a mistake, you must accept responsibility for your actions. Each facet of your life has a price and you, my sons, must be prepared to pay the price for your mistakes." There was a moment's pause to allow the listeners time to ingest what had been said, then Father stated, "It is true that Heaven's laws apply to everyone and that everyone is bound to obey me, but that does not lessen the appreciation I feel for my children. I will never harm any one of you and I will love each of you, always." Father grew quiet for a long moment. "Does anyone wish to add to my speech?"

"Yes. I would like to profess my sincere loyalty to You, My Lord," Raphael announced. He lifted from the ground floor and hovered high over his brothers' heads. "I want to add that Kaela is my hero. And he should be considered a hero by each of you." Raphael pointed to where Kaela sat with Autumn and Archangel Effiel. "Everyone who lives in this kingdom is aware of the northern atrocities. We are aware of the beatings, the slavery, and the loss of angelic lives, the pits and underground prisons where our craftsmen were expected to live, and the spells Sin cast on the northern region that emptied it of its wildlife and destroyed its lush foliage and magnificent trees. Rumor has it that even the fish fled their watery homes to escape the abomination Lucifer birthed at the foot of Father's great white throne.

"But no one knows that Kaela and his crew spied on Lucifer to learn his secrets or how they led thousands upon thousands of slaves to freedom to be healed by our loving Father. I want to put to rest the accusations that he ate slaves. He took slaves from the pits, walked them through the forest to a place of safety, and sent them home to Father's kingdom, where they were healed, bathed, clothed, and fed."

Japeth rose to his feet and lifted into the air with Raphael. "It is true. I and two others, Celone and Ramael, were held prisoner in the pit where Artiff worked. Kaela came to Artiff under the guise of needing a fresh meal." Laughter rose up from the auditorium. Hundreds of brothers who had been held captive in the North confirmed Japeth story. Some, who were enslaved when the tunnel was being excavated, told how they had watched or labored with Kaela as he worked to free captive brothers from the forbidden zone to deliver them safely to God. The auditorium thundered with applause while former slaves paid homage to their liberator.

"And let us not forget the work Autumn did in the North!" Raphael shouted over his cheering brothers. "Autumn kept notes that revealed Sin's evil plans against our region. Autumn left the North without Lucifer's permission to deliver those plans to Scribe Excelsa. Autumn was dragged from the cabin Kaela built and beaten the point of uncreation. God bless Sonnet, Martyr, and all of our fallen brothers who worked in the North to keep us safe." The auditorium roared with cheers and applause.

Scribe Excelsa perched on the balustrade that stretched out before the royal family's booth. "Tonight, in private, Father presented a broach to Kaela with the words *Liberating Angel* inscribed across its front. Our brother no longer wears the dark uniform of the North. He exchanged those solemn clothes to wear, in his leisure time, the pastel robes and cloaks he wore when he taught carpentry to his apprentices." The scribe swiped Zophiel's trumpet, set it against his lips, and blew. The horrible sound of the horn was followed by laughter. Brothers who had mocked Kaela a day earlier were on their feet, shouting his name and cheering him.

A chord was struck by one of Zephon's musicians. Israfel's soprano voice rose like a golden chord in a song written by Bernella especially for Kaela. "Come softly, sweet angel, and please know I understand / the horrors you suffered in that dark, forbidden land./ Let me lead you from your prison through the cold, dark night,/ let me guide you far from peril to Father's healing light"'

When the song ended, Prince Michael stationed himself at Kaela's side. At God's command, batteries of saints surrounded their brother, escorted him to the center aisle, and replaced his robe and cloak with a short white tunic, the hem of which reached to Kaela's knee. "Private Kaela," Prince Michael said, accepting a garment that Archangel Uzziel offered, "I have the pleasure of robing you in this military vest of sapphire blue and gold. The vest's back and its lower hem are embossed with the emblem of a muscular, winged golden lion poised to do battle." The prince took a helmet from Archangel Gabriel's hands. "So that you are recognized as God's trusted saint, I present this helmet to you. Wear it when you are on duty, for it is a vital part of your new uniform."

Archangel Gabriel approached his honored brother. "Kaela, I am aware of your military expertise and that you are proficient in combative maneuvers, therefore, I am pleased to gird your waist with this belt that you designed for Prince Michael's saints while you lived in the North. This belt holds your sword and dagger, your crossbow, and all the tools and weapons you will need to protect and serve the citizens of your globe. Your weapons will be given to you when you report for duty in the morning."

Archangel Gabriel, Prince Michael's first-lieutenant, turned to Kaela's favorite sister. "Goddess Inspiration, you will present Father's gift to our brother."

Inspiration stood on her toes to drape a golden medallion around her courageous brother's neck. "Dearest Kaela," she said softly. Swallowing hard, she subdued her urge to weep with joy. Her silver eyes brimming with tears, she continued, "This golden medallion is awarded to you in accordance with your noble character and the acts of bravery for which you are being honored. The medallion's sturdy chain exemplifies your loyalty to God. Father's coat of arms, the sheaf of wheat bound by one cord, is engraved on the medal's front with the words *Liberating Angel.* Inscribed on the back of the medallion are the words *God's Courageous Lion.* Wear this medallion as a reminder of the love Father and His citizens feel for you." She took Kaela's arm. "I am honored to have the privilege of presenting you to Heaven's King."

Inspiration and Kaela knelt before God.

"My sons of light," Father said in a voice that revealed His love for His children, "behold your brother. Kaela's good and brave deeds earned him a high position in Heaven. From this day forward, this son shall be known as Archangel Kaela."

Word of Kaela's promotion traveled fast. According to one source, Lucifer knew that his beloved warrior had become God's titled angel before the ceremony in the Sacred Region ended. That night, the room in the dark palace that had been reserved for Kaela to use at his convenience was sealed. The following morning, Emperor Lucifer stepped onto his balcony to address his followers.

"Last night, a treasonous act was perpetrated against the North by a new enemy," the false ruler told his citizens. "Kaela, who was a trusted officer in my service, has become one of Prince Michael's soldiers, a member of God's sainted army." Lucifer grew quiet for a long moment. Sin rushed to her heartbroken father's side and whispered in his ear. "Today, a bounty is set on the heads of Kaela and his beloved brother, Autumn. It was they who stole my slaves, leading me to think that my Enemy was more powerful than I believed. It was they who reported all of our plans to Heaven's cruel Dictator and encouraged Him to change our region's climate so that it would not surpass the splendor of His kingdom. It was Autumn who won the hearts of my courtiers so that they trusted him with their secrets. Uncreate the traitors, or bring them to the North alive—it is up to you. But know this, Kaela may be the one who will inherit Heaven's throne, do you really want him for your king?"

Righteous brothers living in the North and acting as Father's spies sent word to Prince Michael that Lucifer and Sin had resumed their ritualistic occult services in their cryptic house of worship. Throughout the services, Sin made promises of eternal life in a new world where followers who volunteered for uncreation received a crown and throne. Slaves stepped forward, offering themselves for sacrifice, not because they lost their faith in Father, but to end their suffering. While sacrificial blood rolled in waves across the mansion's onyx floors, the incestuous witch cast spells designed to transport her victims' courage and wisdom to the great Lucifer, emperor of the North. Through Lucifer's remarkable power of persuasion and promises of renewed greatness, his princes, governors, principalities, dominions, and thrones relieved their shares of the North to him as a show of unity against God and saints.

Kaela's promotion put not only his life in danger but Autumn's life as well. Every day, northern henchmen entered the Sacred Region, hoping to uncreate them. At her angel's insistence, Autumn took refuge in the Holy Castle, where she was watched over by sainted guards. It was during the first days of her exile from Heaven's streets that Lucifer made a second attempt to turn God's citizens against Him.

Standing on the roof of the gazebo in the Holy City's town square, Lucifer shouted, "Citizens of the Sacred Region, I come here to make a public challenge to your cruel Dictator. On an eve in the near future, I shall display my power to create a light in the sky that will rival the Light that sits on a throne atop the Holy Castle. When my powers are displayed throughout this globe, you will long to join me in the North. Know that you are welcome to come to me, pledge your loyalty to me, and worship me as your king. To do otherwise will result in your uncreation." Scowling at the crowd that gathered, Lucifer unfurled his wings and directed his flight toward the North.

Autumn sat in Excelsa's private quarters. She was bored to tears. She wished she had kept her mouth shut about wanting to be a civilian. Now, instead of joining Archangel Kaela in his training exercises designed to teach Prince Michael's solders how to best keep God's kingdom safe, she was sitting here, and why? Because she couldn't keep her big mouth shut.

"Tell me the word's meaning," Scribe Excelsa grumbled. He could not understand this child's inability to learn Father's ancient language. And he hated it when Autumn bit her bottom lip while she studied the word whose meaning she obviously didn't know. "Think Autumn, I need the word's meaning—today, not tomorrow." He thumped his finger on the word, his impatience growing by the second. "I cannot believe that for someone who comes up with colorful metaphors and mind-boggling witticisms, you cannot learn a new language."

Autumn rolled her large gray eyes up to study the scribe's angry face. "I should have stayed in Prince Michael's service. I'm better at horseback riding than I am at figuring out foreign languages." She turned away from her lesson. "Let's forget about teaching me Father's ancient language."

"What is it with you, Autumn?" the scribe complained. "You were always so—"

"Independent," she said, nodding her head. "Excelsa, I need to find something I enjoy doing. I hate trying to interpret Father's ancient language, and between us, I can't read His writing." She studied the scribe's face. "I hear Archangel Effiel has an apprentice. A child named Elbreon. Maybe he could step in and help you handle Father's workload."

She was expressing her desire to work elsewhere, doing anything but this, when her guards knocked at the door. "I am always being watched. I can't go anywhere. I am so bored. I can't go to the shop because I have this price on my head that might endanger my coworkers. I can't live in my cottage because Father feels I'm not safe there. I feel like I'm being punished." Her expression resembled that of a puppy-dog pleading with its master to take it for a walk.

"Oh, stop that!" Scribe Excelsa scolded. "Your guards are here. We're done for the day."

Autumn pushed herself away from the desk. "Excelsa, I worked as scribe in the North. I penned Lucifer's journals and recorded the North's business. I risked my life to keep you and Father informed about the atrocities that took place in the North while I lived there. Please tell me there is something I can do where I can write recognizable words, not words whose letters look like symbols."

Scribe Excelsa sighed. "It was supposed to be a surprise, but Evangeline and the Archangel Effiel are gathering facts about you and Kaela and the work you both did while you lived in the North. I am fairly certain that Evangeline would be especially receptive to whatever details you can offer. Effiel's student, Elbreon, is helping them. They are working in the inner sanctum. If you wait a minute," the scribe said with a smile, "I will walk with you. I have little, if nothing, to do today, so Father won't miss me."

Autumn met Elbreon for the first time since his creation. Yet she knew Elbreon well and was familiar with his desire to be a writer. Feeling more relaxed in the inner sanctum's small library, she talked with her brothers for hours about the night of Sin's birth and described northern atrocities in words that made Excelsa cringe. When the others left for the dining room, Elbreon asked Autumn to walk the castle's grounds with him. Together, they traversed the path that led to God's Meditation Garden. They walked for the longest time, and at every turn they took, Autumn had a new story to tell Elbreon. They visited Sonnet's grave, where she spoke tearfully of the terrifying night that led to his uncreation. From there, they returned to the courtyard where Autumn pointed to the tree she had been tied to when she was captured by Prince Michael's saints.

"I was tied to that tree over there. Archangel Kaela was tied to the tree that stands off to the left and in the front of what I like to call my tree." The pair burst out laughing. Autumn hugged Elbreon's waist. "Would you like to watch the saints' work out? I've been tied to Scribe Excelsa's apron strings for so long that it will be a real treat for me."

Chapter 38

Healing Hands

Autumn and Elbreon entered the stadium through its wide-open doors. They waved at the civilians who gathered in the stands to watch the soldiers on the field being trained in military skills, which included horseback riding, hand-to-hand combat, sword skills, and archery. Autumn scanned the field, looking for Kaela. There he was, scantily clothed like the others, rubbing soil between his hands and preparing for the air skirmish exercises to begin. She nudged Elbreon and pointed to the highest seats in the arena.

"Let's sit up there," she said. "We will be able to use our powerful vision to see our brothers as they work out." She took Elbreon's hand, and together they scaled the stairs that led to seats just below the stadium's decorative balustrade.

The war games began. Hand-to-hand combat, archery, martial arts, sword fighting, charioteer, and horseback training—all these exercises took place on different parts of the playing field at the same time. Over the clanging of swords against shields and the thundering of horses' hooves, a crackling sound caught Autumn's ear. She rose to her feet, looking around the stadium. The sound seemed to be coming from overhead. On the field, officers and saints continued to practice their drills. But the horses stopped their galloping, threw their riders from their backs, and over-turned the chariots they pulled in an attempt to break away and run free. Sainted soldiers rose from the ground where they had been thrown. Still, the noise on the field was too chaotic to hear anything but shouted orders, clanging and banging of swords against shields, and the grunts and groans of brothers who were locked in physical combat.

Autumn stood with her head cocked to one side, her hand resting firmly on Elbreon's shoulder. The ground shook. The horses that were on the field were hoofing the air as they struggled against their thrown riders' determination to mount them. Several horses lost their balance, falling to the stadium's dusty floor. The saints ceased their exercises; they were clearly confused by their steeds' behavior. The ground convulsed. Athletes were thrown off their feet, and spectators lost their seating.

"What is it?" Elbreon asked, and though he was frightened, he remained seated.

Autumn turned away from the sight on the field to gaze at the pure sky above. Shielding her eyes with her wings, she saw a fiery spiral falling through deep space toward Heaven. The crackling sound that drew her attention from the training exercises on the field was unbearable now. The air around her grew warmer by the second, and the landscape grew brighter.

In the last moments of normalcy, Autumn knew that Lucifer had fulfilled his threat to dim God's light by igniting a gaseous planet.

"Take cover!" she screamed. Autumn draped her cloak over Elbreon's head and torso. As the ring of fire settled around the globe like a white-hot belt, she shoved her young brother through the space under their bench. Within seconds, the air was engulfed in flames. Autumn screamed terribly as heat that threatened to suffocate her melted the fabric of her garments into her flesh. Her wings lost their feathers. Her hair fell from her head, strand after burning strand. The stench of burning flesh filled the air around her, and while the terror of what was happening consumed her, the fireball that threatened to devastate the globe grew brighter, brighter, and brighter, until its light robbed the landscape of its colors.

"I have to get out of here!" Autumn shrieked in horror. "I have to get out of here!"

How she arrived at the center of the playing field, she did not know. Maybe she ran to that wide area. She knew she didn't fly; her wings were burned to stubs. Dropping to her knees, she collapsed face-down on the playing field. Through narrowed eyes, she saw the bodies of her stricken brothers lying all around her. Autumn lost consciousness as one angel took her scorched hand in his and pressed its burned flesh to his cheek.

"Autumn, look at me." It was Kaela's voice she heard. "Autumn, look at me." He was sobbing. "Raphael. Over here, I found Autumn. I found Autumn," he repeated, his voice nothing more than a mere whine.

Raphael knelt beside her. "Autumn, please open your eyes and look at me."

Autumn opened her eyes. Kaela gasped, his face lost its color. Autumn's eyes were as red as the deepest red garnet stones. Looking into them, he could not tell where the whites of her eyes ended and her pupils began. Raphael lifted her face in his hands.

"Sweet Raphael," Autumn whispered through lips whose skin resembled the wax of a melted candle.

Kaela turned his head and, through eyes blinded by tears, thank God that Autumn could still see.

"Help me," Autumn rasped through a throat so desperately parch by the fire's heat that it felt it had been scraped raw by a dull, rusty knife. Kaela's tears fell on her burned skin like blocks of salt. Closing her eyes, Autumn gave herself to God. This event, whatever one might call it, was the worst torture she had ever endured in all her days in Heaven. "Father, I'm Yours," Autumn whispered.

"No!" Kaela wept. He wiped his tear-stained face with his hands and surrendered his beloved Autumn to Raphael. "Save Autumn." He loosened his grip on this child he loved more than life. "Autumn must live."

Sweet Raphael spoke soothingly as he touched the fingertips of his left hand against Autumn's charred skin. Lifting his right hand into the air, he called out in a loud voice, "I pray that Heaven's King will lend me His powers so that in His almighty name, I may heal this suffering child." He paused. "In the name of our Lord, I command Pain to release his grip on this brother. Foul entity, I command you to return to the frigid North where you will remain until you are expelled from

Heaven." Again, he paused. "Flesh, heal unscathed. Hair and feathers sprout anew."

Autumn passed out before Raphael finished his holy ritual of healing. She felt someone lift her in his arms. It was Kaela. He had been slightly burned, having hidden under his shield when the air caught fire, but he was well. Autumn slept.

When she awoke, she found Kaela sleeping on the ground beside her. It was morning. Far off in the distance, she could hear her brothers' cries of anguish. Burned angels in the village and in the city were in need of healing. Dazed by her ordeal, Autumn struggled to her feet, only to fall to her knees. Kaela drew her to him. Stroking her hair, he offered her water from a pail set close to where they rested.

"I am so sorry," he whispered. "I forgot that this event would happen unchecked. I should have taken you back to your house in Florida. Once again, I failed you. You never should have experienced this horror." He buried his face in her hair and wept with abandon.

"I needed to be here," she whispered. I had to know what happened on this day. There is one more powerful than you who could have sent me back. Father wanted me here."

Throughout the long, weary day, Raphael returned to see how Autumn was. Now he returned again, one last time, before going to the village to finish his work there. "Here, touch my hands," he said softly. "I am blessed with Father's power to restore my brothers' good health."

Autumn struggled to lift her hand toward him, but she was too weak. She smiled when Raphael met her reach half-way. With his healing hands, he restored her strength.

"Go to our brothers who need you," Autumn said, thankful that he had helped her. "I will be fine. I have Archangel Kaela to see to my needs until I am better able to fend for myself." She hugged the healer's neck before he moved away from her. "Thank you. Thank you so much." She wept.

Turning to Kaela, Autumn asked, "Elbreon?"

"You saved Elbreon from suffering as you, and so many others, did," Kaela replied. He lifted his precious Autumn in his arms and carried her across the playing field toward Father's house. "You will rest today. After I attend Prince Michael's meeting, I will check in on you. I have a feeling that there is much that needs to be done before God's saints will be sent to the North to deal with Lucifer and Sin, so I may be sleeping in my bed tonight." Kaela studied Autumn's face. She was so beautiful, so fair. He wished he could tell Prince Michael and the others that Autumn was from Earth, that she was his guest in Heaven, and how proud he was to say she was his friend.

"How's Autumn?" Prince Michael asked when Archangel Kaela arrived at the conference table.

"Better," Kaela answered. "Much better, thanks to Raphael's healing hands."

"He's a hero, you know?" Michael mentioned, speaking of Autumn, whom he saw as a small male angel.

"Yes, and a good brother," Kaela agreed, speaking of Raphael. Taking his seat at the table, he added, "The first person Autumn asked about was Elbreon." Saints seated at the table with him smiled, nodding. That was to be expected of Autumn; he was always thinking of others.

Prince Michael remained standing throughout the meeting. He spoke in solemn tones about the event that took place the day before. "Our entire region suffered extreme damage from the ring of fire that fell from the sky. Reports are coming in from Heaven's regions located to the east, west, and south of us. They have been hit as badly as we were hit here. We have received no word on northern casualties. Personally, I doubt that Lucifer or his council members will honor us with a report on the devastation that happened in the North since I believe our eldest brother will deny that he is responsible for this catastrophe. So since we have received no word about northern causalities, we will deal with what we know first and move to that region last."

He nodded in Archangel Kaela's direction. "Our new recruit will fill us in on how and why Heaven was engulfed in flames."

Aware that all eyes were on him, Kaela revealed Lucifer's plan to ignite a gaseous planet in deep space. "Our eldest brother's main objective was to dim Father's light in Heaven. He did not care if his ill-conceived plan destroyed Heaven's landscape or injured his unsuspecting brothers. He simply wanted to dim Father's light in Heaven to prove that He has grown weak. Abdiel called in the scientist Savantel, who was clearly opposed to the act, explaining that the heat from the newly lit planet would change Heaven's climate so that it might destroy our globe's plant and ocean life.

"However, in light of what Lucifer did, I am not in favor of putting the North last in our efforts to save our brothers there," Archangel Kaela said. "We have saints working in the North. Some of our sainted brothers are posing as slaves. They have been whipped, starved, and molested by Lucifer's warriors. By denying our righteous brothers a speedy rescue, we are being disrespectful of them. They are our bravest and most courageous citizens. They left our Lord's kingdom to set up shops in the North to teach classes to Lucifer's unskilled supporters, and they are faithful to Father. We should not deny them the assistance they need. We should send a team of saints to the forbidden zone," he said, knowing full well that Prince Michael put restrictions on calling northern Heaven a forbidden region. "We must bring our heroes back home where they can be healed by Father."

Prince Michael nodded. "I agree with you, Archangel Kaela. We do have good brothers who offered their skills to the North, and they are probably wondering when God's saints will come to their rescue. But our first priority lies with the military leaders who sent reports of the damage done to their regions and who requested our immediate aid."

The prince read from his notes. "Fortunately, Father healed our sisters and His council members, who were at their stations in the outdoor throne room when the tragedy struck. As for Nature, who sits on the throne nearest to Father's heart, she, like Father, is made up of all the elements of the universe and was not affected.

After a long sigh, Prince Michael said, "Evangeline, whose office is located on the third floor, was in Father's inner sanctum, working on a book he is currently writing. Scribe Excelsa and Archangel Effiel were with him, since only they are permitted to peruse the journals that line the walls of Father's private library."

And so the briefing continued. The saints learned that Raphael, Jubel, and many others discovered their healing powers when their hearts broke open with compassion for their suffering brothers. They scoured the Sacred Region throughout the night searching for victims who were burned by the fire that fell from the sky, and they were not satisfied until their injured brothers were whole and healthy again. While Prince Michael spoke, Dubbiel arrived with Eae and Eremiel at his side. They had traversed Heaven in search of brothers in need.

"If Father created a prison named Hell for Lucifer," Eremiel, one of God's many golden sons, told Prince Michael and his saints, "then northern Heaven has become our eldest brother's self-created hell. The entire Northern Province is devastated. We did not dare to enter it on foot as we journeyed from our regions to Father's kingdom. Instead, we flew over the North. From the air, we saw mud-covered streets, and for the most part, the region seemed devoid of life."

Zophiel interrupted the meeting. "Prince Michael, I have come to tell you that many of your sainted soldiers and Lucifer's slaves are trapped under the mountain in the tunnel that leads from the North to the Sacred Region." The messenger was clearly upset. "The tunnel's roof caved in when the ring of fire fell from deep space to Heaven. Hundreds of civilians from the village have volunteered to clear away the mud and debris in the hope of finding survivors."

"Prince Michael, I beg your permission to take a battalion of troops to the North to search for and rescue our righteous brothers," Kaela implored as he rose from his seat at the table. "Not everyone in Lucifer's empire is corrupt."

"We have all the hands we need here," Prince Michael told Kaela. "Permission granted. Saints, I pray that our Lord Jehovah, Heaven's one and only King, Creator of the universe and everything in it, will bless each of us with a portion of His strength, courage, wisdom, and understanding to successfully fulfill the needs of our suffering brothers. Lieutenant Gabriel, may God speed you and your troops on your mission. Saints, you are dismissed."

Outside the conference room, Kaela gained permission to see Autumn before leaving for the North. He was in their suite on the castle's first floor, gathering his weapons, when he saw her standing in the doorway. She was watching him.

"Where were you? Are you all right? Do you need anything?" he asked. He stepped back and studied his beloved Autumn. She was wearing her northern uniform—gray shirt, black britches and vest, and on her feet, she wore full-footed black boots that reached to her knees. Over her arm she carried similar uniforms in larger sizes.

"You are not going to the North with me," Kaela said in a firm voice.

She walked across the room, throwing the uniforms onto the back of the sofa. "Oh, but I am," Autumn said, her expression serious, her eyes burning with determination. "I am going to the North with you and your crew. Therefore, I must insist that our saints wear these uniforms."

Kaela felt his face burning with anger. "Yesterday, I held you in my arms and begged Raphael to save you, and today, you tell me that you are going to the North."

"Listen to me," Autumn insisted. "We cannot get past the guards if we are dressed in our sainted uniforms, but we can if we look like a battalion of northern warriors. We have to fit in so that we aren't singled out and uncreated."

She turned when Lieutenant Gabriel entered the room. "I talked with Father when I got wind of your plan to leave the Sacred Region to aid and assist our injured brothers and saints in the forbidden zone. Our Lord agrees that we should take all precautions. He especially liked my suggestion that we dress in northern uniforms during our mission, which He called 'a very principled precaution.' So here it is," she grumbled, handing Kaela his old northern uniform. "There you go."

"There you go," Kaela echoed, glancing across the room at Gabriel. "It's better to blend in with our enemies than to be captured and uncreated by them."

Chapter 39

A Cold, Dark Place

At Heaven's darkest hour, Kaela stood in the castle's courtyard, listening while Archangel Gabriel briefed his troops. He smiled, nodding a greeting to Lindsay who inadvertently made it possible for him to reveal to Prince Michael and God's scribe that he had no intention of returning to the North. Private Lindsay had been his arresting officer on the day Lucifer's foul crew visited the Holy City. Now, Autumn, Joniel, Raphael, and Jubel fell in line beside him.

"Listen up," Lieutenant Gabriel told his troops. "We are the finest saints in God's army, and our mission is to bring our righteous brothers out of the North to be healed in the Sacred Region. We are wearing uniforms that are similar to those worn in the North." He glanced at Autumn before he returned his attention to his saints. "It is better to blend in with our enemies than to be captured by them and uncreated." He nodded in Kaela's direction. "Archangel Kaela, will lead the way. It's going to be a long journey, so stay alert," Gabriel ordered. "And if you get separated from our unit, take cover. Do not try to be a hero while you are alone."

The walk through the northern-most providence was as dark and dismal as it was treacherous. Gabriel commented on the thick mud that threatened to suck the boots from his feet. He stumbled once. Kaela caught him and stood him upright before trudging on in search of their comrades. Autumn wiped tears from her cheeks. The North was once the most beautiful region in Heaven. Its trees sported broad, green well-shaped leaves. Its flowers were the most colorful and fragrant of any flower found in God's kingdom. The North's wildlife were huge, muscular, and fast; and its fish were the most beautiful to look at. She remembered the lakes, rivers, and streams she visited when the North was newly discovered. Back then, she waded through water that shimmered like diamonds, bathed in ponds that mirrored their surroundings, and let the gentle breezes dry her body with its soft fragrant fans.

Autumn pressed her hand to her mouth to stifle a sob. How could Father allow a witch to turn this region into a cesspool? Suddenly, she realized that Father never gave the witch permission to destroy any region on His globe.

"We did it," she whispered. Angelic indifference to the evils that lived in the North made the region the terrible place it had become. She was thinking along those lines when she slammed into Jubel's back. Poking her head to one side, she saw the awful sight that froze her brothers in their tracks.

Octaviel sat on a huge dark throne in a swamp that was fed by the elements. Kaela's brows rose high on his forehead. He studied his friend, who just sat there in the middle of nowhere, doing nothing.

"Octaviel," he called and waited, listening hard for a reply. "Octaviel," Kaela called a second time. Quiet reigned. He leaned and whispered to Gabriel, "I fear our brother has been uncreated. His body may have been put here as a warning to others." He thought for a moment. "Which means Octaviel's reason for being in the North may have been discovered by Father's enemies."

Turning to his troops, he said, "Stay here. I will assess the problem and let you know if it is safe to send in Raphael if indeed his skill is needed."

Kaela left the muddy shore to walk through foul-smelling water that ranged from ankle-deep to knee-high. His feet sank into the soft stinking ground the water covered, making it hard for him to reach his stricken brother as quickly as he hoped. There was no quiet path for him to walk on, and the water announced his intrusion on its territory with each step he took. The odor rising up around him as he waded through the muck and slime that lay on the water's surface grew more offensive with the smallest movements he made. Archangel Kaela stopped midway to where Octaviel sat; he gagged on the stench that engulfed him. The pooling water stretched out far ahead of him. No grass covered this murky bog, no fragrant breezes arrived to sweep away the swamp's foul stench, and Father's warmth was absent from air so cold it sent shivers down his spine.

Kaela stumbled, falling face first into the gore Sin created. He righted himself, wiping the crud from his face. Readjusting his weapons' belt, he trudged over to where Octaviel sat slumped on a false throne.

"Brother," he gasped, sickened by the muck that covered him. "If you live, speak to me now."

"Help me," a trembling voice rasped. A charred hand reached through the night's moist darkness to touch his comrade. "I am so badly burned that when it happened, I prayed to live, but now, I pray that someone or something will uncreate me. Pain feeds on me so hungrily that I should be nothing but bones. And my mind … my mind is filled with more gloom than this dreadful region." He groaned and quit speaking.

Kaela turned to gaze at the area where he left his troops. The gloom conjured by the witch, combined with the clouds Father used to create Heaven's pale night blanketed the region so heavily that he feared he was alone. "Raphael!" he shouted. "Come quickly. Octaviel is alive and needs your healing touch."

Raphael spread his wings, determined that he would not follow in Kaela's footsteps. He thought of hovering in the air, reaching his hand out before him, and instructing his brother to extend his hand upward so that he could clasp it in his. But the sight of Octaviel sitting on the throne, his blackened skin cracked and peeling from his body, his hair burned off, his wings burned to stubs, and the stench that rose up from him caused Raphael to set his feet down in the mire he had hoped to avoid. Taking a deep breath, the healer reached out his powerful hand, touching flesh too tender to be touched. A trembling blackened hand reached to push Raphael's firm stable hand away.

"I need to touch you," Raphael whispered. "Listen to my prayer. Believe, and you will be healed."

Autumn stood in the gloom, not knowing that she was alone. She could hear the distant voices, her brothers' voices, as they searched the area for victims injured by Lucifer's crime. A sloshing sound caught her ear. She turned her attention from the outlying area, where Prince Michael's saints worked in vain to find more of the missing, to the sound of someone making his way through the swamp water to where she stood.

"We need to find cover," a familiar voice told her. "Come with me."

The saints found a cave that wasn't much better than the climate they were seeking to escape. The cavern's inner room was small, but it would serve as a shelter until morning. Archangel Gabriel instructed Lindsay and Citadel to find something dry that could be used to fuel a fire. Autumn took off her cloak, offering it as burning material. The saints smiled at their beloved brother, who always seemed to put the comfort of others before his well-being. One by one, they offered their cloaks, urging Autumn to keep hers. She might have kept it, wrapped up it around her to ward off the North's cold night air; instead, she used it as a blanket to warm Octaviel.

Kneeling in the mud that carpeted the cave's floor, Autumn whispered, "Father, heal Octaviel. Help us to find all our brothers who were injured when the ring of fire fell from the sky. Bless our healers so that we can return to Your kingdom whole and healthy. In Your name, my King, I pray. Amen."

Throughout the night, Autumn ministered to Octaviel. Nothing she did seem to be enough. Her brother needed food and water. His skin and hair had grown back, but both needed to be cleansed to ward off infection. She brushed his hair from his forehead, dusting the dried flesh from his skin with the mere movement of her hand. He stirred slightly.

"Sleep, precious brother," she whispered. It was hard for Autumn to believe that just yesterday she was victimized by a ring of fire that robbed her of her hair and skin. The pain she felt as she lie smoldering on the stadium's floor wore her out. She lost consciousness when sweet Raphael healed her, the relief she felt was that great. She slept most of the day and she was still tired from her ordeal. Autumn's angel, Kaela, was only slightly burned. He had taken cover under his shield when the fire engulfed the globe. His fatigue was caused by the North's brutal climate and unfriendly landscape.

Autumn left Octaviel's side. She walked to where Kaela was sleeping, leaning against the cave's damp wall. Lowering herself to the cave's cold, wet floor, she rested her head against his ribs. She smiled to herself when she felt his arm instinctively pull her closer. He was always warm, and it felt good now to rest her weary bones against her strong gentle angel who towered over her in height and who loved her with all his heart. Autumn closed her eyes and fell into a dreamless sleep that lasted for a few short hours. When she woke, she was covered with her cloak, and the first thing she saw was Octaviel standing over her, smiling.

"It was you who prayed that Father would heal me," Octaviel said in a grateful tone of voice. "I thank you for that, brother Autumn. Without your faith, I would still be weak and unable to fend for myself, but your faith saved me."

"No," Autumn argued. "Raphael and Jubel saved you."

"I will be the one to say who saved me." Octaviel laughed. "And, brother Autumn, it was you. It was your faith in Father's ability to reach through the darkness to heal His faithful son. Your faith in God saved me."

Lieutenant Gabriel reached into one of the packs his soldiers carried on their backs to the North. "We have bread and sweet rolls with us that Kaela stole from Chynella's kitchen." He burst out laughing at the shocked expression on his solders' faces. "No, these rolls were offered by Chynella and his kitchen crew because they feared we might get hungry. And I will admit that I am starving. Enjoy your breakfast." When the troops settled down to eat their chosen breads, Autumn said grace.

Breakfast was a jovial time. All wisecracks and jokes made were aimed at Kaela, who returned wise-crack for wise-crack. When the meal ended, Gabriel turned to Octaviel.

"Brother, tell us how you came to be where we found you."

Octaviel wiped his hands on his tunic. "We were told nothing of Lucifer's plan to ignite the gaseous world," he told his comrades. "We were taken by surprise. The place where you found me, the swamp, and my house used to sit there. I didn't rule the providence from a mansion or palace. I lived in a cabin that I built. Before Lucifer rescinded his council members' ownership of their assigned parcels in this region, I carried out God's business from my home." He shook his head. "I had just returned home from somewhere when a ring of fire entered our globe. Its flames were so intense that I thought my fireplace had blown up.

"It wasn't until I spent the afternoon in that bog that I realized Lucifer had followed through on his threat to ignite a gaseous planet in space, and we were suffering for it." Octaviel's eyes widened. "I forgot to ask, was God's kingdom included in the devastation, or did Father see the threat and extinguish it before it could do harm to His citizens?"

He wept when he heard of his brothers' dreadful injuries but praised Father when he learned they were healed.

"We suspect that no one in the North knew what Lucifer was up to, except his witch." Autumn snorted. "I guess it would be ridiculous to ask if you've heard from Jonathon, considering the condition you were in when we found you."

Octaviel's eyes grew moist. He had forgotten about the righteous brothers who lived in the North acting as spies for God and His holy scribe. "Jonathon," he whispered. "I met with him before Heaven was engulfed in fire. That's where I was. I had just returned home from Jonathon's cabin. Like me, he refused to live in a palace. It was late afternoon when I came home, and all I wanted to do was get warm, eat something, and go to bed."

Lieutenant Gabriel ordered his troops to set out in the direction of Jonathan's cabin. They were trudging through thick mud covered with a skim of green slimy water, the only green in all the North, when Kaela set his foot down on a soft lump that whined like a lost puppy. Reaching his hand down, he grasped the lump in his hand and turned it to face him. Now Sonnet's burial came to mind. Kaela set the whining, shivering clump upright, studying the few features that remained in its burnt and bloody face.

"Gab, I think I just found Jonathan."

Raphael and Jubel rushed forward. Kneeling at Jonathan's side, both healers used their powers to renew his flesh in the hope of avoiding another delay in their journey. Their plan was successful. Jonathan was healed and ready to travel in a matter of a few hours.

More than one hundred injured brothers were found and healed over the following days. Desperate to show their gratitude, they remained in the North to aid and assist in the saints' rescue operation. But the North's cruel climate and the dreadful task of dragging lifeless bodies from the mud added to the trauma they suffered. More often than not, their thoughts turned to home and the comforts they enjoyed in God's kingdom.

Kaela approached his commanding officer with a suggestion. "Sire, we don't need these untrained brothers with us," he said. "Send them home, but before they leave, let them know that a grateful heart owes nothing."

Outside the town that Kaela, Joniel, and their apprentices built, long before Lucifer proclaimed himself the emperor of the North, Lieutenant Gabriel's troops watched as northern warriors stormed the streets, breaking into shops along the way in search of food and clothing. Drenched to the skin by the thick, moist fog that billowed around her like black smoke, Autumn made her way across the street to the building the warriors had just entered. Peeking through the window, she saw that it was the clothing warehouse she visited when she placed orders for uniforms. Hunkering down, she scanned the area with her angelic vision. Seeing that she could safely return to her troops, she hurried away from the building to where Kaela glared at her.

"What was that?" he snarled.

Autumn ignored her angel's question. "Lieutenant Gabriel, I know that building. It's a clothing warehouse. We can find dry uniforms, boots, and capes to change into. Our troops are exhausted. That building will provide us with a warm place to sleep. And I could scout around for food, if you wish." She felt Kaela's hand grasp her arm. She glanced over her shoulder. "I work better alone."

When the last warrior left the warehouse, the saints approached it with caution.

Autumn peeked through the window. "It's clear," she told Gabriel. Turning the knob slowly, so as not make a sound, she opened the door. Peering inside, she saw racks of uniforms, shelves burdened with capes, and the floor lined with boots. "I'm going in." Stepping inside, Autumn made her way through the aisles of clothing that somehow escaped being confiscated by Lucifer's thugs.

"It's clear," she called from the loft overhead. "We can change into fresh clothes and sleep up here. The ground floor of the shop will be a clear field. We will be able to see when warriors enter the building."

At Autumn's suggestion, Lieutenant Gabriel positioned his troops throughout the loft to assure that if some were discovered, others could rise up to defeat their enemies.

That evening, while exhausted saints slept soundly for the first time in days, Lucifer's dark-suited warriors returned to the warehouse. Kaela roused his sleeping brothers to wakefulness. Autumn crawled silently across the floor to where Kaela and Gabriel lay watching the warriors below.

"Stay alert," Lieutenant Gabriel whispered to the saints behind him. "Unsheathe your swords and keep them close." Throughout the long night, God's righteous sons listened for the dreaded sound of northern footsteps on the stairs.

The following morning, Kaela crept down the stairs. The ground floor of the warehouse was empty, but there was no promise that the warriors who slept here last night would not return. He motioned for Gabriel and the others to join him. Cautiously, they made their way down the stairs that led from loft to the ground floor where the weavers' equipment lay overturned and vandalized.

"Step lightly," Gabriel said softly. He turned to Kaela. "These delays have robbed us of valuable time. I am going to send a unit ahead. They will go directly to the tunnel where they will escort recued brothers to the Sacred Region."

The troops left the warehouse, believing in their hearts that the collapsed tunnel had been cleared and their trapped brothers had been freed. It was that faith that encouraged them to split up. While Jonathan led rescued brothers from the North to the safety of God's kingdom,

Lieutenant Gabriel and his saints continued their search for brothers who were hiding from their enemies and were most likely injured. While they search for survivors, they noted the ample destruction Lucifer's attempt to rival Father's light did to the North. Autumn grieved for the shop-keepers, teachers, and weavers, none of whom could be found. The saints left the northern city, taking their search to the outskirts of town to a swampy area that had been a beautiful forest.

"Approach the bog ahead with caution," Lieutenant Gabriel told his team of rescuers. It was here in the dreadful place that they found Prescience working frantically to save his brother Donniel from uncreation.

"Grab my cloak," Prescience called, desperately throwing one end of his cloak across the sloppy top of a muddy bog. "Stop struggling. I can't help you if you sink deeper into that mire." He tossed the end of his cloak a second time. "Grab it, Donnie; grab the end of my cloak."

He was about to stretch his body across the top of the bog when someone grabbed his foot and pulled him back onto solid ground. Prescience spun around, reaching for his sword. His eyes widened. He breathed a sigh of relief. Silently he thanked God, his Father, for sending the help he so fervently prayed would come.

Kaela had already tied his cloak to Prescience's cloak and tossed them across the top of the bog. "Catch hold of the end," he ordered. With Lieutenant Gabriel and Joniel's help, he pulled his weary brother to solid ground and stood him on his feet. "How did you get in there?" Kaela asked, pointing to the bog.

"I was trying hard not to be eaten," Donniel replied. "No. There are no wild beasts in the North. The witch saw to that, didn't she? But the warriors who got separated from their units, who are probably crazed by Pain, hunger, and fear, have become the North's wild beasts."

"Saints, keep a keen eye out for crazed warriors," Lieutenant Gabriel commanded as he scanned the landscape for signs of God's enemies.

The sainted troops had not gone far from where they saved Donniel when northern warriors approached with swords drawn.

"Turn back or be uncreated," the leader, Mephistopheles, shouted at the small band of saints. "You are trespassers in Lucifer's kingdom."

"So he's a self-proclaimed king now, is he?" Kaela chided as he walked to where the warriors stood. "Where is he, this so-called great Lucifer? And where is his witch?"

Mephistopheles lowered his weapon. "Kaela, is that you? I didn't recognize you with all that mud on you. You are labeled a traitor in the North. There is a price on your head and on Autumn's."

"Don't tell me what I already now," Kaela said. "Where are the North's false ruler and his witch?"

"What will you give me for the information you need?" Mephistopheles asked.

"I will give you all the bread that I have in my pouch," Kaela replied. "But first, I need to know if Lucifer and Sin were injured as badly by the devastation they caused as the rest of the globe's citizens were."

"As far as I know, Lucifer and Sin are fine," Mephistopheles said without hesitation. "When the event occurred, we who remain loyal to him believe that the ring of fire fell down through space away from Lucifer, therefore, we suspect that he escaped being burned. As for Sin, she is most likely hidden safely away inside the onyx palace, probably in the deepest underground chamber in the lowest section of mountain's bowels."

Kaela glanced over his shoulder at his commanding officer, before turning his attention back to Mephistopheles. "You don't sound too sure of yourself," he told the warrior. The conversation between the saint and the warrior continued for a short moment longer. When their discussion ended, Kaela removed the pouch from his side that held his moldy, damp bread and gave it to Mephistopheles, who motioned for his warriors to clear the path for God's saints.

"What did he say?" Lieutenant Gabriel asked when Kaela returned to where his troops stood waiting.

"He said for us to stay safe," Kaela replied. "He thinks Lucifer and Sin are well, but he cannot say for sure since he hasn't seen them since Lucifer left for deep space." He motioned for the saints to move out. To Gabriel, he said, "When I left the North, hoping never to return, I believed its climate could not get worse than it was. But standing here, ankle-deep in mud, shivering from the cold, drenched to the skin by rain that never lets up, I must believe that, regardless of what might have happened to Lucifer, Sin is alive and well."

Kaela turned to Autumn. "You will accompany me to the dark palace." He turned to Lieutenant Gabriel. "Take your saints to the tunnel at the mountain's base. Give aid and support to the remainder of the slaves and troops who toil there."

"Prince Michael ordered me to keep five saints with you at all times," Lieutenant Gabriel protested. "And now, you are casually dismissing us as though you are the leader of this mission." His expression was incredulous.

"We work better alone," Autumn told the lieutenant. "Go, do as Kaela said. We will be fine. And if there is trouble, Father will intervene."

Her words, her faith in Father, convinced Gabriel to take his small unit of soldiers to the pit. As they left the clearing, Autumn whispered, "Father, bless us with Your tender mercies."

CHAPTER 40

Loose Cannon

Anyone who was unfamiliar with the North would have mistaken the thick fog and lack of light as a sign that morning was still far off, but morning had indeed arrived in Heaven, and it was time for righteous citizens living in the North to take cover from Lucifer's crazed warriors who patrolled the streets.

Autumn and Kaela lighted in the courtyard outside Lucifer's onyx mansion. Through the fog, they saw forms moving about. If they could see Lucifer's warriors as shadowy forms, Lucifer's warrior could see them. Cautiously, but without missing a step, the pair trudged onward to the door they knew opened to the palace's dark, hostile foyer. They were about to enter the palace when someone touched Kaela's shoulder. Unsheathing his sword, Kaela prepared to battle to his death to protect Autumn.

"WAIT! Archangel Kaela!" Someone hissed in a firm whisper. A hand grasped Kaela's wrist and, with a strength bred of desperation, forced his brother to lower his sword to his side before he could strike. "It is I, Percible." The anger that burned in Kaela's eyes was swiftly replaced with a glimmer of peace. The brothers greeted each other with hugs, pats on the backs, and smiles. "I have engaged the help of your supporters in North. They call themselves liberators. You passed them as you approached the palace. Lucifer is not here. Rumor has it that he abandoned his dark mansion after the ring of fire fell from the sky. Your liberators are hoping to capture Lucifer and Sin should they return and take them back to the Sacred Region where they will be charged for their crimes." He stopped talking to smile down at Autumn. "Where are your troops?" Percible asked.

"Lieutenant Gabriel took our unit of soldiers to the pit," Kaela answered. He pushed the door to the onyx palace open. The threesome slipped into the main foyer. It was dark and smelled of mold. Percible lit a torch he found and handed it to Autumn. The light from the torch's flame was dimmed by the darkness of Lucifer's house, but its glow radiated just enough light to reveal the foyer was littered with papers, broken furniture, and dirty rags. A search of the conference room revealed the table had been upended and its chairs overturned. In the trophy room, display cases had been emptied of their possessions. Desks had been smashed. Awards, falsely proclaiming achievements Lucifer never made, were gone, as were his princely crown and his archangel's trumpet.

Further investigation of the palace rooms revealed that Lucifer's bedroom was the most damaged room in the house. His bedroom furniture was overturned, and his clothing was shredded, which explained the rags that were strewn through the hallway and downstairs to the foyer.

"What is this?" Percible asked. Kaela hurried to his brother's side and found him examining what looked to be a manuscript. "What is this writing? Has Lucifer begun his own language?" He handed a stack of pages to his sainted brother. "Look at this."

Kaela glanced at what was written on the first page of the manuscript before handing it to Autumn.

"Lucifer has forgotten much of Father's ancient script," she said matter-of-factly. "I think he improvised by using words he made up." Autumn smoothed her furrowed brow with her fingertips. "This is so like Lucifer. Everything he's done since I've known him is wrong. Therefore, I must believe that everything he did before we were created was wrong." She glanced at Percible. "This is no new language. It is a childish take on Father ancient language. This may have been Lucifer's first attempt to falsify our Lord's journals. That would explain why he had Belial rewrite them. Belial is fluent in Father's ancient hand."

Her eyes scanned the cluttered room. "Find something we can put this in, something that will keep it dry when we leave this place. We must let our Lord know—"

"I was thinking, Autumn," Percible said. "What if Father already knows? What if this empty house is the result of our Lord's wrath? I mean, look around. Where is everybody? It is as though a divine force moved them from this place to—"

Hell," Kaela said flatly.

Throughout the day, the three saints lingered at the palace. The liberators moved inside the structure and made a thorough search of the premises. Rooms that were locked could not be entered from inside the palace. An investigation revealed the windows were shuttered with steel planks that were obviously bolted from within the rooms to ward off outside intrusion. Making no progress, Kaela, Autumn, and Percible left the palace for the tunnel at the mountain's base. They were curious to see how well the evacuation of the North's slaves and frightened civilians was going.

At the base of the mountain, they were greeted by Raumulis, who escorted them through the mud-covered door of the passageway's first narrow room. Hours later, Percible, Kaela, and Autumn emerged from the darkness of the underground channel to bask in the light that flooded the field that lay beyond the castle's stables and the stadium. The last of Lucifer's slaves walked with God's sainted sons. The rescued sang praises to God and rejoiced that they were safe at last. Autumn walked with her singing brothers, smiling. The mission was a success. The end of the tunnel that lay in the North would be collapsed. Anyone who ventured there to worship Sin or work for Lucifer would remain there or they would escape without the help of Prince Michael's saints.

Prince Michael left the castle to greet his returning brothers. Being in a jovial mood, the prince called to Kaela, "So where is Lucifer's head? I was sure that you would arrive home holding your sword high with Lucifer's head balanced on its tip."

"I am too tired to be amused by your wit," Kaela told his commanding officer in a flat, toneless voice. "I could not find our eldest brother or his witch, so they will live a little longer."

Prince Michael walked with the pair until they reached the castle's fore-hall.

"Autumn has something very important that we think you should see," Kaela told God's prince. "I am inviting you, the scribe, Archangel Effiel, our sisters, and Percible to dine with us this evening. After dinner, the scribe and Autumn can peruse the pages that we believe may have been Lucifer's first attempt to pervert our Lord's sacred journals."

Autumn felt beautiful and feminine dressed in her pale-pink robe with flowers embroidered on its sleeves and around its wide hem. Tossing her long ash-blonde hair over her shoulders, she studied her image in the mirror. She looked good enough to stand before Father's throne. But tonight, she and her angel were hosting a dinner provided for them by God. Leaning toward the mirror, she worried that Kaela would be angry when he saw that she tinted her lips and cheeks pink with strawberry juice and was wearing a garland of pink roses in her hair. It seemed he never complimented her anymore.

A familiar knock at the door interrupted her thoughts. Reaching for the bathroom door's knob, she opened it, just a bit to see Kaela looking back at her. Now, she opened the door wide. Stepping into the bedroom, she twirled on her heels. "How do I look?" she asked.

"It's been an hour. You look late," Kaela grumbled. "Everyone is here." He stormed passed her. "Lay out my clothes, and then go to the living room and talk with our guests while I shower." He stopped briefly. "Are you satisfied with how you look?" He saw her nod. "That's all that counts. Now do what I told you."

Autumn sighed. Kaela always seemed to be in a hurry, rushing by, shouting orders—"Get my clothes!" "Where's my weapons' belt?" "Hurry up!" "Quit looking at yourself," "Where are my sandals?" "Where are my boots?" "Do what I say."

She glanced over her shoulder to the closed bathroom door. Did he see her as a male angel?

Autumn walked to the closet where she removed from it a pale-blue robe, a soft almost white-blue cloak, and matching slippers for her beloved angel's feet. Before leaving the room, she took Lucifer's manuscript from the drawer she stored it in for safekeeping. She would present it to the scribe while Kaela was absent from his guests' presence.

"Father was quite pleased with your prayers, Autumn," Scribe Excelsa said, addressing her the moment she entered the room. He accepted the pages she handed him and encouraged her to sit on the arm of his chair. Together, scribe and Earth angel read from pages that were written half in Father's ancient language and half in Lucifer's made-up jargon.

"I believe this was Lucifer's first attempt to rewrite our Lord's holy books," she told Excelsa. She could tell that he was impressed with her ability to read Father's language. "These pages should be deciphered to find exactly how badly Lucifer longed to change history."

"Change history," Excelsa echoed. He saw Kaela enter the room. "Good, now the rest of you can eat while Autumn and I go over this mishmash of words." The scribe smiled at his former student. "Continue reading, sweet child." He cast the Goddesses a contented look. "I taught Autumn well. I am in for a real treat." That said, he settled back in his chair and closed his eyes. "Read, dear Autumn, I am listening."

"Autumn hasn't had a good meal for days," Archangel Kaela told Excelsa. "This can wait. I suggest that we take our chairs at the table and enjoy the meal Father provided for us."

The conversation at the dinner table was dominated by God's holy scribe. And when the dinner meal ended, the conversation in the living room was dominated by God's holy scribe. Prince Michael longed to hear a detailed account of what happened in the North. He wasn't interested in what went on in the outdoor throne room ages ago. Rising to his feet, the prince gathered his cape and his helmet. He was about to tell Autumn how good it was to see that she fared well in the North when he heard Kaela say, "I will walk you to your apartment."

"Father was pleased that you and Autumn returned home unharmed," Prince Michael told Kaela when they reached his suite. "Will you come in?" He held the door until Kaela motioned that he would follow.

Inside, the prince walked to his desk, lifted a rolled parchment in his hand and gave the paper to Kaela. "I signed it. At our Lord's request and at my command, you are ordered to remain in this region where you will be responsible to train your troops."

"And this paper with your signature on it makes your order a legal command," Archangel Kaela mumbled. Scanning the page, he looked for key words that might declare Michael's order was written in stone, but found none. "Is this how you intend to keep Lucifer and his witch safe? Are you protecting them from knowing the awful torment and misery they caused others? Is that why this paper was drawn up?"

Prince Michael motioned for Kaela to take the chair before his desk. "Father was so worried for you and Autumn. He embraced every prayer from Autumn, every prayer from Lieutenant Gabriel, and every prayer from the others. He waited for your prayer, but it never came. You are the son Father wished He had created first. He admires your strength, your wisdom, your inspiration, your faith, and your charitable ways, and He admires how you love His righteous sons."

"Father told me that once, a long time ago," Archangel Kaela said softly.

"Everything you did in your life exemplifies how Father thinks we, your brothers, should live." Prince Michael lowered his head, thoughtful for a moment, and then he added, "I stepped forward in my desire to exhibit my athletic skills because I admired you. I still admire you, but you are turning into a—"

"Loose cannon." Kaela laughed. He saw Michael's stunned expression. "What?"

"What is a cannon?" the prince asked.

Kaela shrugged. "I don't know. I've heard Autumn refer to Lucifer's warriors as loose cannons, but it's just something my small brothers says when he is trying to be funny."

Prince Michael rose to his feet. "I am curious about that phrase because word reached Father from one of Excelsa's spies that Lucifer and Azazel are building … a cannon." He narrowed his eyes and studied Kaela for a long moment. "Bring Autumn to me. Let's find out what our small brother knows about cannons."

Autumn sat in the small conference room at the foot of the stairs that led to God's outdoor throne room. She was not alone. Prince Michael, Lieutenant Gabriel, Scribe Excelsa, Archangel Kaela, Archangel Effiel and his student Elbreon, were seated at the table with her. Autumn's eyes widened when God's daughters file into the room and positioned themselves behind her chair.

"So what exactly is it that you need from me?" Autumn asked. Her eyes darted from Prince Michael's stern face to Kaela's concerned one.

Reaching for Autumn's hand, Prince Michael patted it and asked, "What is a cannon?"

"Depends on how the word is used in a sentence," she answered.

Scribe Excelsa, Archangel Effiel, and Elbreon dipped the tip of their quills into their ink-wells, ready to scribble her statement into their notebooks.

"A 'loose cannon,' for instance, could be a phrase used to describe someone who irresponsibly takes matters of great importance into his own hands."

"So what kind of cannon is Lucifer and Azazel designing?" Prince Michael asked.

Autumn's brows rose high on her forehead, and she pursed her lips and whistled softly. "Lucifer and Azazel are building *a* cannon? He's building just one cannon, no more than that? If I heard you correctly, I'd say they are planning to do open war in Heaven. Cannons are war machines that spit huge iron balls at anyone standing in their path, and they are powered by gunpowder. Don't ask me how one makes a cannon or where gunpowder comes from. You will have to figure that out for yourselves." She looked around the table. "Can I go now? I'd like to say good night to Paint."

"No. Not yet," Prince Michael said. "Gun-powder? What is gun-powder?"

"Gun-powder is a combustible that is used to fire the cannon," Autumn told him. "Someone puts gun-powder in the cannon, someone else puts the ball in the cannon, and another person lights the fuse. One person can do it all, but it's quicker if it's done by three." She narrowed her eyes. The saints gave her time to think about what she would say next. Prince Michael was about to interrupt her concentration when Autumn offered, "A gun is a small cannon that you carry on your person, meaning, it's yours. You carry it in a holster that is very much like a weapons' belt. Guns work in the same fashion as cannons work. If a gun is perfected, it can be small enough to be concealed."

"How is that?" Scribe Excelsa asked his eyes trained on Autumn's face.

"When a cannon is fired, one knows to take cover," Autumn replied. "When the brother closest to you is hit by a cannon-ball, you don't wait to see if the next ball fired will miss you. Cannons, because they are big, are used outdoors. But guns are small and can be carried in the pocket of one's cloak. A gun can be fired from a distance, or anyone of us could use a gun to uncreate a brother, or brothers, seated with us at this table." She sighed. "That's all I know about cannons and guns. Now can I go to the stables to say good night to Paint?"

"Yes, you may go," Prince Michael said with a smile. "Be careful, and stay close to the Father's house. Don't forget there is a price on your head."

When Autumn was gone, the prince glanced at the brothers who sat with him at the table. "Open war," he said in a hushed voice. "Autumn said if Lucifer is building a cannon, he is planning to do open war in Heaven."

Excelsa motioned to Gabriel, "Bring Father's spy to the table."

Kaela narrowed his eyes and studied Excelsa's face for a long moment, trying to figure the proper way to ask the spy's name. He was about to speak when the lieutenant returned to the conference room with Abdiel. Kaela's mouth dropped open. He rose from his chair, too stunned to speak. Prince Michael motioned for him to be seated.

"I … I think a mistake has been made," Kaela said, dropping into his chair. The prince assured him that his smiling former friend was one of God's most faithful spies. "Excuse me, but I know Abdiel. He is Lucifer's flunky. He fawns over the North's false emperor throughout the day and probably dreams of ruling Heaven from the throne Lucifer reserved for Sin. I truly think a mistake has been made."

"Why, Archangel Kaela? Why do you think a mistake has been made? Do you fear that I am a better spy than you are?" Abdiel asked with a brilliant smile. "Not all of us can be the globe's greatest inventor. Not all of us are so courageous that our goals include heroic works. Someone has to work behind the scenes. Someone has to be good at finding information and hiding his identity so that Father's worst enemies will trust him."

Kaela thought about what Abdiel said. He managed a slight smile. "Well, if I didn't trust you before, I really don't trust you now." He reached for his brother's hand and pressed it to his heart. "You really are good at what you do, Abdiel. I am so sorry for the way I treated you when we lived in the North."

"Contrary to the way you remember your treatment of me," Abdiel said, taking the seat that had been Autumn's, "you were very kind to me. You never hurt me physically, though I must confess, there were times when I longed for your companionship so very much that I was tempted to tell you why I was in the North. And by the way, unlike you, I still live in the North."

"We could have worked together, why didn't you join my forces?" Kaela asked.

"You were a good diversion," Abdiel told him. "But if I told you what I was doing, I would have had too many brothers to answer to. I couldn't chance it. And anyway, you worry too much about Autumn. You would have slowed me down. You had a team that you felt obligated to meet with. And though I was not invited to sit in on the meetings, I would creep around and learn a few minor facts and take those facts to Lucifer. It kept the interest on you while I worked behind the scenes. I never meant for anyone to get hurt. I was simply using your crew as a diversion, doing what I was chosen to do."

Kaela was stunned; his former friend had just insulted him in front of God's highest officials. "I tried to protect as many brothers as I could when I gathered information," he told Abdiel. "How many of our brothers were uncreated because you thought you were doing what you were chosen to do?" Kaela sat down and leaned back in his chair, his eyes fixed on Abdiel. "I admire that you have chosen to remain in the North where you must work closely with Lucifer and Sin, but don't ask me to forgive you for putting others in danger."

"There is the Kaela we all know and love," Abdiel said, his hands extended toward his brother. "He is our protector—"

"Abdiel, we need to know how far Azazel has progressed on the war machine he is building for Lucifer," Prince Michael said. He could see that Kaela was suspicious of Abdiel and that Abdiel had no love in his heart for Kaela. Hoping to stop a confrontation before it began, he asked, "How close to completion is the cannon? And do you know how to build one?"

Abdiel raised one brow high on his forehead and, with a smug grin, replied, "You mean hero Kaela doesn't know how to build a cannon?" He glanced at his brother and shook his head to let Kaela know he was slipping. "He should meet with Inspiration and Wisdom like he did when he hoped to renovate Heaven so our lazy brothers had less reason to become productive and had more time on their hands to make trouble for Father." Abdiel sighed and leaned toward Prince Michael. "In answer to your question: I don't know how far along Azazel is with the cannon. No, like Kaela, I do not know how to build a cannon."

"Where is Lucifer?" Kaela asked. "Where is Sin?"

"Why don't you go back to the North and find them," Abdiel suggested. "I haven't seen them since Lucifer ignited the gaseous planet and almost destroyed Heaven." He shrugged. "As for the cannon, it's almost finished—"

"The cannon is 'almost' finished. I thought you said you didn't know how close to completion the cannon is?" Kaela hissed in a low, impatient tone, his narrowed eyes riveted to Abdiel's face.

"So I did." Abdiel shrugged. He covered his lips with his left hand and, with an innocent expression, replied, "I simply know what I was told: the cannon is almost complete." With a wink, he added, "Remember, Kaela, what Lucifer taught you about the word *almost*?"

"That does not apply here, and you know it," Kaela snorted. "Now how far done is that cannon?" Kaela stood, reached across the table, grasped Abdiel's robe in his hands, and dragged him half-way across the tabletop before Prince Michael and Lieutenant Gabriel stopped him. Kaela released his grip on his former friend. Eyes burning with anger, he told Abdiel, "You had better take this seriously because Father created us, and that being so, He can destroy us. Now tell us what you know about the cannon."

"I know nothing about the cannon," Abdiel grumbled as he straightened his clothing. "I only know what I was told. I never saw the thing. Now I am leaving."

Kaela glanced at Prince Michael. "Surely you aren't going to give him permission to leave? If you keep him here, I can make him talk. I have ways of doing that."

"Let him go." Prince Michael growled.

Without a backward glance at his angry brother, Abdiel left the room.

"Kaela, we are not in the North," Prince Michael scolded. "What was that? Reaching, grasping, and dragging a brother across the table. Do you realize you had your hand drawn back as though you were going to strike Abdiel?"

Prince Michael motioned his sisters from the room. Each silver Goddess kissed Kaela's cheek as they exited. Wisdom paused for a moment to glare at Michael, but he was determined to speak his mind to Kaela, to remind him that he was in the Sacred Region where "having ways of making brothers talk" did not apply.

Chapter 41

The Abduction

With Prince Michael's permission, Autumn left the conference room to go to the stables where she saddled Paint and led him from the stall he was housed in. Outside the stable, she mounted her small pony, spurring him gently in the flanks with her sandaled heels so that he would walk to the field adjacent to Father's back lawn. Autumn exercised Paint for over an hour, her dedication to her pony convinced her sainted bodyguards that they could rest from their duties long enough to enjoy a good meal in the castle's dining room. Together with the stable hand, Adnachiel, the guards made their way across the grounds to castle's back door. Jahoel, destined to become a chief officer in Prince Michael's army, turned briefly to check on Autumn. She would be here when he and Abraxos returned from their break; if not, he knew from experience that he would find her in the stable, caring for her precious little pony.

Autumn kept one eye on her guards. The other eye, she kept on the forest that rose up like a wall on the outer circumference of the Holy Mount's high plateau. When she was certain that she was no longer under surveillance, she dug her heels into her pony's ribs, causing him to break into a full gallop. With reins wrapped securely around both hands, Autumn steered Paint away from the safety of Father's house toward the side of the mountain that opened to a wide field that lay just outside the village below.

Entering the forest, Autumn and Paint disappeared beneath the darkness of the trees' leafy canopy. Paint gingerly made his way down the mountain's slope toward the village. The trip to Kaela's cottage would have been shorter if they had taken the Holy Mount's staircase, entering the village on its jasper streets. But Autumn didn't want to be seen by anyone who might tell Kaela where she was. That being the case, she kept within the parameter of the wooded area that stretched out full and fragrant on either side of the Holy Mount's base. From here, she could easily see the cottage she once shared with her angel. Spurring Paint with her sandaled heels and slapping his hip with her hand, she braced herself for the run of her life. Paint darted across the field that lay behind God's perfect village, and he did not stop until he reached Autumn's beloved cottage.

"Good boy!" Autumn whispered as she lowered herself from his saddle to the ground. "This will be a while, so I'm going to have to tie you out here." She kissed Paint's precious cheek and hugged his neck. "I love you, my darling pony. I'll be back, I promise." Autumn tied Paint's reins to the rail of the back porch, hoping he would be hidden from view by the trees she planted in the yard.

Entering the cottage through the window that opened to the bedroom she shared with Kaela, Autumn went straight to her closet. She planned to spend some time here. Maybe she would pack some of her nicer garments and take them back to the castle. When she opened the closet door, she found her clothing heaped in piles on the floor. Autumn narrowed her eyes. She hadn't been home since Sonnet's burial in Father's garden. And though she was overcome by grief at the time, she couldn't remember leaving her closet looking like this. Confused by what she found, she set about rearranging her wardrobe, taking the time to place her favorite robes, sashes, and cloaks on the bed.

"These, I'll be taking back," Autumn whispered to herself. Kneeling on the floor, she chose sandals to match each robe and cloak she planned to take back to the castle.

Outside, Paint whinnied. Autumn closed her closet's door. "Hold on, I won't be long, sweetheart."

"Really?" a voice behind her asked. "You haven't called me sweetheart ever."

Autumn turned. "Lucifer," she gasped.

She made a dash toward the door, but Lucifer lunged forward, catching the neck of her cloak and robe in his hand. Autumn stumbled backward, almost losing her balance.

"Were you running away from me, Autumn?" Lucifer asked, drawing her face close to his. "That makes me think that maybe, you didn't want to see me today." He twisted the material he held in his hand, smiling when he saw her face turn red. "What's wrong? Can't you breathe?" He loosened his grip slightly. "See, you and I, we're old friends, and I've come to take you home."

"We're not friends, and I am home," Autumn snarled. She struggled to free herself. "Let me go! My brothers are looking for me, they will be here soon, and you'll be sorry."

"Autumn, did you forget? You abandoned your family. You left God's house so that you could come here to see me," Lucifer hissed. Their faces were so close that if she spit on him, she'd get some on her. "Don't look at me like that, you rotten sainted wretch. Rejoice, knowing that you will return to the North with me."

"I am staying right here." Autumn sobbed, struggling to break free.

"You are going back to the North with me, but first, we are going to capture the traitor Kaela," Lucifer snarled. "If you try to resist, I will uncreate you." He tossed Autumn like a rag through the bedroom's door and onto the living room's hardwood floor. Someone else entered the room. While Lucifer ranted, an unseen brother bound Autumn's hands behind her back and placed a gag in her mouth, securing it in place with a piece of cloth that was tied behind her head.

"Get up," Lucifer commanded. He kicked Autumn's side when she refused to move. "Get him up, stand him on his feet," Lucifer ordered.

Autumn lay unmoving, trembling with fear and dread. Someone forced her to her feet. The room was filled with northern council members. Moloch led her to the couch where Sin sat clothed in black canvas. "Sit here. Be quiet, and you won't get hurt."

He turned to Lucifer. "I untied Autumn's pony and sent him back to the Holy Castle. When Kaela sees that Paint has no rider, he will start searching for his beloved brother. Hopefully, when the trail runs cold, Kaela will come here, looking for Autumn. That's when we will take him captive."

"Very good," Lucifer said with a smug sneer on his lips. "Let us make ourselves at home while we wait. Nesroc, check the fruit dish, see if it has been filled. I love the Sacred Region. Food appears, courtesy of Heaven's almighty King. Clothing is cleaned, courtesy of Heaven's almighty King. The cottage is cleaned by unseen hands, courtesy of Heaven's almighty King."

Nesroc entered the living room, the fruit dish in his hands. Grapes, oranges, apples, mangoes, strawberries, and tomatoes were passed around the room.

"Eat, Autumn," Lucifer said. He snapped his fingers. "Oh, that's right. You are gagged and bound, waiting for your hero, Kaela, to come to your rescue." He laughed as he bit into a large red apple. "We may have a long wait ahead of us. I hope you don't get too hungry." His laughter was joined by his council members' laughter, and the room was filled with vile snide comments about Autumn and Kaela's sleeping habits.

While Autumn was held captive by Lucifer and his band of evil thugs, Paint raced desperately down the golden streets of the village toward the base of the Holy Mount. He did not take the winding path that led him back to God's house; instead, he took the one of the many staircases that Nature carved in the four sides of the Holy Mount. He reached an unfamiliar open field where he stopped briefly to survey the landscape that stretched out for miles before him. Hoofing the air, tossing his mane, he glanced back at the staircase he had just ascended. Now, he searched the sky for winged steeds that shared his stable. It was then the small frightened pony saw the banners that rose up from Father's outdoor throne room. Though the banners were a long way off, Paint fixed his eyes on them and ran frantically toward them. He did not stop until he reached the safety of his stall.

Kaela had just left a steaming shower. He slipped a long robe over his muscular body and was about to settle back on the sofa with a large bowl of grapes when someone knocked. Opening his door, he saw the stable hand standing in the hallway.

"I was returning from dinner at the castle when I saw Paint running to the stable," he told Kaela. He looked around the room. "Is Autumn here?" When he learned that Kaela hadn't seen her since she had gained Prince Michael's permission to ride her pony, Adnachiel said, "I spoke with a couple of brothers who thought they might have seen Paint running through the village. They decided it wasn't Paint when he did not take the stairs that led back home."

"Keep our conversation confidential," Kaela ordered. "I'm sure there is no cause for alarm." The archangel watched as the stable hand turned away from his door and made his way down the corridor to the stairs that led to the castle's ground floor. Closing the door to the apartment that had belonged to Lucifer eons ago, Kaela went to his bedroom where he put on his uniform. Buckling his weapons' belt around his waist, he sheathed his sword and dagger. Questions nagged at him. Where were Autumn's bodyguards? Why was Paint seen running through the village alone?

Now Archangel Kaela stood in the wooded area at the mountain's base, looking out across the grassy field that lay behind the cottage he once shared with his beloved Autumn. Moments ago, Father had relinquished His seat in His outdoor throne room to retire to His inner sanctum to create Heaven's pale night. Kaela lingered in the forest a long time, watching his cottage for signs of life. Surely, if Autumn had returned to home, she would light a lantern or two so that she could see better in the darkened rooms of the cottage. When no light glowed from the windows of his former house, Kaela made his way through the field under cover of the clouds that drifted down, thick and moist, from atop the Holy Mount.

At the cottage, Kaela stepped over the banister onto the back porch Autumn built when he had been commissioned to erect dwellings in the North. With great stealth, he crept to the window that opened to his bedroom to look inside. The window was shuttered and locked. Without a sound, he turned and made his way over the narrow wooden porch at the side of the house. As he went, he checked each window. All the shutters were secured from inside. Drawing his dagger from his weapons' belt, he made his way to the front door and kicked it open. Within brief seconds, he was thrown to the porch floor, his weapons' belt removed from his waist, and he was robbed of his sword. The hand that held his dagger was pinned to the floor by someone's booted foot.

"Why, Kaela, I'm so glad you could join us," Lucifer said, removing the blade from the fingers of the hand he stood on. "Oh, I forgot. Pain is not permitted to enter God's sacred kingdom, and whosoever we harm in this region heals too quickly to learn the lesson we hope to instill."

Kaela pulled his hand free and attempted to rise to his feet. He was knocked to his knees, after which he was pinned facedown to the floor. Moloch, Thummuz, and Nesroc held him in a suffocating grip. "Stay down," Moloch ordered.

"Or you will do what?" Kaela hissed. "As your false emperor told me, you are in God's kingdom; nothing you can do will hurt me." He narrowed his eyes and studied Autumn's stricken face. It was clear that she had been crying, probably praying that he would come for her. Sin sat beside her, clutching her arm so that she could not escape. Autumn struggled to free herself. She wanted to be with him. Nesroc pressed Kaela's cheek hard against the floor so that he had to roll his eyes upward to better see his beloved Autumn. Nesroc and Thummuz tied Kaela's hands behind his back, both at the wrists and elbows; his legs were bound at the ankles and just above his knees. Then he was wrapped in a sheet so that he could be more easily transported to the North.

Sin was the first to leave the cottage. Grasping the rags that bound Autumn's hands behind her back, she dragged Autumn toward the door. At that moment, Apollyon looked inside to inform Lucifer that he and the northern delegation should leave the region before God took His throne on the castle's roof. Securing her grip on the rags that bound Autumn's wrists, the witch rose into the air. As Autumn's feet left the ground, she felt her arms being lifted upward behind her, binding her wings so that she could not use them as protection. Her arms were extended so awkwardly that when she was dragged across the northern border, Autumn screamed in pain despite the rag in her mouth.

Sin doubled back through the fog to the field that lay just outside the northern parameter allowing Autumn's pain to subside for an instant. Then she returned to where the guard shacks were located.

Autumn screamed again. The torture continued until Father filled His kingdom with light, and Sin, who feared for her safety, returned to the northern region where her father reigned as the universe's first known dictator.

In the North, Kaela and Autumn were shackled in irons that were burdened with heavy chains, and then they were tossed into a crowded pen whose door was secured with several locks. Seated on the muddy floor, Kaela massaged his beloved Autumn's tender shoulders.

"I'm so sorry," she wept. "I walked right into a trap. If I had known Lucifer, Sin, and their thugs were hiding in our cottage, I never would have gone there." She apologized to Kaela time and time again, blaming herself for his capture. "I put both of us in harm's way. You were safe." Her words broke off in a sob. "I prayed you wouldn't come for me. I prayed that if you did, you would bring Prince Michael's saints to back you up." She shook her head and whimpered," Look what I did to us … look at what I did to us."

Kaela tried to soothe her to no avail. "Try not to think about it."

Autumn turned slightly to glance at him. "Under the circumstances, how do you expect me to do that?" She grew quiet for a long moment. "I was vain," she confessed. "I was so pleased with how I looked last night that I wanted to go to the cottage to check my wardrobe. I wanted to take my beautiful outfits to the castle and wear them at special events. I saw how Scribe Excelsa and Archangel Effiel looked at me. They thought I looked nice." She sobbed miserably. "And then I remembered the old days, when we joined our brothers in the dining room before the concerts. Back then, they looked at me the same way. They admired me, and they were proud to call me their brother."

"We all want the old days back," Kaela said softly. He sighed, peering through the dark gray fog that was so thick it rendered his angelic vision worthless. "I wonder where they will take us. Maybe you should try to sleep." He motioned for her to rest against his side. Though his cloak was damp from the fog, it was better than letting her lie uncovered in the elements. He draped his cloak over Autumn's shoulders and snuggled her close to his body. "Sleep now. I will keep watch, and I will let you know if anyone approaches this cage."

Hours passed, giving Kaela time to think about Abdiel's visit to God's conference room yesterday evening. Did Abdiel know that Lucifer and Sin were in the region? What information did he withhold about the cannon Azazel was building? And would he return to the North to tell Lucifer the saints worried that the weapon would be used against God's citizens? Kaela cradled Autumn in his arms while she slept. "When I get you out of here, I'm going to pay Abdiel a visit." He pressed his lips against Autumn's head and focused on the grounds that lay outside the cage they occupied.

The following morning or maybe it was late afternoon—no one could really tell what time of day it was in the North with its cold, never-ending rains and black dense fogs—Injurious and Turpitude arrived at the pen that housed Autumn, Kaela, and several other captives. Injurious unlocked the pen's barred doors and ordered everyone out. Burdened by iron shackles, the slaves were herded to the courtyard of the onyx palace. Warriors with whips and clubs forced God's sons to submit to Deleterious' vile deed of hacking off their wings with his bloody axe. Injurious tore Autumn from Kaela's arms. Pushing and shoving her to where Deleterious waited, he threw her to the ground, forcing her to kneel.

Sobbing, trembling, gulping back bile, Autumn pleaded with her captors to see that what they were doing to their helpless brothers was wrong. She turned to make eye contact with Deleterious. Turpitude smashed his fist against her jaw, almost knocking her unconscious. Injurious grabbed her hair and set her in a kneeling position, her back to Deleterious. Autumn braced herself against the whip whose braid convinced her to spread her wings to either side of her shoulders. Panic-stricken, she awaited the blow, knowing Pain would feed on her wounds the moment her flesh was cut. Gasping, struggling to breathe, fearful that her rolling heart would stop beating she prayed to wake up so that this nightmare might end.

Deleterious gripped his axe with both hands, lifted it high above his head, and let its blade drop on the narrow part of the wing, attached to the muscle in Autumn's back. Her screams filled the air. Deleterious' eyes moved directly to Kaela, who was on his knees, sobbing, reaching out his hands toward Autumn as though his touch would heal her injuries. The wing should have fallen to the ground, but it was still attached to flesh, muscle, and bone. A second attempt at robbing Autumn of her left wing proved successful.

"Set the slave back on his knees," Deleterious ordered. "I want to get this done sometime today."

Injurious reached for Autumn, who lay curled in a fetal position. As he set her on her knees, he could feel her trembling. She was no longer crying and pleading; she simply knelt to await the blow that robbed her of her right wing. Injurious smiled at Autumn's terror when her right wing fell to the ground but did not detach as it should have. Deleterious inquired if another blow was necessary.

"No, it just needs a good tug," Injurious replied. He grasped Autumn's injured wing and tore it free of the flesh that held it." Autumn screamed and passed out.

Injurious dragged her back to where the slaves were and threw her in a mixture of mud and blood at Kaela's feet. "You promised to protect Autumn, but you failed. Prepare yourself. You are next to test the axe."

Autumn woke in the inky darkness of deep space. The pain in her back had subsided slightly, but the terror of knowing her wings were absent from her body made her turn with a start. She saw Kaela was still chained to her, and she was chained to a long succession of weeping brothers. Clutching the iron cuff she wore around her neck that bound her to chains secured by irons around her wrists and ankles, she asked, "Where are we?" Her question was answered by the sting of a warrior's whip against her bloody stubs. Sobs born of fear and regret clogged her throat, making it almost impossible for her to breathe. Gasping, Autumn whispered, "This was my entire fault. I brought this terror on myself and Kaela."

"Concentrate on the beauty of the universe's vast expanse," a voice inside her head whispered. "There are wonders here that angelic eyes have never seen until now."

Through her tears, Autumn focused her vision on stars that resembled pearls. Clouds of spatial gases that were shaped by interstellar winds glowed in shades of pink, blues, and greens. Awed by her surroundings, Autumn whispered, "Only Father could have created something as beautiful as this."

While Autumn's tearful eyes drank in the beauty of the cosmos, Archangel Kaela did a visual scan of the region for another reason. He had to know the dance of the planets and how they were aligned in deep space so that when he escaped, he could easily find his way back home with Autumn. While he surveyed the universe, Lucifer's warriors dragged their hostages through a supernova's remnants. On the opposite side of the supernova's debris, Kaela saw a dark black hole in space.

Whips cracked, and screams of agony filtered through the vast expanse, their sound lost to any ears that might have heard them. Against their will, God's righteous sons were forced to enter a wormhole's ribbed cavern that flashed with bold electric colors. The brightness of the flashing hues temporarily blinded Lucifer's hostages. The dreadfulness of the wormhole, the drag it had on angelic bodies numbed with pain and weakened by hunger, sapped the life from some; others panicked, screaming wildly, vomiting bile caused by the vertigo of seeing churning waves of rolling colors surrounding them. Had Kaela been free to examine the wormhole's walls, he would have found that though the walls were made of pure air, they were as hard as stone, and they were more dangerous than anything that ever existed in Heaven.

"Do you see that planet over there?" Hagenti, one of Lucifer's rebel warriors shouted. "That is where you are going. Guards who live on the surface of that fiery world will be coming soon. There they are. As soon as they have secured you, you are theirs for eternity."

Autumn narrowed her eyes, focusing on what looked to be another black hole in space. Could Hagenti be mistaken about there being a fiery world he wanted them to see? Maybe he was lost, took a wrong turn, or left Heaven at the wrong location and happened here, thinking he was leading his captives to a fiery world. Her thoughts were interrupted by the sight of horrid-looking creatures floating through deep space in her direction. As the creatures drew nearer, she realized they were brothers clothed in bulky suits that covered their bodies; on their heads they wore helmets with dark face shields. Their helmets were attached to the necks of their suits, and on their hands, they wore thick gloves. Attached to their backs were packs, probably filled with a breathable substance since each pack had a hose that clipped to the back of their helmets.

While the slaves looked on, the commander who just arrived spoke with Hagenti. An agreement was reached. Ownership traded hands. A trumpet's blare filled the region, a signal for Lucifer's guards to return to northern Heaven. Without thought for their captives' safety, the new slave masters dragged their weeping brothers through deep space to the chaotic planet below.

Kaela stared at the dark world he was about to enter. He wondered what a planet without light would do to his brothers. They were already weak, half-starved, and injured. They needed light. Angels were created in the most effulgent light in the universe, and their bodies craved light. But here was this dark planet, a world that would become their prison, a world dark with hate and foreboding.

The descent to the globe's surface introduced God's sons to a new horror—sulfur. The sulfurous fumes that rose up from the globe's surface saturated every cell of their bodies. Noses, mouths, throats, and lungs burned so badly that even swallowing became difficult. Every breath they took made them ill. When they reached the surface, they felt the heat before they even set their feet down. Kaela's first thought was that Pain or a similar entity had accompanied them to this forsaken place to feed on their physical distress. Taking Autumn in his arms, he stood her on his feet, hoping to save her from knowing the soil that glowed red on the planet's surface gave off heat, not light.

"My name is Xaphan," a shrouded warrior called, his voice quieted the slaves who grieved for their lost brothers and who wept because they feared for their lives. "On Sheol, I am Lucifer's general. You were brought here to collect gold for Sin. I will be your commander. I urge each of you to consider your time on this globe as a lesson in self-discipline. While you are here, you will learn that your obedience to Lucifer is your only source of happiness. Had you worshipped the emperor as his laws dictate, you would not be here today."

General Xaphan spread his arms. "Look around you. No one outside this world knows you weep. No one can free you from this prison, and you are so far from Heaven that God cannot hear your prayers. You will do as I say, or you will be uncreated." Xaphan paused for a moment to let the slaves digest what he said. "I do not tolerate whiners or anyone who cannot carry his share of the load." He snapped his heels together and straightened his stance. "Guards, you will lead these slaves to the molten river where they will mine this globe's precious ore."

Guards, two hundred to be exact, jogged across the seething land to where the slaves stood. In their hands, each of the security officers carried four large stone pails by their cords.

"Present the buckets to the slaves," General Xaphan ordered. The guards did as they were told, until each of Lucifer's captives held two pails that could hold five gallons each of ore. "Are there any questions?" None were asked. "Then get to work!"

Lieutenant Rahab was the next to introduce himself to Lucifer's weeping slaves. "You are on Sheol. There is no hiding place on this globe. Escape is inconceivable since you would not survive. Every region on this world resembles this one. To remain in the elements without protective gear for a prolonged period of time is disastrous. I am not worried for your safety. To me, you who support God and obey His laws are pond scum. I could not care less if you perish on Sheol. But, Sin wants her palace decorated in Sheol's gold, and I aim to please our mistress. Therefore, I will see that you are kept alive until the Goddess's request is fulfilled. On completion of your work, you will be uncreated."

Armed guards led thousands of God's most righteous sons over a valley's sizzling floor to a river whose brilliant currents flowed swift and hot. While the slaves received their orders, Kaela tore a strip of material from his tunic and tied it around the bottom half of his face. Brothers, who saw what he did, followed suit. When the briefing ended, the slaves were forced to kneel along the river's scorching banks where they dipped their pails into the fiery ore. Anyone that hesitated from fear or defiance felt the whip's braid on his back.

The heat from the flow, the ore's sulfurous stench, and Pain's constant hunger burdened the slaves' every move. Perspiration ran from their foreheads, stinging their eyes, and blurring their vision, thus hindering their ability to judge how far into the river they should set their pails. From up shore, there came a scream. More screams followed, not of pain, but of astonishment. Word traveled down the line that the skin of Lassarium's hand and arm had been burned off, and the shock of what had happened robbed him of his life.

From the molten river's core, a geyser of flames shot upward. The fount's amber sparks fell in globs from great heights, scarring angelic skin. Injured brothers clenched their teeth, working in tortuous silence. The slaves had to fill their pails with foul-smelling gold regardless of the pain they suffered since the pails had to be emptied simultaneously into waiting drums that would be transported from Sheol to Lucifer's onyx palace. The warriors' blood-hungry whips striped the backs of brothers whose pails were not filled to overflowing, so when the fount sent out globs of fire that fell on those who dipped their pails into the golden river, they continued their work without pause or hesitation.

A grueling half century passed, but it seemed like yesterday that Autumn was dragged through deep space, blood oozing from the stubs that had been her wings and her back stinging from the beating she received, and for what … pledging her allegiance to God. All these many years, Autumn's most faithful companion was the entity Guilt. If she had not been so vain, she and Kaela would still be in the Sacred Region where they would be nourished daily by Father's healing light. But she had grown wiser - being imprisoned on this fiery globe taught her there were worse problems than losing a wing or two to any one of the witch's brutal warriors. The misery of laboring over the molten surface of Sheol's river to mine gold for Sin, the pain of sleeping in a pen on hot soil, and the thirst and hunger she suffered daily erased her fears of being clipped, or beaten. Every day, Autumn worried that she might be uncreated, but every night she feared that if she lived, this nightmare would never end.

Just as Lieutenant Rahab warned, working on Sheol without the benefit of wearing protective suits took a toll on the slaves' physical appearance. They withered like dried twigs, growing gaunt and skinny. Their eyes lost their color, resembling the darkest blood ever bled. Their muscles, though used every waking minute, grew weaker with each passing year. Their lips were parched to a degree that they seemed to have burned off their face. Their teeth went from white to yellow;

some brothers lost their teeth completely. God's enslaved sons were not the beautiful specimens now that they had been on the day of their creation.

Every day, General Xaphan reminded Lucifer's captives that to pray to Father was futile, and so, for years, Autumn fought her urge to pray. But one night, after seeing too many of her brothers uncreated by accidents or acts of hostility, she knelt in the pen and said aloud, "Father, I plead for Your mercy!"

"Autumn, have you gone mad?" Leo asked in a loud whisper. "The guards will hear you, and you will be uncreated."

"Let them uncreate me," she told her weary brother. "I would rather give my life for Father than live another day on Sheol."

She glanced at Kaela. He didn't even resemble the handsome angel he had been. He was scarred from the fire and from the whip. His skin was like leather, and like everyone, herself included, he had lost his thick hair to the heat of this dreadful planet. "I'm going pray. I'm prepared for uncreation of self. Will you join me, Archangel Kaela?" He nodded, crawled to where she knelt, and clasped his hands in a prayerful manner.

"Heavenly Father, You are the universe's purest light," Autumn said, not caring who heard her. "We revere Your name and ask that You do with Your enemy's captive sons what You would do with us if we were in Heaven, for it is Your will, not ours, that must be done. Forgive us, I pray, for becoming Sin's unwitting slaves, and help us to forgive one another and ourselves. Lend us Your mercy, for we are victims of a cruel dictator who hates You because You are righteous and good. Free us from these chains that bind us to this forsaken globe. Help us, I beg You, to leave this darkness behind so that we can bask in Your healing light and do Your bidding. Take us back, oh Lord, to Heaven, for You are our Creator, our Father, our Comforter, our Protector, our King, and our Glory, now and forever. Amen."

When the other slaves heard Autumn's prayer, they dropped to their knees and repeated what she said. Kneeling on the burning soil, surrounded by her brothers with Kaela at her side, her heart felt as though it had been born anew. The sulfur in the air meant nothing to her now, the heat went unfelt, and her soul was lighted by her love for Father in Heaven. Moved by divine fervor, Autumn lay face-down on the smoldering ground, the humblest of all angelic positions, and repeated her prayer a second time.

While she lay there with her forehead pressed against the red-hot soil, a vision presented itself to her. In it, Heaven's King wept tears of joy as sincere prayers that glowed of the purest and most honorable love crossed His holy altar.

"Look, daughters," Father called, "a miracle has happened that is not of my making. Your brothers, those lost souls who worship only me, have gained courage to cry out for my help. These sorrowing children are the source of my deepest admiration, for they shunned evil though it lived all around them. My broken heart has mended. It is time to bring my faithful sons back home."

In her vision, Autumn stood with her Father in the throne room on the castle's highest peak. Heaven's King stretched out His arms and shouted, "I call on the mighty wind that lives in the farthest corner of Infinity's dark basement, come, stand before me."

A faint moan could be heard, a sign that the wind had awakened. The fog that blanketed the mount's plateau retreated to the village, filtering into the Holy City. A second time, God called to the wind. A howl filled the region. Autumn felt the climate change. The sky over Father's kingdom grew black as pitch. Thunder roared. Lightning clashed against the darkened sky. Flowers bent their faces down to the ground, and the branches of the shaggy trees swayed wildly. Autumn clasped her hands to her ears to stifle the roar that promised to become louder.

"Mighty wind," Heaven's King shouted over the gale's uproar, "I order you to do my bidding." The cyclone set its funneled end down on the throne room's tiled floor, but despite its unrelenting power, it did not damage God's precious home. "Go to Sheol and the pits in the North. Find all my captive children. Bring them home to me. In the form of my right hand, lift them from their prisons. Let no harm come to them, return them to my kingdom."

The Holy Father turned to Autumn. "Go, dear child. Be part of this adventure. Witness the joy on my son's faces when they take their place at your side."

Autumn's mouth dropped open. Trembling, she fell to her knees before her Creator. "But this is a vision, yet You can see me."

"I see everyone," He whispered. Heaven's King helped His earthly daughter to her feet. "Go now. Take a seat in the palm of the hand I formed. The wind will not wait forever."

Autumn ran across the throne room's slick floor and flung herself into the hand's airy wind-formed palm. With a fierce roar, the Lord's merciful spirit left the Holy Castle. Cupped between the hand's thumb and index finger, Autumn listened. What is that sound? Listen. The sound grew louder. She rose to her feet. From where she stood she saw the hand fed on the universe's most violent storms. Thunder that had been imprisoned inside the powerful gale pounded like a primitive pulse. Autumn sank down into the hand's palm, leaning her back against its strong fingers.

Autumn surveyed her surroundings. She was in deep space. The stars that she saw before were disturbed by the wind's force and swayed helplessly in its wake. Soon, she would arrive at Sheol where God's wrath would prove victorious over Lucifer's evil. Her brothers would be freed from their prison, and they would return to Heaven where Father would heal them.

"Life will be good, again," Autumn whispered.

"What is that?" a suited warrior shouted. He adjusted his face mask to better see the massive wind that had penetrated Sheol's atmosphere and was headed toward the pens that housed several thousand slaves. "Tell General Xaphan that a cataclysmic atmospheric phenomenon is—" Before he could finish his sentence, flames fanned by the wind's fury leaped up from the planet's surface. Screams of anguish filled the region as waves of fire higher than any wave found in the ocean consumed everyone with the exception of God's righteous sons.

One by one, Autumn's brothers fell into the safety of the divine hand's airy palm. She looked for Kaela. When she found him, they fell to their knees in each other's arms, hugging and savoring the knowledge that, soon, they would be home. The hand carried Sin's slaves through the deepest realms of space and set them down in Father's courtyard where they were greeted by their cheering brothers. Without speaking a word, Father made it clear to Autumn that she was chosen to witness another wondrous event. While Archangel Kaela was welcomed home by his brothers and sisters, Autumn sank down into the hand's spacious palm. At God's command, the airy hand lifted off the ground and directed its flight to the North.

Forneus was assigned to one of the many guard shacks that lined the edge of the northern boundary. From his high perch, he saw what appeared to be a ghostly white hand filled with lightning and roaring with thunder. The phantom was traveling at break-neck speed toward the North. Small at first, the hand grew larger as it drew closer to the border he guarded. Forneus called frantically to Mastema and Mephistopheles, who occupied the neighboring guard house.

"Our enemy, Heaven's vengeful King, seeks to uncreate us!" Forneus leaped to the ground and ran screaming into the wooded area that held nothing but mud and rotted plant life.

Mephistopheles ran from the guard shack. The roaring wind was upon the region. For a brief moment, he panicked; there was no time to warn the great Lucifer of the wind's coming. Collecting his thoughts, the evil angel studied the glowing hand. Currents of light pulsated through its ghostlike veins, giving off an eerie green glow that illuminated the fog shrouding the northern landscape. From where Mephistopheles stood, he could not see where the wind was heading, but he knew this had to be an attempt by God to rescue his imprisoned saints and enslaved sons. Since the tunnel's discovery a little over a decade ago, several of righteous spies had been captured. Some of them had been uncreated.

The great Lucifer ended sainted pilfering of his stock when he commissioned Ornias, who earned the title Deceptive One, to visit the pits throughout the region. Posing as a suffering slave, Ornias was moved from one location to another by pit masters who seemed to treat him as badly as they treated the North's captive slaves. To avoid detection, Ornias surrounded himself with critically ill or severely injured slaves, who he imitated when guards he was suspicious of, approached.

On the night of the tunnel's discovery, Ornias sat in the mud in one of the pits at the mountain's base. It was a quiet evening filled with dark rolling fog and drenching rains that poured a foot of water into the pit's already soft, muddy floor. Ornias found an overhang and settled under it for the night. He was almost asleep when a door that stood unnoticed under a thick coat of mud and vines opened before his eyes. Ornias watched as God's saints emerged from a room deep within the mountain's wall. The saints urged Lucifer's slaves to rise to their feet. Those who couldn't walk or were too weak from hunger were carried from the pit through the door that, until now, no one knew existed. Ornias wanted to call out to Lucifer's warriors, but he did not. Instead, he allowed the saints to usher him through the mysterious door. Inside, he saw a long tunnel that was lighted from front to back with glowing lanterns.

Ornias spent the night in God's kingdom, feasting, bathing, and sleeping in a fresh bed in a room in the Holy Castle; and the following night, he returned to the North. Without hesitation, he led the great Lucifer to the pit where the muddy door opened to a traitor's tunnel. Prince Michael's saints were captured, imprisoned, tortured, and executed. The slaves were confined to pens. The tunnel that led to promised freedom was collapsed. Ornias's discovery brought him great wealth and renown. He was promoted to general and put in charge of hundreds of Lucifer's most blood-thirsty, dark-clad warriors. Mephistopheles wished he had been the one to earn the great Lucifer's respect. He returned to the guardhouse where he watched the sky for signs of the glowing hand's approach.

With Autumn clinging to the airy hand's large thumb it lowered itself into a slave pit. Calling to her brothers, she said, "It is I, Autumn. Father formed this hand in the Sacred Region. It is here to carry you to His kingdom. Leave no one behind, but act swiftly, Lucifer's guards are well aware of our Lord's plan to save His sons, and they will be here shortly." Brothers who were starved, beaten, tortured, and abused were carried aboard the hand by brothers who were weak and malnourished. The divine hand traveled through the North, emptying pits and pens of their sorrowful hostages. When it completed its chore, the hand lifted high into the air, setting its course for the Sacred Region.

On the ground, a company of charioteers stormed through the muddy courtyard outside the onyx palace. Their intent was to take down the wind and regain possession of their emperor's slaves. Autumn saw the chariots' approach but was not afraid. She was certain the wind was too high and too fast to be caught, but when monstrous winged horses effortlessly lifted the warriors' chariots into the air, she lost her confidence in the hand's ability to outrun them. In seconds, hordes of the emperor's dark-clad warriors joined the charioteers in their south-bound flight.

"Father, help us!" Autumn shouted over the wind's thundering roar. The blustery storms that were locked within the giant hand fueled its race from the North toward God's kingdom.

At the onyx palace, in its highest tower, Sin sat on her throne, her dark eyes trained on the glowing object that had stolen her slaves. Her anger burned when she saw her skilled warriors were no match for God's disembodied hand. Scowling, Sin flung herself from the tower's open patio. Like a shadow, she lifted up into the darkened sky. With her cape whipping the air, the witch sped past her warriors. Doubling her speed, she went past the lead charioteer. And now, she was directly behind the wind.

Frighten brothers screamed for the hand to accelerate its speed. The hand exhaled. *Whoosh!* Swiftly, forcefully, the storms that had been pulsating in its veins were expelled. The wind's exhaust propelled Sin backward through the night sky, forcing her back, retracing her flight from the onyx palace. Screaming, clawing at the air, the witch shot like a comet through the northern skies, passing retreating charioteers and warriors. Pushed helplessly through the air like a dry leaf by storms that threatened to consume her, Sin glanced over her shoulder. Oh no. Not this. The onyx palace loomed pitch-black behind her. She braced herself for the inevitable, but nothing prepared her for the pain she felt when her body slammed against the outer wall of the dark building she had conjured from the northern mountain's bowels.

Dazed, Sin clung to a window's sill, screaming for help. She felt her hand slipping. The witch tried in vain to brace herself against the fog-slick onyx wall.

"Lucifer, my beloved—help me."

Unfortunately, the witch's plea was directed to a coward who sat trembling on his bed. Sin tried in vain to lift her broken body into the window. With every move she made, Pain feasted on her wounds.

"Oh," she moaned. Try as she would, she could not become the mist she turned into on the night Father released her into Heaven. Struggling madly, Sin forced her throbbing leg up toward the window. Somehow, she managed to hook her heel over the window's slick sill. Her hand slipped. The loss of its grip sent her plunging head-first down to the ground below. The impact of her fall drove her deep into the mud that carpeted the courtyard's mushy ground.

Above the Holy Castle, thousands of weary souls huddled together in the airy palm of God's powerful right hand. The moment the divine hand rested firmly on the ground, rescued angels rose to their feet, praising their Creator. As they prayed and sang joyful songs filled with words that revered our Lord's awesome powers, their skin mended. Their hair grew thick and full. Even their lost teeth were replaced by new ones. Lifting on wings that were newly healed, they circled the outdoor throne room to honor Father with a dance that resembled the movement of the planets in deep space. Autumn smiled across the wide circle of angels at Archangel Kaela, whose eyes were fixed on her. He winked at her, threw his head back, and laughed aloud. The sights, the sounds, and the scents of the Sacred Region eased the horrid memory of their life on Sheol. Below them, on His throne, Father wiped tears of joy from His eyes. His heart swelled with unconditional love for His sons of light, His most precious creation.

Hours after the angels' dance began, it ended. Father left His throne in His outdoor throne room to retire to His inner sanctum. As nourishing clouds nestled in the tree-tops, sinking slowly down the mountain-side to shroud the Sacred Region in its fertile dews, Archangel Kaela and Autumn returned to their suite in the Holy Castle, where they talked in hushed tones about their ordeal on Sheol and praised God as their savior.

Chapter 42

The Lesson

"While we were on Sheol, I did a lot of thinking," Autumn told her angel. "I looked into my past and I saw myself as a simpering self-pitying whiner who wants her brothers to solve her problems." She studied Archangel Kaela's face. "I left the safety of Father's house to return to our cottage so that I could bring my best outfits back here. I wanted to wear them so that my brothers and sisters would admire my beauty. And look what my vanity caused. We were captured, our wings were axed off our backs, and we were forced to work for Sin on Sheol. I wanted to be admired and respected, but admiration is fleeting, and respect must be earned."

"I would say that your service to God while you were in the North earned you a great deal of respect," Kaela told her. He walked to where she struggled with the sash that girded her robe at the waist. Taking the material in his hands, he drew the ends through the wrapped sections until they fell neatly down the front of her skirt. "Autumn, my dearest angel, our brothers compare your wisdom to that of our Lord's holy scribe. They listen to your words because they love what you say. You are compassionate and understanding. You put the needs of others before your own. When our brothers need someone to talk to, you listen with your heart to what they say. You are not a whiner. You are not self-pitying. If you had not put Father before your own safety, we—all of us—would still be on Sheol or held captive in pits and pens in the North." He lifted her face with his fingertips. "I am very proud of who you are, and so is Father." He smiled when Autumn nodded. "Let's go, we don't want to be late."

It was a night of joy and festivity. The courtyard was brightened by flickering lanterns though Father had not yet left His outdoor throne. Autumn saw cherubs carrying trays filled with food and nectar to tables set up on the castle's lawn. Brothers greeted brothers and shared stories with civilians about their ordeal in the North and on Sheol. Angels traveled the many paths that lay throughout Father's Meditation Garden, and the Goddesses circulated among their brothers, reminding them of their virtuous lessons. At the sound of the trumpet, a blessing was said, and the happy citizens who lived in God's kingdom were invited to enjoy the feast that had been prepared for them.

Within a couple hours, a second trumpet sounded, the theaters' doors opened wide, and everyone was invited inside. When the angels were seated, Father addressed them.

"My precious sons of light," He said, "some of you know, better than others the atrocities that are taking place in the North. Lucifer and Sin are hatching plans to take my throne by force. But soon, I will create One whose strength will be unmatched by God or Goddesses. Only He will rule from my throne, and He will do so with my blessing." Father scanned the audience. The pink hue of their upturned faces told Him that His beloved sons approved of His plan to create His heir. "Remember, when you are troubled or feel threatened, call my name, and I will be there for you. I will never abandon you, and if you should move away from me, return to where you left me. I will be there, happily awaiting your arrival."

The news that Father would create an heir excited Heaven's angels so that they found it hard to sleep that night. Autumn and Archangel Kaela were among those who wandered silently over through the courtyard until they stopped to sit in the garden that grew full and fragrant near the castle's wide porch. Autumn found the bench she and Sonnet claimed as theirs eons ago. Within minutes, she and Kaela were joined by Joniel, Lindsay, Octaviel, and Citadel. Sitting at Autumn's feet on the dew-soaked ground, the brothers talked about the dinner they enjoyed, but mostly, they spoke enthusiastically about Father's announcement that He would create an heir to rule Heaven from His throne rather than chose an heir from among His many advisors.

"Father would never break His own law," Joniel told his brothers. "Our Lord doesn't want an angel to rule in Heaven. But I have to wonder what Father meant when He said His created heir will be stronger than God or Goddess?"

Archangel Kaela shrugged. "It sounds like Father plans to create an heir who is strong enough to protect His righteous sons from harm." He abandoned his seat near Autumn to lie back on the dew-covered grass. This was Heaven's darkest hour, the best time for sleeping. Sleep renewed angelic cells, strengthened their bones, eased their minds, and regenerated their organs. Kaela wished he had gone to his apartment where, by now, he would be asleep. But he was here with his brothers, listening to them marvel over God's plan to bring forth an Advocate whose powers would far outweigh His own.

"Autumn, you studied with Scribe Excelsa," Octaviel said, moving closer to where his small brother sat. "What are your thoughts on Father's statement?"

"We are approaching the dawn of a new millennium," Autumn said. "If Father were to create His heir, this would be the perfect time to do it."

Kaela reminded her that eons had passed since the creation of God's seventh flock, and during those eons, records showed that Lucifer's disobedience to God's laws caused nothing but turmoil. He wondered aloud why Father had waited so long to create His powerful heir.

"I think our Lord sees our weaknesses," Autumn told her angel. "He is aware that our indifference to what we see and hear is the true reason Heaven is on the brink of open war. We let our self-concern, our desire to protect our peace of mind, silence us against what we knew was wrong. We worried that Father would be offended if we exposed our eldest brother's lies." Autumn looked from Archangel Kaela to the others. "Why did we believe our Lord loved one son more than He loved the rest of us?"

Citadel shrugged. Being a seventh-generation angel, he had seen nothing but unrest. "Why did our ancient brothers hold that belief to their hearts for so many eons if it was not true? And why do some continue to fall back on the falsehood that Father loves Lucifer more than He loves us?"

"Lucifer told us that Father sat in unapproachable light to avoid us," Joniel replied. "Nothing could have been further from the truth." He broke a twig off between his fingers and stuck it in his mouth, a habit he brought back with him from the North. "But that still doesn't explain why Father wants to create someone more powerful than Himself."

Lindsay looked from one brother to the next. "We know that Father is a powerful king. Look at what He did. He called a wind from deep space and fashioned it into the form of a hand. He directed that hand to search for, find, and rescue His righteous sons, and He, not our brothers who are blessed with healing powers, healed and nourished every son that was returned to Him from the pits and pens in the North. And let us never forget the brothers Father's air-formed hand lifted from Sheol's molten surface."

No one spoke for a long time.

"When we lived in the North," Autumn finally said, "after Lucifer realized that he still had to answer to Father, we would return to the Holy Castle to enjoy feasts and festivals of light during which our minds and bodies were healed and nourished. The festival took on a serious note when our Lord began to reward His skilled sons with titled promotions." Autumn told the youngsters sitting at her feet about the horror she witnessed when Lucifer gave birth to Sin at the base of Father's pure-white throne. "But know this: Lucifer was evil before Sin was born into Heaven. Sin is benign until a weak or disobedient mind obeys her commands."

"Sin is Lucifer's mentor," Lindsay grumbled. "He is under her influence. She is not under his control."

Autumn spoke up. "Father created us full-grown and wise. Lucifer was given the part of God that I refer to as common sense. Our Lord cannot stop Sin from whispering temptations into our ear. She wants us to leave the path Father set us on to join her on her journey from Heaven to Hell. Lucifer is Sin's power of persuasion. He is the silky tongue that tells us what we want to believe. Lucifer is a vessel of empty promises designed to lead us astray, turn us against what we know is proper, and fill our heads with hopeless dreams. Sin and Lucifer need each other. They are Heaven's evil twins, and soon, they and their supporters will fall from God's grace to the prison He prepared for them."

"How do we know right from wrong?" Citadel asked.

"Sometimes, we believe that God is telling us what to do when, in fact, it is Sin or Lucifer," Autumn said softly. "The way to figure right from wrong is to ask yourself if you would want someone to do to you what you are about to do to him. If the answer is no, then it is wrong to do that to a brother."

"How could Sin have any influence over God's righteous sons?" Lindsay asked.

"Sin visits our bedside in the quiet night," Autumn whispered. "She enters into us as a black mist, and before she leaves, she puts a trace of her foul residue in us. We are infected by Sin. And so we must be obedient to our Lord's laws, faithful to His teachings, and follow His commands. God is the epitome of all that is holy and righteous. He wants for us to be happy and content. He wants us to confide in Him, respect Him as our King, and turn to Him when we are frightened, tempted, or in doubt. To stay righteous, you must make God's laws your body armor, make your faith in Him your sword, and make your respect for Him your shield. By doing that, your war against evil will be won."

Archangel Kaela interrupted. "I am curious if God's heir will be physically different from us."

"He will be beautiful." Autumn sighed. "He will be more beautiful than any angel in Heaven. And whosoever looks on Him will know immediately that He is the Son of God, and we will tremble in His presence, for He will be given the power to see us in such a way that He will know if we are good or bad. Our hearts will either accept Him or reject Him. The heart in those of us who accept God's created Son will soften, while the heart in those who reject Him will grow as hard as a rock. There will be no turning back once our decision is made. We will adore Him, or we will hate Him—there will be no room for political correctness, no room for indifference, no room for flattery or fraud."

"He will be wonderful," Joniel said in awe of what he heard. Tears streamed down his cheeks. "I have waited so long for one to come who will sort us out, who will reward the good, and who will punish the evil."

"Brothers," Autumn said addressing Kaela, Joniel, Lindsay, Octaviel, and Citadel with one loving word, "remember this: trust in Father, accept Him as your Creator, Protector, and King. Your belief in God will keep you safe. Be obedient to our Lord's Laws; be unfaltering in your faith in Him, for your faith in God is your weapon against evil."

To Archangel Kaela, she said, "No matter how fervently we try, we cannot convince Lucifer's followers to surrender to Father or to come home where they can be cleansed of Sin's venom and reintroduced to their old way of life. They are content to follow a weak leader who, through his power of persuasion, has them convinced that our Lord's powers are failing and that Prince Michael's saints are the evil ones."

Kaela addressed his brothers. "Let me add that no matter how passionately we pray for Father to grant salvation to our rebellious brothers, He will not do it until they, themselves, kneel in humble prayer before Him. They must want to be saved from their evil ways. If they do not voluntarily turn to Father, Who loves them, they will know eternal doom."

The youngsters who had joined the archangel, Autumn, and Joniel said nothing; but the expression on their faces revealed that they were considering all that they had been told tonight.

Kaela rose to his feet. "We need to sleep." He knew that angels craved the eight to twelve hours of sleep each night. "Let's sleep on the hope that Father will create a Son who will lead us out of this unrest into peace and happiness. Tomorrow, we will learn what, if anything, Father told Prince Michael and His council members about His plan."

Kaela extended his hand in Autumn's direction and smiled when she placed her palm in his. Lindsay, Octaviel, and Citadel left the garden without a word to anyone. Joniel turned away from the path that led to the castle. He preferred his cottage to a room in Father's house. "I will see you in the morning, brother," Kaela called after him. He smiled at Joniel, who walked backward, waving his hand in the air.

He did not turn in the direction of the staircase that descended from the Holy Mount to the village below until he was sure that Kaela had nothing more to say to him.

CHAPTER 43

The Encounter

On the night Father announced that He would create an heir to His throne, a meeting was held in His inner sanctum. Autumn and Kaela, who had been talking with their brothers following the festival, had just entered the castle's ground floor. They were about to mount the stairs that led to their first-floor apartment when the doors to the holy sanctum opened. The foyer was filled with blinding light from front to back, and when the light dimmed, God's advisors stood outside the sanctum's closed door, talking in hushed tones. The meeting had ended. Lieutenant Gabriel spoke briefly with Prince Michael before leaving the castle to go about his duties. Seeing Autumn and Kaela standing at the foot of the stairs, Michael called to them, "Come with me." He led them to the area of the foyer where plush sofas and chairs set. When they were comfortable, the prince took his seat.

"While you both were imprisoned on Sheol, Father ordered my saints to infiltrate the North to seize the weapons Azazel had built," Prince Michael told the pair. "Father called a summit meeting at the castle. Lucifer refused to attend since he feared he would be arrested for the crime he committed against Heaven's citizens when he ignited that gaseous planet." Michael revealed that the northern delegation met with God. "An agreement was reached that the North would stop building weapons of mass destruction and, in turn, sainted intrusion into their region would end. The agreement was signed by Lucifer, Sin, and Belial, Father, Scribe Excelsa, and me. My saints did not enter the northern region of Heaven until Lucifer broke his end of the bargain.

"Tonight, my saints received word that on Lucifer's orders, Azazel and his apprentices have produced many cannons, large and small. It is rumored that our eldest brother intends to use these weapons on our citizens in the Sacred Region.

"As we speak, Lieutenant Gabriel is briefing his troops on their mission to the North," the prince disclosed. "They will leave tomorrow night when the streets in the North are shrouded in the witch's dark fog and every avenue in Lucifer's false empire is as black as pitch. I will meet with my saints in Father's large auditorium in the morning to fill them in on what's happening. Be there. Until then, sleep well."

That night, Archangel Kaela was awakened from his sound sleep by an unfamiliar presence that entered his suite uninvited. Narrowing his eyes against the light glowing through the slats of the shuttered window, he saw what looked to be a shadowy form at the foot of his bed. The intruder, realizing Kaela was awake, spoke first. "It is I, Abdiel."

The archangel sat up in bed. "How did you get in here?" he demanded. "Where is Autumn? If you harmed Autumn, you will be sorry." While he spoke, he reached for the sword he kept between his bed and his nightstand for times like this. The sword was gone.

"I mean you no harm," Abdiel told his angry brother. "I have your sword." He held the weapon so the light that striped his clothing glinted off the weapon's blade. "Since I am rather fond of my head, I will hold on to your sword for now." He lost his haughty attitude when he felt the tip of Autumn's blade pierce the fabric of his clothing. "Autumn," he said, turning his head slightly while addressing her, "I have no intention of harming either of you. If I wanted to hurt you, I would not have come here alone."

"How did you get in here?" She asked.

"I came in through your living room window," he answered. "When I talk to Prince Michael, I am going to suggest stationing guards on the castle's roof. That way, intruders will be seen on the ground below and in the air above. We must keep our royal family safe from harm."

"You work for Father?" Autumn mused. She glanced around Abdiel at Kaela. "He works for Father?"

"So he claims." Kaela snorted. He leaned across his bed, toward his lantern.

"No," Abdiel said quickly. "Leave the room dark. I can't be seen here."

"All right then, what do you want?" Kaela asked.

"Lucifer is planning a raid on Father's house," Abdiel revealed. "Sin is in a rage because she wanted the raid to happen during the festivities last evening. She wanted our righteous brothers and Prince Michael's saints to know Lucifer has not forgotten that God robbed him of his titles in the Sacred Region." Abdiel waited for Autumn or Kaela to speak. The room reeked of silence. "Kaela, Lucifer must be stopped."

"So when will this so-called raid on Father's house take place?" Kaela asked.

"Soon," Abdiel revealed. "You see, up until now, northern council members had Lucifer convinced that he would undoubtedly be heir to God's coveted throne. But when Father announced that He would create an heir, it changed everything. Now, Lucifer plans to attack the castle and claim the throne as his own. And, no, I am not the informant. Gadreel, who loves both Father and Lucifer, took the news back to the North."

Abdiel covered his hair with his cape. "I must go now. But I leave you with this warning: the assault on the Holy Castle will be devastating if it goes according to Lucifer's plan. Tell Prince Michael to keep God's family safe from harm." He walked to bedroom door. "It was good seeing you both again." Autumn followed him to the living room and watched as he left through the window he used to gain entrance to her suite.

"He's gone," she told Kaela when she returned to their bedroom. "Where are you going?" She didn't expect to find her angel dressed in his uniform, his weapons' belt secured around his waist, and his sword in hand. Sheathing his blade, he walked past her to the living room. "I asked you a question—where are you going?"

"Go back to bed," Archangel Kaela told his beloved Autumn. She followed him into the hallway, watching after him. "I told you to go to bed and get some rest." He could feel her eyes on his back as he descended the stairs that led to the foyer below.

Reluctantly, Autumn returned to their suite. Removing her dagger from the weapons' belt that hung in the hall closet, she made a thorough search of their apartment; she even checked under both beds before she felt safe enough to go to sleep.

Mid-morning, a trumpet sounded. All the soldiers in the region left their posts and reported to the auditorium. When they were seated, Prince Michael took center stage. His lieutenants, generals, and commanders sat at tables that stretched out behind him.

"Please close the doors," the prince said. He waited until the doors were secured before making his remarks. "If you recall, about sixty years ago, we went on a mission to the North during which we confiscated the first cannon and other weapons Azazel built. We brought everything we found to the Sacred Region, and we stored the northern weapons in our Lord's armory for safe-keeping. We learned recently that Lucifer has had Azazel and his metallurgists building weapons to use against those of us living in God's kingdom.

"As a precaution," Prince Michael said, walking to the lip of the stage, "I sent Lieutenant Gabriel to the North to search for and to seize all newly built weapons of mass destruction. I ordered my first-lieutenant to bring the weapons he finds to God's kingdom, where they will be stored."

"Archangel Kaela." The prince waited for his brother to stand at his seat. "I am promoting you to the position of lieutenant. From this moment on, you will be called Lieutenant Archangel Kaela. You have the brutality of the North in you, and we need your combative expertise to assure the safety of our royal family and Father's holy scribe. Are there any questions?" Hearing none, the prince continued his remarks.

"All saints are ordered to protect Father, our sisters, our council members, Scribe Excelsa, Archangel Effiel and his student, Elbreon, with your lives," Prince Michael told his soldiers. "I expect all of you to protect everyone who lives in Father's village and city while you patrol the streets. Saints have my permission to attack trespassers with lethal force." Prince Michael called on Kaela a second time, saying,

"Lieutenant Archangel Kaela, would you like to address this auditorium before we adjourn?"

Kaela rose to his feet. "Brothers, Lucifer and his black-suited warriors are not simply rebels. They are terrorists. Terrorists rely on the element of surprise. They commit atrocities so frightening civilians in all regions of Heaven fear going about their daily lives. Terrorists are too cowardly to target soldiers who can retaliate against them. They attack private citizens who are helpless to fend them off.

"One fact we must remember is that terrorists are always armed when they enter a strike zone. Terrorists trespass against their brothers with the intention of uncreating them before they are discovered, and where you find one terrorist, you will find many." He paused for a moment. "Be fearless. Do not let Lucifer's warriors intimidate you with hateful accusations of discrimination or sainted cruelty. You are God's saints, be brave."

When the meeting ended, Prince Michael's saints left God's house to patrol the streets in the village and the city. Hoping not to arouse civilian curiosity, the saints walked unhurried through the village market-place and the Holy City, stopping occasionally to speak with their brothers before moving on. Sainted training dictated that common angels should be kept unaware of impending danger. Honoring their commanding officer's instruction, saints from each generation greeted civilians with confident smiles and pleasant words. Senior officers from all corners of the globe arrived in God's kingdom to be briefed by Prince Michael on the situation at hand. They were shocked to learn that their eldest brother planned to attack Father's house with weapons unlike any seen in Heaven, until now.

Late that afternoon, Autumn, ripe from training her troops, arrived at the door of her suite to see Kaela walking down the hall toward her. "We have to meet with Prince Michael in his quarters," Lieutenant Archangel Kaela said as he drew nearer to where she stood. He never stopped walking. He simply motioned for her to follow him. Clicking her tongue, she lingered at the door for a moment. She had hoped she would have time for a shower before dinner. She spread her wings slightly. Her angelic ambrosial scent had begun to smell like rotted vegetation. Against her better judgment, Autumn followed Kaela to

Prince Michael's suite, where they were invited to take a seat at his table.

While her angel discussed his battle-shield plans aimed at thwarting Lucifer's attempt to seize Father's throne, Autumn excused herself from the conversation. Without a sound, she left Prince Michael's suite, and when she returned, she was freshly bathed and comfortably clothed in her favorite robe, cloak, and sandals.

Sitting at the prince's table, Autumn noted the appearance of the suite. It was bright, almost cheerfully so. In the corner of the living room sat a broad desk, its top cluttered with maps that were held in place by swords and daggers. The living room walls were covered with maps lined with streaks of ink, designating routes that should be taken when saints scouted the forbidden zone. The back wall of Prince Michael's living room was an arsenal. Weapons of all sorts hung from pegs so that they were easily assessable. And the windows of the suite were barred so that no intruder could enter the prince's private lair. Autumn watched as Prince Michael left his conversation with Kaela to greet his sisters, the scribe, Archangel Effiel, and his student, Elbreon. Soon after their arrival, Chynella's kitchen cherubs entered the suite carrying trays filled with plates of food and pitchers filled with sweet nectar.

After dinner, Prince Michael spoke casually about the day's events, expressing his hope that his commanding officers and their troops would be prepared to defend God's kingdom at a moment's notice.

"Father requested that I leave Lieutenant Archangel Kaela in the Sacred Region. It seems that He has a project that needs our brother's expertise. But, I have news of Lieutenant Gabriel's mission in the North." Prince Michael briefed his guests on the measures Gabriel's troops were taking to stop Azazel from building more weapons. "Several cannons, swords, daggers, and crossbows were found in the northern region. According to my sources, those weapons will be transported to God's kingdom where they will be stored in His armory. I cannot reveal the extra precautions that we plan to take in the future to make our region a safe haven for the Heaven's future King."

"Tell us your plan, saint!" Tumult's voice thundered from outside the barred dining room window, and at the same time, the apartment door was kicked open. Burly northern warriors knocked over furniture in their rush to enter the prince's suite. The Goddesses' screams were subdued by growled threats of uncreation. God's daughters huddled together, silenced by fear. Archangel Effiel, who witnessed the results of atrocities suffered by slaves in the North, put himself between Excelsa and the dark-clad warriors. Elbreon left his chair to shield the Goddesses. Autumn remained seated; unarmed, she saw no reason to call attention to herself. Prince Michael and Lieutenant Archangel Kaela demanded to know the reason for the intrusion.

"Quiet!" Lucifer shouted. The clamor of war roared through the Holy Castle's passageways as saints fought to drive evil from God's house. "I heard that God will appoint an heir to His throne? What is He waiting for?"

"The dawn of the new millennium," Autumn replied, shocked that she spoke.

"Thank you for that, Autumn. Now shut up," Lucifer snarled. His eyes moved from one weary face to the next. "Look at what God has defending His region - an army of buffoons who long for peace and harmony to reign in Heaven." He spit on Prince Michael's boot. "Your so-called God needs someone mighty to rule His world, someone who is not afraid to offend others. He needs someone who can force disobedient sons into submission, if need be."

Though Lucifer's verbal assault had just begun, Kaela could not remain silent another moment. "Do you really think that Prince Michael's saints would allow a fool like you to rule Heaven from Father's throne? Think again, Lucifer. Go back to the North. Tell your supporters and that witch who clawed her way out of your empty skull that their days in Heaven are numbered." The defiant saint, object of God's admiration, drew nearer to his hateful brother. Lucifer stepped back; his armed guards lifted their swords. The northern warriors were prepared to strike Kaela down should he take one more step toward their beloved general.

"Lieutenant Archangel Kaela—is that what the saints call you? You were my sergeant at arms," Lucifer told his former brother. "You chose your meals from my slave pits. How does it feel to sit at a table with civilized brothers who eat fruit and vegetables? Do you hunger for raw flesh? Do you thirst for warm blood? Or was the belief that you were a flesh-eater based on myth?" Lucifer rocked on his toes. "You never fail to amuse me, saint. And now, I see that you envy my accomplishments in the North. That delights me. Look at how far I've come. I was God's first created angel, overseer of my created brothers, first archangel, founder and first director of God's High Council of Angels, first prince, first supervisor of a region in Heaven, first emperor, first commander, first disciplinarian, first war-lord with the first weapons of doom. All those firsts, and you, what are you? You were a carpenter in the Sacred Region, a carpenter in the North, a failure in the northern military, a failure in God's sainted army. What else? Oh, does being 'nothing' count?"

"Give me a sword," Kaela hissed, "and I will show you what I can do with it. Then you will go down in history as being the first braggart, the first liar, the first assassin, the first cheat, the first non-believer, the first warlord to be uncreated by nothing. What a horrible legacy to leave behind. And I will be the honored saint who uncreated an evil, demented creature who tormented its brothers because it lost all its high titles. So what does that make you? Oh, it makes you nothing, Nothing who almost—do you know what the word *almost* means? *Almost* means it didn't happen, it wasn't said, it wasn't accomplished, it didn't get finished—the first nothing who *almost* seized God's throne. It is like saying you never existed, so I will be the honored saint who uncreated a creature whose existence in Heaven did not matter."

Lucifer plunged forward, driving his sword deep into the lieutenant archangel's abdomen. His weapon's blade penetrated the saint's belly, slicing through tissue, muscle, and innards, exiting his back. Burning with anger, Kaela grasped the hilt of the offending blade, closing his bloody hands over Lucifer's hands, and with a steady forward push he forced the blade in backward motion, through the wound, until it exited his body. The two enemies glared fiercely at each other for a brief moment before Kaela quickly over-powered Lucifer, wrenching the sword from his grip.

The angry lieutenant archangel raised the bloody sword over his head, shouting, "Father, permit me to uncreate Your first son." As quickly as he shouted those words, he lowered the sword. "Father, Your will, not mine, shall be done in Heaven."

After speaking those words, Archangel Kaela, second lieutenant of God's sainted army, pressed the sword into the soft flesh under Lucifer's chin. Thick red blood drained from the false emperor's wound. "Father wants someone more powerful than His saints to deal with you. Therefore, you have been spared for the moment, but know this: the nothingness of uncreation awaits you."

"Father loves me more than He will ever love you, Kaela," Lucifer sneered, wincing when the tip of the sword's blade pressed even further into the flesh under his chin.

"Father loves me enough," Kaela growled. "Our Lord's worry is not how much He loves His righteous sons but how much His righteous sons hate you and your witch." He moved Lucifer's face closer using the tip of the sword, which remained in his flesh as his lever. "Your worry is, am I reconsidering my promise to Father to let you live, or will I commit the crime of disobedience to rid Heaven of your presence?" Kaela fixed his eyes on Lucifer's to let him know that he meant what he said. "Order your warriors to leave this room peacefully, or I will have your head on my bed-post tonight, and your flesh will leave my body as waste."

Lieutenant Archangel Kaela had Lucifer right where the saints wanted him, so why was no one making a move to take Lucifer into custody? Had Father ordered them to stand down? Kaela removed the tip of his blade from under his eldest brother's chin. Dragging the edge of the blade upward, through Lucifer's flesh from his chin to his bottom lip, Kaela caused a deep trench to open in his skin. Blood poured freely from the evil emperor's wound, soaking his neck and chest and disappearing against the lapels of his black shirt. "Take your pack of so-called warriors back to your self-proclaimed empire, and forget your plan to seize my Lord's throne."

Lucifer's warriors surrounded him as they backed out of the room and into the hallway. In the court-yard, citizens chased after the warriors until they were well into the air. Kaela ripped open his vest and tunic to check his abdomen. It was healed. He reached for his chalice of nectar - all that remained of the meal he had enjoyed earlier. He downed the warm liquid in one gulp. "If I were you, Prince Michael," Kaela suggested, "I would assign someone to bring the archangels who live in the village and the city to the Holy Castle, where they can be sequestered in the median rooms. I would assign a battalion of troops to guard the outdoor throne room throughout the day to protect our council members, our sisters, Nature, and Father while they are conducting business there. And I would put guards inside the inner sanctum, at every window, and at every door."

Prince Michael's guests were escorted from the room by armed saints. "I need to talk with you, Kaela," the prince said when he saw his lieutenant archangel lift his weapons' belt from the wall peg.

Kaela turned to Autumn. "Go with our sisters to Father's inner sanctum. I will come for you."

"Sit," Prince Michael told him. He poured a goblet of nectar for himself and his fearless brother. Lieutenant Archangel Kaela accepted the goblet, setting it on the table before him. "Did you know that a cavern runs under this house?"

"Autumn told me that he and Sin hid in a cavern under the Holy Mount," Kaela told Prince Michael, referring to Autumn as a male angel who followed the witch on the night of her release into Heaven.

"Well, there is a cavern that opens right under this house," the prince said. "It was accessible from the side of the mountain that leads down the western slope to the village, but no longer. Nature filled it in with dirt and rocks when she learned Sin used it as a hiding place when she toured our region hoping to infect us with her venom."

"Nature knows that evil dwells in darkness, and what better place for evil to hide than in a cave that resides in the deepest recesses of Father's house." Kaela almost hissed.

"Father is not in favor of what the High Council proposed," Prince Michael said. He reached into his bag that set unnoticed under the dining room's long table, until now. "I am not an engineer. My drawings are crude at best, but with the help of skilled others, we hope to erect a dungeon under this house that will be entered by stairs leading into it from the outside of this mansion." He handed his sketches to Kaela. "Preferably the stairs and the doorway to the dungeon will be located on the side facing the backyard and sporting arena. Cells to hold prisoners would have to be erected on the inside." He sat peering across the table, his brows high on his forehead, and his hand resting on his goblet's stem. "Are you willing to accept the task?"

"When does it have to be completed?" Kaela asked. "I mean, you certainly waited long enough—"

"Do you accept the task?" Prince Michael asked.

"I don't see how I can avoid accepting this task, as you call it." Kaela snorted. He had other plans. He and Joniel had drawn up blueprints for a prison that would be shaped like a sphere. If Father approved their plan, a two-story spherical prison would sit on the same side of castle where the dungeon's stairway would be built. The sphere would have one dark chamber and a lighted one. It would hold just two prisoners, Lucifer and Sin. Only Autumn and Joniel knew of his plan to erect a prison that would be unlike any prison Heaven or Sheol would ever know. "When do you need me to start on the dungeon?"

"When do you want to start on it?" Michael asked.

"Tomorrow," Kaela replied. "Joniel and I will commission the aid of our heroic brothers who were enslaved in the North. They will lend their skills to our project. After we remove the rock and soil Nature spilled at the cavern's entrance, we will draw up our blueprints and begin our work."

That night, as they prepared for bed, Kaela told Autumn of Michael's plan for a dungeon. Before falling asleep, he added, "I don't want you coming near the dungeon. Train your troops, exercise Paint." He was still talking when he fell asleep.

Autumn sat on the side of her bed. What a day this had been! Throughout the afternoon and evening, good citizens visited Father's throne rooms. They were loud and angry over Lucifer's behavior. Merchants, craftsmen, weavers, and teachers were suddenly prepared to battle hostile forces to keep their region safe. Autumn yawned. Stretching out on her bed, she smiled knowing that at this very moment, Origen and his weavers were patrolling the streets with Prince Michael's saints. It was good to see everyone in Heaven stepping up to the responsibility of putting an end to what they let happen. Autumn turned on her side, kicked the blankets off her feet and firmed up her pillow by positioning her left arm under it. She closed her eyes and whispered, “Good night, Father. I love You.” Asleep at last, her dreams were filled with visions of riding Paint through flowering fields alive with song-birds and butterflies.

Chapter 44

The Dungeon

The transformation of the cavern under Father's house began the next morning. Kaela had hoped to be among the troops that infiltrated Lucifer's region to confiscate his weapons of war and destruction, but time was of the essence, and he was needed here. Joniel worked faultlessly on the blue-prints that covered the section of the cavern he had been assigned to convert. Brothers Kaela had rescued from the pits and pens in the North lent their skills to the project, thus completing the dungeon in record time. While they worked, they were swiftly reminded that unlike in the North where the work is tedious, time-consuming, and physically draining, work done in the Sacred Region was as easy as gathering a bouquet of flowers.

Within the week, God's saints returned from the North, bringing with them weapons of all persuasions. Just as they had done when they returned home with the treasures they gathered from Heaven's exploration, they tagged the crossbows, long bows, small hand-held cannons, and large cannons before storing them in God's Armory. In awe, saints and citizens alike watched as the building rose up from under Heaven's fertile soil and remained stable while the saints set the small weapons on shelves and dragged the bigger weapons inside, setting them in rows according to their size. When the building returned to the space it occupied underground, it was as though nothing happened at all—the grass, the trees, and the budding flowers were left undisturbed. Now it was time for a tour of the newly finished dungeon under Father's house.

Kaela led a group of saints down the stairs to a door that he unlocked with a large key. "We will keep this door locked at all times to ensure the prisoners will not break free from the keep."

He stepped inside to descend yet another set of stairs that led down to a dirt floor. "I am wearing the key to the keep's outer door around my neck. Each guard who opens the keep's door will be required to do the same." He stepped into a small nook. Pointing to a cabinet located on the wall above a single chair, Kaela said, "This cabinet holds the key that opens all the cell doors." Using the key he wore around his neck, he opened the cabinet. "The cells doors must be unlocked individually, meaning that when this key is used to unlock one cell, the other cell doors remain locked."

Joniel added, "The keep will be heavily guarded. There will be approximately two guards assigned to each cell. And the keys Lieutenant Archangel Kaela showed you will be passed from guard to guard at the end of each shift."

Kaela led the tour group over a dirt path that lay between each row of cells. "As you can see, the paths between the cells are wide. This is so that the prisoners cannot reach through the bars, grab a guard, and hold him hostage. That happened a lot in the North. Of course, Lucifer ordered both the guard and the prisoners uncreated, but that didn't solve the problem—it only added to it." He used the key he took from the cabinet to open a cell. "The cells have no solid walls. We believe it is better to have bars between each cell than to have solid walls."

"I think our prisoners would probably appreciate some privacy," Octaviel suggested.

"Why would prisoners need privacy?" Lieutenant Archangel Kaela asked. "Prison is a lesson in humility, not a second home." He extended his hand toward the rows of cells. "Walls would obstruct the guards' view of the prisoners. This way, one look assures that the prisoners on each cell block are behaving and no measure must be taken to correct them."

"The prisoners are locked inside the cells, so why must the guards see everything the prisoners do?" Zaapiel asked.

"Just taking precautions," Kaela sighed. "If there were walls between the cells, prisoners could hide weapons like sticks or rocks in their quarters. Barred cells eliminate surprises." He studied the faces of the soldiers packed in the aisles that separated one cell block from the other. "Follow me to the back of the keep, and I will show you a few cells that have walls."

He led the group to an area where the cells had brick walls on all sides, including the front of the cell. A small door allowed the prisoner to enter or exit when it was opened by a guard. "This is where our prisoners will go for a time-out. Meaning, when a prisoner cannot be controlled, he will be placed in one of these cells. More will be constructed if necessary. Four guards will oversee each prisoner—not only to ensure that he remains quiet and obeys orders, but to see to his needs should he become ill. We are not imprisoning our brothers to uncreate them. We simply want to hold them until Father decides what we should do with them. Are there any questions?"

Percible stepped forward. "Lieutenant Archangel Kaela, you and your crew are to be commended for the thoughtfulness you put into the construction of this dungeon. I am sure God's saints will agree with me when I say that I can hardly wait to see our eldest brother, his atrocious daughter, and his followers sitting on the metal bunks in each of these cells." He turned slightly toward the troops gathered behind him and set his hands together, cuing them to applaud the work done by Lieutenant Archangel Kaela and his crew.

They were leaving the keep when Prince Michael and his lieutenants arrived for their tour. Percible leaned toward the prince. "These brothers should be rewarded for their work."

"The dungeon is that impressive?" Prince Michael asked. Seeing Percible's nod, he said, "I will speak with Father about commendations for everyone who took part in its construction when I meet with Him in His inner sanctum."

Chapter 45

Northern Aggression

Lieutenant Archangel Kaela stood in the dungeon alone. The cells were empty, their doors stood open, the key that locked all of them was confined to the cabinet that hung on the wall above an unoccupied guard's chair. He walked through the aisles, inspecting each cell as though it would soon hold a member of Lucifer's high council.

"This is wrong," he whispered to himself. He examined the cell designed to hold Sin. The walls were hewn out of stone that had been flattened and polished, not to protect the witch, but to protect the guards she might attack. True, uncreation did not exist in the Sacred Region, but did that rule apply only to those who lived outside this dark, dreary dungeon? Or did it include those who would be locked inside the keep with its prisoners? If the guards were not protected from uncreation, then the prisoners were subject to uncreation too.

Kaela fingered the key he wore around his neck. This key might be the object of open war in Heaven. Unlike the prisoners, the guards would spend hours, not days, here. He tried to imagine what would happen if scores of rebellious northern civilians met their end in the keep. Lucifer and his dark-clothed warriors would seek revenge by wreaking havoc on unsuspecting brothers living in the Sacred Region. And how violently would Sin react to losing her supporters?

"This is wrong," the lieutenant archangel whispered. As quickly as those words fell from his lips, he was up the stairs and outside, locking the dungeon's door. "I have to talk to Father."

"My Lord," Kaela said as entered God's inner sanctum. He was at the throne, shading his eyes with the tips of his wings, and on his knees before the sanctum's doors closed. "My Lord, You created Your sons wise so that we can easily recognize problems before they arise. I am here because I worry that the dungeon may be harmful to our prisoners if they are housed there too long." He moistened his dry lips with his tongue. "Angels love light. Darkness fogs our minds and saps our strength. Whether we are good or evil, we need Your light to function properly. And correct me if I am wrong, but I was always under the impression that we cannot exist in continued darkness."

"My son," the Holy Father said with loving a smile, "though you do not grow physically tired, you need rest so that your dreams can provide answers to your problems. Go to your suite. Get some rest. We will talk more on this subject at a later date."

Kaela rose to his feet. He was almost to the door when he turned to face the throne. This time, he walked forward with his hands shading his eyes. "Give me your permission to build a spherical prison in Your front yard. It will be designed to house just two prisoners in separate cells. The sphere's upper compartment will be drenched in Your pure light, save for the darkness offered it by a single metal panel that will move under the compartment's circular glass roof. The lower compartment will be black as pitch, save for the light offered it by a window that moves along the circular circumference of the sphere."

"And where will you get glass strong enough to keep the prisoners held there from escaping?" God asked, though He already knew the answer.

"I will employ the service of Your faithful council member Anael," Kaela told Father. "He is due to use his skills for more than baubles for our civilians to wear around their necks."

"And for whom is the sphere being built?" Father asked.

Kaela lowered his head for a moment. Then he straightened. "The sphere will house Lucifer and Sin. Lucifer will be in the bottom compartment where he will be nourished so long as he walks in the light the window offers. Sin will be in the top compartment. She will live so long as she walks in the darkness the metal panel offers. The center of the sphere will hold two rooms where the prisoners may freshen up or relieve themselves as needed. Each room will give the prisoners an allotted amount of time before the top room fills with light and the lower room fills with darkness. The sphere will be soundproof so that no voices can penetrate it, and there will be no windows to ensure the prisoners have all the privacy they need to concentrate on staying alive."

"Why would you seek to confine my two most rebellious children to a prison where their only entertainment would be staying alive?" Father asked.

"First, I worry that it may be impossible to keep Lucifer's followers locked up without some of them succumbing to uncreation. That being the case, we may have to find another way to control the prisoners," Lieutenant Archangel Kaela replied. "Second, if Lucifer or Sin perishes in our keep, they will become heroes to their supporters, and we don't need that."

"Lieutenant Archangel Kaela, you have my permission to build the sphere in my yard, but I ask that you make it an object of beauty so that my righteous sons find it attractive," Father said with a nod of His head.

The following morning, a crowd of onlookers gathered in Father's back-yard to watch the construction of a strange new structure. Kaela and Joniel headed the project. Autumn acted as their steward. They were assisted by a great number of carpenters, metallurgists, and masons who had been held hostage in the North and on Sheol. Throughout the day, refreshments were served. In the evening, tables were set up in the yard that the cherubs kept filled with trays of food. When Father left His outdoor throne to retire to His inner sanctum, the work site took on a festive atmosphere as Israfel's choir assembled on the lawn to sing Father's praises, accompanied by Zephon's orchestra.

The workers completed the sphere within a week after its construction began. It was built to Kaela's specifications. The interior of the sphere was framed in wood, and its surface was covered with a metal alloy that assured Lucifer's followers could not rescue him and made it impossible for Sin to escape. The walls were built solid so that the prisoners could not see out, and no one outside could see in. Anael provided the thick, unbreakable glass that was used in the upper compartment's ceiling and floor. To keep Lucifer and Sin from communicating with each other or overhearing conversations carried on by their guards, the sphere was sound-proof. Father contributed to the building of the sphere by lending His light to the compartment that housed Sin and sending His rays through the window that nourished Lucifer.

On the day the sphere opened for inspection, God's Council of Angels were the first to tour the prison built to house the North's rebellious leaders. They marveled at the beautiful designs and decorative swirls that enhanced the sphere's exterior before entering the ground-floor compartment. Standing in pitch-black darkness, Scribe Excelsa asked Joniel to activate its window. "Look, brothers! Here comes the window that offers its beam of light. Let us follow it on its journey through this hallway." With the scribe leading the way, the council members chased the ray of light through the circular hallway of the sphere until they spied a figure standing by what they assumed was the door.

"Who is that?" Scribe Excelsa asked his breathing labored from running.

"It is I, Lieutenant Archangel Kaela," a voice replied. "The sphere is designed to keep our prisoners moving. We don't want them to start feeling at home in their cells."

"Why does my body feel so heavy?" Excelsa asked.

"It is called gravity," the lieutenant archangel told the council members. "Gravity was Father's idea. Shall we continue our tour?"

A study of the upper compartment revealed the light that filtered through a thrice-thick glass roof was one hundred times brighter than the light outside the sphere. When the council members complained that they were blinded by the light's brilliance, Kaela told them, "The magnification of the light in this cell was Father's idea. It is a simple way to control Lucifer's witch."

That evening, his work done, Kaela sat in the dining room with Autumn, Joniel, and their crew of engineers. They were enjoying their meal and one another's company when Prince Michael approached their table. The prince's brows were knitted. And he wore a scowl on his face.

"Well, this can't be good," Kaela told his crew, nodding his head in Michael's direction. "Excuse me. I may need some time alone with my commanding officer."

He lifted his plate and chalice from the table he shared with Autumn and motioned Michael to the table that stood close by. Before they were seated, Kaela said, "Something is bothering you."

"Father wants to speak with you," Prince Michael told him.

Standing before God's throne, Kaela listened to what he was told.

"My son," our Lord said softly, "the dungeon will be off-limits to your civilian brothers. We must avoid a hostage crisis. No one but those who acquire a certificate of authorization signed by Prince Michael can enter the dungeon or the sphere. The prisoners' counselors and legal advisors will be accompanied by two of my counselors and no less than four sainted guards. Visitors to the prisons will leave when their allotted time runs out. And saints as well as northern warriors will surrender their weapons to the guards at the door with the understanding that their weapons will be returned to them when they leave the sphere.

"Now, the reason you are here," Father continued. "I ask that both my errant children be locked in the keep for a while. I will remove Sin's ability to change from solid to vapor so that she cannot escape. There is much to be done, and unlike Prince Michael, I fear the raid that led to the confiscation of northern weapons has simply raised Lucifer's ire toward his sainted brothers. As we speak, my eldest son is planning an assault that he hopes will result in dire consequences for my beloved council members." Father studied the son He confided in. "Go. Tell Autumn what I told you concerning Lucifer. Then begin making your plans to safeguard my kingdom against northern aggression. Our enemies will be upon us sooner than we may know."

In the dining hall, Kaela spoke with Autumn, Joniel, and the brothers who helped him accomplish his sainted tasks at the Holy Castle.

"Our work as carpenters is short-lived," he said with a heavy sigh. He had enjoyed working with his hands to create what was needed in Heaven, but now, Father required his skills as a soldier. "In the morning, we will meet as saints to plan ways to protect our righteous brothers and our royal family from attack. For now, however, I intend to spend this evening with Autumn and all of you who assisted in the excavation of the dungeon and designing the sphere." He glanced from one beloved face to another. "Who among you would like to walk with me for a while?" Several brothers stood at their tables, even those brothers he was not speaking to. Kaela turned see to Michael smiling at him. "It seems I will be busy this evening."

The following morning, as Lieutenant Archangel Kaela prepared to address his troops on the specialized training they would receive in the forest beyond Father's house, he was called to meet with Prince Michael in his third-floor suite. Thinking the meeting was private and that he would receive orders especially drawn up for his troops, he left the courtyard without explanation. When he entered the prince's apartment, there was standing room only. The suite's front rooms were filled to capacity with sainted officers who listened intently to what Lieutenant Gabriel had to say.

The lieutenant pointed the tip of his sword to one of the many maps that decorated the long wall of Prince Michael's apartment. "We suspect that the lumber-yard, Father's outdoor throne room, and the courtyard behind and around the castle are crucial points of interest to our eldest brother and his crew of rebels." He glanced from the maps at the faces before him. "I suggested, and Prince Michael agreed, that we would be wise to put our best-armed guards in place here." Gabriel set the tip of his sword against a large blue-print of the outdoor throne room, pointing out several strategic points where guards would be positioned. "To protect Father, our sisters, our council members, Scribe Excelsa, Archangel Effiel, his student Elbreon, and Heaven's empty throne."

"Where is Lieutenant Archangel Kaela?" Cerviel, a commander from Heaven's southern region asked. "We need his input on this since his troops are trained in what Autumn calls special ops."

"I am here," Kaela called from the back of the room.

"Well, you should be up front," Commander Cerviel grumbled. "Make way for Lieutenant Archangel Kaela."

The soldiers divided so the Kaela could easily make his way to where Gabriel stood. "I have no idea what you want from me, Commander Cerviel. I usually take my orders from Prince Michael or do Father's bidding."

"Just listen to what your brother is saying, and then you can give us your input," the commander told him.

Lieutenant Gabriel resumed his briefing. "It is believed that Lucifer will arrive in the outdoor throne room while Father is creating Heaven's day. Likewise, it is feared that in a show of arrogance, he will launch an assault on Nature in an attempt to seize her throne." Some of the generals, commanders, and other high officers questioned aloud why Lucifer would attack a gentle entity like Nature.

Kaela, being created of the first flock and who had visited the throne room on several occasions, gained permission to speak. "The throne of which Lieutenant Gabriel spoke is the throne that is positioned to the left of Father's high seat. Our sisters refer to it as the throne of love. Lucifer craved that throne, not because Nature held it, but so that he could prove to us that Father loved him best. Most of our brothers who never visited Father's outdoor throne room think that when Lucifer lost his crown due to his disobedience to God's laws, the throne was destroyed so that no one else could occupy it.

"The truth is the throne always belonged to Nature as her reward for the duties she performed when Heaven was being created. She is the one who built the Holy Mount. When she finished building this mountain, Nature built a castle on its highest peak. She designed the outdoor throne room especially for Father so that He could illuminate Heaven with His brilliant glow. Our Lord encouraged Nature to build a second throne, one nearest to His heart. When her task was finished, Father asked her to occupy His throne of love. Lucifer claimed that throne for a short season. But when he betrayed our King by amassing supporters and encouraged them to commit atrocities against our brothers, he lost his titles and his throne in Heaven.

"The thrones in Father's inner sanctum were set up in a similar pattern. But recently, a third throne has been erected in both locations of the castle. No one knows who the third throne is for, but it is positioned closest to our Lord's powerful right hand, and if I may venture a guess, I would say it is reserved for the One who will become Heaven's future King."

Not a word was spoken by anyone for the longest time. Perhaps during this moment of silence, all minds turned to when Lucifer lived in the Sacred Region, right here, in God's house. Maybe Kaela's explanation brought to mind the times they heard Lucifer speak out in haughty tones about how Father's powers were failing. It could have been that they suddenly realized they should have done something then to curve their brother's hateful desire to rule Heaven from God's coveted throne. And when they saw how Lucifer behaved the night Father set a princely crown on Michael's head, well, maybe they should have left their seats, chased after Lucifer, dragged him to the inner sanctum, and demanded that God punish him for his transgressions. They knew at the time that Lucifer was deceitful, even vengeful, but they did nothing to stop their eldest brother's attempts to remove Father from Heaven's creation, His high seat, and possibly, from existence.

"Who sat in the throne of love after Lucifer?" a saint seated in the back of the room asked.

"Nature," Kaela responded. "Nature is the rightful owner of the throne that sits closest to our Lord's heart." He pointed to a saint who sat with his hand raised.

"Did anyone ever claim the throne that sits closest to our Lord's power?" the saint asked.

Prince Michael stepped forward. "For a short season, when I served as director of God's High Council, I sat in a chair that was located closest to Father's power," he told his sainted brothers. "When the northern uprising sprang out of control, I gained our Lord's permission to do what I am best suited for, and that is to train my soldiers to protect our civilian brothers against northern atrocities. After I left the throne room, a third throne was added. It remains unoccupied to this day."

"Lucifer is fully aware that three thrones are erected on this building's spacious roof," Kaela told his brothers. "He craves Father's high seat for himself. He wants the seat to the left of God's throne for Sin. The one to right, he has reserved for Belial."

Prince Michael took the floor. "A curfew will be set starting this evening. All brothers will be in their homes immediately after their dinner meal here at the castle. They will not be permitted to walk the streets of the city or the village, and Father's courtyard is off-limits to them when the dining room, café, cafeteria, and the castle's shops close for the evening. If we find one civilian breaking curfew, he will be stored in one of the dungeon's many cells until I see fit to release him."

"Why are we punishing our citizens?" Lieutenant Archangel Kaela asked, barely able to contain his anger.

"To keep them safe," was the prince's response. "Are there any other questions?" Hearing none, Prince Michael closed the meeting. After the last saint left, Lieutenant Archangel Kaela remained.

"Kaela," Michael said, setting his weapons' belt on his desktop, "you know Lucifer's plan. If he is victorious against our Lord, three sources of evil will sit on Heaven's thrones. Presently, our archangels who have no military training have been removed from their homes in the city and the village. They are here, in the castle's median rooms on the second floor. Our intention is to keep them safe. But our sisters, Scribe Excelsa, Archangel Effiel, Elbreon, and our high council members must sit with Father night and day."

"I will station my troops at strategic points to ensure their safety," Kaela said as he lowered himself into the chair that sat before the desk.

"No." Prince Michael stated, "I have a plan."

While business went on as usual in the shops, cafeteria, dining hall, and cafés that lined the Holy Castle's lobby, God's civilian sons noticed that sainted presence had increased. Autumn led her troop of cherubs through the foyer and up the castle's staircase. Lieutenant Archangel Kaela arrived with thirteen of his most skilled saints. They, too, mounted the stairs. And even more curious to the castle's visitors was the appearance of God's high council members, the Goddesses, Scribe Excelsa, Archangel Effiel, and his student Elbreon, all of whom reported mid-morning to Father's inner sanctum.

Saints, tall and small, assembled in the large conference room on the castle's third floor. There, artists who had joined Prince Michael's service years before discovering their skills prepared to put their talents to good use. Lieutenant Archangel Kaela glanced around the room. Autumn was nowhere in sight. He breathed a sigh of relief. He loudly protested the part of Prince Michael's plan that might have put Autumn in harm's way. He was glad to see that the prince had reconsidered the role his beloved Earth angel would play in the possible capture of Lucifer and Sin.

"Line up," Kaela ordered. "The artists are prepared, and the transformation is about to begin." He could think of a million things he would rather do than this.

Each saint moved from where he stood to the table where an artist waited. Then the magic began. Saints who never visited Father's outdoor throne room and those who saw it only when they flew over the castle during training exercises would now see it up close for the first time. Lieutenant Archangel Kaela smiled as artists slathered the little cherubs' faces, arms, and legs with sparkling white paint.

"Don't forget their chests," he told the artists. "Our sisters' silver robes are cut low." He felt himself blush as a thought sprang to mind. It didn't matter how low the necklines of the Goddesses' gowns were; none of them could fill out a top like Sin could. He cleared his throat. "I'm going to find Autumn."

"You're next," one artistic saint told him. "You are going nowhere."

"Well, I guess, I'm staying here then," he chuckled.

Kaela passed the table, smiling down at the taller well-proportioned cherubs who took on the guise of his virtuous sisters. He took his seat at the table where a talented brother began disguising him as one of God's civilian council members.

"Prince Michael wants you to sit close to the throne, sire," the artist said, making small talk while he worked. "Therefore, your appearance must be perfect." Kaela glanced up at him. "I must make you resemble council member Archangel Uriel, whose seat on the council sits closest to our Lord's high seat." The artist began by clipping Kaela's tousled hair closer to his head. "This will grow back, sire," he assured, brushing the cut hair to the conference room floor. "Hold very still while I apply this sparkling gold paint to your face and—"

"Don't forget his chest," one cherub teased. Kaela turned to see seven painted cherubs standing in a row wearing silver skin-tight gowns, silver slippers, and long, white, flowing hair borrowed from a horse's mane and tail. He burst out laughing when he saw their borrowed hair was adorned with white peacock feathers. "Yeah, well, let's see how good you look painted gold," the cherub teased. "You are already uglier than you usually are."

"Keep that up, and I'll put you on report." Kaela laughed. He sat back and let the artist transform him into Uriel.

When the saints were sufficiently disguised for the part they would play, they paraded into the throne room where they knelt before God before taking their assigned seats. Though Kaela sat closer to Father's throne than his brothers, he was not as close to it as he thought he would be. And the placement of sainted weapons, on the floor at their feet—this was bad. Could they get to their swords in time to save anyone from a hostile attack? He was half-tempted to reach for his sword, grasp it in his hand, and spring up from his seat; but what would that look like to Father? Kaela sighed and sat back. Now a new question arose in his mind: why would Father allow Nature to remain seated on her throne during a threat of danger?

Using his powerful vision, Lieutenant Archangel Kaela studied the beloved entity. His close inspection revealed his worse fear. Autumn, more feminine and more beautiful than he had ever seen her before, occupied the throne closest to God's sacred heart. Suddenly, Kaela knew the council seat he sat in was too far from Father's throne for him to save Autumn, or anyone else, for that matter.

Using his inborn carpentry skills, he did a virtual measurement of the distance that separated him from his beloved Autumn. Could he save her if Lucifer and his warriors attack the castle's outdoor throne room? He was about to order her from the throne room when one of the artists assigned to disguise Prince Michael's saints called to her. Autumn took Father's hand in hers and said something that only He could hear. Kaela watched as she left the throne room. Maybe Michael found a more suitable double to play Nature. No, he had not. In seconds, Autumn returned, taking her seat next to God's throne. Kaela studied her disguise to make sure that her true identity was well hidden.

From where Kaela sat, he saw that Autumn wore a sunny red wig that flowed softly to her waist. She was dressed in all the colors that Nature loved—earth tones, ocean blues, and various shades of greens. He smiled when he saw that Autumn's wig and gown were decorated with colorful leaves and flowers. Yes, she was lovely to see, and he could not stop looking at her. But he wasn't Autumn's only admirer. Father lifted the back of her hand to His lips and kissed it tenderly.

"You are the most beautiful angel in Heaven, my child," the globe's precious King told His darling daughter.

Autumn's eyes glistened with tears. "Thank you, Father. I am honored by Your words." She swallowed hard. "I feel beautiful," she whispered softly. "And I am proud that You chose me to impersonate Your precious Nature."

According to the book written by Archangel Effiel, Nature, fair and beautiful, is beloved by God and sons. God's Word, years after He became flesh, credited Nature for painting, forming, shaping, and perfuming every leaf, every blade of grass, and every flower in Heaven and on every foreign globe He blessed with His gift of life. Nature chose the color of the beasts' coats, the fishes' fins and scales, and the birds' feathers. In Heaven and throughout the universe, she determined the breeding cycle, and she was there when wildlife creatures gave birth to their young. Though Father and His Word breathed life into barren globes, Nature made them beautiful.

Now, during these troubled times in Heaven, when war loomed on the horizon and sainted tensions were high, the days in the outdoor throne room passed without conflict. To safeguard the parameters of the Sacred Region's borders, Prince Michael's set his saints in plain sight of Father's enemies to ward off northern intrusion. On the streets of God's kingdom, saints disguised as civilians frequented the market-places, the shops, and the castle's courtyard.

Each morning before Father took His throne to create Heaven's brilliant day, Lieutenant Archangel Kaela met with his small battalion of troops in the castle's third-floor conference room. There, amid briefings, wise-cracks, and laughter, they strapped their daggers and swords around their waists, slipped into tunics that covered their weapons' belt, draped wide banners worn by the council members around their necks, donned partial robes, and topped their costumes with a soft-blue cowl decorated with golden stars. The change of attire was requested by Kaela, who informed Prince Michael that the long robes and cloaks worn by the council members and the seating, not to mention the positioning of their weapons, put the saints posing as member of the royal family in harm's way.

"Saints," Lieutenant Archangel Kaela called. The soldiers grew quiet. "Before we leave for the outdoor throne room, be aware that this may be our final day of guarding our beloved royal family, their scribe and his assistant, and those who stand close by our Father's throne. I must say that I am honored to have each of you at my side while we perform our duty to keep our family safe." Kaela gave the same speech every morning, fearing he might be struck down before he could tell his soldiers how he felt. "Each of you is truly the best of Prince Michael's saints, and I am humbled by your skills, your performance, and the dignity with which you handle yourselves when you are called to arms." Applause filled the room. "That applause is yours, not mine. Now let us position ourselves in the throne room, where we are needed."

Lieutenant Archangel Kaela led his saints to the foot of God's throne, where they knelt in humble reverence.

"Arise, my faithful sons," Father called, "and take your positions in the throne room."

Autumn was already seated. She took on the demeanor of a queen while she impersonated Father's beloved element.

"I hate that I might be somewhere else tomorrow," she told Father in all honesty. "I love dressing like this. It's like attending a costume ball every day, and I hate that our talks might end so abruptly. I will still pray to You, You know that, but our discussions—"

"Visit my throne when you can, child," Father said with a smile. "You are always welcome." He patted her hand the way loving parents do when they comfort a child whose heart is filled with disappointment. "But please, let us continue the conversation we started yesterday just before Kaela dismissed you and his troops."

Kaela sat with his eyes narrowed as though lost in thought, but it wasn't his thoughts that had his undivided attention; it was his curiosity. Where were those screams of terror and angry shouts coming from? Were they coming from the village or the courtyard below?

"Saints," he called from his seat, "prepare to defend this room, its thrones, and all who occupy this place. The northern attack on God's kingdom has begun." He reached under his tunic and unfastened the clasps that secured his dagger and his sword. Expectantly, he raised his eyes to the sky, searching for signs of rebel intrusion.

While the saints sat ready to do combat with an arsenal of weapons hidden under their costumes, Autumn was unarmed. Now she wished in her secret heart that she had bowed to Kaela's fear that something might happen before Father could intervene. If she had listened to her angel, a sword would be leaning against her throne, right where she could get to it if need be. Autumn glanced around the room. Her cherubs, dressed like Goddesses, were completely without protection. There was no way to fit crossbows and casings of arrows, daggers, and swords under their tight-fitting garments.

Autumn's breathing quickened. Her thundering heart rolled in her chest. Only when she felt Father's hand close over hers did she grow calm. Now, she watched and listened as the sounds of war grew louder.

The battle was in the castle now. Lucifer's warriors had broken through every sainted stronghold and were about to make their presence known to God and His council members. A battery of rebels flew low over the outdoor throne room. The unit, led by Lucifer, tumbled gracefully from the sky to light before the King's coveted throne. The self-proclaimed northern emperor paced before his Creator, his lips curled in a sneer and his eyes narrowed in hatred.

"So you put an element on the throne I once occupied," Lucifer hissed. Autumn sighed. Her disguise was a success. Lucifer drew his sword, butted the tip of its blade against the floor, and leaned lightly on the hilt of his weapon. "How dare You seat a pile of weeds and stinking flowers on the throne of beauty and nobility that is my birthright? I was created to become Heaven's almighty King." He reached out and swiftly tossed Autumn to the floor. "Stay!" he ordered when she attempted to right herself. He set his blade against her cheek. "Father, should I uncreate this creature while I am here?" To Lucifer's amazement, the gentle force rose from the floor and, without so much as a glance at him, defiantly took the throne. "Not to worry. Soon, I will be king, and you will be gone."

"You were not created to be Heaven's King," Father thundered. He leaned forward, glaring at His false son. "Kneel before my throne and ask forgiveness for the atrocities you committed, or leave this region, for your presence in this place upsets all that is pure and sacred."

"The fact that You are worshipped by some has made You vain," Lucifer snarled. "Do You remember when I was Your best-loved pet? I achieved greatness, earned titles based on my beauty, and I had a birthright. When You saw that I amassed a following larger than Yours, You sent me away. You put me in the North to fend for myself, and I became greater than You. To belittle me, to make me feel less than I truly was, You gave my titles to Michael. You placed a crown on his head and made him the leader of Your broken army. My warriors are defeating Your saints as we speak." Lucifer glared at God. "Angels shall not procreate. I performed a miracle. I gave birth to Sin in this room, at the foot of the very throne You occupy. Soon, Heaven will be mine, and You will be banished from this globe forever."

"Heaven will always be mine," Father told His errant son. "I will never concede to evil by leaving my throne. I will not betray the pure love of my faithful sons to appease a malcontent who seeks to instill fear, not respect, into his brethren to obtain his goal of leadership. You are a failure, and you will continue to fail in all you do unless you kneel before me, confess your atrocities, ask the brothers you wronged for their forgiveness, and atone for your crimes by working for Heaven's good. Accept that you will never be Heaven's King since cherubs are created to serve their Master."

"I am not a cherub," Lucifer hissed. He had always hated those fat, ugly little brothers.

Father leaned toward His hateful son. "In rank, you are now equal to a cherub. Continue talking, and you will be far less."

Lucifer grew quiet for a long moment. Then without word or warning, he lifted the tip of his blade from the floor, and in one dreadful move, decapitated Citadel. Before the youngster's head fell to the floor, Kaela threw off his saintly robes, and with his sword drawn, he attacked Lucifer at the foot of God's throne. Lucifer's eyes were wide and wild with realization as the council members rose in like form and attacked the members of his unit.

"It's a trap!" the false emperor screamed as he fought for his life. "Retreat!" But it was too late; the battle was on.

The sound of steel clashing against steel slashed through the mantel of peace. The air around warring soldiers grew warmer as their battle intensified. Using both hands, Kaela forced the blade of his sword down the blade of Lucifer's sword until the cross-guard of his weapon locked with the quillon of Lucifer's weapon. Then with a swift circular motion of his wrist, Kaela sent Lucifer's blade crashing to the floor, out of reach. The emperor recoiled at the sight of his enemy coming at him in full advance, slicing his weapon through the air.

"Uncreate me, Kaela," Lucifer growled his eyes wide and wild with anticipation. "Show Father your true self."

Hearing his eldest brother's words and knowing that he would play into Sin's hands if he fulfilled Lucifer's request for uncreation, Kaela dropped his sword to the floor. Swiftly, unexpectedly, Lucifer leapt from the floor, threw Kaela down on his back, and took a seat on his chest. With his left hand locked around Kaela's throat, the northern emperor pulled a dagger from a band of material that was tied around the calf of his leg. While he attempted to strangle the saint with one hand, he struggled to plunge the dagger into Kaela's heart with the other. Kaela clasped both his hands around the emperor's wrist in a desperate effort to fend off the foul weapon.

"Worthless saint," Lucifer snarled against Kaela's face, "prepare for your uncreation." He lifted the dagger again with the intention of slicing through his brother's heart with its blade. For what seemed an eternity, Kaela fought to keep the dagger's sharp glistening tip from meeting its mark.

"Not today, Lucifer," Kaela gasped. "I will not be uncreated today." Swiftly, he released his grip on Lucifer's wrist. The evil emperor lost his balance, and his dagger plunged onto the throne room's tiled floor. Its jagged blade broke in half. A piece of the blade bounced up, slicing Lucifer's cheek before it dropped onto the tile next to Kaela's ear.

From where Kaela lay, he could see the misty silhouettes of thousands of warring angels. For good or evil, a battle had been waged in Heaven. Fearing that Lucifer might be strengthened by his followers' loyalty, Kaela rolled him over until he had him on his back. Cramming one knee into Lucifer's chest, Kaela slammed the villain's head against the floor until he lost consciousness. Shaken by the ordeal, the saint rose to his feet. Four of his troops rushed to where Lucifer lay, bound him, and received God's command to house him in the dungeon. A trumpet sounded. Word of Lucifer's arrest was announced, and the evil angels retreated to the North.

Kneeling before Father's throne, his knees reddened by the blood of his noble brothers, Kaela asked permission to retire from the outdoor door throne room to a place of privacy and seclusion. "I cannot stay here a moment longer," he told his Creator." After gaining permission to return to his suite of rooms in the Holy Castle, the lieutenant archangel took his leave.

Autumn sat trembling on the throne located closest to Father's loving heart. Her eyes scoured the outdoor throne room's bloody floor. "Why didn't You intervene?"

"I did not make Lucifer a tyrant," Father said softly. "I gave him the titles he craved, but his brothers, through their indifference to my laws, gave him his power over them. Had they taken a stand for what they knew was right, had they resisted Lucifer's lies with a toss of their head and a wave of their hand—as they should have—I could have helped them deter their eldest brother's desire to rule in Heaven. But even the most faithful of my sons chose to accept Lucifer's lies. They accepted that he set himself above them, and they allowed him to do it. They accepted when he told them that I sit in unapproachable light to avoid them. They accepted when he said my powers were failing, and those who did not accept that lie did not try to correct him. They remained silent." Father sighed. "No. I did not bring this on my sons—they brought it on themselves. Therefore, they are responsible to correct this situation and return peace to Heaven."

"You gave us a peaceful world, and now we are getting what we deserve," Autumn said. She turned her head away from the sight of

Citadel's disembodied head being wrapped in a pure-white cloth while his blood continued to drain from the wound in his neck.

"No, child, my sons deserve so much better than this," Father said, His eyes brimming with unshed tears. "They are simply responsible, directly and indirectly, for perverting this globe with evil, and they must correct what they allowed to happen."

"May I be excused, Father?" Autumn asked.

"You may, my precious darling daughter of mankind," Father said.

It was Autumn's turn to run from the outdoor throne, disrobe as she raced down the stairs, and toss her costume into an artist's hands. The saint would have embellished her in praise if she had slowed her pace for just a moment. A sob escaped her throat as tears streamed down her cheeks in rivulets.

"I'm so sorry, Father," she repeated until she stood outside the door of the suite she shared with Kaela. Wiping her hands over her face, she smeared the makeup that had been applied so expertly just a few hours ago. Resting her right hand on the door's latch, she broke it down. Standing in the living room, she called out, "Kaela. Kaela! Oh, please be here."

She hurried to the bedroom where she found Kaela, lying face-up on his bed. He was still covered in golden paint, his bloody sword at his side and his knees still caked with Citadel's blood. Autumn lay down beside him, pressed her face into his side, and sobbed one wracking sob after the other until she fell asleep.

That evening, emotionally drained from the day's events, she and Kaela slept. While needed sleep nourished her body, her mind was tortured with dreams of her troubled past. Under Autumn's closed eyes, she saw Lucifer's face, then Sin's. They were in the cottage. She was bound, beaten, and she was kneeling in the North's cold climate. Mud welled up around her knees, and she struggled to remain upright. The scent of blood made her gag. Her wings were gone.

"Wake up," a distant voice called. Autumn struggled to open her eyes, but she was paralyzed by torturous sleep. The nightmare continued.

Autumn dreamed of Sheol. She saw the lava, smelled the sulfur, felt the globe's unrelenting heat as it burned her skin; and she could smell her hair burning off her head. Sheol's fires rose up in torrents, burning white-hot. Far off in the distance, Autumn heard angry words being shouted, whips cracking, cries of pain, and screams of anguish.

"Wake up," someone whispered. If only Autumn could open her eyes. If only, she could leave this horror behind her and bask in God's light; she would not feel so weak, so sick, so tired.

Across the blackened landscape, fluorescent-red rivers of lava threatened to close her lungs forever. She gasped. A sword appeared from nowhere, its blade leveled at her neck. Screaming Autumn bolted upright in bed, her fearful eyes opened wide.

She cried out Kaela's name, but he was gone. A small slice of parchment lay beside her. "He left me a note," she whispered to no one there.

"Autumn," the note read, "Prince Michael sent Zophiel to our room with a message. While we slept, Sin and several northern leaders were imprisoned. They were captured when they returned to the Father's kingdom to rescue Lucifer from the dungeon. I am with the prince and Lieutenant Gabriel. Freshen up and go back to bed. You need to rest."

Autumn did as the note told her to do. Pulling the sheet to her waist, she closed her eyes.

"This will end soon. We have Lucifer and Sin where we want them," she whispered softly to herself. Relieved that Prince Michael's saints captured the witch and her minions, Autumn fell into a deep healing, dreamless sleep.

Chapter 46

The Sphere

Within hours of Sin's capture, a multitude of evil angels arrived in the Sacred Region. With Belial as their leader, they gathered in the Holy City's town square where cruel speeches were made against God. Armed warriors threatened righteous brothers with uncreation, simply to ensure there would be no retaliation to their trespass. Lucifer's council members gathered on street corners, speaking loudly on his behalf, demanding their false emperor's swift release. Doubtful and disbelieving souls living in God's kingdom added to the chaos by challenging Father to reveal His strength or relinquish His throne to Lucifer. Frightened citizens and merchants moved from their homes and shops to the safety of Father's house. The courtyard filled with angry saints who took an oath to protect and defend all that was righteous. The pounding of their steeds' hooves against the tiled porch floor that led to the auditorium echoed through the castle's wide hallways. In the small conference room on the third floor, Prince Michael and his officers prepared for war.

While the Sacred Region broiled in hatred and while northern warriors threatened Father and His righteous sons, Prince Michael's lieutenants visited every populated region in Heaven. Their mission: to recruit and enlist innumerable brothers to aid them in their fight against evil. Military posts were set up in all regions, except in the North, where the saints were not welcome. Lieutenant Archangel Kaela, proficient in weaponry and martial arts, trained newly enlisted soldiers living in the eastern region of Heaven. He was about to dismiss his troops after a day filled with grueling exercises when Zophiel arrived with a startling message. "The Holy City is burning to the ground. Prince Michael is calling for reinforcements."

When Kaela's troops arrived in town, the fabric shop was engulfed in flames. Skeins of yarn and various materials, as well as tools the weavers used to make garments and wall hangings, littered the sidewalk. Origen knelt in the center of the street, his face buried in his hands. His life's work was gone. His apprentices gathered round him, helping him to his feet. Disheartened weavers, burdened at the thought of having to start over, watched as flames shot through the shop's roof, leaping into the air.

Down the street, billowing clouds of smoke lifted upward, casting a dark hue over a sky illuminated by God's pure light. Zephon's warehouse was burning out of control. The wealth of musical instruments he stored there could not be saved. The musician paced the sidewalk across the street, his weary eyes fixed on the burning building. Two blocks away, Atonal and Bernella fought the rising flames that ravaged their storage loft; ancient poems and compositions that were revered as classics by God and His angels were destroyed in a matter of minutes. Throughout the day, the Holy City was fraught with flames. When one fire was extinguished, a new one sprang to life.

While the saints rallied to save God's town, Asmadai and Adramelech, former co-rulers of one-seventh of the southernmost quadrant of the northern region, baffled the crowds with their fraudulent speeches. Adramelech publicly accused Prince Michael's saints of being prejudice toward Lucifer's followers. "We are called rebels, our emperor is accused of being a criminal, Sin is referred to as a witch, and they call the North a forbidden zone. Our governing techniques are called atrocities, and because we do not worship the God of this region, we are called non-believers, doubters, and idolaters. Where is the North's freedom of choice? Where is our right to self-expression? I appeal to Mercy to free our lord, the great Lucifer, from his prison."

Asmadai spoke next. "Soon, an heir will follow in God's shaky footsteps. Heaven will have two weak leaders. If God is so powerful, why does the Sacred Region play host to its enemies? The present lack of leadership only confirms my belief that your future King will be as cowardly as His Father. Will you follow a leader who backs down from His enemies, trembling at the sight of them? Or will you rise up against your King to follow Lucifer? Look around! God has allowed an opposing force to enter His land. Be thankful to Lucifer that we did not come to take hostages, for if we did, this land would be ours. Join our cause. Take up arms against Heaven's fading King. Free yourselves from His shameful reign."

Beelzebub spoke to the crowd. "On my way to this place, I observed Mercy as she left God's castle. She planned to tell the masses that her Father's prejudice against Lucifer is justified. Yet your Lord claims His sons are created equal. In opposition to His own claim, God gave your brother Lucifer meaningless titles while He bestowed active titles upon His chosen prince." Beelzebub stopped addressing the crowd to shout orders to the warriors gathered behind him. "Stand the Goddess Mercy before her brothers. We will force her to confess God's crimes against Lucifer to everyone who lives in this region."

The crowd gasped in horror when Flagitious dragged Mercy from the place where she was held captive to where Beelzebub stood. "Tell them!" he shouted in the weeping Goddess's ear. "Tell them how God demeans Lucifer's powers to you, your sisters, and Prince Michael's cowardly army."

Wracked by heart-wrenching sobs, Mercy struggled to free herself while northern supporters took the bandstand to tell lies about God and Prince Michael. "Do not believe these brothers!" she shouted. "They are evil. They are doomed to perish in a prison called Hell."

That night, during a lull in the battle, Uzziel met with Kaela in the castle's main foyer to discuss the events of the day. "Did you hear about Autumn's heroic actions?" Kaela indicated that he had not. "We were searching for Raphael. He and his healers were caring for citizens who fell victim to northern aggressors. Autumn and I were joined in our search by Prescience and Stephon. As we passed over the town square, we received news that Mercy was being tortured—"

"Mercy was being tortured?" Kaela asked. He was astonished at what he heard.

"Yes, Goddess Mercy, our sweet sister, was being tortured by Beelzebub," Archangel Uzziel replied. "When we reached the gazebo in the town square, Mercy was screaming in terror. She was urging our brothers to ignore what Beelzebub told them about Father, calling Beelzebub a liar and a fraud. Before our eyes, Beelzebub hit our sister. He hit Mercy like you or I would hit an attacker to fend him off. Before I could react to what I saw, Autumn bolted like lightning from the sky toward the gazebo, slammed into Beelzebub, knocking him off his feet, thus freeing Mercy from his grasp.

"Flagitious grasped Mercy by the arm. Autumn flew into his face, feet first. I never saw anything like it. The blow knocked the northern counselor out of the gazebo, onto the ground. Seeing his chance to save Mercy, Autumn caught our precious sister around her waist, and with a downward drag of his mighty wings, he lifted Mercy high above her hateful enemies. Autumn brought our sister here, to the castle, where he delivered her to Father's protective arms before reporting for duty." Uzziel smiled. "I think a commendation is due."

"Why would pure hearts stand idly by while a traitor demeans our Lord and abuses our sister?" Lost in thought, he did not speak for a moment. "Was Raphael found?" Kaela asked.

"Yes, Archangel Uriel found Raphael in the village." Uzziel sighed. "He was healing fallen brothers when a group of Lucifer's dark-clad warriors arrived. The rebels were carrying a severely injured brother that they wanted healed. After Raphael restored the northern warrior's health, he and his comrades became threatening. They left when Archangel Uriel descended to the ground a few feet from where they stood." Uzziel turned to Kaela. "Where were you that you didn't know about any of this?"

Lieutenant Archangel Kaela was out of touch with the events of the day because he was guarding the prisoners who had been confined to the keep. Running his hands through his thick blond hair, he told Uzziel, "I should have been patrolling the streets. Tomorrow, I will order one of my saints to guard Father's prisoners." The lieutenant archangel glanced at the foyer's wide open doors. "There's a hazard," he said. "We need to position guards throughout the lobby to see that Lucifer's officers and warriors do not enter Father's house."

Archangel Uzziel left the sofa he sat on and lifted his helmet from a stand's mirroring top. "I see some of our brothers have arrived for the conference," he said referring to the meeting to be held in Father's sanctum. Turning back to his conversation with Kaela, Uzziel confessed, "I worry that the disbelievers and doubters who live in this region will abandon Father to join Lucifer's forces. We as saints should encourage our citizens to shun Lucifer's warriors and to ignore what they say."

"I'll be on patrol tomorrow," Lieutenant Archangel Kaela told his sainted brother. "I will make anyone who breaks Father's laws or anyone who harms our righteous brothers sorry he was ever created."

Uzziel nodded in agreement. "You will learn many new words. Each one defines hate, bigotry, injustice, intolerance, and treason. These words are not used by our citizens to define Lucifer, his warriors, or his northern delegation. These hateful words are being used by Lucifer's followers to describe how they feel about God and His saints."

"Then let us send the northern warriors to Hell, where they belong," Lieutenant Archangel Kaela grumbled under breath. "This globe was created by Father for His righteous sons, and if it means my life, I will keep it free."

During their conversation, Uzziel and Kaela made a vow to God to protect His kingdom, His family, His citizens, and Heaven from Lucifer's hateful warriors. Their conversation ended when they joined their comrades outside the inner sanctum's closed doors.

When God's righteous sons were invited into the sanctum, they entered two abreast. They took their seats in the section reserved for Prince Michael's saints. Lieutenant Archangel Kaela was the last to enter the room. As he walked to his chair, the candles that lined the room and surrounded God's throne flickered; the torch that was positioned above the Father's holy altar glowed brighter. The northern counselor's eyes scoured Kaela's face and the clothing he wore. He saw that the traitor wore a sainted uniform. Sainted words were engraved across the front of his chest plate: "We rise or fall together." The short blue cape hanging down his back to the hem of his knee-length garment was attached to his chest plate at each shoulder by a golden chain.

Belial sneered. He did not doubt that Kaela falsely declared his loyalty to Heaven's Dictator as he had declared his loyalty to Lucifer when he lived in the North. He turned away in disgust.

"Your citizens are hostile toward our leaders," the northern counselor told Father. "I am speaking of Lucifer and Sin. And worse, a traitor who plays a role that influences brothers on both sides of this conflict is present in the room. And now that he has declared his loyalty to You, he will not hesitate to uncreate our leaders." He glanced in Kaela's direction. "I think we know of whom I speak."

Lieutenant Archangel Kaela pretended to be oblivious to Belial's accusation, probably because it was the first time in a long time that he had heard the counselor speak the truth. A glance around the room proved that every titled saint and every titled warrior was present. Uzziel set his hand on Kaela's shoulder, pointing to the empty chair next to Autumn. She must have arrived early because she had a front-row seat. Kaela motioned for Uzziel to help himself to the chair if he so desired.

"I'm staying here," Kaela whispered. Uzziel left the seat he sat in to claim the one next to Autumn. Kaela smiled to himself. From where he sat, he could clearly see Belial standing before Father's shrouded image; better still, from here, he had the advantage of uncreating any rebels that might attempt a heroic attack in Lucifer's name.

"My son," Father said. "Why did you call this meeting?"

"We, the counselors of the North," Belial began, referring to himself, Beelzebub, Flagitious, and Mammon, "are concerned for our leaders' well-being. They have been confined to Your dungeon, a dark, damp hole that is the design of the warped and twisted mind of a traitor who sits among us." Belial paced as he talked to the Holy Father. "We approached Prince Michael, begging him for our leaders' swift and immediate release from the keep, but our request was denied. We do not ask for their freedom to roam Heaven's streets, but we plead with You to free them because their incarceration may lead to their uncreation."

"I did not release the prisoners because they cannot be trusted," Prince Michael said on his behalf. Rising to his feet, he added, "Father, it is on my orders that Lucifer and Sin shall remain in the keep where they will be safe—"

"Safe from what?" Belial demanded. "Are they in danger?"

"Father, it is true that some of our citizens are more than a little upset about the damage northern warriors did to their homes and shops," Prince Michael said in regards to Belial's question. "Brothers who were held hostage in the North and on Sheol have threatened to uncreate Lucifer and Sin. Therefore, I have refused to release the criminals to their counselors until this unrest passes."

"You have our leaders locked in a keep underground because you know that our forces have entered your region and their generals have turned your most faithful followers against God and saints!" Belial shouted. "We have run your citizens out of their homes, destroyed their shops, and robbed them blind, and all your God does is talk about when Heaven's peace is restored. You and your officers are cowards!"

Saints and warriors rose to their feet, their weapons drawn.

"Stop it!" God thundered. "There will be no bloodshed in this room."

Belial pointed toward the inner sanctum's curtained windows. "Look outside, almighty King. Your citizens have fled their homes with whatever they can carry on their backs, but it did them no good, did it? They are trapped here, in Your courtyard, because while they fled, Lucifer's warriors followed them and set up camp outside Your walls." Belial turned to the saints, who sat glaring at him through narrowed eyes. "We, the citizens from the North, are trying to right the incredible wrong God did that brought this destruction on His region. Our presence here is evidence that God is a weak leader, so expect chaos and mayhem until Lucifer takes his rightful throne in Heaven."

Truth leaped to her feet so furiously that her royal chair over turned behind her. "Father has done nothing wrong, Belial," she snarled. "Your eldest brother craved titles because he wanted to set himself apart from his brothers. Father had hoped that Lucifer would use the titles responsibly, but he did not. Instead, he used his titles to convince malcontents to break with God and join him in the North. Father did not send Lucifer away. Lucifer chose to leave this region so that he could amass an army that would help him seize Father's throne."

"Lucifer has yet to seize God's throne." Belial snorted. "Lies told to demean Heaven's first prince, Heaven's first—"

"My son," Father interrupted, "Lucifer's titles are invalid. He is no more than a common angel. By attacking the castle and beheading one of my most promising young sons, Lucifer is lower than any beast of the field in Heaven. Nothing he says matters. Nothing he does for or against Heaven will bring him victory. He is a worm who was an angel, and all that remains of what he was is his physical appearance. Now, why are you standing before me?"

Belial cleared his throat. "The northern delegation asks Your permission to visit our emperor who is incarcerated in Your keep. We wish to assess the great Lucifer's situation. We want to know if he is being treated well, if he is being fed well, and if he is being kept clean. And we want to see how well his health is holding up."

"Your request is granted," Father told His former counselor. "My saints will escort you, Beelzebub, and Flagitious to the dungeon. They will be present while you speak with Lucifer. Immediately following the meeting, my saints will report to Prince Michael. They will tell him everything that was discussed."

To Lieutenant Gabriel, Father said, "The meeting between the members of the northern delegation and their clients will take place at Heaven's eleventh hour. You will see that Lucifer and Sin are shackled by thick chains and that the chains are secured by iron plates that are bolted to the floor." Father glanced around the room. "Are there any suggestions or requests that need addressed before the meeting in the keep convenes?"

Wisdom stood at her throne. "Dearest Father, allow Lieutenant Archangel Kaela to be present at the meeting that will be held between Lucifer, Sin, and their counselors." Having stated her suggestion, the Goddess took her seat.

Belial stood in the center of the floor, his head swiveling from Father's throne to where Kaela sat. "Do not allow that traitor to enter the keep with me!" he shouted. "Kaela is the reason for all this unrest. He robbed Lucifer of his citizens while they worked in the North for Sin."

Kaela stepped forward to address his angry brother. "I saved slaves who were beaten, starved, and used as experiments from uncreation." Turning his attention to Father, he said, "I am willing to remove my weapons' belt outside the door of the keep, and I will submit to a weapons search by our guards, not by any of the perverse warriors who support Lucifer. I humbly suggest that everyone who enters the keep do the same to ensure that the guards will not be forced to uncreate anyone before the meeting winds down."

"Scribe Excelsa, let Lieutenant Archangel Kaela's offer to remove his weapons before entering the keep be spread across the minutes as well as his suggestion that everyone, regardless of rank or position, do the same," Father told His scribe. God grew quiet for a moment. "Belial, if there is an uprising, an attempt by the counselors to illegally free our prisoners, an attempt on the prisoners' part to flee, or an attempt to uncreate the armed guards stationed in the keep, my saints have my permission to attack with lethal force to preserve what little peace Heaven has left. Do you understand what I am saying?" Seeing Belial's nod, Father ended the summit meeting.

The angels, beasts, birds, and some insects were sleeping soundly when God's saints escorted Belial, Beelzebub, and Flagitious through the courtyard to the keep. Saints and counselors submitted to a weapons search before being led down a long narrow staircase to a steel door. A young soldier called out the code that was being used this evening to gain clearance to the keep. The thick door opened to reveal a second set of stairs that led to a flat concrete floor. The saint who guarded the metal box holding the one key that opened every cell in the dungeon greeted the delegation. He pointed to a table set close by the stair-case that led to freedom. The saints took their seats. Belial and his associates stood, watching the darkness that stretched out before them for signs of Lucifer's approach.

Kaela sat with his hands folded on the table in front of him. He knew in his heart that this would not be a good visit. Lucifer had been here for days. He refused to go to the courtyard where he would be nourished by Father's light. He refused food and water, and he rarely left his cot. When Lucifer entered the area where he would meet with his advisors, he was sick and weak. No chains were needed. The guards who walked on either side of him held him up so that he did not fall to the cold, gray floor. Concern lined the faces of saints and northern delegation members alike. The guards gently lowered Lucifer, who shivered from the cold and who was swiftly losing his will to live, into his chair at the table.

From a cell located in the center of the keep, a howl rose up that disrupted the thoughts of those who felt concern for Lucifer. Sin, raging and horrible to see, was dragged from the darkness, forced to walk past cells that set empty, and into the light where she was shoved into a chair made of iron. The chains rattling from her cuffed wrists were locked to bolts located on the chair's armrest. Thick metal clamps held her upper arms so that she could not move them to her sides or lift them above her head. The clamps assured the guards that the witch would not flee. Her lower legs were clamped against the lower front of the metal chair in the same fashion. To please Father, saints locked the chain hanging heavy from the witch's neck brace to the thick round ring that rose up from the center of an iron plate bolted to the floor.

"God's saints put me here so my followers will not see my uncreation," Lucifer rasped. "When I am gone, uncreate all God's sons who refuse to worship me. Win them however you must. Fill their heads with empty promises of wealth, titles, and false worth. When they learn of your deceit, tell them they misunderstood your intentions. Give them false hope, and if they are too wise to fall for your lies, behead them and anyone who associates with them."

"You shall not perish," Belial promised, patting Lucifer's hand. Feeling the cold, stiff flesh of the emperor's hand beneath his palm sent shivers down the counselor's spine. The skin on Lucifer's hand felt the same as the skin on the hands of the slaves they uncreated in the North. "I can promise you this," Belial whispered, "I will talk to Heaven's Dictator about your waning health, and if He does nothing to change your situation for the better, your followers will burn this region to the ground."

Father was about to leave the inner sanctum to take His throne on the castle's highest peak when Belial streaked through the door, shouting threats and demands. In a desperate attempt to force God to listen to what he had to say, he drew a dagger, threatening to uncreate the scribe. Guards raced to where Belial stood clutching Excelsa by his cloak. Lieutenant Archangel Kaela watched the scene explode into a screaming frenzy before he stepped in to stop the disturbance.

"Stand down," he told the guards, who surrounded Belial, their swords drawn and ready to strike. Turning to the angry counselor, he said, "Release Excelsa, Belial. Have you forgotten the events of Excelsa's abduction from God's kingdom to the North? Sheathe your dagger and leave this room."

Belial tossed Excelsa to the floor and made a mad run toward Kaela. God's sainted son grasped his brother's wrists in his hands. Locking his left leg firmly behind his attacker's leg, he took him to the floor and confiscated his weapon. "I have always been fond of you, Belial," Kaela said softly as he helped the trembling counselor to his feet. "But I will uncreate you as easily as I will uncreate any brother who threatens my Lord or the members of His royal family." Straightening Belial's cloak, Kaela continued to speak to him in soft tones. "Leave this room, go to your northern brothers, and tell them that Kaela will speak to Father on Lucifer's behalf. I will save your false emperor from uncreation. He will not perish in the keep or anywhere in the Sacred Region." He felt the tension in Belial's body ease. "None of us in this region want our eldest brother to waste away until he is gone forever."

"Will you ask for his freedom?" Belial whispered.

"Lucifer has been arrested and imprisoned, and rightfully so," Kaela said softly. "I will do my best to better his condition so that he does not perish. I promise you that, and nothing more."

Belial stepped back. "Lucifer's followers hate you, Kaela. They want you uncreated. They want your head on a post. I will see that happens if our emperor is uncreated in the keep you built to cage your northern brothers." He tossed his head and set his dagger back in his belt. "The protests will begin anew. There is nothing you or your saints can do to stop us. And from time to time, I will return to the keep to check on Lucifer's condition. The longer he is locked up in that hole under this house and the worse he gets, the more cottages and shops will burn to the ground."

Belial stormed out of the inner sanctum, slamming both heavy doors behind him.

"Father," Kaela said, kneeling before God's throne, "I must speak with You about Lucifer's waning health and Sin's growing strength."

"Speak, my son," Father urged.

Kaela rose from his kneeling position. "Father, if Lucifer should perish during his imprisonment in the keep, Belial will label him a hero. He will bombard our citizens with lies about You. Lucifer's popularity will grow. His generals will hold rallies that will escalate into the blasphemous worship of a worm that ruined Heaven simply because he set himself apart from his righteous brothers." Without taking his eyes off Father's effulgent glow, Kaela added, "If the northern delegation convinces the doubters and disbelievers who live in the Sacred Region to join them, they will have the strength they need to seize Your throne, and Heaven's peace will never be restored."

"So what do you suggest we do?" Father asked.

"I suggest that we move the prisoners to the sphere I built in Your backyard," God's admired son replied. "It will provide the darkness Sin seeks to keep her well, and it will provide enough light to nourish Lucifer."

Father rose from His throne. "I make this proclamation: to keep Lucifer from becoming exalted among Heaven's doubters, disbelievers, his followers, and northern warriors, he and Sin will be moved this day from the dungeon to the sphere where their needs will be met." Father's image faded until it disappeared from sight.

Outside the inner sanctum's long, narrow windows, the landscape brightened, birds awoke to sing their songs, nocturnal insects ceased their chirping, and bees left their hives to pollenate Nature's abundant flowers.

Late that morning, the evil pair was led in separate processions through God's flowering courtyard to their new prison. Bolstered by two sainted soldiers, Lucifer threw off his scarlet cloak and tossed his topaz-colored robe onto the lawn before him. Standing over his discarded clothing, Heaven's first created angel basked in God's pure light. His guards prodded him to move forward. Lucifer fell to his knees on the ground. Intent on doing their duty, saints forced the self-proclaimed northern emperor to his feet and dragged him up the stairs that led to his cell. When the threesome reached the top step, the thick iron door was opened. The cell's dark interior leaped out at Lucifer. Screaming obscenities and blaspheming God's name, the prisoner was tossed into the sphere, and the triple-locking door was closed behind him.

Below the Holy Castle, inside the dungeon's gloomy cell, Sin cloaked herself in a black hooded robe that had been provided for her by Belial. Before the keep's heavy door was opened, twelve muscular angels shackled themselves to the vile Goddess. Cautiously, they escorted Sin from the dungeon to the castle's lighted courtyard. From under her darkened shroud, the foul witch directed her anger at her Holy Father. Righteous on-lookers felt that Sin was more annoyed at God's light than she was frightened by His impending wrath.

In a futile attempt to escape, Sin disregarded the safety of her heavy cloak and bolted up toward Heaven's crystalline dome, but she could go only as far as her chains allowed her. While her skin burned and flaked from her body, horrified saints were lifted off the ground—so great was her strength.

Frantic voices erupted. "Get reinforcements!" Prince Michael's brave saints had lost their battle to keep the witch anchored to the ground. Straining her muscles, Sin lifted higher into the air. The horror of her skin burning and flaking from her body, the flames that rose up from her hair and scalp, brought screams from the saints who tried to drag Sin down to safety.

"Help us! The witch is burning! We need reinforcements!"

Civilians rushed forward. Hands reached up to grasp the thick chains attached to the witch by heavy metal cuffs. Sin lost her will to fight as God's pure light threatened to uncreate her, and she sank to the ground like a wilted leaf.

Prince Michael's saints dragged the scorched witch to her feet, forcing her to walk to her lighted cell. Desperate to be free, Sin clung to the frame of the prison's thick iron-clad door. She shrieked obscenities as Michael's determined saints pried her fingers loose, slammed the door shut, and quickly bolted it. Trapped inside her lighted cell, God's eighth daughter filled the prison's upper story with her horrible screams.

That evening, Kaela gained Prince Michael's permission to speak with Lucifer. Flanked by Stephon and Patrician, he climbed the short set of stairs that led to the emperor's cell.

"Lieutenant Archangel Kaela," Stephon said. "Sire, did you forget? Saints and civilians must drop their weapons at the door of the sphere if they wish to visit Lucifer or Sin. According to the scribe that law is yours, not Father's. You put a second law in place that visitors must submit to a weapons search—" he stopped talking when he saw the anger in his commanding officer's eyes.

Lieutenant Archangel Kaela did not appreciate a youngster he trained reminded him that his suggestions were adopted as laws that had to be obeyed. Kaela grumbled something under breath as he removed the belt that held his dagger and sword. Patrician searched his clothing for hidden weapons. When his young brothers were satisfied that he was not a threat to Father's enemy, Stephon said, "You may enter the sphere, sire." He lowered his head. "I'm sorry but, it has to be this way."

"You are a good soldier, Stephon," Kaela said, patting the child's upper arm. "This is your world now, not mine. I am an ancient angel who, like Father, closed my eyes to a budding tyrant. I should have killed Lucifer the day Archangel Uzziel introduced him to the North. But in my heart, I believed his lie that Father loved him more than He loved the rest of us."

Patrician fumbled with the door's lock. His hands were shaking. It was obvious the youngster feared Lucifer.

"Here, let me undo the lock so that I can get on with the rest of my evening." Lieutenant Archangel Kaela took the key from between Patrician's fingers and opened the door. "See that while I am here, my conversation with Lucifer is not interrupted. I will not be long, I promise."

A young soldier named Raguel stepped forward. "Sire, on Prince Michael's orders, I cannot allow you to enter the sphere alone." The child's dark green eyes searched Kaela's face for signs of approval.

Kaela nodded. "We don't want to arouse the prince's anger, do we?" With Raguel in tow, he crossed the cell's threshold, walking directly to where Lucifer laid face-down on the floor. Kaela called the emperor's name as he knelt beside him.

"Are you sleeping?" Kaela asked resting his hand against Lucifer's back.

Lucifer sat up and looked at him.

"How are you? Have you eaten?" Kaela could see by the abundance of fruit on the tray at Lucifer's side that he had not touched his food. "You need to end your hunger-strike, or you will perish." He offered Lucifer a northern pear. When Lucifer turned his head away, Kaela bit into the fruit. "It is very good." He sat down, resting his back against the wall, peering into the darkness. Where was the window? Evidently, the sphere's internal works had not been activated. "They tell me that Sin is fine. Do you have a message for her?"

Lucifer sneered into Kaela's face. "Why are you here?" He took a bunch of grapes from the tray and scooted against the wall Kaela occupied. "You are not interested in my survival. Look at what you did to me. I almost died in that underground prison you built. You are cruel. No, you are perverse. Only a perverse mind would condemn a light-loving brother to darkness." Lucifer popped a grape into his mouth. "You betrayed me, Kaela. The small betrayals, the tricks you played on me to amuse my hateful Enemy, were nothing compared to this." Lucifer reached for an orange. He peeled it and offered half of it to Kaela. "Sin is all right?"

"Yes, I told you, she is fine. I am going to visit her momentarily. Do you have a message? Anything you would like to share with her?" Kaela saw Lucifer's expression change many times as he thought about what he might tell his child.

"You are trying to trick me again," Lucifer suddenly accused. "Listen." Though sound could not filter through the sphere's steel-covered walls, the North's false emperor swore he heard the whispered shouting of voices, the stifled clattering of chariots, and the muffled poundings of horses' hooves. "Listen." Lucifer slid his back up the wall until he stood upright. "My warriors have arrived. Soon, they will conquer this region and set my flag in place." He put his finger to his lips. "Listen. Do you hear the blood-curdling screams of sainted cowards meeting their uncreation?" He pressed his ear against the wall, smiling.

Kaela listened. Hearing nothing, he decided it would be best for Lucifer to know the cold, hard truth even if it did break his heart. "Your supporters are content that you have been moved from the dungeon to a place that sets you apart from your imprisoned companions," he said, watching Lucifer's face closely for signs of emotion. "They left the region. They have returned to the North, and those who are imprisoned are not cheering you, nor are they seeking ways to save you and your witch. They are too concerned with their own well-being to worry about the two of you."

"Then what is it I hear that sounds so joyous?" Lucifer asked, his eyes brimming with tears, fearful of what Kaela's answer might reveal.

"You are hearing a festival that is being hosted by Father and Prince Michael to honor our brave saints," Kaela replied, knowing full well that no festival was being held. "Our saints scored so many warriors' lives during the attack you launched against our Lord that we are celebrating our good fortune." He cupped his hand to his ear. "Listen. Can you hear the shouts of praise and cheers of admiration for the athletes who are marching onto the playing field? Our prince raided the North. He freed our brothers from your pits and pens. As we speak, Prince Michael is being hailed as a hero, and his saints are receiving prestigious awards for their courageous acts of valor and honor."

Lucifer cupped his hand around his ear. He heard nothing now.

Kaela studied Lucifer's face. Even the sphere's darkness could not hide the despair the false emperor felt. God's favored son patted his eldest brother's shoulder, saying, "Soon, Zephon's orchestra will play a song that Sonnet wrote, the words of which praise our Lord's leadership and strength. Israfel will lead the citizens of this region in songs of praise and hail Father, who sits in nourishing light. His strength is ours by day. His love is ours by night. Glory to God Jehovah! He will create a new King to rule in Heaven. His name shall be known to every living creature, even to the beast, fowl, insect, and aquatic creatures on this globe."

"Oh, Heaven," Lucifer wept. "I hoped to rule this globe from God's throne, but I am here, imprisoned in this odd contraption, listening to whispered songs that praise an heir who is not yet created." Lucifer leaned his head against the wall. "If only Heaven's hateful Dictator would have mercy on me and create me anew. I could start my life over. I might prove to be a righteous son with no crimes in my past to haunt me." He turned to Kaela. "Was I ever, in my entire life, as charming and as beautiful as Heaven's new King will be? How did I lose my birthright, Kaela? Did I even have a birthright, or was my inheritance an imagined gift?" Lucifer wept bitterly. "Perhaps if Father had drawn up stricter laws, I would have turned out differently."

"Only righteous souls obey God's laws," Kaela told the weeping emperor as he prepared to leave the cell. "Stricter laws would not have kept you from becoming a criminal. The stricter the law, the more inclined you would have been to break it. You are evil throughout. The crimes you committed resulted from your weak character and lack of self-respect. In my opinion, discipline cures defiance. Father would have done better by you if He had enforced His laws. Have you forgotten your northern motto 'Fear breeds respect'?" Kaela walked to the door. "Prepare to be disciplined, Lucifer, for our new King shall suffer no fools."

"I might still be king, Kaela!" Lucifer screamed. "My followers will avenge me."

"I doubt that you will ever be anything more than what you are, Lucifer," Kaela snarled as the door slammed shut behind him. To the guards, he said, "On my mark, activate the window in sphere's lower story." Kaela ascended to the prison's roof. A window there gave him visual access to the prisoners in both cells. Lucifer lay motionless on the floor of his darkened cell while Sin, clothed in heavy garments, sat in God's pure light.

"Activate Lucifer's cell."

The evil general was lost in self-pity when, through the ceiling, a narrow beam reached down to touch him. Its warmth soothed his hands and dried his tear-stained face. Standing upright, Lucifer watched the beam move ever eastward. Its glimmering ray shone like a beacon of hope. God's foul son hurried behind it until he matched its speed. At last, in perpetual movement, he fed on the beam's fertile glow. Kaela descended from the sphere's roof to the stairs leading to Sin's cell. He and Raguel walked through the lighted hallway, searching for the witch. They found her huddled against the wall, her dark cloak had been returned to her, and she had it drawn over her from head to toe.

"Sin," Kaela called, "can you hear me?"

"I have not perished, if that's what you mean." The witch opened her cape so that one eye peered out at him.

"Lucifer sends his love." Kaela knelt beside her. "He wants you to know that he is sorry for having drawn you into his crimes." He reached inside Sin's cloak and felt her trembling hand close around his. "In a meeting that was held before I visited Lucifer, Father informed His saints that you are with child. By our Lord's strict mandate, your baby will not be born in Heaven. Therefore, I have been sent here to offer you uncreation in return for information that might help us expel Lucifer from Heaven. If you do not comply, you will be eternally damned to a foul prison known as Hell."

"Uncreation means that I will cease to be," Sin whispered. "What about my child? Will he be uncreated too?" She studied Kaela's face for a long moment. "You would uncreate a mother and her unborn child? What kind of monster are you?" Sin rose to her feet. "What kind of monster is God? He offers His daughter uncreation or eternal damnation? Well, my baby shall be born in Heaven, and he will reign with his parents at his side."

"Your child is an abomination, and he will perish if he is born on this globe," Kaela told his evil sister. "He is a creature of darkness, and darkness cannot thrive in Heaven." To prove his point, he rose to his feet and robbed Sin of her cloak. When she reached for it, he withdrew it farther from her. "Accept my offer; information in return for uncreation. Do what is best for Heaven and for your evil child." Foul Sin gazed at her light-withered hands and gave up all hope for survival. She asked if Lucifer knew of God's plan for his unborn son.

"No, he knows only that you are well." Kaela draped the witch's cloak over his arm. "You will not need this." He walked to the door. "Think about it. Hell is an awesome place. I hear that Hell is worse than the planet Sheol." He turned to look at the witch. Her bald head was glowing red; her skin appeared to be melting off her bones. God's light was taking its toll on Sin's body. "Think about the offer of uncreation or damnation. I expect your answer by tomorrow."

"Or what!" Sin screamed. "What will you do?" When Kaela did not reply, the witch made a demand. "I must speak with Lucifer. I need his opinion on this matter. Do you hear me?" Kaela left the compartment. Sainted guards closed the triple-locking door and set a heavy bar across it. Raguel, having fulfilled his orders, returned to his station on the ground floor while Kaela flew to the top of the sphere. Through the window that revealed all, he saw the witch. She pounded her fists against the wall until a panel cast its shadow on her skin like a welcomed phantom. Sin ended her tantrum to watch the panel move in constant westward direction. Filled with hope, Sin ran behind the darkness the panel lent, her arms outstretched, reaching for its vague gloom.

Battle in God's House

Voices filled with emotion filtered up from the Holy Castle's courtyard to its outdoor throne room. The desperate voices belonged to God's righteous sons who longed for Heaven's peace. The angry voices belonged to Lucifer's supporters, who had just learned that their leaders had been escorted from a life-sapping dungeon to a sphere built by a traitor. When Father retired to His inner sanctum, northern warriors went to the Holy City where they stole what merchants managed to salvage following previous attacks and burned what was left of most of the shops. An assault on the village sent smoke curling upward from the valley that circled the Holy Mount's broad base. A battle between saints and warriors raged on for hours, and neither side seemed to be winning.

To end the violence in the streets, Prince Michael sent a fleet of His most trusted military personnel to all the posts located in Heaven's newly populated regions. When the saints returned home, they brought with them innumerable volunteers whose battle skills were honed by experienced leaders. To the civilian eye, their numbers looked great, but truth was, the soldiers recruited to protect Father's righteous sons simply added enough fighting power to equal the number of dark-clad warriors who pledged their allegiance to the North's false emperor and his perverse daughter.

Faithful sons led by Dubbiel from the east, Chayyliel from the south, and Eae from the west arrived in the Sacred Region. These three commanders had, in the past, lent their fighting skills to Prince

Michael during the first northern invasion that nearly destroyed God's city. Now, they and their troops arrived in the Sacred Region during the day to make a show of their presence in Father's kingdom. Some soldiers walked the distance; others sat on the broad backs of prancing horses or the sleek muscular backs of glistening unicorns.

The procession wound its way through the streets of the Holy City, traveled the twisting, turning lanes of the village, and climbed the long, broad staircase Nature honed in the sides of the Holy Mount. As they made their way to Father's house, talented brothers and skilled craftsmen left the remnants of their homes and shops to greet them. When the soldiers reached the courtyard, they were met with deafening cheers from brothers who had taken refuge in Father's house to escape the fighting and chaos that went on around them.

Commander Dubbiel stationed his troops on the walls that surrounded Father's mansion; Chayyliel stationed his saints at the parameters of the wooded area that bordered the wide-open field where the stables were located, and Eae posted his saints around the full circumference of the stadium where the games were held. Armed troops were assigned to patrol the streets of the village and the city. For the first time in what seemed to be forever, frightened civilians enjoyed a reminder of peaceful times when merchants and shop-keepers set up their tables in the courtyard to display new items that skilled brothers crafted.

Zophiel sounded his trumpet. The crowd grew quiet. God's messenger unrolled a scroll he held in his hand and read, "Father invites all His sons, peaceful or rebellious, to attend a Festival of Light to be held in the stadium on His lawn." The messenger's voice was as loud as thunder. "This night, our great Lord God Jehovah will reveal to Heaven's citizens the name of the One who will inherit His throne." Cheers rose up, songs of praise were sung, and for a moment, it seemed like old times again.

Lieutenant Archangel Kaela sat at his desk in the apartment he shared with Autumn. For the second time, he read over the report he was required to write for Prince Michael concerning his visit in the sphere with Lucifer and then with Sin.

"I am pleased to report that the visit with Lucifer went well," he wrote. "During our conversation, I encouraged him to break his hunger strike. His imprisonment in the dungeon has affected him in ways that I cannot define. He hears his supporters cheering him when the sphere is sound-proof and its walls block all view of the surrounding area where it sits." Concerning Sin, he wrote, "The witch is with the child. It is obvious that she will not accept uncreation to lessen her burden or to save the abomination she carries inside her from the terror of being dissolved at birth by God's pure light." About the sphere, he wrote, "The sphere is working well. Both the windows and the panels are doing what they were designed to do." After applying his signature to the bottom of the page he had written, Kaela set his pen aside and left his apartment. He had one more task to complete before he could join Autumn at the stadium.

Prince Michael gave Kaela orders that he was to brief Commanders Dubbiel, Chayyliel, and Eae on the unrest that Lucifer's dark-clad warriors wrought throughout God's kingdom. Lieutenant Archangel Kaela learned from Dubbiel that while he journeyed to Father's house, he and his troops saw rebels lurking in the rolling hills that skirted the village. Eae added that his troops saw rebels hiding in the remnants of burned town houses in the Holy City. Chayyliel added his angry voice to the conversation.

"Our brothers should return to their homes and take up arms to protect their belongings," he said. "Instead, they hide in Father's house, too frightened of their enemies to fight for what they know is right and just. By leaving their homes and shops, they have given northern criminals places to lurk in."

Autumn sat on a bleacher in the stadium watching the festivities. She had a place saved for Kaela, who promised he wouldn't be long, but then, she knew he had much to do now that the commanders of the West, East, and South were in the region. She, too, had duties to perform that she otherwise never would have had if so many soldiers had not arrived in Father's kingdom at once. Autumn and her small sainted brothers shed their uniforms to work in the kitchen and the dining room. Theirs was an all-day chore. First, they worked in the kitchen, helping Chynella and his cherubs prepare innumerable meals;

then they helped Atella's crew serve the soldiers nectar and fresh water. Three meals were served throughout the day to an untold number of sainted brothers. After dinner, many of the troops lingered at their tables, leaving just moments before the festival was scheduled to begin in the stadium. Autumn worried that she would not be able to attend the festivities. But somehow the trays, plates, goblets, and silver were washed, dried, and put away in time to catch the end of Father's Festival of Light.

Autumn sat on a seat in the bleachers with a space beside her reserved for Kaela. Her eyes were fixed on the stadium's open double doors.

"Come on, Kaela," she whispered impatiently. "Father has an important announcement to make, and I want for us to be together when He makes it."

Lieutenant Archangel Kaela arrived just as the awards ceremony was about to begin. Smiling down at Autumn he took his place beside her. Across the playing field from where they were seated, Zophiel perched on the balustrade that towered over the stadium's highest row of seats. Setting his trumpet's mouthpiece to his lips, he blew. The horn's blare drew everyone's attention to the royal family's booth. Father left His seat, making His way to where six righteous sons knelt in humble reverence.

"Arise, my wonderful children," God said as He accepted the medallion Love offered. "Sarandiel, a vision awakened you from your sleep during the twelfth hour of Heaven's night. Your vision warned that my enemies had left their fortress in the North and were marching toward my kingdom. You left your bed, armed with nothing more than your love for your Creator and your concern for your brothers. You flew on outstretched wings over the streets in the village and the city, crying out to your brothers to leave their homes to take refuge in my house.

"You noted who left their cottages and town houses and who stayed hidden inside. You went door-to-door, forcing the remnant of your frightened brothers into the streets, and after that, you gathered them, one and all, and led them to the safety of the Holy Castle." Father slipped a golden medallion's chain over Sarandiel's head. "With this medallion, I proclaim you to be the Ruling Angel of Heaven's Twelfth Hour of Night."

With tears streaming down his cheeks, his fingers clutching the medallion that lay against his chest, Sarandiel knelt before His Creator. He and five others were honored this evening. Father proclaimed Varhmiel, Ruler of the Fourth Hour of Day; Vequaniel, Ruling Angel of the Third Hour of the Day; Zaazenach, Ruler of the Sixth Hour of Night; Tartys, Ruling Angel of the Second Hour of Night; and Suriel, who healed as many brothers as Raphael, received the Medallion of Healing Powers and had a new meaning put to his name.

"In my ancient language, Suriel means 'God's Command,'" Father said. "From this day forward, your name shall bear that meaning." He spread His arms wide open as He spoke to those who gathered in the stadium to attend this special Festival. "The sons you see kneeling before me earned their awards through their strength and courage. Each one, through his determination to save lives, did so with little or no regard for his own safety. Their loyalty to their King, and their unwavering need to courageously see to their brothers' safety became their body armor against those who sought to cause them harm. They have fortitude, which is the strongest, boldest form of faith anyone can possess."

Cloaked in thick clouds, Father said, "Arise, my sons. Turn, face your brothers, and accept your much-deserved acclaim." The stadium erupted in applause. Wisdom, Devotion, Charity, Love, Inspiration, Truth, and Mercy escorted Sarandiel, Varhmiel, Vequaniel, Zaazenach, Tartys, and Suriel to their seats before returning to take their place beside their loving Father.

Father signaled for silence. A blast from Zophiel's trumpet quieted the crowd.

"Tomorrow starts a new chapter in Heaven's history," God told His sons. "Your dreams will introduce you to my heir, your future King. When you awaken, you will know Him well. Immanuel's presence in this region will bring about unrest like Heaven has never known before, and it will continue until He becomes King. When I set my crown on my heir's head, all doubt will be gone from this globe, forever. You will either love your new King or you will hate Him. Once your decision is made, your feelings will be engraved in your heart, and there will be no turning back. Pray that you are among those who love and admire Immanuel. When He rules in my place, even the fish, insects, birds, and beasts on this globe will kneel before Him. Unlike me, He will suffer no fools."

That night while the angels slept, they met the One who would rule Heaven from Father's powerful throne. He was tall and handsome, His hair was the color of the richest spun gold, and His eyes were bluer than Earth's skies on a clear day. He called Himself Immanuel, and when He spoke His voice quickened and calmed the heart at once. Immanuel's expression was one of extreme peacefulness. Unlike the saints, who suffered so much strife, Immanuel's face was not lined by worry or dismay.

In her dream, Autumn reached her trembling hand toward Him. Dropping to her knees, she whispered, "My Lord, it is I, Your servant, Autumn. I loved You even before I met You. Every problem in my life, here and elsewhere, has flown, and in Your presence, I am at peace."

"I know you, my loyal servant," Immanuel said softly as He caressed her cheek with His silky cool hand. "I am in your heart, and I will be with you always." Immanuel's whispered promise filled her heart with joy. The dream faded.

Autumn woke up smiling. She turned over in bed and kicked one leg out from under the covers, rubbing her toes on the blanket's cool silky border. A breeze, sweet and fragrant, entered through her window to caress her face.

"Immanuel," Autumn said softly. "My beloved Brother, welcome to Heaven."

She turned on her side, facing Kaela's bed. It was empty. She sat up. Now she could hear the clatter and clamber of war. The Sacred Region was under attack.

"KAELA!" she screamed.

Without hesitation, Autumn leaped from her bed, and with trembling hands, she dragged on her military uniform. Securing her weapons' belt around her waist, she bolted into the hallway. Though she stood alone on the marbled floor of her Father's glorious house, voices from every staircase echoed the dreadful words: "The castle is under siege."

Lieutenant Gabriel was the first of her sainted brothers to dart passed her. Hearing the sound of feet pounding over the floor behind her, Autumn turned to see a battalion of saints running in her direction. Unsheathing her sword, she led the way to the staircase that descended to the foyer on the castle's ground floor. Once there, Autumn gripped her sword's hilt in both her hands. Diving into the fray, she drove back one warrior after another. All around her, saints locked in combat with Father's enemies shouted, "Victory to the Lord God Jehovah!" And suddenly, there was a lull in the battle. This slender thread of idleness gave Autumn a chance to assess the situation.

Across the room from her, her sainted brothers locked swords with Lucifer's dark-clad thugs, pushing them forward to the foyer's wide-open porch in an effort to secure the inner sanctum's tightly closed doors. So far, the battle was one of stomping feet, shouted insults and profanity, and the dreadful sound of metal clashing against metal. But when the first saint fell, uncreated, to the floor, Prince Michael gave his troops the command to attack their northern brothers with deadly force. Now the battle turned bloody. From where she stood, Autumn caught a glimpse of Kaela. He was scoring warriors as quickly as they could approach him. It seemed to her that the northern warriors were lining up, hoping to be the one to brag that he had uncreated God's Liberating Lion.

With her sword clasped securely in both hands, Autumn defended herself against Vine and Ose, two of Lucifer's most loyal supporters. She was overpowering them when they turned away from her to chase after Vassago, a northern civilian. Autumn watched after them, curious about why they would retreat from combat to pursue an innocent member of Sin's court. She shook her head. She had no time for this; she had to secure Father's home.

Now a new distraction rumbled through the foyer. Zophiel's voice thundered over clashing metal, angry shouts of defiance, and screams of trapped civilians, that the key to Father's underground armory was missing.

Autumn made the dreadful mistake of lowering her sword in her effort to hear God's messenger. Catching her off guard, Vual and Gylle assaulted Autumn with brute force. Together, they knocked her off her feet onto her back. Clutching her sword tightly in her hand, she scooted backward, toward the stairs, and into the throng of battling angels. She knew that she had to regain her footing if she hoped to ward off these two horrid spirits. But just when she thought her way was clear to strike, Vual knocked her onto her back on the stairs. He was fast, too fast. Glaring down into her face, he pressed his foot against her stomach. She felt his sword's tip pierce the skin on her chest, just slightly above her beating heart.

"If I must die today, Father, I am honored to have served You," Autumn whispered. Closing her eyes, she prepared to receive the deadly blow.

Lieutenant Archangel Kaela had been battling his way across the foyer to where he thought he saw Autumn. At that time, she was engaged in combat with two northern civilians, neither of whom was trained in swordsmanship. But immediately following Zophiel's message, Kaela lost sight of her. When he found her, she was sprawled on her back on the stairs, in dire need of help. Vual was leaning over her, teasing her with his sword.

"You like to play!" Kaela shouted. He shoved his blade through Vual's back so fiercely that its tip exited his stomach. "Play with that," he snarled. Withdrawing his sword, he dragged Autumn to her feet.

"Go!" he shouted at her. "Go to the inner sanctum."

She knelt on the stairs, trying to wrest her sword out from under the fallen warrior. Gylle saw his chance to strike Autumn down, but with one vicious sway of his blade, Kaela stopped the warrior's attack before his sword met its mark.

Losing his patience with Autumn, Kaela grasped her hand in his and dragged her down the stairs to the foyer. Shoving saints and rebels from his path, he got her safely to the sanctum's closed doors. Placing her behind him, he shouted, "Pound on the door with your fist or kick it with your foot if you must. Make yourself heard by our brothers who are locked inside." The lieutenant archangel staved off an attack by Caim and Furcas, both of whom proved to be formidable foes to all saints in Prince Michael's army.

"Let me in!" Autumn screamed. She was terrified of the scene that was unfolding before her eyes: saints and rebels falling to the floor in pools of their own blood, their eyes dazed, their mouths gaping, their life ebbing from their bodies.

Kaela crashed his sword down on Caim's shield, knocking him off his feet. Behind him, Autumn stood sobbing. Kaela felt the outdoor air being drawn toward him from the foyer's open porch. Turning slightly, he noticed the door to the sanctum was cracked open. "Take Autumn!" he shouted. A hand reached around the door, grabbed Autumn's weapons' belt, and dragged her inside.

Across the foyer, close by the kitchen, Vassago cowered under a dining room table. He measured the span that lay between him and the kitchen door. Could he make it to the door without being seen by Vine or Ose? Lifting the floor-length cloth, he peered out from under the table. From his hiding place, he could see that the fight was fast moving from the foyer to the castle's courtyard. Hugging his knees, he waited until he heard Nesroc's trumpet blare. The northern general had sounded retreat, calling his warriors from God's kingdom. Now Vassago left his hiding place, hoping that he might find an abandoned cottage somewhere in the village. He could rest there, knowing that all his needs would be met by God's invisible hands. But as fate would have it, Vassago didn't see the little saint who left the inner sanctum to retrieve his sword from the stairs where he dropped it.

"Vassago," Autumn called, sheathing her sword. "Wait. I want to talk to you." Everyone in Heaven knew that while Vassago lived in the North, he used his inborn skill to find lost or stolen objects that belonged to Sin and Lucifer. The problem was if the object was stolen, not only did Vassago find it, but he revealed the name of the thief. His revelation resulted in the severe punishment of many saints who worked for Father. "Why were those brothers chasing after you?" Autumn asked.

Vassago lowered his head. He knew this would be bad. When he was questioned by a curious brother, he could not tell a lie. "They were chasing after me because I know the whereabouts of the key and the names of those involved who took it." He cringed when Lieutenant Archangel Kaela, accompanied by Lieutenant Gabriel, First Officer Percible, and Private First-Class Stephon entered the castle's dining hall.

"Who took the key?" Autumn asked.

Vassago studied the sainted unit through tear-filled eyes. "Last night, during the ceremonies, Nefarious and Malfeasance were commissioned by Belial to fly to the roof of this house and remove the key from God's throne." He turned his attention to Kaela. "I am aware that you and your apprentices built all the furnishings for this house and that your apprentices decorated the furniture with etchings. But Nature built God's ancient throne. She carved a scene on the side of your King's high seat that depicts two globes joined by a golden bridge. She thought if she hid the key in plain sight, no one would see it." He saw Kaela and Autumn look from him to where their commanding officer stood. "No, you don't understand. The bridge in the etching is the key.

"Nature thought that God's effulgent light would block the details of the etching from our eyes," Vassago explained. "The scene went unnoticed and was not mentioned to anyone. But Belial, who acted as counselor to God's high court for eons, was familiar with the scene, and he was present when the key was set in place."

"Where is Belial now?" Lieutenant Gabriel asked.

Vassago rolled his eyes from one side of the hall to the other. "He is in his old neighborhood here, in the Sacred Region. He has taken up residency in the town house where he lived when he served God. He not only has the key to God's armory, but he is in possession of many of God's journals. He stole them from the King's private library the night he flew northward to pledge his loyalty to my emperor, the great Lucifer."

"You are a good brother," Autumn said as she took Vassago's hand in hers. "Join our forces. We could use someone with a skill like yours."

"You don't understand," Vassago said. "Even though I will never lift a weapon in my hands with the intention of harming a brother, I will never lower myself to kneel before God or Immanuel. I do not believe that God created Heaven. I doubt that He created the angelic race. I believe that His heir will be weak and will be crushed by Lucifer, who is the rightful heir to Heaven's throne."

"You opinions are your own, but know this," Lieutenant Gabriel said, "when Father levels His sentence upon Lucifer and Sin, their supporters will suffer their leaders' fate."

"I am aware that God is unfair in His feelings toward me and brothers like me," Vassago sadly admitted, "but it will be an honor to share whatever punishment God deems fit for Lucifer."

"Take Vassago to a private room in the castle, and put guards at the room's doors and windows," Prince Michael's first officer told the saints. "And keep this discussion private."

To Vassago, he said, "You will be safe for now."

Turning to Lieutenant Archangel Kaela, Gabriel issued a command. "You and your unit of saints will arrest Nefarious and Malfeasance, but you will allow Belial to go free. God has a purpose that he must serve in Heaven before he receives his rightful punishment."

On the night of Vassago's revelation to Gabriel and his saints, a spirit swifter than Mercy, purer than Heaven's air, far more transparent than the witch's dark mist, and more obedient to God than His most faithful saints, entered Belial's town house. While the northern counselor slept, invisible hands lifted the key to God's armory from his desk's cluttered top. Those same unseen hands gathered our Lord's holy journals from the floor where they lay scattered about like fallen leaves. Within moments of completing His mission, the spirit materialized before God's nocturnal throne. Immanuel knelt in humble reverence and with deep respect for His beloved sacred Father. He placed the objects He recovered from Belial's town house on the floor at His Creator's feet. With the King's permission, the Holy Son rose to take His seat closest to God's power.

The morning following the battle in Father's house, saints gathered in the dining hall. Prince Michael's table was filled to capacity. No plates sat before him or his guests. They were locked in a deep private conversation that was meant to be kept just that—private. Among those seated with the prince were Commander Eae, Commander

Cerviel, Sergeant Eremiel, First Officer Hofniel, Lieutenant Archangel Kaela, Autumn, and Lieutenant Gabriel.

"So you heard my gripe," the prince said, looking from one guest's face to the other. "Give me some input."

To everyone's surprise, Autumn spoke first. "Sir, Lucifer's incarceration confirmed our worse fears - we cannot keep our rebellious brothers confined in the keep. We learned, too, that our civilian population is at risk of attack every day, but they are not cowards—well, not all of them are cowards. And, I am pleased to report that Joniel, his apprentices, and our metallurgists have combined their skills to build a number of barred cells on the western parameter of the holy mount."

"So why didn't I receive your report sooner? Why did you wait until now?" Prince Michael asked. He was clearly annoyed that Autumn had not passed this information on to him sooner.

"Well, in case you hadn't noticed, sir, I was busy all day yesterday defending our Lord's house," Autumn replied firmly, but respectfully. "And when the battle ended, I helped Lieutenant Archangel Kaela and his First Officer Percible arrest Nefarious and Malfeasance. After which, I patrolled the streets in the city and the village. I hope my explanation for why my report is late in coming is acceptable to you, sir."

The officers looked from Autumn to their commanding officer. "Continue your account," Prince Michael said with a wave of his hand.

"The problem the craftsmen encountered is that they do not have enough material to build more cells to accommodate the number of criminals we have in custody in the keep," Autumn told her sainted brothers, "which, if I might add, has become a noisy stinking hole filled with loud, vulgar, demanding rebels." She stretched her hands out on the table top. "To add to the problem, Father wants these criminals to receive fair treatment. He wants us to question each of our vile brothers to determine if they feel they have been justly incarcerated."

"Of course these criminals have been justly incarcerated." The prince said with a hint of anger in his voice. "Father knows that. Look at what they did to the Holy City, this house, and the village. I need suggestions."

"We could uncreate them for their offenses," Eremiel suggested. "We know they are criminals, some more so than others, so why are we feeding them, exercising them, and seeing to their needs? This is what we do with our horses, not our enemies."

"I agree with Eremiel," Hofniel said after a long silence. "Let's rid ourselves of this menace once and for all." When no one neither agreed with nor objected to what the pair said, Hofniel added, "How long have we waited for Father to intervene? How much longer must our region suffer at the hands of its enemies until Father decides to restore Heaven's peace?"

Lieutenant Archangel Kaela spoke next. "Look around this room. See how different we are from each other. Some of us are tall, some are small, some are white in color, and some of our brothers are golden. We don't look alike. Who in the universe but our Holy Father could create innumerable sons who are so different and yet belong to the same race?

"And even though we are different in looks, temperament, and skills, our Lord passed a law that encourages us to love one another as He loves us. Can you imagine the love that swells up in His heart when He recalls the day we awakened in His laboratory and called Him Father? Just looking around this room, can you imagine how long it took Him to make each of us full-grown and wise? Did it take minutes, hours, or days for our Lord to fashion Prince Michael so that he would become a great athlete, explorer, and commander of a sainted army?"

Commander Cerviel interrupted. "It takes Father one night to create an entire flock, Kaela, so where are you going with this?"

Kaela shook his head. "None of us know for sure if Father took one night, one hundred nights, or one hundred years to create a flock. No one knows if we slept for one night and awaken the next morning to a flock of new brothers or if our Lord caused us to sleep for one hundred years before we woke up. What is the meaning of one night to God? Is our day a second of His time, or is it an eternity?" He looked around the room. "All I know is this: yesterday, I cut each of my rebellious brothers down in less than a minute. I never stopped what I was doing to consider how long it took our Lord to create the warriors I scored while I battled to clear the Holy Castle of its intruders."

"So what are you trying to tell us?" Commander Eae asked. "Are you saying that we should not uncreate those who seek to uncreate us, our brothers, Father, and His royal family?"

"I'm not saying anything like that," Kaela said in a stern voice. He apologized to his sainted brothers for his impatience. "What I think I'm trying to say is, Father created us, and He feels it is His obligation to be fair, just, and kind to us all. Even though the northern warriors consider our Lord their enemy, He is still their Creator, their King, and their Holy Father. We are the reason for Heaven's unrest, as surely as our northern brothers. Because of our indifference to Lucifer's hateful lies, our Lord is going to let us solve the problems that we brought on ourselves.

"We can pray to Him to give us victory over our brothers, but that is not what He wants to hear. Father wants to hear prayers that thank Him for what He has given us. He is our Father. He loves us as our Father, and though He appreciates what His saints are doing to restore our globe's peace, He doesn't favor one of us, good or evil, over the other. Our Lord will not take sides."

"As much as I hate to admit it, that sounds right," Prince Michael agreed. "Maybe that is why Father created His heir. And speaking of our future King, we must prepare for this evening's festival during which our Lord will introduce Immanuel to us."

Commander Eae spoke from his seat. "Our Lord invited everyone, just like He did when He held His festival last evening. Two festivals held in the midst of utter chaos, hours apart. In the past, in peaceful times, our Lord hosted two festivals a month." He glanced at Kaela. "I doubt that Lucifer's bunch will be there. I fear they will be too busy fabricating ways to make our lives miserable."

CHAPTER 48

The One

The hour of the festival was fast approaching. Prince Michael distributed the scribe's hand-written notes describing the activities that were planned for the opening ceremony. There was no time for practice, so sporting events that would be held this evening rested squarely on the athletes' broad shoulders. In the auditorium, Israfel and his choir reviewed the songs they would sing when Father introduced Immanuel to Heaven's angels. Conductor Zephon's chalk-board was filled with instructions that his musicians were encouraged to memorize. In the stadium, Yofiel, Prince Michael's most trusted sport angel and military commander, put the athletic teams through their paces. Autumn chose the open field close by the stables, away from the shouted commands, marching feet, and noisy clanking of chariot wheels, to train her precious cherubs. Archangel Gabriel and his crew of trained equestrians worked in that very same field with timid unicorns, brawny steeds, and muscular flying horses to ensure that all of Heaven would remember this festival forever.

While all this preparation was taking place, Lieutenant Archangel Kaela walked toward the barred cells that sat on the western lawn of Father's house. In his hand, he clutched a scroll that held an order he was loathed to obey. Handing the scroll to Puriel, who was in charge of a small battalion of saints who guarded the cells, he waited. The child read the orders once, glanced at Kaela through narrowed eyes, and read the orders a second time.

"I will have to get what is written in the scroll verified," he told Kaela. It was obvious to other guards that the young saint did not trust the lieutenant archangel. "You wait here, sir, we will see what happens when I return."

Lieutenant Archangel Kaela nodded his approval for Puriel to speak to his commanding officer. The child returned to holding area. "I am to give you the sole key that unlocks every door here," he grumbled. "I had to hear it from my commanding officer since I did not—"

"Trust me," Kaela said, ending the saint's sentence. He took the key in his hand. "You don't know how I feel about being the one who was elected to do this. I know that I am not trusted by youngsters created of the seventh flock."

"You are not trusted by anyone, sir," Puriel informed. "If you, not God, were our creator, I would be on Lucifer's side right now. That is how much I distrust you."

Lieutenant Archangel Kaela smiled at the arrogant young saint. "I didn't choose to live in the North. I was happy with my life as a carpenter in Father's kingdom. I was drafted into serving God by Scribe Excelsa long before I enlisted in Prince Michael's service. I worked as a civilian with a crew of brave brothers that I returned safely to this region after we freed Lucifer's slaves." He wrapped his arm around the child's shoulders. "So here is my suggestion to you: show those of us who worked for God in the North some respect, for the day is fast coming when you will have no choice over what it is that you must do in our Lord's name, just as I have no choice over what I must do now."

Puriel walked with the lieutenant archangel to the first cell. "You have to admit it is strange that Father gives you all the questionable duties that I, being a faithful son, would never think to perform."

"You would disobey Father?" Kaela asked. "Well, there's one for the books. As questionable as I am, I have never once considered disobeying my Lord."

He reached for the small trumpet at his side and blew into it. When the evil angels heard the noise the trumpet made, they turned to see who it was that required their attention. "Listen up," Kaela told the mob that had stopped its howling, swearing, and chanting to hear what he had to say. "Father wants all His created sons to be present at the event that will introduce our future King to us.

"Personally, I hope by inviting you to this solemn ceremony, God will show how powerful Immanuel is by having His heir turn all of you to dust. But I don't know that will happen since our Lord wants to keep the event peaceful. Then again, He is arming all His saints, and we will be on horseback. So who knows? Father might think that luring all of you to the stadium where you will be uncreated would be great entertainment for Lucifer's former slaves." The ruckus that reverberated through the quiet field began anew.

For a second time, Lieutenant Archangel Kaela sounded his trumpet. The northern rebels turned their attention from their fears and worries to the object of their hatred. "Anyway," Kaela said, pacing before the weary criminals. "God gave Prince Michael orders that I am to come to these shining barred cages, which remind me of the cages we used when we transported dumb beasts to God's kingdom from all over Heaven, but my orders are to open these cages and let you to walk free."

A gruff warrior shouted, "We will fill the Holy City with our chants, and if restoration has begun, we will destroy it again!" Cheers rose up when his evil brothers heard his words.

"I am really hopeful you will do that," Kaela said, smiling at Puriel's shocked expression. "Immanuel is more powerful than Father, and according to our Lord, our newly created brother will suffer no fools. That means Immanuel won't tolerate Lucifer's warriors or his supporters. What fun it will be to watch as He uncreates all of you—*poof*, into oblivion you go."

"Will you get on with what you have to do, sir?" Puriel scolded. "Just do it."

"This child doesn't trust me," Lieutenant Archangel Kaela said, unsheathing both swords that he carried on his back. "I don't think any of you trust me." He paced back and forth before the cells. "Word on the streets has it that I scored about fifty of you when you attacked the castle. I restrained myself from uncreating as many of you as I would have since I was in my Father's house, but here, in this wide-open field, I might score at least one hundred of you."

"Sir, please, just free them!" the young saint shouted.

"The cub is getting all excited." Kaela teased the young saint as surely as he teased the warriors. "I am going to hand one of my swords to him." Turning to Pruiel, he asked, "You are proficient in swordsmanship, I hope?"

"Yes, I am," Puriel growled. "Can you just get this done, sir?"

Lieutenant Archangel Kaela walked to the door of the first cell. "When you step out, step away from me, and keep moving, unless, of course, you hope to be uncreated like Vaul and Gylle." Word of the warriors' gruesome deaths swept through Heaven like a wind-kissed flame, causing good and evil brothers to shudder at the description of their demise. The lieutenant archangel unlocked the first cell.

The warriors who left the cell spit at Kaela, glared at him, snorted at him, bared their teeth at him, but no one moved toward him in a threatening manner. And so it was with the warriors in the remaining twenty cells.

"Go now!" Kaela shouted as they walked toward the forest. "Find a place where you will be safe and hide there because if Immanuel does not uncreate you tonight, I will uncreate you in the morning."

He turned to Puriel. "If you need me, I will be in my suite preparing for the evening's festivities. And I would appreciate it very much if you returned my sword."

Puriel handed the weapon to Kaela and watched in disgust as his questionable brother slipped both his swords into the scabbards on his back-pack. "I'll see you at the stadium."

Autumn and Kaela reached their apartment door at the same time. They both sighed. Each had tried to be the first one home.

"I'm in the parade," they said in unison.

Autumn stepped away from the door, allowing Kaela to open it for her. He expected her to make a bee-line to the bathroom where she would remain until just minutes before the parade would begin. Instead, Autumn walked to the window, unsheathed her sword, and checked it for smudges.

"Your uniform is laid out on the bed. Your medallions are on the dresser. Start getting ready." She spit on the cloth she wiped over her sword's blade. "Tonight, I want my sword to be blindingly brilliant in God's light."

The area outside the stadium's doors was in pure chaos. Prince Michael approached Autumn. "You are going to lead your military cherubim into the stadium. Your unit will be followed by the taller brothers who are foot soldiers. The saints on horseback will follow the foot soldiers, and behind them, the charioteers will enter the stadium." He handed her a sheet of paper filled with instructions and diagrams.

"Cherubim, form lines in accordance to your rank," she ordered. Pacing before her troops, she said, "We are here to make Father proud. He is introducing our new King to us, and He is, no doubt, nervous. So to ease our Lord's mind, we are going to be on our best military behavior." Autumn walked to one cherub and straightened his vest. "Check your uniforms. A good appearance shows that we take our vows to protect and defend our citizens seriously." She opened the page that she had crushed in her hand while she talked. "We are going to go through our entry into the stadium by marching in place. That means, we will pretend that we are at the stadium's doors and that we are entering the playing field, but we will not move from this spot."

The practice began. Little cherubs marched in time as Autumn called out, "We are entering the stadium. Heads up, eyes front, shoulders squared. March in time. Left, right, left, right—very good! Keep that up. Now, we have reached the area before our Lord's family booth. Kneel. Very good! Rise to your feet. Turn to the left. We are going to take our seats in the bottom rows of the bleachers that lay straight ahead. I will be leading, so just follow me." Applause rang out from the saints who watched Autumn put her cherubs through their paces. Autumn turned toward her brothers, bowed from her waist in their direction, and straightened with a smile on her face.

It was time. Autumn stood directly outside the stadium's wide double doors. Her heart beat so fiercely she could hear it pounding in her ears.

"Don't show off," she called to her troops. "Do it like we practiced. Stick with what we know, and don't call attention to your selves. Be part of a whole." She took a deep breath. Music filled the air. Cheers drown out the music. A spark caught Autumn's eye. She glanced up to see saints with torches in their hands seated on the broad backs of flying horses circling above the stadium. A trumpet's blare signaled the entertainers and saints that the royal family had taken their seats and the ceremony was about to begin.

The stadium doors opened. From where Autumn stood, she saw Zephon and his musicians file off the field followed by Israfel and his choir.

"Follow me!" was Autumn's shouted order to her troops. The audience rose to its feet as she and her cherubs marched onto the field.

Autumn led her unit up the center of the playing field, stopping directly in front of Father's family booth. While her cherubs knelt on both their knees, Autumn unsheathed her sword. Kneeling on one knee, her sword raised above her head she said in a loud, clear voice, "Immanuel, my favored Brother, Father's gift to His faithful sons, Heaven's future King, Your military cherubs salute You, and we pledge our loyalty to You forever and ever."

Amid a thunderous applause, Autumn and her cherubs rose to their feet simultaneously and marched across the stadium floor to seats that were reserved for them.

Lieutenant Archangel Kaela led his foot soldiers down the stadium's playing field where they knelt before the royal family. "My Lord, sole reason for my happiness, I thank you for the gifts You have given me. My saints and I declare our eternal loyalty to You and our future King, Immanuel." The audience rose to their feet, wildly applauding their hero and his soldiers. Lieutenant Archangel Kaela and his saints marched across the playing field to take their seats behind Autumn and her military cherubim.

Lieutenant Gabriel led his equestrians onto the playing field. Seated on his steed's broad back, he assembled his saints in direct line with the royal family booth. At the sound of Gabriel's trumpet, the horses dropped onto their front knees. Cheers and applause exploded throughout the audience.

"Father, Your sainted equestrians declare our loyalty to You and to our beloved brother, Immanuel, forever and ever." His piece said Lieutenant Gabriel led his saints to the left side of the stadium, past the section where Autumn and her cherubs sat, down the playing field, and out the stadium's double doors.

Now the charioteers entered the stadium. A brief speech was delivered by Archangel Uzziel, who took the route Gabriel laid to the stadium doors. Equestrians and charioteers would return to the stadium after the horses and unicorns were secured outside the arena.

Israfel's choir sang songs that honored Heaven's outgoing King and songs that honored the heir to Heaven's throne. While the angels sang, the horse soldiers and charioteers returned to the stadium to take their seats in the audience.

When the last saint was seated, Father addressed His sons. "My precious children," our Lord said, "Thank you for this wonderful evening. I am touched that so many of you could attend this ceremony at a time when Heaven's peace has been so sorely disrupted. Your loyalty to me and to my heir, Immanuel, the love you have shown your precious sisters, and the respect you have for Scribe Excelsa, Archangel Effiel and his student Elbreon and the historian Evangeline, fills my heart with joy.

"I am pleased to say that the northern warriors have returned to the North with Belial as their new leader. Lucifer and Sin are locked securely in the sphere built by Lieutenant Archangel Kaela and Joniel. And for now, Heaven's peace has been temporarily restored. We have a long way to go before our globe returns to what it was so many eons ago." Father paused for a moment. "I want my sons of light to know that I did not create Immanuel because I do not love you. I created Immanuel because I love all of you equally. And with that, my children, I am honored to introduce your future King, my created heir, Immanuel."

Immanuel rose from His seat. He kissed His Father's cheek and waited for Him to be seated. "Jehovah God is our King, our Creator, and our Father. He is the sole reason for our happiness. In the future, I will wear His crown, own His scepter, and I will be honored to rule

Heaven from His throne. The day will come when I will purge this globe of evil and I will restore Heaven's peace.

"I will love anyone who sincerely loves Father, and I will sincerely hate anyone who despises Father. His enemies are my enemies. We have good brothers in the North who need to come home to the Sacred Region. They are loyal sons who would gladly give their lives for our Lord. Brothers who pledged their loyalty to Lucifer and Sin are doomed to eternal misery. If they repent of their wrong-doing, they will be saved."

Immanuel took His seat next to Father. Zephon's orchestra played music while Prince Michael's saints prepared to close the ceremony. Every step that was taken to bring the troops in was done in reverse. Saints on winged steeds with fiery torches in their hand rose into the air to circle the area above the royal family booth. Chariots rolled through the stadium's wide-open doorway and circled the field before exiting. Lieutenant Gabriel led his saints on horseback through the stadium where their steeds knelt before God and Son. Lieutenant Archangel Kaela followed suit. And last but not least, Autumn and her little cherubim marched onto the field where they knelt in humble reverence before their King and His future heir. Amid cheers and applause, Prince Michael's saints exited the stadium through its wide-open doors. The festival had ended, but the celebration continued long into the night.

Brothers who ate too much, danced too long, and sang until they were hoarse left the Holy Mount to make their way down the staircase to their homes in the village and the city. Those faithful sons who were too afraid to return to what was left of their cottages and town houses retired to the Holy Castle's median rooms. Autumn and Kaela visited Father's garden where they—with Joniel, Octaviel, Stephon, Phillip, and Percible—retreated to their favorite spot to talk about the night's events. Surprisingly, they were joined by Puriel, who, when the others left, lingered behind.

"Lieutenant Archangel Kaela," the youngster said, "I had the opportunity to talk to some of the brothers who were held hostage in the North. They told me about the slave pens and pits. And they told me about how you served God while you lived there." He lowered his head for a minute as though considering what he would say next. "I owe you an apology, sir. I behaved very badly when you arrived at the barred cells to release our prisoners. I would like to make that apology now."

Lieutenant Archangel Kaela smiled, resting his hand on the child's shoulder. "Never apologize to anyone for doing what you think is right. You are an obedient and dutiful son. You are a good soldier, and someday, you will excel to greatness. Follow your inborn common sense, be proud of who you are and what you know, and always have the grace to admit that you may have been wrong, but never apologize—especially not to me."

"Thank you for your advice," Puriel said. "I will try to make you proud. With that, I will say good night." He turned away from Autumn and Kaela, leaving them to watch after him.

"So what now?" Autumn said, stretching her arms above her head.

"I have to return you to the gazebo in Florida," Kaela told her. "A storm has risen up and I must keep you safe." He smiled at her disappointment. "Your husband will be home soon. He will be looking for you. He wants to keep you safe, too."

Those were the angel's final words to Autumn. She glanced around the gazebo. Her notes were plastered against the structure's screened walls, the wind raged, huge thick bolts of lightning streaked across the sky, and it started to rain. Autumn frantically grabbed her notes. She ran across the gazebo's floor, kneeling to rescue whatever it was that she had written before she was swept away to Heaven as Kaela's guest.

"Autumn, leave this stuff here," David said. He was standing inside the gazebo. "I came home, and I'm glad I did. Come on, let's get to the house." He took her notebook from her and motioned her toward the door. Together, they ran through the driving rain to the safety of their house. Pulling the front door closed, David said, "When I came home, I thought you were in the office, running off recipes. It was lightning, so I turned the printer off." He listened. "I think it's still running."

"I have to put this stuff away," Autumn said. "I'll check the printer. It's unplugged, you say?" She saw David's nod. "Yeah, I better check it to see what's wrong with it."

In the den, she studied the printer through narrowed eyes. "This is You, isn't it, Kaela? You are doing this to ensure that I have the first few chapters of my book done." Autumn glanced up to see David enter the room. He was looking at the floor that was carpeted with printed pages. "It's a book I wrote," she told him.

"Isn't the printer supposed to be plugged into the outlet?" David asked.

"Oh, it's having a little problem. It's nothing," Autumn said. By now, David was tracing the printer's power cord from the back of the device to the idle plug he held in his hand.

"How is this happening?" David asked as the last page of text fell to the floor he knelt on.

The printer was silent now. Reaching past David, Autumn picked up a page that lay away from the other pages that fell to the floor. She read aloud, "Autumn heard her angel's promise and knew that he spoke the truth. Kaela would return; together, they would testify at Lucifer's trial, and they would celebrate a hard-won victory for God and Son."

This final page was God's way of letting Autumn know her story had not ended.

www.ingramcontent.com/pod-product-compliance
Lightning Source LLC
Chambersburg PA
CBHW021602120626
46545CB00001B/25
9798896390787